REFUGEES, ASYLUM SEEKERS AND THE RULE OF LAW

The contributors to this volume examine how the legislative, executive and administrative arms of government have responded to issues concerning the rights and status of refugees and asylum seekers in five common law jurisdictions: the UK, Australia, Canada, the USA and New Zealand. Who and what determine the legislative agenda in this context? Is the legislative agenda driven by the legislators, or are the responses of the jurisdictions driven by the international context? We evaluate the responses from a human rights perspective and assess the integrity and coherency of legal responses as shown by their impact on the rule of law.

SUSAN KNEEBONE is a Professor of Law and a Deputy Director of the Castan Centre for Human Rights Law at the Faculty of Law, Monash University, Victoria, Australia.

REFUGEES, ASYLUM SEEKERS AND THE RULE OF LAW

Comparative Perspectives

Edited by
SUSAN KNEEBONE

CAMBRIDGE
UNIVERSITY PRESS

CAMBRIDGE
UNIVERSITY PRESS

University Printing House, Cambridge CB2 8BS, United Kingdom

One Liberty Plaza, 20th Floor, New York, NY 10006, USA

477 Williamstown Road, Port Melbourne, VIC 3207, Australia

314-321, 3rd Floor, Plot 3, Splendor Forum, Jasola District Centre, New Delhi - 110025, India

103 Penang Road, #05-06/07, Visioncrest Commercial, Singapore 238467

Cambridge University Press is part of the University of Cambridge.

It furthers the University's mission by disseminating knowledge in the pursuit of education, learning and research at the highest international levels of excellence.

www.cambridge.org
Information on this title: www.cambridge.org/9780521889353

© Cambridge University Press 2009

This publication is in copyright. Subject to statutory exception and to the provisions of relevant collective licensing agreements, no reproduction of any part may take place without the written permission of Cambridge University Press.

First published 2009

A catalogue record for this publication is available from the British Library

ISBN 978-0-521-88935-3 Hardback

Cambridge University Press has no responsibility for the persistence or accuracy of URLs for external or third-party internet websites referred to in this publication, and does not guarantee that any content on such websites is, or will remain, accurate or appropriate.

CONTENTS

Contributors   *page* vi
Foreword   ix
Preface   xi

Introduction: Refugees and Asylum Seekers in the
International Context – Rights and Realities   1
SUSAN KNEEBONE

1   The Rule of Law and the Role of Law: Refugees and
    Asylum Seekers   32
    SUSAN KNEEBONE

2   Asylum and the Rule of Law in Canada: Hearing the
    Other (Side)   78
    AUDREY MACKLIN

3   Refugees, Asylum and the Rule of Law in the USA   122
    STEPHEN H. LEGOMSKY

4   The Australian Story: Asylum Seekers outside the Law   171
    SUSAN KNEEBONE

5   The Intersection between the International, the Regional
    and the Domestic: Seeking Asylum in the UK   228
    MARIA O'SULLIVAN

6   Conclusions on the Rule of Law   281
    SUSAN KNEEBONE

Appendix   310
Bibliography   312
Index   329

v

CONTRIBUTORS

SUSAN KNEEBONE is a Professor of Law and a Deputy Director of the Castan Centre for Human Rights Law at the Faculty of Law, Monash University, Victoria, Australia. Susan teaches Forced Migration and Human Rights, International Refugee Law, and Citizenship and Migration Law. She has organized several conferences and workshops, made submission to public inquiries, and frequently handles media enquiries on these issues. She is the author of many articles on these topics and the editor of the following books:

- *The Refugees Convention 50 Years On: Globalisation and International Law* (Ashgate, 2003)
- *New Regionalism and Asylum Seekers: Challenges Ahead* (with F. Rawlings-Sanaei; Berghahn, 2007).

Susan has twice been a Senior Visiting Research Fellow at the Refugee Studies Centre, Oxford (2003, 2006), and in 2006 was a visitor at the Centre for International Studies (CERIUM), University of Montreal. In May 2008, Susan organized a major international conference on 'Best Practices for Refugee Status Determination: Principles and Standards for State Responsibility' at Monash University Centre, Prato, Italy.

STEPHEN H. LEGOMSKY is the John S. Lehmann University Professor at the Washington University School of Law in St Louis. He is the sole author of two Oxford University Press monographs, and of *Immigration and Refugee Law and Policy* (now in its fourth edition), which has been adopted as the required text for immigration courses at 163 US law schools. Stephen founded the immigration section of the Association of American Law Schools, has testified before Congress, and has been a consultant to President Clinton's transition team, the first President Bush's Commissioner of Immigration, UNHCR, and several foreign governments.

AUDREY MACKLIN teaches at the Faculty of Law, University of Toronto, Canada. Her research includes national, international and comparative dimensions of migration and citizenship law. Her scholarship includes articles and chapters on gender-related persecution, trafficking, credibility in refugee determination, and the securitization of migration and citizenship regimes. She recently co-authored *Cases and Materials in Canadian Immigration and Refugee Law* (Toronto: Emond Montgomery, 2007).

MARIA O'SULLIVAN is a Lecturer in the Law Faculty, Monash University. She holds a BA/LLB (Hons) degree from the Australian National University and a LLM in International Human Rights Law from the University of Essex. She has worked in various legal positions, including as a researcher with Matrix Chambers, London, and as a legal adviser with the Refugee Review Tribunal. Her primary research interests are administrative and refugee law. She is currently completing a doctorate on the cessation of refugee status, under the supervision of Susan Kneebone.

FOREWORD

The 'Rule of Law' is a sophisticated constitutional principle, crucial in many countries to the proper demarcation of the roles of national parliaments, the judiciary, and the executive structures. It is also, more broadly, a notion at the heart of national debates around certain of the more complex, multilateral issues confronting our modern world – terrorism, transnational crime, irregular migration and asylum among them.

If its importance is undisputed, in the experience of the Office of the United Nations High Commissioner for Refugees (UNHCR) its nuances and permutations are nevertheless many. In some of the societies where we work, conflict or human rights violations have rendered the rule of law very relative, to a point where the machinery of protection and of justice have lost their legitimacy, if they continue to exist at all. The rule of law has painstakingly to be reconstructed, institution by institution, law by law, capacity by capacity. In certain other more developed societies, particularly where security is driving the operation of asylum systems, the rights of refugees are moving to the periphery of the rule of law notion. International law standards may be applied very inconsistently within and between countries; arbitrary detention, not subject to judicial review, is leaving many asylum seekers in a sort of legal limbo; and the world of borders can be particularly immune – with interception, turnarounds and *refoulement* taking place outside the frame of proper scrutiny. The rise of populism in some countries has proved to be a big obstacle for refugee protection to overcome, as it tends to go hand in hand with racist, anti-foreigner campaigns. These are contributing to the growth, in many parts of the world, of more intolerant societies, which in itself challenges basic law and order precepts.

Undeniably, the concerns for governments in managing their borders, in the face of a growth in transnational crime and illegal migration, as well as the threat of terrorist attacks, can be daunting. Making the right and necessary distinctions is not always easy. UNHCR has long been involved in supporting the development of efficient and responsive asylum systems in many countries, as one additional contribution we can make to advancing the rule of law. Our offices provide governments with advice on new legislation. They visit reception and detention facilities, monitor access to asylum procedures at land, sea and air borders, and promote compliance with international and regional norms.

I welcome the choice of core topic for this publication, which is how to foster and maintain the integrity of modern asylum systems. The analyses in it will, I hope, assist us all in healing what in the following pages is elaborated upon as the general malaise of the rule of law when it comes to the protection of asylum seekers.

Erika Feller
Assistant High Commissioner –
Protection, UNHCR

PREFACE

This book arises from a project funded by the Australian Research Council entitled 'The Asylum Seeker in the Legal System: A Comparative and Theoretical Study'. The purpose of this project is to conduct a comparative study of the responses of five national legal systems, including that of Australia, to the problem of reconciling the rights of asylum seekers with the 'integrity' of the rule of law. The overall aim is to conduct a theoretical inquiry into the normative principles or values underlying the five legal systems. The project's specific aims are to identify:

- the responses of each of the three branches of government (the executive, the legislature and the judiciary) to the problem, and their relative significance as a response in each legal system, and comparatively;
- the significance of differences in the nature and structure of decision making at the administrative level in determining the response in each legal system;
- in this context, the differences in, and the significance of, constitutional and other legal guarantees of human rights in each legal system;
- the 'community' and its significance in determining the values that underpin the different legal systems.

The philosopher Ronald Dworkin's 'interpretive theory of integrity' is used as a comparator and framework for analysis. In particular, the following issues are examined:

- Is there a coherent legislative principle? (Of what significance is the method and extent of incorporation of international law obligations into the legislation of the national legal system?)
- Of what significance are differences in the nature and structure of decision making at the administrative level?

xii PREFACE

- How integral is the adjudicative process? Of what significance are differences in the Constitution and the human rights framework for the adjudicative role? What values underpin judicial reasoning? Are the courts deferential to executive policy in their approach to refugee law?
- The community and its role. What is the relationship between the executive arm of government and refugee advocates, including non-governmental organizations (NGOs) in the formation of policy?

Initially, the participants in this project were asked to prepare written responses to the questions set out in the Appendix to this book. We then met at the Faculty of Law at the University of Montreal, Canada, in August 2006. The responses and the discussion at the Montreal round table were the basis of the proposal for this book. The original participants at this round table (in addition to me) were Rodger Haines QC, Colin Harvey, Stephen Legomsky and Audrey Macklin. The round table was generously hosted by François Crépeau of the Centre for International Studies (CERIUM), University of Montreal, who also arranged a follow-up open forum on *Refugees, Asylum Seekers and the Rule of Law* which involved a number of members of the NGO community and other academics and practitioners.

I organized a second meeting in Melbourne, Australia, in August 2007 attended by Rodger Haines QC and Stephen Legomsky in person, and Audrey Macklin by video link-up. This was also followed by an open round table on the 'Rule of Law' at which John Gibson, the Honourable Anthony North and Maria O'Sullivan participated, together with a number of members of the Refugee Review Tribunal, academics and practitioners.

I thank all participants at both meetings and follow-up forums in Montreal and Melbourne for the time and commitment they put into attending these meetings, and for their contributions to the project. Their ideas have contributed to the outcome – the current book. Although there have been some changes between the original participants and the final contributors to this book, it draws upon the summaries and comments provided at those initial meetings. In particular I thank those who have made written contributions to this volume.

I thank Audrey Macklin and Donald Galloway, who provided insightful comments on Chapter 1. I am particularly grateful to Maria O'Sullivan, who wrote Chapter 5, entitled 'The Intersection between the International, the Regional and the Domestic: Seeking Asylum in the UK' at short notice, and who has read and commented on the chapters I have written for this book. Maria has been a most supportive colleague on this project. I thank Robert Thomas and Gareth Morell, who read and commented upon Chapter 5 at short notice, and who provided detailed and helpful comments.

Various research assistants have helped at different stages of the project. In chronological order, they include Edwina Howell, Katie Mitchell, Stephanie Booker, Ellen Roberts, Bronwyn Polson and Madhavi Ligam. Extra special thanks are owed to Bronwyn Polson, who worked closely with me for several months overseeing the editing process with efficiency, calm and an unfailing sense of proportion and humour. Her assistance was invaluable.

I thank the Law Faculty at Monash University for granting me a period of study leave in 2006 to pursue this project, and the Refugee Studies Centre in Oxford where I was a Senior Visiting Research Fellow in October and November 2006, and where much of the thinking for this project took place.

I also thank Finola O'Sullivan at Cambridge University Press for her unflagging interest, support and encouragement for the book.

I thank my husband, Richard Kneebone, for his continual support and encouragement, and for assisting with the bibliography and in a myriad of other ways.

Finally, I express my thanks to the Australian Research Council for awarding me the grant which made this book possible.

Susan Kneebone
Faculty of Law
Monash University
Melbourne, Australia
May 2008

Introduction: Refugees and Asylum Seekers in the International Context – Rights and Realities[1]

SUSAN KNEEBONE

This book uses the idea of the 'Rule of Law' to illuminate how the legal systems in five industrialized countries which share a common legal heritage – namely Canada, the USA, Australia, New Zealand and the UK – have responded to issues about the rights and status of refugees[2] and asylum seekers.[3] This is a particularly important issue in its own right because, as explained in Chapter 1, the rule of law, which is the cornerstone of the concept of democracy and of modern legal systems, is challenged by its application to refugees and asylum seekers. It is also important for a second reason. The rights of refugees are defined in international law, but are subject to state discretion as to their implementation in national legal systems.[4] As the chapters in this book reveal, implementation is being done in such a way as to deny refugees the

---

[1] This expression is also used in the following title: Frances Nicholson and Patrick Twomey (eds.), *Refugee Rights and Realities: Evolving International Concepts and Regimes* (Cambridge University Press, 1999).

[2] In everyday parlance a 'refugee' is a person in flight, a person seeking refuge. However, in international law a 'refugee' is a person who comes within the definition in Art. 1A(2) of the Convention relating to the Status of Refugees, Geneva, 28 July 1951, in force 22 April 1954, 1989 UNTS 137 (Refugee Convention) and the Protocol relating to the Status of Refugees, New York, 31 January 1967, in force 4 October 1967, 19 UNTS 6223, 6257 (Refugee Protocol).

[3] An 'asylum seeker' is a person seeking asylum from persecution who has yet to be recognized as a 'refugee' as defined in Art. 1A(2) of the Refugee Convention. But note that the United Nations High Commissioner for Refugees (UNHCR) takes the view that a person who satisfies that definition is a 'refugee' without the need for a determination to that effect. This is known as the 'declaratory' theory – see UNHCR, *Handbook on Procedures and Criteria for Determining Refugee Status under the 1951 Convention and the 1967 Protocol relating to the Status of Refugees* (Geneva: UNHCR, 1979, re-edited 1992) (UNHCR Handbook), para. 28.

[4] This is known in international law as the 'margin of appreciation', the idea that national differences in interpretation of treaties must be allowed, subject to two limitations: necessity and proportionality.

2   REFUGEES, ASYLUM SEEKERS AND THE RULE OF LAW

rights which are due to them under the international regime of refugee protection. Thus the international rule of law is also being eroded by implementation at the national level.

This raises the issue of the interconnectedness of the national and the international rule of law. Should the rule of law be regarded only as a 'national enterprise', as Audrey Macklin queries?[5] How can coherency between the national and the international rule of law be achieved? These are issues addressed in this book.

While there is much scholarly discussion about the content of the international rule of law[6] as it applies to refugees and asylum seekers,[7] there is also a need to focus upon the national rule of law which shapes the immediate responses to the issues which refugees and asylum seekers raise. The focus upon the national rule of law is therefore important for yet another reason. As explained in Chapter 1, this focus provides a clear picture of the role of law; of how the law operates in relation to refugees and asylum seekers.

The purpose of this introductory chapter is to put the issues which are discussed in this book into context. This will be done by describing both the rights which apply under international law to refugees and asylum seekers, and the development of the international system of refugee protection in the second half of the twentieth century. It will highlight the significance of national legal responses in shaping that system. In particular it will be explained that although refugees are persons in flight, and in need of protection, and as such are exceptions

---

[5] See Audrey Macklin, 'Asylum and the Rule of Law in Canada: Hearing the Other (Side)', Chapter 2 in this volume.

[6] In this context it is generally accepted that the 'International Rule of Law' for refugees comprises at least the 1951 Refugee Convention and the 1967 Refugee Protocol. The issue of which other international instruments are relevant is a matter of some debate. James C. Hathaway, *The Rights of Refugees Under International Law* (Cambridge University Press, 2005), p. 8 argues that, in addition to the Refugee Convention and the Refugee Protocol, the rights regime that applies to refugee entitlements includes the two 'foundational treaties of the international human rights system', namely the International Covenant on Civil and Political Rights, New York, 16 December 1966, in force 23 March 1976, UN Doc. A/6316 (1966), 999 UNTS 171 (ICCPR) and the International Covenant on Economic, Social and Cultural Rights, New York, 16 December 1966, in force 3 January 1976, UN Doc. A/6316 (1966), 99 UNTS 3 (ICESCR).

[7] For example, there are divergent views held on many issues by the authors of two leading texts in this area, namely: Hathaway, *The Rights of Refugees*; Guy S. Goodwin-Gill and Jane McAdam, *The Refugee in International Law*, 3rd edn. (Oxford University Press, 2007).

INTRODUCTION 3

to the usual rules of migration and for admission to territory,[8] the reality today is that many states view refugees as nothing other than ordinary migrants. That is, the special status which is accorded to refugees under international law is not respected.

In a nutshell, we see that the common trend of industrialized receiving states is to erode the notion of international refugee protection and state responsibility by restrictive measures aimed at deterring or deflecting asylum seekers. Such measures include denying asylum seekers access to territory to claim asylum and denying access to refugee status determination procedures.

The current policies of industrialized states towards refugees are made in the context of concerns about the high level of 'irregular' international migration, and security. Often these two concerns are conflated when it is assumed that all irregular or undocumented migrants are security risks. This leads to policies which discriminate against refugees by containing them in regions of origin and preventing 'secondary movements', or denying them entry at a destination for processing.[9] In particular, in the context of international migration, refugees are often juxtaposed with 'mere' 'economic' migrants. The 'migration–asylum nexus', which is employed in this context, concentrates upon the fact that there are 'mixed flows' of asylum seekers and irregular (economic) migrants. The effect of the migration–asylum nexus is to treat the protection needs of refugees as a secondary consideration to migration controls.

At the global level, the international system of refugee protection in the post-World War II period has mostly developed in reaction to refugee crises and mass outpourings, rather than as responses to individual refugee needs. In this context, there is an inherent tension between the rights of refugees and the political realities of refugee policy. For example, in this chapter it will be shown that one consequence of the restrictive policies of industrialized receiving states has been the 'containment' of refugees in regions of origin and an overall decline in respect for the concept of refugee rights and protection. The figures (discussed in the text below) show a decline in the number of refugees

---

[8] Michael Walzer, 'Membership' in *Spheres of Justice: A Defence of Pluralism and Equality* (Oxford: Basil Blackwell, 1983), p. 31 – discussed in Chapter 1 in this volume.

[9] Matthew J. Gibney, 'Forced Migration, Engineered Regionalism and Justice Between States' in Susan Kneebone and Felicity Rawlings-Sanaei (eds.), *New Regionalism and Asylum Seekers: Challenges Ahead* (Oxford: Berghahn Books, 2007), Chapter 3.

4   REFUGEES, ASYLUM SEEKERS AND THE RULE OF LAW

seeking asylum in industrialized states, but an increase in the number of those living in 'protracted refugee situations', and an increased number of internally displaced persons (IDPs, or 'internal refugees' as they are sometimes termed). While it may be simplistic to draw a direct correlation between these three trends, there is evidence that the decline in the number of refugees seeking asylum in industrialized states is connected to the latter two trends.

Until recently, the number of persons seeking asylum in industrialized countries had fallen steadily since the beginning of the twenty-first century,[10] but at the same time the total number of people 'of concern'[11] to the United Nations High Commissioner for Refugees (UNHCR) has steadily increased. In December 2006, UNHCR calculated this category at 32.9 million,[12] which represented a 56 per cent increase during 2006 alone. Significantly, this figure includes those living in 'protracted refugee situations' and an increased number of IDPs.[13]

This chapter will first outline the development of the international system of refugee protection in the post-World War II period, and the individual rights and state responsibilities that evolved under that regime. This is followed by tracking the implementation and development of the international system of refugee protection by receiving states in response to subsequent global crises. For that purpose, the discussion will concentrate on the Cold War period and the post-Cold War period, respectively. In the discussion of the latter period, it will be

---

[10] UNHCR, *Statistical Yearbook 2006, Trends in Displacement, Protection and Solutions* (Geneva: UNHCR, 2007), p. 7 states that the number of refugees has increased for the first time in five years to 9.9 million. See www.unhcr.org/statistics.html (accessed 26 March 2008). See also UN High Commissioner for Refugees, *Note on International Protection: Report by the High Commissioner*, Geneva, 29 June 2007, A/AC.96/1038. The increase noted was from 8.7 million at the end of 2005 to 9.9 million at the end of 2006. This increase was attributed to new refugee populations in Jordan, Syria and Lebanon from Iraq. This correlates with the number seeking asylum in industrialized countries – UNHCR, *Asylum Levels and Trends in Industrialized Countries 2007* (Geneva: UNHCR, 18 March 2008), p. 4 points out in this study of forty-three industrialized countries that the number of asylum seekers had increased by 10 per cent in 2007 and that this is the first increase in five years. See www.unhcr.org/statistics/STATISTICS/47daae862.pdf (accessed 26 March 2008).

[11] The UNHCR mandate includes seven classes of persons: refugees, asylum seekers, and IDPs in certain states which agree to their intervention, returned refugees and IDPs, stateless persons, and 'other persons of concern'. See UNHCR, *Statistical Yearbook 2006*.

[12] UNHCR, *Basic Facts*, www.unhcr.org/basics.html (accessed 14 April 2008).

[13] UNHCR, *Statistical Yearbook 2006*, p. 7 puts the figure at 12.8 million. See www.unhcr.org/statistics.html (accessed 26 March 2008).

INTRODUCTION 5

shown that refugees have evolved from being a protected class at the end of World War II, to being discriminated against in the context of irregular international migration. Refugees now compete for international attention with other categories of 'forced' migrants such as IDPs. The question considered in the discussion is the link between these trends and the responses of the legal systems of industrialized states. To what extent are they a product of a lack of responsibility to refugees in the developing world?[14]

Part one: development of the international system of refugee protection – rights

The 1951 Refugee Convention, which was negotiated in the aftermath of World War II, was intended to deal with the European problem of 1.25 million refugees arising out of the post-war chaos. In particular it was directed at the victims of Nazi and other fascist regimes. This is recognized by the definition which describes a refugee as a person with an individual 'well-founded fear of being persecuted' as a result of 'events occurring before 1 January 1951' (Art. 1A(2)). Signatories to the Convention could choose to interpret this as referring to events in Europe 'or elsewhere' (Art. 1B(1)) but largely, in fact, read it as being subject to geographical limits. As a result of the 1967 Protocol relating to the Status of Refugees, the temporal and geographical limits were removed.[15]

The Refugee Convention not only provided an individualized definition of a refugee but also made it clear that it was an instrument for human rights protection. The Convention which arose from European events, and which was brokered (largely) by European nations, was also a manifestation of the development of a system of international law and institutions intended to provide responses and solutions to a global problem. The importance of the establishment of the UNHCR in 1951 to administer the Convention under the United Nations General Assembly should not be underestimated. This development was part of a package of far-reaching human rights instruments and measures which were intended to recognize the universality of human rights.

---

[14] Of the 32.9 million 'persons of concern', 11.1 million were from Asia and 10.1 million were from Africa. See UNHCR, *Statistical Yearbook 2006, Trends in Displacement, Protection and Solutions*, p. 7, www.unhcr.org/statistics.html (accessed 26 March 2008).
[15] This development is discussed later in this chapter.

6   REFUGEES, ASYLUM SEEKERS AND THE RULE OF LAW

The Refugee Convention is an instrument of human rights protection which was intended to implement the basic right to flee persecution and to seek and enjoy asylum, and to enshrine the right against *refoulement* (Art. 33(2)). The refugee definition in Article 1A(2) refers to a person with a 'well-founded fear of persecution' who is outside her/his country, and who is persecuted for one of the five reasons specified in the Article. This was a significant development, as previous instruments had provided a generalized, descriptive refugee definition.[16] It is now well established that the meaning of 'persecution' should be interpreted within a human rights framework which includes reference to the standards provided by the main human rights treaties.[17] As James Hathaway has said, the Refugee Convention was 'rarely understood to be the primary point of reference' for refugee rights.[18]

It is sometimes remarked that the problem with refugee policy makers is that they cannot count from one to thirty-three. This refers to the fact that, whereas a lot of attention is given to the refugee definition in Article 1A(2) of the Refugee Convention and to the *non-refoulement* obligation in Article 33, very rarely is reference made to any of the other rights and responsibilities referred to in the Convention. In fact the Convention confers tiers of rights on 'refugees' according to the relationship or status of the refugee in the state from which asylum is sought. Those rights adhere to refugees according to a hierarchy of human rights ranging from basic rights to life and liberty to include social and economic rights. In his most recent book, Hathaway has analysed the rights recognized

---

[16] James C. Hathaway, 'The Evolution of Refugee Status in International Law: 1920–1950' (1984) 33 *International and Comparative Law Quarterly* 348.

[17] Michelle Foster, *International Refugee Law and Socio-Economic Rights: Refuge from Deprivation* (Cambridge University Press, 2007), Chapter 2. The main treaties which are advocated by Hathaway and Foster are Universal Declaration of Human Rights, Paris, 10 December 1948, GA Res. 217 A(III), UN Doc. A/810 (UDHR), ICCPR, ICESCR, plus Convention on the Elimination of All Forms of Discrimination against Women, New York, 18 December 1979, in force 3 September 1981, UN Doc. A/34/46, 34 UN GAOR Supp. (No. 46) at 193 (CEDAW), Convention on the Rights of the Child, New York, 20 November 1989, in force 2 September 1990, UN Doc. A/44/49, 44 UN GAOR Supp. (No. 49) at 167 (CROC) and International Convention on the Elimination of All Forms of Racial Discrimination, New York, 21 December 1965, in force 4 January 1969, UN Doc. A/6014 (1966), 660 UNTS 195 (CERD). The role of 'soft' law and 'customary' law are less clear. Hathaway, *The Rights of Refugees*, argues for a 'positivist' approach to international law and prefers to apply an understanding of international law as 'a system of rules agreed to by states' (p. 10). This approach is indicated by his view about the status of the *non-refoulement* principle discussed later in this chapter.

[18] Hathaway, *The Rights of Refugees*, p. 5.

INTRODUCTION

by the Refugee Convention in the light of the relevant human rights instruments.[19]

In recognition of the 'declaratory' nature of refugee status,[20] some basic rights adhere under the Refugee Convention to all refugees, irrespective of status. These include the negative rights against *refoulement* (Art. 33) and discrimination as to 'race, religion or country of origin' (Art. 3).[21] To this can be added Article 31, the non-penalization provision which applies to refugees 'unlawfully' in the country; that is, those who have entered or attempted to enter the territory without permission.[22] Additionally all refugees are entitled to free access to courts of law 'on the territory of all Contracting States' (Art. 16(1)).

Generally, under the Refugee Convention, social and economic rights adhere to a refugee as the status of the person becomes more settled. Thus for example, those refugees whose presence is simply 'lawful' have a right to be self-employed, a right to freedom of movement, and the right not to be expelled except on security grounds.[23] But lawful 'stayers' are entitled to freedom of association, freedom of employment, eligibility for the 'liberal professions', housing, public relief, labour law protection and social security, and travel documents.[24] However, there are some rights in this category which apply to all refugees. These rights arise from the requirements to treat refugees on the same footing as 'aliens generally' (Art. 7) in relation to property rights and advanced education (Arts. 13, 22(2)) and on the same footing as 'nationals generally' in relation to rationing, elementary education, and taxes (Arts. 20, 22(1), 29). Hathaway says that, in drafting the Convention, a deliberate decision was taken not to require any 'attachment' or lawful status for property rights, rights in relation to tax, and free access to courts of law, because the drafters wished to ensure that asylum seekers could claim these rights even if not physically present.[25] At the other

---

[19] Hathaway, *The Rights of Refugees.*   [20] UNHCR Handbook, para. 28.

[21] See also Refugee Convention Art. 4 – freedom of religion and Art. 8 – exemption from exceptional measures on the ground of nationality.

[22] Guy Goodwin-Gill, 'Article 31 of the 1951 Convention Relating to the Status of Refugees: Non-penalization, Detention, and Protection' in Erika Feller, Volker Turk and Frances Nicholson (eds.), *Refugee Protection in International Law: UNHCR's Global Consultations on International Protection* (Cambridge University Press, 2003), pp. 185–252 explains that Art. 31 covers persons attempting to enter a territory on the basis of de facto control or jurisdiction.

[23] Refugee Convention, Arts. 18, 26, and 32 respectively.

[24] Refugee Convention, Arts. 15, 17, 19, 21, 23, 24 and 28 respectively.

[25] Hathaway, *The Rights of Refugees*, p. 162.

8   REFUGEES, ASYLUM SEEKERS AND THE RULE OF LAW

end of the spectrum, Article 30 of the Refugee Convention applies to resettled refugees and refers to the transfer of assets. Clearly the drafters of the Refugee Convention were alive to the need to protect the rights of all refugees in a variety of situations, including during flight.[26]

As stated above, there are some protections which apply to all refugees irrespective of their status under national law. These include freedom from detention (Art. 31(2) refers to refugees 'unlawfully' in the country of refuge), non-discrimination (Art. 3 – which is amplified by Art. 7 and Arts. 20, 22(1), 29 – the right to be treated equally to 'aliens' and 'nationals' in the areas referred to), free access to courts of law (Art. 16(1)), and the provision of adequate procedures to protect against *refoulement* (Art. 33). These provisions impose obligations upon states to respect the rights of refugees. Additionally, Article 35 of the Refugee Convention requires Contracting States to cooperate with the UNHCR – an obligation which is also recognized in the Preamble of the Convention.

The Preamble refers to the pre-1951 agreements on refugee flows, and to the fact that 'the grant of asylum may place unduly heavy burdens on certain countries, and that a satisfactory solution of [the] problem . . . cannot therefore be achieved without international cooperation'. Finally, the Preamble notes the role of the UNHCR to supervise the international refugee protection regime, with the cooperation of state parties (which is recognized as a specific state obligation in Article 35 of the 1951 Refugee Convention, as already mentioned).

Of the rights referred to above, the right to seek asylum and the right against *refoulement* are often described as the twin key precepts of refugee protection. As is well known, over the last decade and a half this protection has been weakened through a range of measures adopted at state levels as responses to the refugee 'problem', including non-entrée measures, interceptions, interdictions, offshore processing, restrictive application of the refugee definition, and application of 'safe third country' concepts which are based upon the false understanding that there is no responsibility to process an asylum seeker if protection can be sought in a safe alternative country.[27]

The legality of these measures under international law is a matter of some debate, fuelled by the fact that the 1951 Refugee Convention did

---

[26] Susan Kneebone, 'The Legal and Ethical Implications of Extraterritorial Processing of Asylum Seekers: The "Safe Third Country Concept" in Jane McAdam (ed.), *Forced Migration and Human Rights* (Oxford: Hart Publishing, 2008), Chapter 5.

[27] Including safe 'country of origin'. See Kneebone, 'The Legal and Ethical Implications of Extraterritorial Processing'.

INTRODUCTION 9

not actually spell out a 'right' to asylum. Further, there is debate over the nature and scope and status of the *non-refoulement* obligation and the extent to which states are in breach of such obligation when they carry out restrictive measures. The arguments about each of these precepts are now summarized, in order to demonstrate the gaps in the 'International Rule of Law' in these areas, and the opportunities for states to exploit them.

The 'right' to seek asylum

The Refugee Convention defines persons who are 'refugees' in international law, prescribes the rights which flow from that status, and describes the obligations of State Parties to the Convention. While it does not prescribe a 'right' to asylum as such, it arguably presupposes it. The Preamble, for example, assumes that refugees will be accorded the fundamental rights and freedoms of the Universal Declaration of Human Rights (UDHR),[28] which include Article 14, the 'right to seek and to enjoy in other countries asylum from persecution'. Importantly, Article 14 is preceded by the provision about freedom of movement in Article 13 of the UDHR. Article 13(2) of the UDHR (which is replicated in the International Covenant on Civil and Political Rights (ICCPR)[29] Arts. 12(2) and 12(4)) describes a right to leave and to return to one's own country.[30] Notably, the right to be free from persecution, which is implicit in the Refugee Convention, is reinforced by UDHR Article 5: 'No one shall be subjected to torture or to cruel, inhuman or degrading treatment' (see also ICCPR Art. 7). This right to be free from persecution arguably forms the basis of the right not to be 'refouled' in the Convention Against Torture and Other Cruel Inhuman or Degrading Treatment or Punishment (CAT)[31] Article 3[32] and in Article 33 of the

---

[28] Universal Declaration of Human Rights, Paris, 10 December 1948, GA Res. 217 A (III), UN Doc. A/810.

[29] International Covenant on Civil and Political Rights, New York, 16 December 1966, in force 23 March 1976, UN Doc. A/6316 (1966), 999 UNTS 171.

[30] Note that this presupposes that a person has a nationality. The problem of stateless people is of great concern to the UNHCR – see UNHCR, *Statistical Yearbook 2006*, p. 7 – by the end of 2006 there were 5.8 million stateless persons 'of concern' to UNHCR.

[31] Convention Against Torture and Other Cruel Inhuman or Degrading Treatment or Punishment, New York, 10 December 1984, in force 26 June 1987, UN Doc. A/39/51 (1984), 1465 UNTS 85 (CAT).

[32] While CAT is directed at freedom from 'torture' defined as 'severe pain or suffering, whether physical or mental . . . intentionally inflicted', the meaning of 'persecution' under the Refugee Convention is arguably broader.

10   REFUGEES, ASYLUM SEEKERS AND THE RULE OF LAW

Refugee Convention. Self-evidently, in order not to be refouled, a person must be granted an opportunity to seek asylum.

Despite these efforts to state that people should be able to flee persecution, and not returned to places where they face persecution, Article 14 of the UDHR is said to contain an empty right without a corresponding duty.[33] As the provisions of the international instruments discussed demonstrate, while there is freedom to leave one's country and to flee persecution, there is no corresponding duty upon a state to admit a refugee. The Refugee Convention does not contain a specific right to seek asylum and is similarly silent on the matter of refugee status determination procedures.

The issue of asylum thus becomes one of state responsibility and of characterization of that responsibility. Hathaway says: 'In pith and substance, refugee law is not immigration law ... but rather a system for the surrogate or substitute protection of human rights'.[34] Hathaway explains: 'Refugee status is a categorical designation that reflects a unique ethical and consequential legal entitlement to make claims on the international community'.[35] But states may choose to interpret such a view as an injunction to resettle refugees and point to the lack of such obligation under the Refugee Convention.[36]

This appeal to the ethical status of refugees is similarly one that has had little effect on states. Guy Goodwin-Gill and Jane McAdam have described how political attempts to enshrine a 'right' to asylum in international law in the post-World War II period foundered in the face of claims for territorial sovereignty.[37] They say that, while there is no right under international law to asylum, states have a duty under international law not to obstruct the right to seek asylum. They suggest that the legality of many non-arrival measures adopted by states can be called into question under international law.[38]

---

[33] Gregor Noll, 'Seeking Asylum at Embassies: A Right of Entry under International Law?' (2005) 17 *International Journal of Refugee Law* 542 at 548.

[34] Hathaway, *The Rights of Refugees*, p. 5.

[35] James C. Hathaway, 'Forced Migration Studies: Could We Agree Just to 'Date'?' (2007) 20 *Journal of Refugee Studies* 349 at 352.

[36] *Ruddock v. Vadarlis* [2001] FCA 1329; (2001) 110 FCR 491 at 521 (para. 126) per Beaumont J. Note that Goodwin-Gill and McAdam, *The Refugee in International Law*, p. 9, say in relation to the 'surrogate protection' theory, that 'the role of theory not always helpful'.

[37] *Ibid.*, pp. 355–64.   [38] *Ibid.*, p 358.

INTRODUCTION 11

As they say in their Introduction: 'Refugee law ... remains an incomplete legal regime of protection, imperfectly covering what ought to be a situation of exception.'[39]

By contrast, regional instruments entered into after the 1951 Refugee Convention recognized the gap in the 1951 Convention and were more direct in their recognition of the principle of asylum. But that story must be deferred for the moment until we have examined the status of the *non-refoulement* principle in international law.

The 'right' not to be refouled

The *non-refoulement* obligation is expressed in Article 33 of the Refugee Convention which provides:

> No Contracting State shall expel or return ('*refouler*') a refugee in any manner whatsoever to the frontiers of territories where his [sic] life or freedom would be threatened on account of his race, religion, nationality, membership of a particular social group or political opinion.

So fundamental is this principle to the concept of protection underlying the Refugee Convention that no reservation from this provision is permissible.[40] It is established that the principle of *non-refoulement* covers admission and non-rejection at the border of a state[41] and is thus the corollary of the right to seek asylum. In theory, the principle applies to all persons regardless of whether they meet the strict definition of refugee within the meaning of Article 1A(2) of the Refugee Convention,[42] and 'good faith' implementation of the principle[43] requires states to consider whether a person is entitled to protection before returning them.

---

[39] *Ibid.*, p. 1.   [40] Refugee Convention, Art. 42(1).

[41] Goodwin-Gill and McAdam, *The Refugee in International Law*, p. 207. Cf. *Ruddock v. Vadarlis* [2001] FCA 1329; (2001) 110 FCR 491 at 521 – Beaumont J considered that Art. 33 only applied to *expulsion* of a person who has established refugee status.

[42] This flows from the declaratory nature of recognition of refugee status in international law: Brian Gorlick, 'The Convention and the Committee against Torture: A Complementary Protection Regime for Refugees' (1999) 11 *International Journal Of Refugee Law* 479; Goodwin-Gill and McAdam, *The Refugee in International Law*, p. 244; Sir Elihu Lauterpacht QC and Daniel Bethlehem, 'The Scope and the Content of the Principle of *Non-Refoulement*' in Erika Feller et al. (eds.), *UNHCR's Global Consultations on International Protection* (Cambridge University Press, 2003), Chapter 2.1, p. 116.

[43] This refers to the principles of interpretation in the Vienna Convention on the Law of Treaties, Vienna, 23 May 1969, in force 27 January 1980, 1155 UNTS 331, Art. 31(1) discussed in Chapter 1 in this volume.

12   REFUGEES, ASYLUM SEEKERS AND THE RULE OF LAW

The principle of *non-refoulement* thus applies to all asylum seekers irrespective of their immigration status.[44] That is, it applies to persons both lawfully and unlawfully in a state or attempting to enter a state.[45] The principle is not limited to acts committed upon a state's territory but extends to the idea of 'chain' *refoulement*, that is, it covers indirect removal to a place of persecution.[46] It imposes a high standard to ensure that there is no possibility of a subsequent removal to a third country where the person might be at risk.[47]

The *non-refoulement* principle is mirrored in other treaties which prohibit torture and cruel, inhuman or degrading treatment or punishment, such as the ICCPR.[48] The *non-refoulement* principle is also affirmed in the CAT,[49] which contains a prohibition against torture. The fact that the *non-refoulement* principle goes beyond Article 33 of the Refugee Convention supports its status as an implied component of a customary prohibition on torture and cruel, inhuman or degrading treatment or punishment.

One particular challenge to the *non-refoulement* principle is the issue of extraterritoriality. It is common for states today to adopt practices such as interdictions, interceptions and offshore processing of asylum seekers. These practices challenge the *non-refoulement* principle. For example, in *R v. Immigration Officer at Prague Airport; ex parte European Roma Rights Centre* (*European Roma Rights Centre*),[50] it was decided that the *non-refoulement* principle did not apply to a group of Czech Roma people who had been refused permission at Prague airport to leave the Czech Republic in a UK-operated pre-clearance scheme. The House of Lords held that Article 33 of the Refugee Convention did not apply in these circumstances and limited its operation to acts at the border or within a border. In their view, these people were not refugees within the meaning of the Refugee Convention Article 1A(2), as they had not left the Czech Republic.

---

[44] Goodwin-Gill and McAdam, *The Refugee in International Law*, p. 233.
[45] Thomas Musgave, 'Refugees', in Sam Blay et al. (ed.), *Public International Law: An Australian Perspective* (South Melbourne: Oxford University Press, 1997), p. 317.
[46] Lauterpacht and Bethlehem, 'The Scope and the Content of the Principle of *Non-Refoulement*', p. 110.
[47] *Ibid.*, pp. 122–23.
[48] ICCPR, Art. 7. Goodwin-Gill and McAdam, *The Refugee in International Law*, p. 209.
[49] CAT, Art. 3. This treaty provides that a person shall not be returned to a place of torture. Goodwin-Gill and McAdam, *The Refugee in International Law*, p. 208.
[50] [2004] UKHL 55; [2005] 2 AC 1.

INTRODUCTION 13

Despite that decision, most academic commentators take the view that the Article 33 principle of *non-refoulement* has extraterritorial application.[51] The basis of this view is that extraterritorial jurisdiction is engaged when a state exercises control or authority over a territory or individuals.[52] Although the contrary view was expressed by a majority of the US Supreme Court in *Sale* v. *Haitian Centers Council Inc.* (*Sale*),[53] this much criticized decision relied almost solely on the terms of national legislation, and it has not altered the opinion of commentators about the extraterritorial application of Article 33 of the Refugee Convention. The issue of extraterritorial application is a difficult one which is bound up with the question of whether the principle of *non-refoulement* has the status of customary law. Goodwin-Gill and McAdam conclude their study of the practices surrounding both Article 33 and the other treaties as follows:

> The principle of *non-refoulement* can thus be seen to have crystallized into a rule of customary international law, the core element of which is the prohibition of *return in any manner whatsoever* of refugees to countries where they may face persecution. The scope and application of the rule . . . thus [regulates] State action *wherever* it takes place, whether internally, at the border or through its agents outside territorial jurisdiction [emphasis in original].[54]

There is debate about the status and scope of *non-refoulement* as a customary principle of law.[55] Some consider that Article 33 embodies a principle of customary international law, or *jus cogens*, binding on all members of the international community regardless of whether or not they are a signatory to the 1951 Refugee Convention.[56] Sir Elihu

---

[51] Goodwin-Gill and McAdam, *The Refugee in International Law*, pp. 244–53.
[52] ICCPR, Art. 2. Goodwin-Gill and McAdam, *The Refugee in International Law*, p. 245.
[53] 509 US 155 (1993) – see Stephen Legomsky, 'Refugees, Asylum and the Rule of Law in the USA', Chapter 3 in this volume. Goodwin-Gill and McAdam, *The Refugee in International Law*, pp. 247–248 stress that the decision did not and could not alter the state's international obligations. They also note that the Inter-American Human Rights Commission on Human Rights subsequently found the USA to be in breach of Art. 33(1).
[54] Goodwin-Gill and McAdam, *The Refugee in International Law*, p. 248 (emphasis in original). See also p. 346. This calls in question the activities of the Australian government under the 'Pacific Plan' – see Chantal Marie-Jeanne Bostock, 'The International Legal Obligations Owed to the Asylum Seekers on the MV Tampa' (2002) 14 *International Journal of Refugee Law* 279 at 291.
[55] Goodwin-Gill and McAdam, *The Refugee in International Law*, pp. 345–58.
[56] Donald Greig, 'The Protection of Refugees and Customary International Law' (1984) 8 *Australian Year Book of International Law* 108 at 133–34 cited in Nick Poynder, 'Recent Implementation of the Refugee Convention in Australia and the Law of

14 REFUGEES, ASYLUM SEEKERS AND THE RULE OF LAW

Lauterpacht and Daniel Bethlehem argue that the content of *non-refoulement* as a customary principle of law includes the prohibitions in the complementary protection treaties (such as the ICCPR and CAT).[57] But Hathaway rejects the view that *non-refoulement*, however defined, is part of customary international law.[58] Goodwin-Gill and McAdam suggest that there is only a 'minority of commentators' who deny it this status.[59] In their view, each state is thus considered to have an indirect responsibility to guarantee that an asylum seeker will not be subject to torture, inhumane or degrading treatment upon return to their country of origin or transit country.

Due to the debate over the status and scope of *non-refoulement*, it is open to states to interpret the principle restrictively as the *European Roma Rights Centre* case and the *Sale* decision illustrate. Moreover, apart from the debate about the customary status of the principle, and the debate about its extraterritorial application, there is also scope for states to apply the principle according to their own meaning. The various components of *non-refoulement*, the meaning of 'life or freedom', of 'torture' and 'cruel, inhuman or degrading treatment or punishment' are all open to interpretation at the state level (as are the various elements of the refugee definition).[60]

On a practical level, the UNHCR suggests that the problem with the *non-refoulement* principle is one of implementation by states, not one of standards.[61] In support of this, Goodwin-Gill and McAdam cite many examples of situations, including those in Rwanda, Thailand, Bangladesh and the former Yugoslavia, where the principle has been breached in recent decades.[62] It is to these realities of refugee protection that we now turn.

Accommodations to International Human Rights Treaties. Have We Gone Too Far?' (1995) 2 *Australian Journal of Human Rights* 75 at 89.

[57] Lauterpacht and Bethlehem, 'The Scope and the Content of the Principle of Non-Refoulement', para. 253. cf. Goodwin-Gill and McAdam, *The Refugee in International Law*, p. 348 – while torture might be covered by both treaties, query whether 'inhuman degrading treatment' is incorporated into a customary principle.

[58] Hathaway, *The Rights of Refugees*, pp. 36 and 366. Note that Goodwin-Gill and McAdam, *The Refugee in International Law*, pp. 351–358 critique this interpretation of the *European Roma Rights Centre* case.

[59] Goodwin-Gill and McAdam, *The Refugee in International Law*, p. 354.

[60] Jari Pirjola, 'Shadows in Paradise – Exploring *Non-Refoulement* as an Open Concept' (2007) 19 *International Journal of Refugee Law* 639.

[61] Mr McNamara, UNHCR, UN doc. A/AC.96/SR.522 (1997), para. 61 cited in Goodwin-Gill and McAdam, *The Refugee in International Law*, p. 229.

[62] Goodwin-Gill and McAdam, *The Refugee in International Law*, pp. 229–32.

Part two: development of the international system of refugee protection – realities

The Cold War period

In the Cold War period, crises such as the Hungarian crisis of 1956 and the Czech uprising in 1968 emphasized the ideological basis of the individualized concept of refugee protection in the 1951 Refugee Convention. But from the 1970s onwards, refugee crises in other parts of the world, largely in Africa and Asia, suggested that the refugee problem was not unique to Europe and that it required different approaches. The UNHCR promoted the 1967 Refugee Protocol to enable it to deal with new situations of refugees en masse, such as Chinese refugees fleeing communism, and refugees from African states affected by decolonization, civil wars and independence movements. However, whereas the Refugee Protocol recognized the global nature of the problem, the universality of the rights of refugees, and the possibility of global solutions,[63] it did not grant the UNHCR the extra powers it wanted in order to deal with groups of refugees.[64] The legacy of this episode was to create a distinction between refugees who flee individualized persecution (and who can claim refugee status under the 1951 Refugee Convention), and those who flee generalized violence (who may have difficulty in proving that they are persecuted as individuals). The process surrounding the Protocol also showed the tension between state interests and the UNHCR, which is dependent on the same states as donors for its operations.

As a result of the failure of the Refugee Protocol to extend the UNHCR's mandate, it was left to the regions themselves to deal with the refugee problem as best they could. In the course of doing so, the regional initiatives demonstrated the problems and weaknesses of the system of protection which had developed around the Refugee Convention.

For example, the central importance of asylum was a feature of the 1969 Organization of African Unity Convention Governing the Specific Aspects of Refugee Problems in Africa (OAU Convention),[65] which

---

[63] Laura Barnett, 'Global Governance and the Evolution of the International Refugee Regime' (2002) 14 *International Journal of Refugee Law* 238 at 248.

[64] Sara E. Davies, 'Redundant or Essential? How Politics Shaped the Outcome of the 1967 Protocol' (2007) 19 *International Journal of Refugee Law* 703.

[65] Organisation of African Unity, Convention Governing the Specific Aspects of Refugee Problems in Africa, Addis Ababa, 10 September 1969, in force on 20 June 1974, 1001 UNTS 45.

16   REFUGEES, ASYLUM SEEKERS AND THE RULE OF LAW

arose in the context of independence movements and massive displacements during the period of decolonization in Africa.[66] Article II of the OAU Convention, headed 'Asylum', deals specifically with asylum, *non-refoulement*, and durable solutions. Article II(1) states that:

> Member States of the OAU shall use their best endeavours consistent with their respective legislations to receive refugees and to secure the settlement of those refugees who, for well-founded reasons, are unable or unwilling to return to their country of origin or nationality.

Although the right of asylum is qualified by the requirement that it be 'consistent with their [domestic] legislations', it is an advance on the Refugee Convention. To take the political 'sting' out of asylum, Article II(2) states that the grant of asylum is 'a peaceful and humanitarian act'. The *non-refoulement* obligation is contained in Article II(3) and is applicable to persons whose 'life, physical integrity or liberty' would be threatened for the reasons set out in both refugee definitions.

The 1969 OAU Convention was a direct inspiration for the 1984 Cartagena Declaration on Refugees adopted at a Colloquium held at Cartagena, Colombia, in November 1984 (Cartagena Declaration),[67] which relates to the 'refugee situation' in Central America. This was a response to mass refugee influxes, in this case arising from political and military instability in Central America in the 1970s and 1980s. As in the OAU Convention, the refugee definition in the Cartagena Declaration is linked to root causes.[68] The Declaration also confirms that the granting of asylum is 'humanitarian' in nature, and reiterates the importance and meaning of the principle of *non-refoulement*. The Declaration reflected the then current experiences of refugees by expressing its 'concern' at the problem raised by military attacks on refugee camps and settlements

---

[66] Between 1963 and 1966 the number of refugees in Africa rose from 300,000 to 700,000: Micah B. Rankin, 'Extending the Limits or Narrowing the Scope? Deconstructing the OAU Refugee Definition Thirty Years On', UNHCR, *New Issues in Refugee Research*, Working Paper No 113 (April 2005) at p. 2.

[67] Cartagena Declaration on Refugees, Cartagena, 22 November 1984, OAS/Ser.L/V/II.66, doc.10, rev.1, 190–3.

[68] Article I(2) of the OAU Convention states: 'The term 'refugee' shall also apply to every person, who owing to external aggression, occupation, foreign domination or events seriously disturbing public order in either part or the whole of his country of origin or nationality, is compelled to leave his place of habitual residence in order to seek refuge in another place outside his country of origin or nationality.'

INTRODUCTION 17

in different parts of the world.[69] Additionally, going beyond the 'legal' refugee issue, it expresses its 'concern' at the 'situation of displaced persons within their own countries'.[70]

The importance of asylum as a measure for achieving 'durable solutions' was reinforced during the refugee crisis in Indo-China in the 1970s and 1980s, when up to 3 million people fled from Indo-China in the two decades after 1975. The Comprehensive Plan of Action for Indo-Chinese refugees (CPA), which was agreed upon in Geneva in June 1989 by the UNHCR, countries of first asylum and 50 resettlement countries in the West, followed a renewed surge in Vietnamese departures in the period 1987–8. An important factor in the success of the CPA was the granting of asylum by countries in the region.[71] However, another factor in the success of the CPA was that the countries of first asylum were assured that their obligations were temporary, as resettlement would follow. Thus the CPA demonstrated the pragmatic realities of refugee policy.

'Durable solutions'

In the immediate post-World War II period, the emphasis of refugee protection under the Refugee Convention was upon integrating and resettling refugees in a new country. Today the preferred 'durable solution' is repatriation to the country of origin. The evolution of this approach began during the Cold War period.

In the early 1980s, when it became clear that the post-World War II rapprochement on refugee protection was fading, the expression 'durable solutions for refugees' first appeared in the UNHCR's Executive Committee's (ExCom) Conclusions. This was the period in which there was a substantial rise in the number of worldwide refugees. In 1974 the UNHCR estimated that there were 2.4 million refugees worldwide, but by 1984 the figure was 10.5 million.[72] In 1996 this figure had risen to 27 million, although the figure now included IDPs under the UNHCR's

---

[69] Cartagena Declaration, para. III(7). [70] Cartagena Declaration, para. III(9).

[71] UNHCR, 'Flight from Indochina' in *The State of the World's Refugees 2000: Fifty Years of Humanitarian Action* (Oxford University Press, 2000), Chapter 4; Rick Towle, 'Processes and Critiques of the Indo-Chinese Comprehensive Plan of Action: An Instrument of International Burden-Sharing?' (2006) 18 *International Journal of Refugee Law* 537.

[72] Barnett, 'Global Governance' at 249.

18   REFUGEES, ASYLUM SEEKERS AND THE RULE OF LAW

expanded mandate. The important point about this discussion is that in the Cold War period, as the number of refugees increased, refugees became recognized as a 'problem' and one which had to be 'solved'.

In the 1980s, as refugee crises escalated, the emphasis of refugee protection changed from an 'exilic' basis to a 'source control bias' through policies of containment and temporary protection.[73] UNHCR ExCom Conclusion 22 (XXXII)-1981, which dealt with the 'Protection of asylum seekers in situations of large-scale influx',[74] emphasizes the need to protect asylum seekers according to 'basic human standards' and 'fundamental civil rights', even while providing temporary protection. However, eight years further on, the tone of UNHCR ExCom Conclusion 58 (XL)-1989 on 'The problem of refugees and asylum seekers who move in an irregular manner from a country in which they had already found protection'[75] is quite different. While it refers to the need to respect 'basic human standards'[76] in relation to irregular 'movers', its focus is upon the 'destabilizing effect' which such movements have 'on structured international efforts to provide appropriate solutions for refugees'. Conclusion 58 reflects the escalating crisis in Indo-China and the perceived need to halt 'secondary movements' by asylum seekers. Around this period, the emphasis of refugee protection changed to 'containment' in countries of origin.

At all times, voluntary repatriation has remained the preferred UNHCR solution for refugees. For example, UNHCR ExCom Conclusion 58 (XL)-1989 on 'The problem of refugees and asylum seekers who move in an irregular manner from a country in which they had already found protection'[77] states that governments should, 'in close co-operation with the UNHCR':

(i) seek to promote the establishment of appropriate measures for the care and support of refugees and asylum seekers in countries where they have found protection pending ... a durable solution and

---

[73] T. Alexander Aleinikoff, 'State Centred Refugee Law: From Resettlement to Containment' (1992) 14 *Michigan Journal of International Law* 120 at 125.

[74] UNHCR ExCom, 'Conclusion no. 22 (XXXII)', (1981) *Protection of Asylum Seekers in Situations of Large-scale Influx*, UN doc. A/AC.96/601, para. 57(2).

[75] UNHCR ExCom, 'Conclusion no. 58 (XL)', (1989) *The Problem of Refugees and Asylum Seekers Who Move in an Irregular Manner from a Country in Which They Have Already Found Protection*, UN doc. A/AC.96/737, part N.

[76] *Ibid.*, para. (f).   [77] *Ibid.*, part N.

INTRODUCTION 19

(ii) promote appropriate durable solutions with particular emphasis firstly on voluntary repatriation and, where this is not possible, local integration and the provision of adequate resettlement opportunities.[78]

Thus, while voluntary repatriation was still emphasized in this period, the focus was changing to 'local integration'[79] or 'containment' in the country or region of first asylum.

The Cold War period was characterized by regional and UNHCR efforts to respond to new refugee crises *and* to the interests of its state donors. In this period, there was a great deal of emphasis on 'durable' solutions, suggesting that the 'problem' could be solved. But in the post-Cold War period it became clear that the problem was entrenched and that there was no easy 'quick fix'.

The post-Cold War period

The break up of the Soviet Union at the end of the 1990s and the end of the Cold War are commonly seen as definitive factors in the refugee 'problem'.[80] The change in the geopolitical landscape also coincided with the rise in the number of IDPs and a developing awareness of the issues that this category of 'forced migrants' raised. At the same time, the problem of 'protracted refugee situations' increased, but so also did the level of international migration. We discuss each of these trends in turn and relate them to the policies of industrialized states. But first it is necessary to describe the general effect of the end of the Cold War.

One consequence of the end of the Cold War was a change in the geopolitical role of states. Julie Mertus describes this as an important aspect of 'the new refugee regime' which became evident in the 1990s at the close of the Cold War.[81] In her words:

> [T]he new refugee regime reflects the trend away from the State and strict notions of sovereignty but also the staying power of the statist paradigm.[82]

In other words, concern with territorial sovereignty prevailed in the context of decentralized and weak states. Further, the root causes of

---

[78] *Ibid.*, para. (d).   [79] *Ibid.*, para. (e).
[80] Julie Mertus, 'The State and the Post-Cold War Refugee Regime: New Models, New Questions' (1998) 10 *International Journal of Refugee Law* 321.
[81] *Ibid.*   [82] *Ibid.* at 323.

20　REFUGEES, ASYLUM SEEKERS AND THE RULE OF LAW

displacement were perceived to be qualitatively different. As Mertus expresses the point:

> Today, refugees are often victims of violence or natural disasters, not ideological persecution.[83]

Moreover, as Mertus observes:

> Receiving States talk less about the human rights of the uprooted and more about their own rights.[84]

Goodwin-Gill has pointed to the difficult role of the UNHCR in the 1990s in this context, and to what he refers to as ' "Depoliticisation" [sic] of the refugee and the challenge of relevance'.[85] As the UNHCR itself has observed,[86] there has been a lack of interest in addressing the refugee issue since the end of the Cold War. It points out that this rubs off on countries of first asylum, which tend to be the poorer countries, where refugees are seen as a costly burden. This general decline in respect by states (both industrialized and in regions of origin) for the institution of asylum, and their unwillingness to help refugees, has been blamed for the rise in the number of IDPs and protracted refugee situations.[87] However, the finger has been pointed at the industrialized states as the leaders in constraining the international refugee regime.[88]

The IDP issue

The first major international recognition of an IDP issue was the Security Council authorization for Allied intervention in Iraq to protect the Kurds in 1991, although the issue had been acknowledged since the end of the 1980s in the context of difficulties in repatriating Cambodian and Afghani

---

[83] *Ibid.* at 326.　　[84] *Ibid.* at 328.

[85] Guy S. Goodwin-Gill, 'International Protection and Assistance for Refugees and the Displaced: Institutional Challenges and UN Reform', paper presented to Refugee Studies Centre Workshop, Oxford, 24 April 2006, p. 4, http://refugeelaw.qeh.ox.ac.uk/pdfs/guy-goodwin-gill-institutional-challenges.pdf (accessed 14 April 2008).

[86] UNHCR, *The State of the World's Refugees: Human Displacement in the New Millennium* (Oxford University Press, 2006), Chapter 5, available at www.unhcr.org/static/publ/sowr2006/toceng.htm (accessed 14 April 2008).

[87] Jeff Crisp, 'Forced Displacement in Africa: Dimensions, Difficulties and Policy Directions', UNHCR Research Paper No 126 (July 2006), p. 4.

[88] *Ibid.*; Catherine Dauvergne, 'Refugee Law and the Measure of Globalisation' in Savitri Taylor (ed.), *Nationality, Refugee Status and State Protection: Explorations of the Gap between Man and Citizen* (Special edition of *Law in Context*, Federation Press, 2005) 62 at 64.

refugees. Thomas Weiss and David Korn[89] point to UN Resolution 1992/73, which authorized the appointment of Special Rapporteur Francis Deng and which commissioned a study of the IDP issue as the beginning of the development of a 'mandate' on the issue.[90] Throughout the 1990s, the advocates for resolution of the IDP issue sought to keep the issue out of the UN, while the UNHCR fought to retain the integrity of its protection mandate. At the same time, the UNHCR further expanded its 'good offices' mandate to provide humanitarian assistance to IDPs,[91] often to critical acclaim,[92] as for example in the Balkan crisis.

Although it has been suggested that this episode of UNHCR intervention is evidence that IDPs arise from policies of containment, it has been pointed out that the IDP issue pre-dated the Balkan crisis. The link between restrictive state policies of admission and the IDP issue is thus difficult to prove, although it is often assumed.[93] In reality, the IDP issue is greatest in situations where there are failed states and internal conflict (such as in West Darfur, Sudan and Chad). In these situations, the distinction between IDP and refugee is fluid and technical, depending upon whether a person has managed to cross a border. Certainly IDP and protracted refugee situations often coexist on different sides of a border, particularly in Africa.

However, while it is difficult to prove a link between a downturn in support for refugees in industrialized states and the increased attention given to IDPs in the 1990s, it is clear that the two trends coincided with a preference for containment. Moreover, there was a greater willingness on the part of the international community to intervene in situations of displacement. As Roberta Cohen says:

> Greater access at the end of the Cold War to people uprooted in their own countries, coupled with changing notions of sovereignty, enabled the international community to step in when governments proved unable or unwilling to provide for the security and well-being of their displaced populations.[94]

---

[89] Thomas G. Weiss and David A. Korn, *Internal Displacement: Conceptualization and Consequences* (London: Routledge, 2006), Chapter 1.

[90] *Guiding Principles on Internal Displacement* E/CN.4/1998/53/Add.2, 11 February 1998.

[91] Guy S. Goodwin-Gill, 'International Protection and Assistance for Refugees and the Displaced: Institutional Challenges and UN Reform'.

[92] Michael Barutciski, 'A Critical View on UNHCR's Mandate Dilemmas' (2002) 14 *International Journal of Refugee Law* 365.

[93] UNHCR, *The State of the World's Refugees*, Chapter 7.

[94] Roberta Cohen, 'Response to Hathaway' (2007) 20 *Journal of Refugee Studies* 370 at 372.

22 REFUGEES, ASYLUM SEEKERS AND THE RULE OF LAW

Another reason for the separation of the IDP issue from refugee protection is pointed out by Josh DeWind:

> [I]n recent decades most refugees have sought protection en masse and, out of practical necessity, have been provided for as groups with camps and programmes that effectively deprive individuals of the ability to choose how they would like to cope with their predicament.[95]

As DeWind says, 'the realities of refugee circumstances and the politics of response diminish . . . individual refugee autonomy'.[96] Nevertheless, as pointed out above, the industrialized states have special responsibilities in the area of refugee policy, and the increase in the number of IDPs coincided with a decline in ideological and material support for refugees.[97]

It has been calculated that in 1982 the ratio of IDPs to refugees was 1:10, but that by 2006 it had reversed to 2.5:1.[98] The issue was the subject of an *Expert Seminar on Protracted IDP Situations* jointly hosted by UNHCR and the Brookings-Bern Project on Internal Displacement in Geneva, June 2007,[99] at which the similarities and differences between protracted IDP and refugee situations were discussed. The participants acknowledged that there is an important advocacy role to bring the issue to the attention of the international community, which bears responsibility for resettling refugees.[100]

Protracted refugees

The UNHCR has estimated that 'more than 60% of today's refugees are trapped in situations far from the international spotlight'.[101] Moreover, the 'vast majority are to be found in the world's poorest and most unstable regions'.[102] UNHCR estimated that the number of 'protracted refugee situations' (which it defines as situations involving more than 25,000 people for at least five years) rose from twenty-seven in 1993 to thirty-three in 2004.[103] They point out that most of the refugees

---

[95] Josh DeWind, 'Response to Hathaway' (2007) 20 *Journal of Refugee Studies* 381 at 382.
[96] *Ibid.*   [97] Crisp, 'Forced Displacement in Africa', p. 4.
[98] Weiss and Korn, *Internal Displacement*, p. 1.
[99] Brookings-Bern Project on Internal Displacement, *Expert Seminar on Protracted IDP Situations* (Geneva: 21–22 June 2007) – the figure quoted at p. 1 is 14.2 million. In 2005 it was calculated that the UNHCR's mandate covered 8.7 million refugees and that the total IDP population was 23.7 million. In 2006 the total IDP population had risen to 24.5 million. See *ibid.* Table 1 on p. 22.
[100] *Ibid.*, p. 13.   [101] UNHCR, *The State of the World's Refugees*, p. 106.
[102] *Ibid.*   [103] *Ibid.*, pp. 108–109.

INTRODUCTION 23

originated from countries where conflict persists and/or the state is in collapse. The crises in the Balkans, Somalia, The Great Lakes Region, Darfur/Chad and Iraq are the main sources of these refugee populations.

The issue of 'protracted refugee situations' illustrates the results of policies of containment which evolved in the 1990s. This is recognized in the Agenda for Protection,[104] which arose out of the UNHCR Global Consultations on International Protection of 2000.[105] It has a large emphasis on durable solutions, especially for protracted refugee situations. In particular, it recognizes that policies of containment have led to inequalities in the distribution of the burden of the refugee problem, and have resulted in human rights abuses. In the final section of this chapter, the legal responses of industrialized receiving states in the decade leading up to the beginning of the twenty-first century are described and linked to issues of 'forced migration'. This is the context in which restrictive measures towards asylum seekers and refugees are practised by industrialized states.

International migration and the migration–asylum nexus

Meanwhile, another trend which was signalled by the end of the Cold War was an increase in human mobility as states and borders collapsed or controls were not enforced. Already increasing, international migration became an entrenched feature of the global picture. One estimate is that the number of international migrants grew from about 100 million in 1960 to 175 million in 2000.[106] It is currently estimated that worldwide the number of people living outside their homeland stands at 200 million.[107] The majority leave their place of birth because they are unable to earn a living and because there is a demand for their labour elsewhere.[108] But this cohort includes both regular (legal) and irregular migrants. This is not surprising, as it has been pointed out that the conditions that cause economic migration are closely linked with those that cause forced migration, leading to the migratory movement of people with 'mixed motivations'. Further, both economic migrants

---

[104] Agenda for Protection, A/AC.96/965.Add.I, 26 June 2002.
[105] *Ibid.*, Declaration of State Parties, Preamble cl. 2.
[106] UNHCR, *State of the World's Refugees*, Box 1.1, p. 12.
[107] Antonio Guterres, UN High Commissioner for Refugees, 'Human Movement: It's About Taking Care of People', *The Age*, 11 December 2007, p. 13.
[108] *Ibid.*

24 REFUGEES, ASYLUM SEEKERS AND THE RULE OF LAW

and asylum seekers tend to follow the same routes and use the same mechanisms for mobility.[109]

In its 2005 report, the Global Commission on International Migration[110] referred to the growth of global social networks and diasporas as a factor which aided this process.[111] This process is sometimes referred to as 'globalization'. It involves 'large scale flows of goods and services, financial assets, technology and people across international borders'.[112] An important consequence of this process is that it highlights inequalities between regions in the global North and the global South.[113] For example, it has been estimated that 63 per cent of the international migrants referred to above were in developed countries.[114]

This migration–asylum nexus dominates current policy responses of industrialized countries. As one writer has said:

> To some extent ... the migration–asylum nexus is a self-fulfilling prophecy: by ignoring the fundamental causes of migration and treating all entrants with suspicion and restrictiveness, governments themselves help to erode the distinction between economic and forced migrants, which is a cornerstone of their policies.[115]

But nevertheless, the response of developed states to this issue is arguably disproportionate.[116] For example, the International Organization for Migration (IOM) estimated in 2000 that 150 million people live outside their country of birth, but point out that this is about 2 per cent of the global population.[117] Moreover, the distinction between 'economic migrant' and 'refugee' is not as distinct as policy makers might

---

[109] Stephen Castles, 'The Migration–Asylum Nexus and Regional Approaches' in Kneebone and Rawlings-Sanaei (eds.), *New Regionalism and Asylum Seekers*: Challenges Ahead, Chapter 1.

[110] Global Commission on International Migration, *Migration in an Interconnected World: New Directions for Action*, Report (2005), www.gcim.org/en/ (accessed 14 April 2008).

[111] *Ibid.*, Introduction, para. 11.

[112] UNHCR, *State of the World's Refugees*, Box 1.1, p. 12.

[113] Erika Feller, 'Asylum, Migration and Refugee Protection: Realities, Myths and the Promise of Things to Come' (2006) 18 *International Journal of Refugee Law* 509.

[114] UNHCR, *State of the World's Refugees*, Box 1.1 p. 12.

[115] Castles, *New Regionalism*, Chapter 1, p. 30.

[116] For example, there is evidence that receiving states exaggerate or overstate the numbers of asylum seekers who arrive by boat in order to secure political support for restrictive measures. See Elspeth Guild, 'The Europeanisation of Europe's Asylum Policy' (2006) 18 *International Journal of Refugee Law* 630.

[117] Stephen Castles, 'Towards a Sociology of Forced Migration and Social Transformation' (2003) 37 *Sociology* (No 1 – *Global Refugees*) 13 at 15 citing (IOM) 2000 *World Migration Report 2000* (Geneva: International Organisation for Migration, 2000).

INTRODUCTION 25

think. There are many examples of discrimination on the basis of social or economic grounds which can be described as 'persecution' under the Refugee Convention.[118] Stephen Castles argues that most 'forced migration' (which includes refugee movements) is linked to economic development rather than to specific crises. He argues that politicization of the issues disguises their foundation in global inequality.[119] Nevertheless the response of industrialized states has been to attempt to prevent all irregular international migration.

In recent years there has been a direct emphasis on controlling the movement of asylum seekers through another legal regime which has been developed to control the activities of smugglers and traffickers in the context of 'irregular' international migration. This refers to the creation of the United Nations Convention against Transnational Organized Crime (CTOC framework)[120] in late 2000. This framework reflected the growing concerns of the international community over the trafficking of persons and migrant smuggling. The two Protocols which supplement it, and which were adopted at the same time, demonstrate these concerns. These are the Protocol to Prevent, Suppress and Punish Trafficking in Persons, Especially Women and Children (the Trafficking Protocol)[121] and the Protocol against the Smuggling of Migrants by Land, Sea and Air (the Migrant Protocol).[122] Under this framework, smuggling and trafficking in persons is perceived as an aspect of transnational organized crime associated with the phenomenon of 'irregular' international migration.

Although the rights of asylum seekers (who are termed 'migrants' for these purposes) are preserved in theory under the Migrant Protocol,[123] there is also provision to prevent them from leaving their country by unauthorized or irregular measures, and for them to be prosecuted for

---

[118] Foster, *International Refugee Law and Socio-Economic Rights*.
[119] Castles, 'Towards a Sociology of Forced Migration and Social Transformation'.
[120] United Nations Convention against Transnational Organised Crime, New York, 15 November 2000, in force 29 September 2003, UN Doc. A/55/383.
[121] Protocol to Prevent, Suppress and Punish Trafficking in Persons, Especially Women and Children, New York, 15 November 2000, in force 25 December 2003, UN Doc. A/55/383, Annex II.
[122] Protocol Against the Smuggling of Migrants by Land, Sea and Air, New York, 15 November 2000, in force 28 January 2004, UN Doc. A/55/383, Annex III. A third Protocol against the Illicit Manufacturing of and Trafficking in Firearms, Their Parts and Components and Ammunition further emphasizes the transnational organized crime context.
[123] Migrant Protocol, Art. 19.

26 REFUGEES, ASYLUM SEEKERS AND THE RULE OF LAW

such attempts.[124] These measures, which curtail freedom of movement and the right to seek asylum, may be justified by states under ICCPR Article 12(3) on the basis of 'national security' or 'public order'. This demonstrates how the issue of 'irregular' international migration can be used to justify restrictive measures against asylum seekers.

Part three: the introduction of restrictive legal measures for asylum seekers

The waning support for the concept of asylum, as discussed above, is reflected in legal responses and developments in refugee law in the 1990s. The rise in the number of international migrants led to the placing of asylum within the discourse of immigration policy (the migration–asylum nexus) and highlighted three trends:[125]

- greater sophistication of the administrative state
- growth in administrative bureaucracies with a preference for order
- containing forced migrants in country of origin (as discussed above).

In this section, two brief examples of the trend to order and 'control' are mentioned, namely, the introduction of the 'safe third country' notion and the further 'containment' of refugees.

One clear example of a restrictive trend to asylum seekers which arose as a response to increased international migration is the 'safe third country' notion,[126] which has its origins in collective European practices dating from the 1990s aimed at restricting access to national asylum procedures. This was historically the period when 'asylum fatigue' began to set in as the number of asylum seekers in Europe escalated. In this period, a number of other restrictions such as sanctions on carriers, detention, and abbreviated asylum procedures were introduced. In 1993 the influential German scholar, Professor Kay Hailbronner, published an article entitled 'The Concept of "Safe Country" and Expeditious

---

[124] See Art. 6(4) and cf. with Art. 5. See Colin Harvey and Robert P. Barnidge, 'Human Rights, Free Movement, and the Right to Leave in International Law' (2007) 19 *International Journal of Refugee Law* 1.

[125] Andrew Shacknove, 'From Asylum to Containment' (1993) 5 *International Journal of Refugee Law* 516.

[126] This is a concept which rests upon the premise that the obligation or responsibility to process the asylum seeker rests with another country. Stephen H. Legomsky, 'Secondary Refugee Movements and the Return of Asylum Seekers to Third Countries: the Meaning of Effective Protection' (2003) 15 *International Journal of Refugee Law* 567 at 570.

INTRODUCTION 27

Asylum Procedures: A Western European Perspective'[127] supporting the use of the safe third country notion to prevent the European asylum system from collapsing.[128]

Official recognition of the safe third country notion dates from the 1990 Dublin Convention[129] and the 1992 EU Ministers' statement.[130] Under the terms of the EU Resolution, Member States of the EU agreed to incorporate the 'host third country' principle into their national legislation. The effect of this was to impose an obligation on a Member State to identify whether such a country existed before undertaking a substantive examination of the application for asylum.

Furthermore, as the scale of international migration rose in the 1990s, receiving states began to focus on the costs of establishing systems for refugee status determination and started to introduce further measures to 'warehouse' or 'contain' refugees. Attention was also focused upon the status granted to applicants for refugee status. The malaise of the international refugee protection system was summarized by Hathaway and R. Alex Neve in an article published in 1997.[131] The features they singled out for attention included the costs of 'individuated' state responsibility, the 'warehousing' of refugees in regions of origin, and the creation of non-entrée systems. In particular, they pointed to the expectation of permanent resettlement as a point of contention on the part of states. In their article advocating that refugee law needed to be made 'relevant again' by concentrating on 'collectivized' and 'solution-oriented protection', Hathaway and Neve focused in particular upon the benefits of temporary protection, and advocated a scheme of burden-sharing involving 'interest-convergence' groups.

---

[127] Kay Hailbronner, 'The Concept of "Safe Country" and Expeditious Asylum Procedures: A Western European Perspective' (1993) 5 *International Journal of Refugee Law* (No 1) 31.

[128] Rosemary Byrne and Andrew Shacknove, 'The Safe Third Country Notion in European Asylum Law' (1996) 9 *Harvard Human Rights Journal* 185 argue that the introduction of the notion coincided with the rise of the administrative state in developed countries.

[129] Convention Determining the State Responsible for Examining Applications for Asylum Lodged in One of the Member States of the European Communities, Dublin, 15 June 1990, entered into force 1 September 1997.

[130] Resolution on a Harmonized Approach to Questions Concerning Host Third Countries, London, 1 December 1992 (the EU Resolution).

[131] James C. Hathaway and R. Alex Neve, 'Making International Refugee Law Relevant Again: A Proposal for Collectivised and Solution-Oriented Protection' (1997) 10 *Harvard Human Rights Journal* 115.

28   REFUGEES, ASYLUM SEEKERS AND THE RULE OF LAW

The Hathaway and Neve article produced a vigorous response[132] which pointed out the risk that such measures would be unlikely to achieve the suggested outcomes, that they would lead to further 'containment', and that they could affect stability and peace in those regions. The authors suggested that any savings achieved were unlikely to be diverted, in whole or in part, to support refugee communities in regions of origin. Unfortunately the call of Hathaway and Neve for more burden-sharing has not been taken up by industrialized states. Subsequent practices fit the description of burden-shifting rather than burden-sharing as, for example, demonstrated by Australia's 'Pacific Plan'.[133] The problem of 'containment' of refugees and IDPs has become endemic. Although the Member States of the European Union (EU) are developing an external policy based on assisting refugees in regions of origin, this is a new development, encouraged by the UNHCR.[134]

Part four: conclusions – an intractable problem?

The persistence of 'protracted refugee situations' demonstrates that lasting or 'durable' solutions are yet to be found for the unstable state conditions in which the majority of today's refugee populations live. In this context, three interlinked factors are involved. First, there is the reality of the North–South divide, and the reluctance of industrialized states to see the issues from a global development perspective. Secondly, there is the problem of authority and legitimacy in this context. The UNHCR struggles to enlist the support of donor states, who as parties to the Refugee Convention have agreed to cooperate with it. For their part, states rely on their so-called sovereign rights to determine who will enter their territory, and on their practical ability to implement the Refugee Convention in national legal systems. In this context, industrialized states must bear responsibility for positive solutions, and need to work with the UNHCR and other organizations to achieve parity between regions.

As mentioned above, in 2002 the UNHCR launched its Convention Plus initiative, which was intended to shore up international refugee

---

[132] Deborah Anker, Joan Fitzpatrick and Andew Shacknove, 'Crisis and Cure: A Reply to Hathaway/Neve and Schuck' (1998) 11 *Harvard Human Rights Journal* 295.

[133] Savitri Taylor, 'The Pacific Solution or a Pacific Nightmare? The Difference between Burden Shifting and Responsibility Sharing' (2005) 6 *Asian-Pacific Law and Policy Journal* 1. See further, Chapter 4 in this volume.

[134] See Alexander Betts, 'Towards a Mediterranean Solution? Implications for the Region of Origin' (2006) 18 *International Journal of Refugee Law* 652.

INTRODUCTION

law with a normative framework for global burden-sharing. As the initiative winds up, an assessment of it concludes, rather gloomily, that Convention Plus 'fell far short of expectations'.[135] It was envisaged that Convention Plus would provide 'soft law' agreements as substantive outcomes, but they did not materialize. Reading the subtext of the 'report', it appears that the 'North–South' divergence was a large factor in the (negative) outcomes of Convention Plus. Northern states basically wanted to protect their interests and Southern states felt that their interests and needs were being overlooked.[136]

In this context, if the international regime of refugee protection is to be sustained, the burden is on Northern states to act responsibly. This includes using their legal systems to support rather than to deny protection to asylum seekers where appropriate. But rather than beginning with that premise, states have typically insisted on their sovereign rights to determine who will enter their territory. Although the human rights context of refugee law is widely acknowledged, it is applied inconsistently.[137] Current indications are that refugee law is inconsistent between states at the national level. It seems that states are using refugee law at the national level to achieve their own aims. Erika Feller, the Assistant High Commissioner – Protection, UNHCR, recently referred to the asylum 'lottery' and remarked that:

> Finding asylum can become a matter of chance in some regions, due to inconsistency by States in applying Convention standards.[138]

One indication of this is the wide divergence between recognition rates for refugees among different countries and tribunals.[139] For example, in 2002, the recognition rate in Canada was 55 per cent, in contrast to Greece, whose recognition rate was less than 2 per cent. In the USA and the UK, recognition rates were around 30 per cent, whereas in Australia, Belgium and Sweden, the rate was 20–25 per cent.[140] These figures (taken at face value) suggest that national legal responses are significant in

---

[135] Alexander Betts and Jean-Francois Durieux, 'Convention Plus as a Norm-Setting Exercise' (2007) 20 *Journal of Refugee Studies* 1 at 2.

[136] *Ibid.* at 6.

[137] Michelle Foster, *International Refugee Law and Socio-Economic Rights*, p. 28.

[138] Erika Feller, UNHCR, 'Statement', 58th Session of the ExCom of the High Commissioner's Programme, agenda item 5(a) in introducing the 2007 Note on International Protection, Doc AC.96/1038, 3 October 2007.

[139] See Legomsky, Chapter 3 in this volume.

[140] Ninette Kelley, 'International Refugee Protection Challenges and Opportunities' (2007) 19 *International Journal of Refugee Law* 401 at 428.

30 REFUGEES, ASYLUM SEEKERS AND THE RULE OF LAW

translating the international regime of refugee protection into practice. They demonstrate the interconnectedness of the international and the national rule of law. They suggest the important role of national legal systems in implementing the international law rights of refugees and asylum seekers and the opportunities that exist for interpreting and implementing those rights according to 'domestic' or national under-standings, given the 'imperfectness' of the regime, as described in this chapter.[141] The way that the rule of law operates at the national level in relation to refugees and asylum seekers determines the extent to which their rights are respected.

It is for that reason that this book explores national legal responses and the rule of law. The issue of the rights and status of the asylum seeker in the legal system raises fundamental questions about how to maintain the 'integrity' of the rule of law when it is under challenge, and the role of the state in protecting individuals who are not 'nationals'.

This book is important for a second reason – because it exposes the challenge that national legal responses pose to the international regime of refugee protection. As explained in this chapter, the Refugee Convention imposes the basic obligation of *non-refoulement* on states. However, as detailed in this book, as a result of general policies aimed at deterring spontaneous asylum seekers, many categories of individuals are excluded from the right to an individual determination of their status, which the Refugee Convention envisages. States are avoiding engagement with that obligation by denying the right to seek asylum, or by granting other forms of 'complementary' protection.[142] If states are bypassing the international system of refugee protection, this has implications for the development of policy responses at the international level.

In the next chapter, entitled 'The Rule of Law and the Role of Law: Refugees and Asylum Seekers', the meaning of the rule of law, and how it fits with ideas about the operation of a legal system comprising three independent arms of government is explained. This will assist with an evaluation of the role of law in this contested area of policy. It also explains the link between the international and national law rule of law in this scheme. In particular, that chapter introduces the reader to

---

[141] Another indication of the asylum 'lottery' is the differing interpretations of aspects of the refugee definition, divergent approaches to credibility assessments and varying standards of proof.

[142] That is, protection afforded to states by persons who fall outside the definition of a refugee in the Refugee Convention, Art. 1A(2). This issue is discussed in Chapters 4 and 5 in this volume.

Ronald Dworkin's idea of 'law as integrity' as one tool in an evaluation of the role of national legal systems and the interconnectedness of the international and national law rule of law.

Following that general discussion of the rule of law, subsequent chapters outline the national legal responses in different jurisdictions, beginning with Canada (Chapter 2), followed by the USA (Chapter 3), Australia (with some New Zealand comparison, Chapter 4), and concluding with the UK (Chapter 5). The final chapter (Chapter 6) draws together the themes and material presented in the book.

1

The Rule of Law and the Role of Law: Refugees and Asylum Seekers

SUSAN KNEEBONE

The purpose of this chapter is to explain some meanings of the rule of law, and how they fit with ideas about the operation of a legal system comprising three independent arms of government. This will assist with an evaluation of the role of law in this contested area of refugee and asylum law and policy. In particular, this chapter introduces the reader to Ronald Dworkin's idea of 'law as integrity' as one tool in such an evaluation.

The focus of this book upon the rule of law arises from an overall concern with how national legal responses to refugees and asylum seekers have developed, and what they reveal about the operation of the rule of law. The way that the rule of law operates at the national level in relation to refugees and asylum seekers determines the extent to which their rights in international law (especially, as explained in the previous chapter, the right to seek asylum and the right against *refoulement*) are respected. That is, it is important for practical reasons, as it has been left to state parties to international treaties to acknowledge and to implement the rights and status of asylum seekers and refugees. As explained in the previous chapter, the international rule of law is imperfect, and it is open to individual states to interpret and implement it according to their own needs and understanding.[1] This book is concerned about the integrity or coherency of 'dualist' legal systems. The rule of law is important for that reason, but also because it shows how national refugee policy is developed, and the subtext that underlies national policy.

---

[1] United Nations High Commissioner for Refugees (UNHCR), *Handbook on Procedures and Criteria for Determining Refugee Status under the 1951 Convention and the 1967 Protocol relating to the Status of Refugees* (Geneva: UNHCR, 1979, re-edited 1992) (UNHCR Handbook), para. 28 assumes that an administrative decision about refugee status is merely declaratory. See 'Introduction: Refugees and Asylum Seekers in the International Context – Rights and Realities' (Introduction) note 4 for a summary of the doctrine of margin of appreciation.

THE RULE OF LAW AND THE ROLE OF LAW   33

In this context, Ronald Dworkin's idea of 'law as integrity' is appealing as a comparator and framework for analysis because it contains a concept of an integrated rule of law, reflecting the operation of a legal system. The idea of 'integrity' in a legal system also has a popular meaning associated with values of justice, equality and procedural fairness, and the independence of the three branches of government.[2] It implies the existence of a morally coherent legal system which emphasizes the rights of individuals. But governments also use this term to describe the aims of their restrictive policies in relation to asylum seekers when the 'national interest' is invoked. When they talk about the 'integrity' of the asylum system, they often use the term to refer to inviolable territorial borders, and to policies which allow them to decide who is allowed to enter their territory and to share the benefits that they provide to the political community.[3] Clearly this is another view of integrity which focuses upon the distributive consequences (the costs and benefits which accrue to the community) of policies in relation to refugees and asylum seekers. This other view of integrity looks to protect the 'rights' of the community *from* refugees and asylum seekers.

In this chapter, Dworkin's integrated rule of law will be described as an addendum to the system of 'checks and balances' which is provided by three independent branches of government. The chapter begins with an explanation of different versions of the rule of law which embody formal and substantive (or normative) visions of law, and their application to refugee and asylum law and policy. Part Two, which focuses upon theories of adjudication, stresses the significant role of judges to protect the rights of refugees against *refoulement*. In this context, the implications of the difference between formal and substantive explanations for the concepts of judicial review and procedural fairness and the value of neutrality are discussed. In Part Three, the discussion turns to the role of the legislature and the idea of the 'legislative principle' – which can be equated to the responsible exercise and interpretation of legislative power. This part includes a discussion of how principles of legislative interpretation bring international law into our 'dualist' legal systems. Part Four discusses the role of 'the community' and of national boundaries in defining the rights of asylum seekers. In this part, we

---

[2] Justice James Spigelman, *The Integrity Branch of Government* (2004) XLVIII Quadrant 7–8 at 50–7 suggests that administrative law through the doctrine of judicial review performs this role.

[3] See Legomsky, Chapter 3 in this volume.

34   REFUGEES, ASYLUM SEEKERS AND THE RULE OF LAW

move away from legal concepts and from Dworkin's theory to discussion of the political and ethical implications of excluding asylum seekers from legal systems. The combination of these arguments provides a better picture of how legal systems operate, and how national responses to issues about refugees and asylum seekers might be shaped.

Part one: contested meanings, overlapping consensus[4] on the rule of law

The 'Rule of Law' is a phrase redolent with meaning and significance for lawyers and political scientists alike. The American legal philosopher, Ronald Dworkin, has described the rule of law as an 'aspirational' but 'contested' concept or 'ideal'.[5] So, it may be asked, why do we concentrate on this concept which is so contentious and which, moreover, has been treated with such scepticism by other recent commentators?[6] It is precisely because of that scepticism and the need to understand the meaning of the rule of law, because of the significant consequences that it has for asylum seekers and refugees, that we embark upon this route. In this part, it is explained that the concept embodies both formal (or procedural) and substantive (or normative) visions of law. This has important implications for evaluating the way in which judges decide cases about asylum seekers and refugees in national jurisdictions.

In its most simple and non-contentious sense, the 'rule of law' refers to the idea of *rule by law*, but this then begs the question of the significance of the expression 'rule *of* law'. What is the essence of 'law' and, for that matter, what are 'laws'? Is a valid law simply one that arises from a legitimate and recognized source, and which conforms to formal criteria (such as procedural requirements and clarity), or do other criteria also determine its validity? And what do these ideas tell us about the nature of 'law' and of a legal system? These are all very important questions without easy answers, but which have enormous relevance to

---

[4] Liam Murphy, 'Concepts of Law' (2005) 30 *Australian Journal of Legal Philosophy* 1 at 18.
[5] Ronald Dworkin, *Justice in Robes* (Cambridge, MA; London: The Belknap Press / Harvard University Press, 2006), p. 5.
[6] See David Dyzenhaus, 'Recrafting the Rule of Law' in David Dyzenhaus (ed.) *Recrafting the Rule of Law: The Limits of Legal Order* (Oxford: Hart Publishing, 1999), Chapter 1, p. 1 citing Judith Shklar who refers to the rule of law as 'ruling-class chatter': Judith N. Shklar, 'Political Theory and the Rule of Law', in Allan C. Hutchinson and Patrick Monahan (eds.), *The Rule of Law: Ideal or Ideology* (Toronto: Carswell, 1987), p. 1.

THE RULE OF LAW AND THE ROLE OF LAW 35

the problem of determining the rights of asylum seekers and refugees who depend upon states for implementation of their rights. Thus they raise one set of issues which challenge the limits of contemporary legal systems. To find some answers to these questions, we need to go back a little in legal history.

The well known late-nineteenth century English jurist, Albert Venn Dicey, famously employed the term 'rule of law' in two senses: first to embody the idea of lawful constraint of authority (the idea of 'rule by law'), and secondly to signify the right to equal individual subjection to the law.[7] But these twin ideas, summarized as 'authority' and 'equality', do not always lead to the same practical solutions where individual rights are concerned. There are many examples in the context of refugees and asylum seekers, as highlighted in the chapters of this book, where their rights have been denied in the 'name of the law'. This brings to mind the well-known aphorism: 'The existence of law is one thing; its merit or demerit another'.[8] That is to say, self-evidently law and justice are not synonymous.

The contrast between authority and rights in Dicey's formulation leads us to another idea – the distinction between law and politics. It reminds us that political scientists are also interested in the concept of the rule of law, and that law and government are inextricably interconnected. The idea of authority suggests a 'formal' or 'thin' vision of the rule of law – the fact that officials and citizens alike are bound by and required to act consistently with the law. In this vision of the rule of law, it might be said that a law *is* a law because it is a validly enacted. On the other hand, the notion of rights which arises from ideas of equality, citizenship and democracy, and the corresponding duties or responsibilities of the state, refers to the exercise of government power. It suggests that something more than formal validity is needed to make a *law*. This could be called a 'thick' or substantive vision of the rule of law,[9] as it embodies values and norms.

---

[7] Albert Venn Dicey, *Introduction to the Study of the Law of the Constitution*, 10th edn. (London: Macmillan, 1959). Contrast Dyzenhaus, 'Recrafting the Rule of Law', p. 2 who makes a similar distinction between 'institutional restraints' and the 'rule of reason'.

[8] John Austin, *The Province of Jurisprudence Determined and The Uses of the Study of Jurisprudence* (London: Weidenfeld and Nicolson, 1954), pp. 184–185 cited by Brian Z. Tamanaha, *A General Jurisprudence of Law and Society* (Oxford University Press, 2001), p. 145.

[9] Brian Z. Tamanaha, 'A Concise Guide to the Rule of Law', Legal Studies Research Paper Series, Paper 07-0082, September 2007, p. 3.

36   REFUGEES, ASYLUM SEEKERS AND THE RULE OF LAW

Each of these views is a simplification of more complex ideas but, set out in this way, it can be seen that the dichotomy between the thin and the thick visions of the rule of law runs parallel to a division between law and politics. As Trevor Allan[10] points out, in addition to the twin concepts of authority and equality set out above, Dicey's Rule of Law also expressed political ideals, namely the 'legal doctrine of parliamentary sovereignty and the political doctrine of the sovereignty of the people'. We return to these important ideas later in this chapter, where we discuss the role of the community and the rule of law. For the moment it is important to note that the meaning of 'sovereignty' under the rule of law can be either a legal ('parliamentary sovereignty') or a political ('sovereignty of the people') concept, and perhaps a combination of the two when we talk about 'democracy', for example. These are not issues that we can examine in detail here, but the reason for mentioning them is to show that the answer to the question: 'What is the essence of "law"?' needs to take account of these legal and political concepts.

Returning for the present to the twin ideas of authority and equality in Dicey's theory, we can describe the 'thin' vision of the rule of law as one which stresses *posited* law or authority. This leads to enquiry into the nature of a legal system and the requirements of valid laws. This is described as legal positivism, and is regarded as the leading modern legal philosophy.[11] Its most famous exponent is the English philosopher, Herbert L.A. Hart, who claimed that his theory of law was both descriptive and conceptual.[12] Hart said that a legal system exists if a basic rule of recognition (or locus of authority), *accepted* by the system's officials, is in place, and if the rules applied in that system as valid rules according to that rule of recognition are *generally obeyed*.[13] While Hart's concept of law is avowedly politically neutral, his most persistent critic,[14] Ronald Dworkin, proposes a model of 'law as integrity' which

[10] Trevor R.S. Allan, *Law Liberty and Justice: The Legal Foundations of British Constitutionalism* (Oxford: Clarendon Press, 1993), p. 11. Note that Allan suggests that both Dicey and Dworkin were concerned with 'overall coherence and unity of the legal system'.

[11] Brian Z. Tamanaha, 'The Contemporary Relevance of Legal Positivism' (2007) 32 *Australian Journal of Legal Philosophy* 1 at 1.

[12] Herbert L.A. Hart, *The Concept of Law* (Oxford: The Clarendon Press, 1961).

[13] Brian Bix, 'Legal Positivism' in Martin Golding and William Edmundson (eds.), *The Blackwell Guide to the Philosophy of Law and Legal Theory* (London: Blackwell, 2005), Chapter 2, p. 10 (emphasis in original).

[14] Tamanaha, *A General Jurisprudence of Law and Society*, p. 133.

THE RULE OF LAW AND THE ROLE OF LAW 37

is essentially focused upon political morality (in the sense explained below).

The law–morality debate has been defused to a certain extent by the development of two schools of legal positivism;[15] namely the exclusive and the inclusive versions. These, it is claimed, were shaped by a defensive reaction to Dworkin's critique of Hart.[16] The exclusive or 'hard' version claims that what law is and what law ought to be are two different questions. To qualify as law under this version, 'something must be *posited* through some social act or activity, either by enactment, decision or practice [emphasis in original]'.[17] By contrast, the inclusive or 'soft' version of legal positivism allows some operation for moral principles. It claims that, while there is no necessary moral content of a legal rule, a particular legal system may make moral criteria necessary or sufficient for validity *in that system*.[18] Hart accepted this version of positivism in the posthumously published postscript to *The Concept of Law*.[19] Brian Bix suggests that the strongest argument for inclusive legal positivism is the 'fit' with the 'way both legal officials and legal texts talk about the law'.[20] Inclusive legal positivism accepts that moral criteria may be either a sufficient or necessary ground for legal validity in many circumstances. For example, the principles of equality and due process (which are discussed in Part two below) *necessarily* have a moral basis.[21]

This somewhat abstract discussion demonstrates several points. First, there is a range of views about the relationship between law and morality, which as we will see, affects views about how judges decide cases or *should* decide cases (this relates to theories of adjudication, discussed in Part two). Secondly, it is difficult to describe the difference in views as a dichotomy; rather there is an overlapping consensus on the relationship between law and morality. In this context, the idea of a continuum of views may be a better analogy.[22] Thirdly, this brief discussion illustrates the evolutionary nature of the rule of law.

---

[15] Tamanaha, 'The Contemporary Relevance of Legal Positivism'; Liam Murphy, 'Concepts of Law'.

[16] Tamanaha, 'The Contemporary Relevance of Legal Positivism' at 24.

[17] Scott Shapiro, 'Law, Morality, and the Guidance of Conduct (2006) 6 *Legal Theory* 127 at 127 cited by Tamanaha, 'The Contemporary Relevance of Legal Positivism' at 23.

[18] Bix, 'Legal Positivism', p. 20.   [19] *Ibid.*   [20] *Ibid.*

[21] *Ibid.*, p. 21. Inclusive legal positivism accepts that the use of moral criteria is a choice of the officials, not a characteristic of the legal system.

[22] Dyzenhaus, 'Recrafting the Rule of Law', p. 3.

38   REFUGEES, ASYLUM SEEKERS AND THE RULE OF LAW

This last point is an essential one. The ideal of the rule of law is a dynamic one that has responded to and been shaped by particular political and constitutional events. For example, when Dicey wrote, he was responding in part to the imminent rise of the administrative state and to the defects that he saw in the French system of separate administrative courts. Before Dicey's time, the idea of the rule of law was debated by political philosophers as the framework of our modern constitution took shape and the powers of the King developed into a concept of state. Our shared constitutional history was shaped by contests between the different arms of government. Indeed, it is said that Jeremy Bentham, the 'father' of legal positivism was inspired by a desire to curb the power of 'activist' judges.[23] Today, the issue of the rights of refugees and asylum seekers provides yet another challenge to the rule of law when executive and judiciary battle for control of the issue, and reactive legislatures use legislation to implement the executive's agenda.

The idea that law and politics are separate is a subtext which underlines legal positivist thinking.[24] As David Dyzenhaus reminds us, the development of legal positivism led to the severance of the link between political theory and legal theory.[25] While Dworkin's theory is self-described as embodying political morality, it implies 'politics' in a special sense as elaborated below. By contrast Hart's theory was purposefully apolitical and uncritical of the state.[26] However, in a statement which encapsulates a popular view, Dennis Galligan (who critiques Hart's theory) points to the limits of that view:

> Modern legal orders are based on ideas and values that ought to win support and protection. The idea that law is *relatively* distinct from politics, that legislatures are limited in the use of their legislative authority, that officials hold power on trust and should answer for their use of it, and that law should be used as an instrument for both stability and achieving positive social goals, all warrant our support [emphasis added].[27]

As the discussion in this book illustrates, it is doubtful whether law and politics can be entirely separated in the context of the rights of refugees and asylum seekers.

---

[23] Margaret Davies, *Asking the Law Question* (Sydney: Thomson Lawbook, 1994), p. 49.
[24] David Dyzenhaus, 'Reuniting the Brain: The Democratic Basis of Judicial Review' (1998) 9 *Public Law Review* 98.
[25] *Ibid.*   [26] Murphy, 'Concepts of Law' at 9–10.
[27] Dennis J. Galligan, *Law in Modern Society* (Oxford University Press, 2007), p. 21 (emphasis added).

THE RULE OF LAW AND THE ROLE OF LAW   39

To summarize the discussion up to this point: while there is agreement on the need for a rule of law, there is disagreement on what the rule of law comprises. In simple terms it can be said that the rule of law embodies both formal (or procedural) and substantive (or normative) visions of law. The formal vision of law approximates to the idea of legal positivism within which a second consensus has formed on the relevance of morality to understanding the nature of the rule of law. But while there is some consensus on the point of morality, the relevance of political concepts to the rule of law is one that continues to divide legal philosophers.

In his approach to political morality, Dworkin provides a substantive vision of the law which has, in turn, inspired many other philosophers to question aspects of the positivist tradition, such as the nature of rules and discretions.[28] But, before proceeding further, it is necessary to explain Dworkin's ideas a little more fully, as they are central to understanding the distinction between formal (or procedural) and substantive (or normative) visions of law which are discussed in this chapter. They are also essential to understanding the discussion of the 'legislative principle' and the importance of 'community' in Parts three and four, respectively, of this chapter.

Dworkin's interpretive theory of law as 'integrity'

As explained above, Dworkin rejects the positivist idea that a legal system is explained simply by the existence of binding obligations. His theory has developed over the years after long reflection and debate. For example, in *Taking Rights Seriously* (1977),[29] Dworkin was concerned to identify the policies and principles (values) which determine how legal systems function, as opposed to thinking about law as a system of rules. In *A Matter of Principle* (1985),[30] Dworkin discussed the application of the principle of procedural fairness or 'due process' in adjudicating the rights of individuals. In *Law's Empire* (1986),[31] Dworkin focused on

---

[28] Dennis J. Galligan, *Discretionary Powers: A Legal Study of Official Discretion* (Oxford: Clarendon Press, 1986).
[29] Ronald Dworkin, *Taking Rights Seriously*, 2nd edn. with a Reply to Critics (Cambridge, MA: Harvard University Press, 1978).
[30] Ronald Dworkin, *A Matter of Principle* (Cambridge, MA: Harvard University Press, 1985).
[31] Ronald Dworkin, *Law's Empire* (Cambridge, MA: Belknap Press, 1986).

40   REFUGEES, ASYLUM SEEKERS AND THE RULE OF LAW

the role of judges in adjudicating and deciding issues in the legal system, particularly in 'hard cases'.

Dworkin looks for the underlying principles or values which lead to a united or coherent legal system. Dworkin's idea of 'law as integrity', although not unrelated to the popular meaning described at the beginning of this chapter, has a special meaning which focuses upon the operation of the rule of law. His theory of law is that the nature of legal argument lies in the best moral interpretation of existing social practices.[32] His theory of justice is based upon the principle of equality of all human beings.[33] His idea of 'law as integrity' is an *interpretive* theory of law which concentrates upon the role of judges in a legal system and upon their responsibility to decide cases by reference to precedent and basic principles or values. Dworkin requires judges to evaluate the justifying purpose or goal or principle to be applied.[34] In his view, judges have to be politically neutral (in the sense of partisan) but not morally neutral. But on the other hand, his idea of justice, being based upon equality, reflects his view about political morality.[35]

In *Justice in Robes* (2006),[36] Dworkin explains that his interpretive theory functions by seeking the 'best' or 'moral' 'justification' in practice. This has two dimensions, which Dworkin terms the 'fit' and the 'value' of a practice:

> First, a justification must roughly *fit* what it purports to justify . . . Second, . . . it must also sufficiently describe some sufficiently important *value* that the practice serves [emphasis added].[37]

For example, in the context of constitutional adjudication, he said:

> Integrity asks them to find and apply the principles of constitutional morality that provide the best justification of their past decisions, not one by one, but as a body of constitutional law.[38]

In *Law's Empire*, in addition to an adjudicative principle about the role of judges, Dworkin also recognized a legislative principle which asks law

---

[32] Stephen Guest, *Ronald Dworkin* (Edinburgh University Press, 1992), p. 1.   [33] *Ibid.*
[34] Dworkin, *Law's Empire*, pp. 87–8; Dyzenhaus, 'Recrafting the Rule of Law', p. 9 says that Dworkin 'illuminated the justifactory' characteristic of the rule of law.
[35] Guest, *Ronald Dworkin*, p. 1; Charles Covell, *The Defence of Natural Law: A Study of the Ideas of Law and Justice in the Writings of Lon L. Fuller, Michael Oakeshot, F.A. Hayek, Ronald Dworkin and John Finnis* (New York: St Martin's Press, 1992), p. 145.
[36] Dworkin, *Justice in Robes*.   [37] *Ibid.*, p. 15 (emphasis added).
[38] James Allan, Charles Fried and Ronald Dworkin, '"The Supreme Court Phalanx": An Exchange' (6 December 2007) 54 *New York Review of Books* 19.

THE RULE OF LAW AND THE ROLE OF LAW   41

makers to make morally coherent 'sets of laws'.[39] Dworkin explains that 'law as integrity' asks judges to assume, 'so far as this is possible, that the law is structured by a coherent set of principles about justice and fairness and procedural due process'.[40] This theory is based on the assumed existence of coherent community goals and policies which are moral and fair, that is, 'integrated'. This aspect of his theory raises a dilemma, as explained further in this chapter. Although his theory was not framed with the issues of asylum seekers in mind, it has the potential to be used to exclude 'outsiders'.

Dworkin's views have divided the community of legal philosophers. On the one hand, his supporters point to the notion of substantive rights implicit in the theory of political morality, arising from his overall concern with the value of equality. This is an aspect of his view that all persons should be treated with equal respect and concern. For example, it has been suggested that the antecedents of his views are a long line of legal humanists.[41]

But his detractors have critiqued the non-positivist focus of his interpretive theory. For example, it has been said that:

> Dworkin urges the citizenry to adopt a Protestant attitude to the law, figuring it out for ourselves rather than take it on authority. . . . Unlike the claim that it is not the case that all law imposes overriding duties to obey, the claim that we should not give the state the benefit of the doubt about what law is seems resistible.[42]

In other words, although Dworkin describes his theory as one of 'political morality', it is found lacking as a theory about state power.[43] Instead of discussing the idea of state power and its institutions, Dworkin focuses upon the concept of 'community', as explained further below. Another criticism is that the idea of 'law as integrity' depends on there being 'initial agreement' between the legislature, the courts, the administrative agencies, and the constitution.[44] This reflects Dworkin's concept of 'community' but also demonstrates that he does not view

---

[39] Dworkin, *Law's Empire*, p. 176.   [40] *Ibid.*, p. 243.
[41] Mark D. Walters, 'Hercules as Legal Humanist: Historicising Dworkin's Jurisprudence', Queen's Faculty of Law, Legal Studies Research Paper Series WP No. 07–01 (September 2006), http://ssrn.com/abstract=989609 (accessed 9 May 2008).
[42] Murphy, 'Concepts of Law' at 13.
[43] Notably, he was also critical of Hart's theory on that basis.
[44] Sheikh Shaghaf, 'The Empire Strikes Back: A Critique of Ronald Dworkin's Law's Empire', April 2007, p. 15, http://ssrn.com/abstract=976312 (accessed 13 May 2008).

the legal system as comprising three *competing* arms of government. Rather it is an *integrated* system of government sourced back to the community.

Recently, in *Justice in Robes*, Dworkin defended his interpretive theory of law. He said:

> A proposition of law is true, I suggest, if it flows from principles of personal and political morality that provide the best interpretation of other propositions of law generally treated as true in contemporary legal practice.[45]

It is important to appreciate that, in contrast to Hart's theory of *analytical* jurisprudence, Dworkin's theory is about legal practice. As others have pointed out, they were each talking about different aspects of the rule of law.[46] However, the fact that Dworkin focused upon the practice of law has had an enormous impact in its own right.

Dworkin's views have inspired the articulation of rule of law issues for discussion in this chapter and in this book. These are explained next.

Rule of law issues

There are many pressing issues which are highlighted in the chapters of this book in relation to the practical operation of the rule of law and the balance between the three arms of government. In the remainder of this chapter, the implications of these issues for the rule of law are discussed, using both the distinction between formal and substantive visions of law and by reference to Dworkin's views. These can be grouped under the following headings:

- The judicial processes: Are the courts deferential to executive policy in their approach to refugee law? Is such deference shown in respect to certain types of decisions? Is the principle of procedural fairness respected in relation to refugees and asylum seekers? In the process of interpreting international treaty obligations, are the courts respecting human rights obligations?
- The administrative structures for decision making and their impact on the rule of law. As several chapters in this book indicate, there are serious issues about the independence of decision-making institutions

---

[45] Dworkin, *Justice in Robes*, p. 14.
[46] Michael Steven Green, 'Dworkin v. The Philosophers: A Review Essay on *Justice in Robes*' (2007) 5 *University of Illinois Law Review* 1477 at 1491.

THE RULE OF LAW AND THE ROLE OF LAW 43

at this level and the quality of their decisions. Is independence a value in its own right? Does it apply at this level of governance?

- Is there a principle of neutrality in operation in this context (both at the administrative and at the judicial levels)? Are refugees and asylum seekers treated with equal respect in comparison with nationals in the legal system? If not, what justifies the distinction between these groups?
- The often excessive and hasty use of legislation to achieve policy objectives in this highly contested area of policy. Is such power exercised responsibly as a public trust, as Galligan's statement set out above requires? Related to that is the issue of incorporation of obligations under international human rights treaties: Are states using their legislative powers responsibly to incorporate such obligations or, conversely are they failing to incorporate such obligations?
- Flowing from these queries is how to explain the exclusion of refugees and asylum seekers from legal protection. Is such response explained by how a particular legal community values refugees and asylum seekers? What legal doctrine justifies discrimination in this context?

To elaborate upon these issues, the remainder of this chapter focuses first upon judicial processes, because they are most relevant to the idea of formal and substantive concepts of law introduced in this section and to Dworkin's theory. We then turn to the idea of the 'legislative principle', which includes an important discussion about incorporation and interpretation of international law obligations. Finally we deal with the more 'political' issue of why asylum seekers and refugees are excluded from legal protections.

Part two: integrity and adjudication

In this part we discuss the implications of formal and substantive explanations of the concepts of judicial review and procedural fairness, as these are two all-important concepts which protect asylum seekers and refugees from *refoulement*. This also incorporates a discussion of the value of neutrality and its place in formal and substantive visions of law. The significance of this discussion is that it shows that formal and substantive thinking about how the rule of law operates lead to different outcomes for refugees and asylum seekers.

The role of the courts and judges as one set of 'officials' in the legal system challenges legal positivist thinking, which prefers to operate under 'posited' laws. This is particularly the case in the context of refugees and asylum seekers, where policy is contentious. For example, governments are inclined to think that the courts, judges and administrative decision makers are undermining the will of parliament, whereas refugee advocates claim that the courts and judges are too deferential to government policy. Here it is argued that a substantive adjudicative role can be justified as conforming to the underlying human rights basis of refugee law.

Hart and Dworkin: theories of adjudication

In recent years several important debates about the role of judges in a democracy have shaped theories of adjudication around the role of judges in statutory interpretation. These issues are highly relevant to refugees and asylum seekers, as their rights and status are defined in national laws and constitutions which the courts and judges are called upon to interpret in the light of international human rights obligations.

In this section, the distinction between Hart's and Dworkin's theories of adjudication is explained by reference to the formal (positivist) and the substantive versions of the rule of law, and the implications of this distinction are elucidated. The positivist theory of statutory intention links the judge's role back to the sovereign legislature so that legislative intent is interpreted as the will of parliament, and parliament is conceived as representing the majority of the polity. This can be described as a formal view of the law. But the theory is challenged by decisions in which the judicial role is more 'activist' – where a purposive interpretation is given to a constitution or statute or Bill of Rights, or where the application of customary law (rather than parliament's edict) is involved.[47] In the context of refugees and asylum seekers where international law and human rights are involved and 'good faith' interpretation is required of treaty obligations, this imposes an additional challenge to legal positivist theory.[48]

In relation to constitutional review (where there is a written constitution), there is debate over whether a constitution should be interpreted according to a fixed or historical meaning, or whether contemporary circumstances should be taken into account.[49] This is the 'originalism' debate about whether the objective or subjective intentions of the

---

[47] Bix, 'Legal Positivism', p. 26.

[48] As explained in Part Three of this chapter, this process is also linked back to parliament.

[49] Joseph Raz, 'The Authority of Constitutions and the Authority of its Authors' in Larry Alexander (ed.), *Constitutionalism: Philosophical Foundations* (Cambridge University Press, 1998), Chapter 4, pp. 157–193; *Singh* v. *Commonwealth* (2004) 222 CLR 322.

THE RULE OF LAW AND THE ROLE OF LAW 45

makers of the constitution are relevant. Dworkin's view on this debate is clear. He said that the role of judges is to uncover the existence of fundamental moral and political rights in the exercise of an independent judicial role.[50] The difference between these views loosely accords with the formal–substantive divide, with the 'original' approach approximating to the positivist view. Dworkin's view about the constitutional review function of judges also reflects his views about the 'polity'. It grew out of a political philosophy that rejects the idea that democracy can be reduced to the simple formula of majority rule.[51] Dworkin's concept of political morality which derives from the 'community' is a theory about the sovereignty of the people.

It is unsurprising that Hart did not develop a theory of adjudication beyond a formal view of the role of judges. Under his concept of law, judges are officials bound by the rule of recognition under a system of law comprised of the union of primary and secondary rules. Under his 'conventional' approach, judges – like other officials – are bound by a 'pact' to accept and apply the laws.[52] His theory has been described as one about 'sources' or 'pedigree'. He did not delve into how judges apply the law. For Hart, the 'internal point of view' was simply 'the practical attitude of rule acceptance'.[53] But for Dworkin this was not enough – he wanted to know more about the process of adjudication in the legal system, about how judges conceive the 'internal point of view'. Dworkin critiqued Hart's model based on 'pedigree' as 'conventionalism', pointing out the underlying values of predictability and stability in such a model.[54]

By contrast, Dworkin's focus was on the protection of substantive values, as the following discussion demonstrates. In *Taking Rights Seriously*,[55] Dworkin developed a theory of adjudication that stressed the role of the judge to apply principles and policies. In his attack on positivism, Dworkin stressed the need for the application of standards in legal reasoning. He replaced the concept of rules with principles and policies. In particular he analysed and explained the important role of

---

[50] Covell, *The Defence of Natural Law*, p. 152.
[51] David M. Beatty, *The Ultimate Rule of Law* (Oxford University Press, 2004), p. 26.
[52] Scott J. Shapiro, 'What is the Internal Point of View?', 14 October 2006, http://ssrn.com/abstract=937337 (accessed 1 May 2008).
[53] *Ibid.*
[54] Bix, 'Legal Positivism', p. 32. It has been pointed out that this critique prompted the development of inclusive legal positivism: see Bix, 'Legal Positivism', p. 33.
[55] Dworkin, *Taking Rights Seriously*.

46   REFUGEES, ASYLUM SEEKERS AND THE RULE OF LAW

judicial decision making as an application of standards. Dworkin's theory of adjudication made a valuable contribution to the understanding of the role of the judge. Dworkin argued that the rule of recognition could not account for legal principles, nor could it differentiate between those that were useful and those that were not.[56]

In *Law's Empire*,[57] Dworkin explains that 'law as integrity' requires judges to assume, 'so far as this is possible, that the law is structured by a coherent set of principles about justice and fairness and procedural due process'.[58] This is an aspect of his theory that law is interpretive – that it is both the product of and the inspiration for comprehensive interpretation of legal practice.[59] This interpretive theory of integrity is based on the assumed existence of community or communal goals and policies which are moral and fair or 'integral'.[60] Because the community has evolving needs, he stresses that the standards have to be compromised by what 'is possible'.

Dworkin's standards of integrity and procedural due process are sourced back to a political community, and are based upon substantive, universal values. For Dworkin, integrity is a principle over and above justice, fairness and procedural due process. It presupposes that legal rights and duties were created by a single author – the community personified – expressing a coherent conception of justice and fairness.[61] Justice refers to the outcome and involves an 'ought' evaluation of moral and political rights. Fairness relates to the structure for making decisions. It is concerned with consistency and 'due process'.

In *Law's Empire*, Dworkin's main concern was with the adjudicative principle.[62] There we see his concern with a coherent legal system in which judges make interpretative decisions under his rights-based concept of the rule of law. But in discussing the role of judges in relation to legislation, Dworkin recognized the link with the legislative principle. He stressed that judges were bound by the principle of legislative supremacy to accept the legitimacy of statutes. But he also stressed that the criteria of 'fit' and 'value' apply to justify a decision.

As he explained in *Justice in Robes*, this requires the formal rules (such as constitutional principles and other matters of procedure) to be taken

---

[56] Bix, 'Legal Positivism', pp. 15–17.   [57] Dworkin, *Law's Empire*, Chapters 6 and 7.
[58] *Ibid.*, p. 243.   [59] *Ibid.*, p. 226.
[60] Cf. the critique of Trevor Allan, 'Justice and Fairness in Law's Empire' (1993) 52 *Cambridge Law Journal* 64.
[61] Dworkin, *Law's Empire*, p. 225.
[62] *Ibid.*, p. 176. See also Dworkin, *Taking Rights Seriously*.

THE RULE OF LAW AND THE ROLE OF LAW 47

into account. But Dworkin explained that judges may disagree about the underlying values that a practice incorporates. In relation to legislative meaning he says:

> The reasons we have for supposing that a body constituted as that body is constituted has the power to make laws are reasons of political morality, and if lawyers disagree about the precise character of those moral obligations they will inevitably disagree on at least one occasion about what law the legislature has in fact made.[63]

In this passage Dworkin suggests that while it is for judges to check that legislation conforms to constitutional norms, such as the principle of equal protection, the judges cannot question the authority of the legislation as such. However, the judge must look for its underlying values. In relation to legislative interpretation he said:

> [W]e must defend our choice as the best justification of the complex practice of legislation, and that will require us to defend it in a particular conception of democratic or other political morality.[64]

These views make an interesting contrast with those of Sir Gerard Brennan when he was a Justice of the High Court of Australia. Relevantly, Sir Gerard expressed a view about the role of judges in interpreting legislation. In an article entitled 'Courts, Democracy and the Law',[65] Sir Gerard discussed the relationship between the three branches of government. In particular, he was concerned to reconcile the judicial review role of the judiciary (which he termed 'the third branch of government') with the doctrine of the separation of powers. In a passage which clearly recognizes the formal–substantive dichotomy, he said that the rule of law ensures that the text of a statute is interpreted in accordance with the values of the common law, but that the courts are powerless to remedy injustice in the face of unjust legislation enacted within power.[66] In this and other contexts, he made it clear that in cases of conflict between valid legislation and the common law, the legislation would prevail.

In contrast to Dworkin's approach, Sir Gerard's view suggests an unquestioning acceptance of the formal validity of legislation, rather than a preliminary review of its content for consistency with fundamental norms.[67] It suggests that judges have no role in determining the

---

[63] Dworkin, *Justice in Robes*, p. 16. [64] *Ibid.*, p. 17.
[65] Hon Mr Justice Gerard Brennan (1991) 65 *Australian Law Journal* 32. [66] *Ibid.* at 37.
[67] As explained below, this process should occur when there is an issue of legislative interpretation of treaty obligations.

content of the law. This, as explained in this book, is often the predominant approach of courts on issues which concern interpretation of both executive powers and refugee rights. In such cases, the courts often defer to executive power.

By contrast, Dworkin's approach is that legal interpretation 'pretty much always involves moral judgment since determining what the law is requires us to make moral sense of otherwise inconclusive legal sources'.[68] As the discussion about judicial review in the next section illustrates, Dworkin's theory of adjudication, which focuses upon the 'justifactory' role of judges and upon substantive values, has influenced the thinking of a generation of scholars.[69]

Judicial review and the democratic state

The crucial point about the judicial review debate (which essentially mirrors the argument about theories of adjudication) is that a formal (positivist) theory emphasizes parliamentary sovereignty whereas a substantive theory explains and justifies the role of the judge to interpret the law in the light of fundamental principles or values. As the discussion in this book demonstrates, the availability of judicial review is essential to protect refugees and asylum seekers from *refoulement*, particularly as there are widespread concerns over the quality of administrative decisions. It is therefore disturbing to see that in four of the jurisdictions discussed in this book (the USA, Canada, the UK and Australia), the national governments have attempted to limit or restrict access to judicial review by refugees and asylum seekers in an attempt to curb the rising number of applications for review.

The judicial review debate, which arose in the late 1980s in response to an increase in the volume and scope of judicial review of administrative decisions, framed the challenge about the role of judges in terms of formal versus substantive theory.[70] In this debate, the protagonists delved deep into the history of the 'ultra vires' doctrine[71] and the theory of separation of powers. In simple terms, the protagonists were divided according to whether they believed in a formal or substantive explanation for judicial review.

---

[68] Murphy, 'Concepts of Law' at 2.

[69] E.g. Paul Craig, 'Formal and Substantive Conceptions of the Rule of Law: An Analytical Framework' (1997) *Public Law* 467; Dyzenhaus, 'Recrafting the Rule of Law'.

[70] This section is based on Susan Kneebone, 'What is the Basis of Judicial Review?' (2001) 12 *Public Law Review* 95. The debate is explained more fully in that article.

[71] Dawn Oliver, 'Is the Ultra Vires Rule the Basis of Judicial Review?' (1987) *Public Law* 543.

THE RULE OF LAW AND THE ROLE OF LAW   49

In Dawn Oliver's 1987 article, it was argued that judicial review has moved on from the ultra vires rule to a concern for the protection of individuals, and for the control of power per se, rather than powers or vires as such.[72] That is, there was an implicit rejection of the 'red light' theory of judicial review,[73] namely that the purpose of judicial review is predominantly remedial, to contain administrative action within the bounds of legality.[74] This article is the root of the view that judicial review is a common law principle rather than a principle of parliamentary sovereignty.

Subsequently, a spirited defence of the parliamentary sovereignty principle was advanced.[75] It was argued that the ultra vires doctrine is best explained as a principle of parliamentary sovereignty or supremacy, that is, as based on legislative intent, while at the same time acknowledging that the modern law of judicial review is a judicial creation.[76] This view was justified by the need to maintain the principle of parliamentary sovereignty as a basic constitutional doctrine. It used the analogy of the fig leaf to explain that it 'preserves decencies'.[77] For that reason, it described the ultra vires doctrine as a 'gentle but necessary discipline'[78] for the judiciary.[79] Its major concern was to harness the opportunity for unbridled judicial creativity.[80]

Paul Craig, who is firmly on the other side of the debate, rejects the 'fig leaf' metaphor for the ultra vires doctrine.[81] Craig argues on the basis of the historical development of the remedies and the *grounds* of judicial review, in particular jurisdictional error and natural justice,

---

[72] See also Dawn Oliver, 'The Underlying Values of Public and Private Law' in Michael Taggart (ed.), *The Province of Administrative Law* (Oxford: Hart Publishing, 1997), pp. 217–242.

[73] Carol Harlow and Richard Rawlings, *Law and Administration* (London: Weidenfeld and Nicholson, 1984), Chapter 1.

[74] This is an idea which fits with the 'authority' or formal/positivist explanation of law.

[75] Christopher Forsyth, 'Of Fig Leaves and Fairy Tales: The Ultra Vires Doctrine, the Sovereignty of Parliament and Judicial Review' (1996) 55 *Cambridge Law Journal* 122.

[76] *Ibid.* at 134.   [77] *Ibid.* at 135.   [78] *Ibid.* at 137.

[79] See also Mark Elliott, 'The Ultra Vires Doctrine in a Constitutional Setting: Still the Central Principle of Administrative Law' (1999) 58 *Cambridge Law Journal* 129.

[80] See Jeffrey Jowell, 'Of Vires and Vacuums: The Constitutional Context of Judicial Review' (1999) *Public Law* 448.

[81] Paul Craig, 'Ultra Vires and the Foundation of Judicial Review' (1998) *Cambridge Law Journal* 63; Paul Craig, 'Competing Models of Judicial Review' (1999) *Public Law* 428; Paul Craig, 'Public Law, Political Theory and Legal Theory' (2000) *Public Law* 211. See also Dyzenhaus, 'Reuniting the Brain'; Peter Bayne, 'The Common Law Basis of Judicial Review' (1993) 67 *Australian Law Journal* 781.

50   REFUGEES, ASYLUM SEEKERS AND THE RULE OF LAW

that the doctrine has a common law foundation. He refers to this as the 'traditional' view, as opposed to the 'modern' or statutory interpretation ('fig leaf') view described above.

This debate reflects the difference between the views that judges on judicial review primarily exercise delegated legislative authority, as distinct from common law authority which is concerned with individual rights.[82] The parliamentary sovereignty argument supports a positivist theory, whereas the rights argument is a substantive argument. As Dyzenhaus expresses it, the two corners of the ring represent the institutional restraint model versus the rule of reason (as embodied in Dicey's twin ideas, authority and equality).[83] As Dyzenhaus explains, the advantage of the latter (rule of reason) 'liberal antipositivist' view is that it emphasizes that judges have a crucial role in upholding the values of the legal order.[84]

The next sections of this part deal with the related concepts or principles of neutrality and procedural fairness. Importantly, both these principles, which have enormous practical relevance to refugees and asylum seekers (because of the ever present risk of *refoulement*), are supported by both formal and substantive visions of the rule of law, which fits with the 'inclusive' legal positivist view that equality and due process *necessarily* have a moral basis. But in the case of procedural fairness, there is another factor which is used to limit its application to refugees and asylum seekers.

Neutrality and judicial (institutional) independence

In the orthodox statement of the common law principle of natural justice or procedural fairness which is discussed in the next section, due process and *decisional* neutrality are twinned concepts. The focus in this section is upon neutrality as a value applied to institutions.[85] Neutrality is tremendously important for asylum seekers and refugees for two

---

[82] This argument is explained more fully in Kneebone, 'What is the Basis of Judicial Review?' at 97–99.

[83] Dyzenhaus, 'Recrafting the Rule of Law', p. 2.

[84] David Dyzenhaus, 'The Politics of Deference: Judicial Review and Democracy' in Taggart (ed.), *The Province of Administrative Law*, Chapter 13. Dyzenhaus explains this term as reflecting Blackstone's theory that the common law is the legal repository of moral values, and that the common law is itself a creation of the people. He contrasts this with 'democratic positivism'.

[85] See Susan Kneebone, 'Is the Australian Refugee Review Tribunal "Institutionally" Biased?' in François Crépeau et al. (eds.), *Forced Migration and Global Processes* (Lanham, MD: Lexington Books, 2006), Chapter 10.

THE RULE OF LAW AND THE ROLE OF LAW   51

reasons. First, because access to a neutral hearing is the foundation of the right to seek asylum and, secondly, because it guarantees the right to *non-refoulement*. Yet as the chapters in this book reveal, industrialized states perceive their legal systems as being at risk of inundation and abuse by refugees and asylum seekers and do their best by direct and indirect legal means to minimize their attempts to access territory and to use the legal system. The indirect means include the use of accelerated and 'fast track' procedures for those who turn up at the borders. Such procedures, as discussion in this book details, compromise the standard of the hearing.

Neutrality, like procedural fairness, can be justified for both formal and substantive reasons. As an instrumental or formal concept, neutrality is justified for reasons of efficiency or accountability.[86] In this sense, neutrality as accountability is associated with judicial independence and the separation of powers doctrine, to support the idea that judges should be free from political interference. The neutrality or impartiality of judges (and decision makers at other levels) is a value which is respected by legal positivists in its own right as freedom from political interference leading to the best outcomes (see Legomsky, Chapter 3). Judicial independence and neutrality are thus objectives of the separation of powers.

Sir Gerard Brennan, whose views were discussed above, had a particular approach to the role of the courts as 'the third branch of government', which supports the idea that judicial independence is a principle of public policy tied to the concept of neutrality. He stressed the role of judges as apolitical, neutral and legitimated by public or community confidence.[87] Judicial review (which he intended in a broad sense), he said 'has no support other than public confidence'.[88] He did not rest the adjudicative function upon the inherent role of the courts to review delegated legislative action, but rather upon 'the assignment . . . of that function by the general consent of the community'.[89] That is, he

---

[86] Dyzenhaus, 'Recrafting the Rule of Law', p. 7 points out that Bentham subscribed to this ideal as a fact of political control.

[87] Hon Mr Justice Gerard Brennan, 'Limits on the Use of Judges' (1978) 9 *Federal Law Review* 1; Hon Mr Justice Gerard Brennan, 'Extra-Judicial Notes' (1998) 17 *Australian Bar Review* 9.

[88] Hon Mr Justice Gerard Brennan, 'The Purpose and Scope of Judicial Review' in Michael Taggart (ed.), *Judicial Review of Administrative Action in the 1980s: Problems and Prospects* (Auckland: Oxford University Press, and Legal Research Foundation Inc, 1986), pp. 18–35.

[89] *Ibid.*, p. 18.

52   REFUGEES, ASYLUM SEEKERS AND THE RULE OF LAW

supports judicial independence or neutrality as a political or democratic value. This view fits with Dicey's concern to counter arbitrary power in accordance with a system of governance which operates by separation of powers.[90]

In the jurisdictions covered in this book, important decisions about refugee status are made at the administrative level of government. And in all jurisdictions, concerns are raised about the neutrality and independence of decision making at that level, which include concerns about the fact that governments prioritize efficiency over 'administrative justice' (as O'Sullivan expresses it in Chapter 5). It is therefore important to be able to argue that neutrality applies at that level of decision making, and that it is not simply an attribute of judicial independence.

It is interesting to see that, in this book, Legomsky primarily supports the ideal of neutrality for administrative decision makers on the basis of separation of powers, and additionally on the basis of protection of individual (substantive) rights. Macklin (in Chapter 2) points out substantive reasons for applying a concept of neutrality in this context. This is because refugees and asylum seekers are outsiders in the legal system. Yet neutrality applied as a principle of equality of treatment ensures that non-citizens are treated equally to nationals. Neutrality as a principle of equality or non-discrimination thus has substantive outcomes.

This discussion shows us that neutrality in institutional decision making is important for both instrumental and substantive reasons, which in principle apply to both judicial and administrative decision makers.

By way of comparison, there is an important point in Dworkin's theory which indicates his underlying substantive premise. While Dworkin agrees that judges must be politically independent, he made it explicit that judges cannot be *morally* neutral. He said that he expects judges to apply the principles of political morality. This is an integral part of his theory of adjudication and 'law as integrity'. His idea of justice, being based upon equality, reflects his view about political morality.[91] In other words, he agrees that *political* neutrality means better substantive outcomes.

---

[90] Colin Harvey, 'Refugees, Asylum Seekers, The Rule of Law and Human Rights' in David Dyzenhaus, *The Unity of the Public Law* (Oxford: Hart Publishing, 2004), Chapter 8, p. 19; Mark D. Walters, 'The Common Law Constitution and Legal Cosmopolitanism', in Dyzenhaus, *The Unity of the Public Law*, Chapter 16, p. 433.

[91] Guest, *Ronald Dworkin*, p. 1; Covell, *The Defence of Natural Law*, p. 145.

Neutrality and procedural fairness

In this section we highlight the importance of *decisional* neutrality in the sense of an impartial decision, as embodied in the requirement of an individual unbiased decision under the natural justice or procedural fairness principle. This is important for refugees and asylum seekers, for ensuring access to a hearing and protection against *refoulement*, as stated above. It is also necessary to comply with the Convention relating to the Status of Refugees (Refugee Convention),[92] which contains a definition of 'refugee' that focuses upon an individual's fear of persecution,[93] as explained in the previous chapter. Yet it is the application of this principle which best illustrates the tension in contemporary legal systems. In the jurisdictions surveyed in this book, governments have been concerned about the pressure that the requirement to give individual hearings to large numbers of asylum seekers poses to their legal system, and have attempted to limit the number of hearings conducted, either by direct or indirect means (or to limit access to judicial review from such hearings, as mentioned above).

This discussion of procedural fairness and decisional neutrality highlights another important challenge to the rule of law as it applies to refugees and asylum seekers in this context, namely their status as non-citizens in national legal systems. Thus this discussion links to Part four below, namely the exclusion of non-citizens from legal systems under a theory of communitarian liberalism.[94]

To get to that point it is necessary to first explain the meaning of procedural fairness, how it has both formal and substantive rationales, and why it might be argued that it does not apply to non-citizen refugees and asylum seekers. In this respect we begin to see the limits (and the scope) of the rule of law and of Dworkin's theory.

Two different aspects can be extrapolated from the natural justice principle (which is these days referred to as 'procedural fairness').[95]

---

[92] Convention relating to the Status of Refugees, Geneva, 28 July 1951, in force 22 April 1954, 1989 UNTS 137.

[93] *Ibid.*, Art. 1A(2).

[94] This defines liberal justice in terms of the application of community standards. It can thus lead to exclusion of non-members of the community. See Catherine Dauvergne, 'Beyond Justice: The Consequences of Liberalism for Immigration Law' (1997) 10 *Canadian Journal of Law and Jurisprudence* (no 2) 323.

[95] For further discussion, see Susan Kneebone, 'Natural Justice and Non-Citizens: A Matter of Integrity?' (2002) 26 *Melbourne University Law Review* 355.

54   REFUGEES, ASYLUM SEEKERS AND THE RULE OF LAW

First, it represents an ideal of justice (this can be referred to as 'the justice value'), which is of unquestionable antiquity.[96] In this sense it clearly embodies a universal substantive standard. As explained below, it also contains instrumental or procedural standards. Secondly, it is a principle of practical application available to those to whom the threshold right to be heard is extended. This can be referred to as 'the participation principle'. The important point about extending natural justice to an individual is that it enables the person to participate meaningfully in the process of decision making.

The justice value defines the natural justice principle by reference to both universal *substantive* and *procedural standards*, whereas the participation principle implicitly limits the right to participate in a hearing by reference to *distributive justice* principles as explained below.[97] It is the participation principle which best explains the limits of the reach of the universal doctrine of natural justice, and its non-application to non-citizens.

The 'justice value' stems from the fact that the rules of natural justice incorporate fundamental ideas or values about the substance of the principle. These include: equality, non-discrimination, impartiality and basic fairness. The natural justice principle also has an inherent instrumental value which highlights the value of fair procedures for securing accurate outcomes. In this sense, the justice value incorporates both substantive and procedural standards, which are interconnected.[98] The fact that when conducting judicial review the courts explain their role as being to determine whether procedural rather than substantive fairness was accorded does not detract from that proposition. That is, the courts emphasize the limits of the process of judicial review, and eschew interfering with substantive outcomes.[99] To define that role, the courts have, in recent years, preferred the term 'procedural fairness' to natural justice.[100]

---

[96] *R v. Chancellor of the University of Cambridge (Dr Bentley's case)* (1723) 1 Str 552 at 567 (93 ER 698 at 704) citing the example of Adam and Eve in the Garden of Paradise. See also *Dr Bonham's case* (1610) 8 Co Rep 113b (77 ER 646).

[97] That is, principles about how the benefits of a society are distributed or shared. If this is combined with a theory about who comprise that society or polity it becomes a political theory, e.g. under liberal democratic theory based upon the concept of government by consent as discussed in Part Four of this chapter.

[98] Peter Cane, 'Mapping the Frontiers' in Peter Birks (ed.), *The Frontiers of Liability, Vol I* (Oxford University Press, 1994).

[99] E.g. *Haoucher v. Minister for Immigration* (1990) 169 CLR 648 per Dawson and Gaudron JJ dissenting.

[100] E.g. *Kioa v. West* (1985) 159 CLR 550.

THE RULE OF LAW AND THE ROLE OF LAW   55

Natural justice thus incorporates a theory of *substantive* procedural justice, rather than merely being a mere procedural rule about the distribution of benefits, or of distributive justice.[101] However, the participation principle limits the right to participate in a hearing by reference to distributive principles of a different kind; namely, as Macklin expresses it,[102] participation in democratic processes. But as Macklin points out, asylum seekers and refugees are not part of 'the polity'.[103] For that reason, as she says, they are heavily dependent on the judiciary to protect their rights. Under common law legal systems, limitations on the universal or common law right to natural justice are defined by reference to legislative intention,[104] or parliamentary sovereignty. That method of limitation can be rationalized as, or analogized to, a political or constitutional principle that provides an opportunity for citizen participation in a democracy. The non-citizen is therefore prey to the application of that limitation. Although, in many decisions, the courts have made no distinction between citizens and non-citizens,[105] the decisions are not consistent.[106] There is no guarantee of a right of non-citizens to participate in the making of decisions that affect them.[107]

Macklin discusses the Canadian decision of *Singh* v. *Minister for Employment and Immigration*[108] in which natural justice (or procedural fairness) was applied to a group of asylum seekers, as a principle of universal and 'fundamental' justice which applies to citizens and non-citizens alike. Importantly, in the *Singh* decision, the court rejected the government's 'instrumental' arguments about 'administrative convenience' as a criterion for denying the claimants access to a hearing, and focused instead on the effect that denial of the right would have on the claimants (that is, *refoulement*). Macklin's discussion in Chapter 2 illustrates both the formal (procedural, instrumental) and substantive ('deontological') values of procedural fairness, and shows how the Canadian court extended such rights to non-citizens.

---

[101] John Rawls, *A Theory of Justice*, revised ed. (Oxford University Press, 1999), pp. 73–78. Rawls' is a theory which applies to a society conceived as a closed or bordered system separate from other societies. Rawls uses a 'refurbished' version of the social contract argument.

[102] Chapter 2 in this volume.   [103] *Ibid.*   [104] *Kioa* v. *West* (1985) 159 CLR 550.

[105] E.g. *Ibid.*; *Heshmati* v. *Minister for Immigration* (1991) 31 FCR 123; *Somaghi* v. *Minister for Immigration* (1991) 31 FCR 100.

[106] Cf *Simsek* v. *Minister for Immigration* (1982) 148 CLR 636; *Salemi* v. *MacKellar* [No 2] (1977) 137 CLR 396.

[107] *Wu Fu Fang* v. *Minister for Immigration* (1995) 136 ALR 583.   [108] [1985] 1 SCR 177.

56   REFUGEES, ASYLUM SEEKERS AND THE RULE OF LAW

As we will see in Part four, the exclusion of non-citizens can be justified under a theory of communitarian liberalism.[109] That is, on the need for closed societies and borders. As outsiders in a community, it is suggested that non-citizens do not have the right to share our institutions and resources. Although the natural justice principle can be justified in terms of instrumental outcomes, as suggested above, or even in terms of social justice,[110] often the justification for exclusion of the right to participate is broadly political. It can be linked to distributive justice principles to the exclusion of instrumental values, as explained in Part four.

This discussion highlights the fundamental importance of judges and other decision makers (and legislatures) to ensure that procedural fairness is observed for refugees and asylum seekers for whom the outcome of denial is the very real risk of *refoulement*. However, ironically under national legal systems, the fragility of the principle in relation to such refugees and asylum seekers stems from their very status as non-citizens. In the last section of this chapter, we explore further the reasons for their exclusion from participation in legal procedures, and in particular why they are denied access to a hearing and the right to be processed for asylum.

Before concluding this part, we consider briefly what guidance we can take from Dworkin's views on procedural fairness. In *Law's Empire*, Dworkin described procedural due process (which he equates with procedural fairness) as a matter of principle. That is, it is a standard to be observed as a requirement of justice or fairness,[111] rather than a goal to be achieved. But, as we noted above, Dworkin's standards of integrity and procedural due process are sourced back to a political community. For Dworkin, integrity is a principle over and above justice, fairness and procedural due process. It presupposes that legal rights and duties were created by a single author – the community personified – expressing a coherent conception of justice and fairness.[112] This view, as we shall see, may lead us back to the same conclusion about exclusion as with the participation principle.

---

[109] This defines liberal justice in terms of the application of community standards. It can thus lead to exclusion of non-members of the community. See Catherine Dauvergne, 'Beyond Justice'.

[110] Gerry Maher, 'Natural Justice as Fairness' in Neil MacCormick and Peter Birks (eds.), *The Legal Mind: Essays for Tony Honoré* (Oxford: Clarendon Press, 1986), Chapter 6.

[111] Dworkin, *Taking Rights Seriously*, p. 22.

[112] Dworkin, *Law's Empire*, p. 225.

THE RULE OF LAW AND THE ROLE OF LAW 57

By contrast, in considering the interpretive and adjudicative role of judges in relation to statutory interpretation and judicial review, the difference between formal and substantive theories of adjudication is important. Whereas a formal theory of adjudication might lead to a deferential approach, Dworkin's interpretive theory of law as 'integrity' focuses upon equality of rights and the substance of the law.

We turn now to the examination of a second aspect of Dworkin's interpretive theory of law – the legislative principle, which is one of the two basic sub-principles or standards of integrity that he recognizes. This principle, as we will see, is linked to the adjudicative principle and is enormously important in implementing the rights of refugees and asylum seekers in national legal systems.

Part three: the legislative principle

One of the issues addressed in this book is whether, in the context of the rights of refugees and asylum seekers, there is a 'coherent legislative principle' in operation. Under Dworkin's theory this is a principle directed at both legislators and at interpreters of legislation. It requires that law makers make morally coherent 'sets of laws', and it requires judges and those who apply legislation to interpret such legislation in accordance with his interpretive theory of law. In *Justice in Robes*, he describes legislative interpretation as involving judgements of political morality, of determining what interpretation is consistent with the limits of power as interpreted.

As the chapters in this book explain, in this context there are concerns about the use of legislative power and about the interpretation of such power. There are concerns about the circumstances in which governments legislate (or fail to legislate), about compliance with formal and democratic processes, and about the interpretation of legislation implementing refugee rights in national legal systems.

As Galligan points out, the idea that public power is held on trust for achieving 'social goals' is important. Galligan suggests that legislative powers should be used to pursue 'social goals for the common good'. He suggests that powers which are used for 'capricious' reasons or which are 'captured by special interests' might not conform to that test.[113] In Chapters 4 and 5 (Australia and the UK), the extensive use of legislation is highlighted. This use of legislation to achieve the ruling government's

---

[113] Galligan, *Law in Modern Society*, p. 258.

58   REFUGEES, ASYLUM SEEKERS AND THE RULE OF LAW

policy agenda in this context is troubling.[114] Whilst positivist theory characterizes legislation as the embodiment of parliament's will as the elected representatives of the people, behind-the-scenes reports suggest that in the relationship between the legislative and executive arms of government, the balance of power has swung to the executive arm of government.[115] Indeed, it may be that the executive is overly responsive to populist views.[116] O'Sullivan in Chapter 5, discussing the UK, describes such legislation as 'reactive'. Dworkin's principle of legislative integrity presupposes that the legislature coherently expresses the community's conception of justice and fairness.[117] It is unclear whether this is always the case, as the discussions in this book illustrate.

One question considered in this part is whether legislators are exercising their powers responsibly in relation to the incorporation of treaty obligations which affect the rights of refugees and asylum seekers, especially the Refugee Convention. The issue of the extent of incorporation of treaty obligations raises the question of whether the 'trust' imposed on legislators is being properly carried out. Another question concerns interpretation of legislation which incorporates treaty obligations.

The use of legislation to overturn judicial decisions whose outcomes the executive disapproves of (this has occurred in both Australia and the UK) is another feature of the use of legislative power in this context. This is objectionable for different reasons. As Colin Harvey has expressed it, by such action governments show their 'lack of concern for principle in the face of public policy imperatives'.[118] Such use of the legislative power threatens the principle of judicial independence and neutrality discussed above. Under Dworkin's concept of law it shows a lack of integrity; an absence of an integrated legal system.

In addition to the broad use of legislative power, there are also concerns about compliance with the formal processes for the

---

[114] Contrast Robert Thomas 'The Impact of Judicial Review on Asylum' (2003) *Public Law* 479 at 483.

[115] E.g. Hon Sir Gerard Brennan, 'The Impact of a Bill of Rights on the Role of the Judiciary: An Australian Response' in Phillip Alston (ed.), *Towards An Australian Bill of Rights* (Canberra: Centre for International and Public Law and HREOC, 1994), pp. 177–186.

[116] Adrienne Millbank, *The Problem with the 1951 Convention* (Canberra: Department of the Parliamentary Library, 2000–2001), Research Paper 5, www.aph.gov.au/library/pubs/rp/2000–01/01RP05.htm (accessed 1 May 2008).

[117] Dworkin, *Law's Empire*, p. 225.

[118] Colin Harvey, 'Asylum Seekers, Ultra Vires and the Social Security Regulations' (1997) *Public Law* 394 at 399.

THE RULE OF LAW AND THE ROLE OF LAW 59

introduction of legislation in this context. These are issues about transparency. For example, in Chapter 5, O'Sullivan details issues about lack of consultation and scrutiny in the UK, and about the use of secondary legislation rather than primary legislation where fundamental rights are affected. That is, the detail about rights is contained in legislation which has not been subjected to parliamentary scrutiny.[119] In Chapter 4, which tells the Australian story, there are tales of extensive public inquiries leading to recommendations for legislative changes which have been ignored by the government. Another Australian feature is the extensive conferral of broad discretionary powers, which are difficult to challenge. The conferral of broad discretionary powers is also common in the USA, as shown in Chapter 3.

For Dworkin, legislative integrity is a formal virtue which is part and parcel of his view of the community as composed of fraternal members, with reciprocal obligations.[120] That is, it embodies his conception of the state as a distinctive collective entity, rather than as a body governing by the implied consent of the people.[121] In *Law's Empire*, Dworkin gives the example of 'checkerboard statutes' as the 'most dramatic violation' of the ideal of integrity. He requires that there be equal treatment of all persons under his principle of equality.[122] Specifically, he pointed to the inconsistency between statutes permitting slavery and the guarantee of equal protection in the 14th amendment of the US constitution.[123] That is, the legislative principle should guide legislators to respect the right to equal protection.[124] In *Law's Empire*, Dworkin argues that the legislative principle is so much part of our political practice that no competent interpretation of the practice can ignore it.[125]

Incorporation of treaty obligations

The legislative principle has a potentially important role in determining the relationship between national and international law. Under the 'dualist' systems of law which operate in all the jurisdictions discussed in this book, there is a need for specific legislative incorporation of such

---

[119] Contrast Legomsky's account (Chapter 3 in this volume) of the USA where the parliamentary model does not operate. As he explains, Congress has spelt out the detail of the legislation.

[120] Covell, *The Defence of Natural Law*, pp. 163–164.   [121] *Ibid.*, pp. 164 and 167.

[122] *Ibid.*, p. 164.   [123] *Ibid.*, p. 184.   [124] *Ibid.*, p. 185.

[125] Dworkin, *Law's Empire*, p. 176.

60 REFUGEES, ASYLUM SEEKERS AND THE RULE OF LAW

(which arises from the principle of parliamentary sovereignty in the Westminster systems). The usual explanation for this is that the rule of law is based upon the separation of legislative, executive and judicial powers.[126] On a strict view of the separation of powers, it follows that, as entry into a treaty arises from executive action, it requires a specific act of legislative incorporation to become part of domestic law.[127]

In practice, as the comparison of Australia and New Zealand in Chapter 4 illustrates,[128] the extent and the manner in which a state chooses to incorporate its obligations under the Refugee Convention has a strong impact on the extent to which the rights of refugees are respected in the national legal system. By contrast, in the UK (see Chapter 5), there is evidence that the incorporation of the European Convention of Human Rights (ECHR)[129] through the Human Rights Act (UK) has had the practical effect of expanding the scope of protection beyond that provided by the Refugee Convention.

Many states, such as Australia, subscribe to a strict 'positivist' or 'statist' view of their international treaty obligations.[130] That is, they regard treaty obligations as governing the relationship between states at the international level, rather than as creating obligations or enforceable rights for individuals. While fundamental human rights are matters of international obligation, states bear the primary responsibility for the protection of human rights.[131] As Guy Goodwin-Gill says, 'the challenge lies in the space between obligation and implementation'.[132] Thus the manner and extent of incorporation does matter.

---

[126] *Walker v. Baird* [1892] AC 491; *Attorney-General for Canada v. Attorney-General for Ontario* [1937] AC 326 at 347.

[127] Note that in the USA a similar principle operates. There the distinction is between self-executing and non-self-executing statutes. In practice, very few statutes are considered to be self-executing.

[128] Chapter 4 in this volume.

[129] European Convention for the Protection of Human Rights and Fundamental Freedoms and its Protocols, Rome, 4 November 1950, in force 3 September 1953, ETS 5, 213 UNTS 221 (ECHR).

[130] In relation to Canada, it has been suggested that there is an inclination to treat all international law as 'inspirational' but not 'obligatory' – Jutta Brunnée and Stephen J. Toope, 'A Hesitant Embrace: Baker and the Application of International Law by Canadian Courts' in Dyzenhaus (ed.), *The Unity of the Public Law*, Chapter 14.

[131] Guy S. Goodwin-Gill, 'Forced Migration: Refugees, Rights and Security' in Jane McAdam (ed.), *Forced Migration, Human Rights and Security* (Oxford: Hart Publishing, 2008), Chapter 1 at p. 13 citing World Conference on Human Rights, Vienna Declaration and Programme of Action 1993, UN Doc. A/CONF.157/23 (12 July 1993) s. I, para. 1.

[132] Goodwin-Gill, 'Forced Migration: Refugees, Rights and Security', p. 13.

THE RULE OF LAW AND THE ROLE OF LAW   61

Because states regard treaty obligations as a matter between states, they often choose not to incorporate them fully, or at all. In such situations, the issue of whether there is effective implementation is raised. International law requires the 'good faith' implementation by a state of its international obligations. This principle is expressed in Article 26 of the 1969 Vienna Convention on the Law of Treaties (Vienna Convention): 'Every treaty in force is binding upon the parties to it and must be performed by them in good faith.'[133] Moreover Article 27 of the Vienna Convention plainly states that: 'A party may not invoke the provisions of its internal law as justification for its failure to perform a treaty.' Arguably, the 'margin of appreciation' doctrine – the discretion that states are given for implementing treaties in national law – is conditioned by this principle of good faith.[134]

In particular, in many jurisdictions there is legislative modification of the Refugee Convention definition of a refugee which not only waters down obligations but also hinders 'transnational judicial conversation',[135] and international effort to achieve consistency in interpretation of the refugee definition.[136] However, in addition to the question of the extent of incorporation of treaty obligations, the issue of compliance with the 'legislative principle' arises in relation to interpretation of national legislation which incorporates treaty obligations, or national legislation which impacts upon treaty obligations.

Interpretation of treaty obligations

Article 31(1) of the Vienna Convention requires that a treaty 'shall be interpreted in good faith in accordance with the ordinary meaning to be given to the terms of the treaty in their context and in the light of its object and purpose'. Although the Vienna Convention postdated the Refugee Convention, it is important to note that this approach to interpretation accords with the Preamble of the Refugee Convention,

---

[133] Vienna Convention on the Law of Treaties, Vienna, 23 May 1969, in force 27 January 1980, 1155 UNTS 331 (Vienna Convention).

[134] See also Vienna Convention, Art. 18, which requires states to refrain from acts which would defeat the object and purpose of a treaty.

[135] James Hathaway, *The Rights of Refugees under International Law* (New York: Cambridge University Press, 2005), pp. 1–2 explains the need for such conversations to achieve consistency across jurisdictions.

[136] Michelle Foster, *International Refugee Law and Socio-Economic Rights: Refuge from Deprivation* (Cambridge University Press, 2007), p. 28 has described international jurisprudence as 'patchwork'.

62   REFUGEES, ASYLUM SEEKERS AND THE RULE OF LAW

which makes it clear that its object and purpose is to assure to refugees 'the widest possible exercise of . . . fundamental rights and freedoms'.[137] In relation to interpretation of the Refugee Convention, it seems that the 'dominant view' is that its provisions should be interpreted within a human rights framework.[138] This applies, in particular, to the elements of the refugee definition in Article 1A(2) of the Refugee Convention, which are themselves undefined. Therefore, if states fail to interpret the definition within a human rights framework, it can be argued that they are not complying with this 'good faith' obligation. This is an issue in Australia, where the courts are inclined to give primacy to the national legislation, rather than to the Refugee Convention (see Chapter 4). In other jurisdictions also, there is a tendency to review exercises of power under administrative law principles.

At the *national* level, it is well established that legislation implementing treaty obligations must be interpreted consistently with the treaty. This presumption can be traced back to the nineteenth century.[139] However, being a mere presumption, it can be overridden by contrary legislative intention, thus preserving the principle of parliamentary sovereignty. In recent years, the most important debates about interpretation have taken place around the scope of unincorporated treaty obligations. These debates raise fundamental issues about the relationship between national and international law, and about the role of human rights in national legal systems. As the discussion in this book illustrates, there are important differences between states which reflect national perceptions about the role of international law in national legal systems.

As a substantial proportion of specific treaty obligations (including most of the Refugee Convention) are unincorporated in most of the jurisdictions covered in this book, principles about their interpretation are highly relevant. In the case of unincorporated treaties there are two

---

[137] Guy S. Goodwin-Gill and Jane McAdam, *The Refugee in International Law*, 3rd edn. (Oxford University Press, 2007), p. 8.

[138] Foster, *International Refugee Law and Socio-Economic Rights*, p. 28. See also *ibid.* Chapter 2. But note that there is disagreement about which human rights treaties are relevant and, in particular, about the relevance of customary law. That is, some refugee lawyers take a more 'positivist' view than others about what 'the International Bill of Rights', as it has been termed, comprises. See the discussion of the scope of the *non-refoulement* principle in the Introduction to this volume.

[139] Claudia Geiringer, '*Tavita* and all that: Confronting the Confusion Surrounding Unincorporated Treaties and Administrative Law' (2004) 21 *New Zealand Universities Law Review* 66 at 75 citing *R* v. *Keyn* (1876) 2 Ex D 63 at 85 and *Murray* v. *Schooner Charming Betsy*, 6 US 64 (1804).

sets of principles which govern their interpretation under the general or common law. There is, first, the presumption that a statute is not intended to be in conflict with international law and should be interpreted as far as possible consistently with such law (the presumption of consistency).[140] Secondly, there are common law presumptions about fundamental rights.[141] These presumptions are sometimes referred to collectively as the 'principle of legality'. However, in common law jurisdictions, the principle of parliamentary sovereignty can ultimately trump treaty obligations under a 'dualist' system of law.[142]

Thus, similar presumptions about conflicting rules of national and international law apply to both incorporated and unincorporated treaty obligations. It is presumed that, in the absence of a contradictory provision, statutes are not to be in conflict with international law. This has given rise to the proposition that, in cases of ambiguity in legislation, the courts should prefer an approach that favours the treaty. In Australia, the application of this principle of ambiguity has led to conflicting judicial interpretation of legislation governing the rights of asylum seekers and refugees, in relation to mandatory detention.[143]

In New Zealand, Canada and the UK, the presumption which applies in cases of ambiguity has been codified. Under the New Zealand Bill of Rights Act 1990, s. 6, judges have a positive obligation to interpret statutes consistently with the rights and freedoms contained in the Bill of Rights. A similar position applies in the UK, where the Human Rights

---

[140] *Daniels* v. *R* [1968] SCR 517 at 541; *Mabo* v. *Queensland* (No 2) (1992) 175 CLR 1 at 42 per Brennan J; *Koowarta* v. *Bjelke-Peterson and Others* (1982) 153 CLR 168; *Polites* v. *Commonwealth* (1945) 70 CLR 60; *New Zealand Airline Pilots Association* v. *Attorney-General* [1997] 3 NZLR 269. One New Zealand authority suggests that an unincorporated treaty obligation is a mandatory relevant consideration: *Tavita* v. *Minister for Immigration* [1994] 2 NZLR 257 (see Geiringer, '*Tavita* and all that'). For discussion of the general principles of interpretation, see Rosalie Balkin, 'International Law and Domestic Law' in Sam Blay (ed.), *Public International Law: An Australian Perspective* (Melbourne: Oxford University Press, 1997), Chapter 5; James Crawford and William R. Edeson, 'International Law and Australian Law' in Kevin W. Ryan (ed.), *International Law in Australia*, 2nd edn. (Sydney: Lawbook, 1984), Chapter 4.

[141] E.g. *Coco* v. *R* (1994) 179 CLR 427 at 437; *Bropho* v. *Western Australia* (1990) 171 CLR 1 at 17–18.

[142] E.g. in *Lim* v. *Minister for Immigration* (1992) 176 CLR 1 (discussed in Chapter 4 of this volume) it was decided that the Migration Act 1958 (Cth) s. 54T which provided that the amendments in issue in that case were to apply despite 'any inconsistency with Australian law' displaced the presumption. As O'Sullivan notes in Chapter 5, the UK Human Rights Act 1998, s. 6(2) reflects the principle of parliamentary sovereignty.

[143] See the discussion of *Al-Kateb* v. *Godwin* (2004) 219 CLR 562 in Chapter 4 in this volume.

64   REFUGEES, ASYLUM SEEKERS AND THE RULE OF LAW

Act 1998, s. 3, requires courts to interpret legislation 'so far as possible' to be compatible with the ECHR. However the Canadian Charter of Rights and Freedoms is more far-reaching, as it permits the Supreme Court to invalidate legislation for inconsistency with the Charter. In Canada it has been decided that the presumption of consistency is not dependent on an ambiguity.[144]

The issue of the normative or substantive effect of international law in the national legal systems covered in this book has played out not through discussion of human rights principles but through the application of administrative law principles, in many cases involving legislation and the rights of refugees and asylum seekers. As discussion in this book reveals, varying approaches have been adopted in the different jurisdictions. This shows the contested nature of the national–international law relationship.

This discussion in this part demonstrates concerns with the health of the legislative principle as it applies in this context. It illustrates the interconnectedness of the 'national' and the 'international' rule of law and the role of national legislators in determining that relationship. It raises the question, as Macklin expresses it in Chapter 2, of whether the rule of law is only a state-based or national concept. As the discussion in Part Four demonstrates, arguments for the rights of asylum seekers and refugees may need to go beyond state-based explanations in order to protect their rights under international law.

Part four: liberty, equality, and fraternity: the rights of outsiders

As various chapters in this book demonstrate, there are many practices, including restrictive entry measures, which states utilize in order to keep refugees and asylum seekers away from the territory and national legal systems. Such measures are often taken to implement 'border control' in the 'national interest' (see Chapters 2, 3 and 5 in particular). In the introductory chapter of this book, 'Introduction: Refugees and Asylum Seekers in the International Context – Rights and Realities', it was explained that the 'right to seek asylum' does not correspond to any duty on the part of a state to permit entry to refugees and asylum seekers, or indeed an obligation to process them. The right to freedom of movement is a qualified one, in which international law privileges nationals

---

[144] *Baker* v. *Canada* (Ministry of Citizenship and Immigration) [1999] 2 SCR 817 at para. 70.

THE RULE OF LAW AND THE ROLE OF LAW   65

and persons 'lawfully within the territory'[145] ahead of non-nationals. The territorial sovereignty which states exercise over outsiders ensures that the notion of a boundary is a practical obstacle to exercise of the right to seek asylum.

The legal status of refugees and asylum seekers as non-citizens or as 'illegal immigrants' is often central to state responses. In the USA and Australia, in particular, there is a clear relationship between the status of asylum seekers as 'aliens' and the application of immigration law and policy. In both these states there are policies which run counter to the rights of asylum seekers, directed at controlling the border and the problem of 'illegal immigrants'. It seems that through these policies and the implementing laws, refugees and asylum seekers are defined into national legal systems as outsiders, by way of 'exclusionary inclusion'.[146] That is, they are defined by way of exclusive rather than inclusive concepts, as non-citizen aliens.

Despite the principle of non-discrimination which the Refugee Convention applies to all refugees, the principle of equality manifestly is not applied evenly to such persons within the legal system.[147] Linda Bosniak has referred to this as the law's 'conflicted understanding of the difference that alienage makes'.[148] This is because for some purposes the law treats these aliens as equal to nationals or citizens, but for others it does not. Bosniak asks:

> [T]o what extent is discrimination between citizens and aliens a legitimate expression of the government's power to regulate the border and control the composition of membership of the community? How far does sovereignty reach before it must give way to equality?[149]

Further, although the concept of human rights which governs the rights of refugees and asylum seekers focuses on persons not citizens, such

---

[145] International Covenant on Civil and Political Rights, New York, 16 December 1966, in force 23 March 1976, UN Doc. A/6316 (1966), 999 UNTS 171, Art. 12(1). Frederick Whelan, 'Citizenship and Freedom of Movement: An Open Admission Policy?' in Mark Gibney (ed.), *Open Borders? Closed Societies? The Ethical and Political Issues* (New York: Greenwood Press, 1988), pp. 3–39.

[146] Susan Kneebone, 'Strangers at the Gate: Refugees, Citizenship and Nationality' (2004) 10 (1) *Australian Journal of Human Rights* 33.

[147] Refugee Convention, Art. 3. For an elaboration of this principle see Hathaway, *The Rights of Refugees*, pp. 1–13.

[148] Linda Bosniak, *The Citizen and the Alien: Dilemmas of Contemporary Membership* (Princeton NJ: Princeton University Press, 2006).

[149] *Ibid.*, p. 39.

66   REFUGEES, ASYLUM SEEKERS AND THE RULE OF LAW

rights require translation into national legal systems under our 'dual' legal systems. The legal doctrine of parliamentary sovereignty also links refugees and asylum seekers and their human rights to the nation through the legislative principle in the 'contested' ways described above.

There is a legal impasse between the notion of territorial–parliamentary–state–sovereignty which reinforces the lack of a legally enforceable right to seek asylum, and the non-extraterritorial application of the right against *refoulement*.[150] This has given rise to a theoretical debate between supporters for and against the notion of 'open' versus 'closed' borders.[151] For example, to argue for broader respect for the right to seek asylum is seen as an argument for 'choice' and as advocating for 'open' borders. Similarly, support is also seen to arise for open borders from 'cosmopolitans' who stress the importance of global justice and universal human rights in determining the rights of refugees.[152]

To extract ourselves from this *legal* impasse, it is helpful to turn to political doctrines to seek an explanation for the exclusion of 'outsiders'.[153] The purpose of this discussion is to seek explanations for the exclusion of 'outsiders' by states. The first broad doctrine that comes to mind is the *political* concept of the sovereignty of the people, the idea of government by consent. In this framework, there are a number of complex ideas largely focused upon the ethical or moral rights of individuals and states. The concept of 'community' is central to these ideas. They include arguments about the right of states to self-determination, to determine who shall 'belong' to their community. There are also

---

[150] *Sale* v. *Haitian Centers Council, Inc,* 509 US 155 (1993); *Ruddock* v. *Vadarlis* (2001) 110 FCR 491 reversing *Victorian Council for Civil Liberties Incorporated* v. *Minister for Immigration* (North J) (2001) 110 FCR 452 (special leave to appeal to the High Court was refused: (2001) 205 CLR 694) and *R* v. *Immigration Officer at Prague Airport; ex parte European Roma Rights Centre* [2004] UKHL 55; [2005] 2 AC 1. See Goodwin-Gill and McAdam, *The Refugee in International Law,* p. 247. This issue is discussed in the Introduction to this volume.

[151] Michael Walzer, *Spheres of Justice: a Defence of Pluralism and Equality* (Oxford: Basil Blackwell, 1983), pp. 31–63 and Joseph Carens, 'Aliens and Citizens: The Case for Open Borders' (1987) 49 *The Review of Politics* 251 represent the arguments for closed and open borders, respectively.

[152] Peter and Renata Singer, 'The Ethics of Refugee Policy' in Mark Gibney (ed.), *Open Borders?,* Chapter 4, pp. 111–30.

[153] For the purpose of this discussion, it is assumed that refugees and asylum seekers are 'security neutral', that they do not pose a risk to the community for reasons of security. It is not intended to discuss the provisions in the Refugee Convention (Arts. 1F, 31(2), 33 (2)) which deal with exceptions to refugee status on the basis of (loosely) security issues. These issues are considered in Chapters 2, 3 and 5 of this volume.

THE RULE OF LAW AND THE ROLE OF LAW

arguments about justice, that is, about the distributive implications of an 'open' versus a 'closed' border policy. Such arguments need to be balanced against the needs of refugees and asylum seekers, which are recognized by the human rights framework.

The argument for closed borders is one that resonates with state interests. It has two relevant aspects: it assumes the existence of a 'bounded' territory and the right of the 'community' to exclude those who are not its members. The first feature is familiar in legal language – it is explicitly represented by the legal argument for territorial-sovereignty nexus, which was referred to above. The second feature, the idea of 'community' and the right to confer membership on new-comers is implicit in refugee law. As stated above, refugees are con-sistently defined in state or national policy by exclusion, that is, as persons outside the legal system. They are defined by way of 'exclu-sionary inclusion', as non-citizens. To structure this discussion, we look first at liberal arguments for exclusion and liberal understandings of the 'community'. We then situate Dworkin's views within that under-standing. After reaching yet another impasse with those views, we turn to broader ethical arguments and explanations for the exclusion of refugees and asylum seekers.

Liberal theory and the community

The political philosophy of government by consent incorporates the liberal notion that members of that society are free to act within the confines of the rights recognized by that society. However such theory runs into difficulty in attempting to construct an argument in favour of refugee rights. This is because refugees are not part of the compact – they cannot consent because they are outsiders. The paradox of liberal theory is that it presupposes a bounded community or society whose rights are put ahead of the universal rights of refugees. This idea, known as 'communitarian liberalism', leads to a conflict between liberal princi-ples and the autonomy or liberty of the individual. Catherine Dauvergne argues that, because liberal theory first presumes a community and then explores theories of fairness and justice within that concept, it does not yield a standard of justice which is useful for assessing the rights of refugees.[154]

---

[154] Catherine Dauvergne, 'Beyond Justice'.

Michael Walzer is one of the political philosophers critiqued by Dauvergne.[155] Walzer's discussion of community membership is the classic work which attempts to explain the philosophical justification for bounded communities and exclusionary immigration policies. Walzer starts from the idea of a bounded world in order to examine the concept of distributive justice.[156] He explains that, as members of a political community, we must distribute and share, and that membership (or citizenship) is the 'primary social good' which we can confer on outsiders. He suggests two principles upon which membership is conferred. First, the principle of 'mutual aid' involves an objective or external and collective 'cost–benefit' analysis of the risks and costs involved in admitting a new member. The second is an internal principle under which the existing members decide which individuals should become the new members, on the basis of 'neighbourhood', 'family' and 'club' analogies. That is, the existing members look for persons with shared characteristics.

Walzer's principle of 'mutual aid' creates a link between national identity and territory. It involves an objective or external and collective 'cost–benefit' analysis of the risks and costs involved in admitting a new member, which can operate roughly as a 'Good Samaritan' standard. Walzer ties this to the fact that states control territory. He supports the sovereign right of a state to decide who shall become a member of the society within its territory. He recognizes that sometimes the first (individual) principle discussed above and the second (collective) principle can conflict. Importantly, he says that the idea of national identity involves a link between the people and the land.

Thus Walzer argues that our understanding of what membership means in our community is an issue of distributive justice. His is an argument for closed borders subject to the 'need' of the community.[157] Rather than taking a strict utilitarian approach (which looks to maximize benefits), Walzer takes the principle of mutual aid as the basis upon which a community can distribute membership. However, he concedes that refugees are 'one group of needy outsiders whose claims cannot be met by [the principle of mutual aid by] yielding territory or exporting wealth – only by taking people in'.[158]

---

[155] Catherine Dauvergne, 'Amorality and Humanitarianism in Immigration Law' (1999) 37 *Osgoode Hall Law Journal* 597 at 601.

[156] Specifically he took Rawls' 'refurbished social contract' as his base argument.

[157] Contrast Donald Galloway, 'Liberalism, Globalism and Immigration' (1993) 18 *Queens Law Journal* 266, who argues for a self-determining needs-based approach.

[158] Walzer, *Spheres of Justice*, p. 48.

THE RULE OF LAW AND THE ROLE OF LAW   69

This attempt to argue for refugee rights highlights that such exist as an exception to the legal entitlement and states can, and do, exclude such rights, as the discussion in this book highlights. Although refugee rights are universal human rights, they are often not recognized by national legal systems. Dauvergne concludes that 'communitarian liberalism', which emphasizes the 'beneficence' or discretion of states in recognizing such rights, fails to provide principled guidance for legal systems. She says that such policy is based on humanitarianism and that it is amoral for this reason in not recognizing universal human rights.[159]

As Christina Boswell says 'liberal theories run the risk of over-reaching themselves' – such theories set up expectations about 'individual and collective ethical agency' which cannot be redeemed in practice.[160] The notion of bounded communities defeats our efforts to construct a rights-based approach to refugees which is not an argument for open borders. We therefore turn back to Dworkin's concept of the 'community' and its role in relation to outsiders.

Dworkin and the community

The concept of a fraternal, personalized community is crucial to Dworkin's theory of integrity. The theory of integrity presupposes that legal rights and duties were created by a single author – the community personified – expressing a coherent conception of justice and fairness.[161] In his view, the community is a 'distinct moral agent because the social and intellectual practices that treat the community in this way should be protected'.[162] His interpretive theory of law, as explained, is sourced back to this idea of community. As Dworkin was at pains to point out in *Law's Empire* and in *Justice in Robes*, his theory also requires a coherency between the legislative and adjudicative functions which is sourced back to a political community. In particular, he explained the need for justification in his interpretive theory of law. But who are the members of this community and what rights do 'outsiders' have under this conception?

Dworkin's community is not based upon liberal theory (the sovereignty of the people) but is rather an anti-liberal approach, based upon the idea of a collective, fraternal entity. Dworkin rejects both a social

---

[159] Dauvergne, 'Amorality and Humanitarianism in Immigration Law' at 620–23.
[160] Christina Boswell, *The Ethics of Refugee Policy* (Aldershot, UK: Ashgate Publishing, 2005), p. 1.
[161] Dworkin, *Law's Empire*, p. 225.   [162] *Ibid.*, p. 188.

70   REFUGEES, ASYLUM SEEKERS AND THE RULE OF LAW

contract theory of individual natural rights and a utilitarian approach pursuant to which the needs of the majority prevail, as they conflict with his maxim of equality.[163]

The right to participate as a member of the community is central to Dworkin's theory of integrity (and of procedural fairness). Dworkin's theory is internal or communal in the sense that it is intended to explain the meaning of integrity within a cohesive political community, rather than across boundaries or in an international community. It was not intended to apply to the context of strangers in a community, so what follows is somewhat conjectural.

Dworkin's principle of procedural due process requires the consistent weighting of moral harm, and amounts to the right to be treated equally. His view is that the participation of any member of a democratic community ought not to be limited by assumptions about worth, talent or ability.[164] It is limited to the concept of community and compromise solutions, rather than to an abstract, absolute right to equality. In relation to procedural due process, Dworkin recognized that this did not give an individual the right to as much protection as a decision maker could provide. As with his basic principle of integrity, he acknowledged the overriding standard of the community.

According to Dworkin, membership of the social group or community carries with it mutual obligations based upon reciprocity and mutual concern.[165] The community or group must show equal concern for the well-being of others in the group in the interests of integrity. The wishes of each member of the group or community are to count on a par with the wishes of any other member.[166] Thus, potentially under his theory, persons can be excluded by the community if it is in the community's interests. Dworkin admits that on occasions the principle of integrity requires that the community be unfair to others outside the group – but for reasons that are good for the group. On such occasions, integrity conflicts with justice and fairness, but his view is that an outcome consistent with political integrity will always be principled.

He acknowledges the overriding political community standard. Thus, he suggests, those whose concept of justice is based on concern for those outside the group treat their association as only a de facto accident of

---

[163] Guest, *Ronald Dworkin*, Chapters 3 and 9 explain this as a concept of 'egalitarian utilitarianism'.
[164] *Ibid.*, p. 100.   [165] Michael Walzer, *Spheres of Justice*, pp. 31–63.
[166] Guest, *Ronald Dworkin*, p. 232.

THE RULE OF LAW AND THE ROLE OF LAW 71

history or geography, and not as a true associative community.[167] That is, integrity, although an ideal or principle, has to be applied in a realistic way – Dworkin uses the phrase 'so far as this is possible' frequently in explaining the concept of integrity, so as to recognize the compromises that have to be made. This means that judges may sometimes be required to defer to popular morality.[168] He explains that integrity would not be needed as a distinct political virtue in a utopian state. He thus envisages that, for political reasons, a community might decide to exclude certain persons or groups of persons from the right to participate.

As mentioned above, Dworkin's theory of integrity has been critiqued for its failure to analyse the nature of legal institutions and for its lack of theory about the state.[169] In *Justice in Robes*, Dworkin recognizes that 'politically important values like liberty and equality are in deep conflict with one another so that compromise among them is necessary'.[170] After characterizing that conflict as itself a 'fundamental value', he continues:

> In the end some unguided and subjective choice among values is necessary, and that fact challenges my assumption that one interpretation of overall legal practice or even some local area of law can sensibly be defended as overall best.[171]

It is unclear whether the critique of communitarian liberalism which is made against Dworkin is justified.[172] It may be that he would admit asylum seekers to the community where it did not harm the collective but enhanced its fraternal characteristic. But this may then lead him in the same direction as Walzer, in terms of allowing only a limited number to take up membership. There does not seem to be a significant difference between the liberal version of the 'rights of strangers' and Dworkin's anti-liberal approach.

The above discussion highlights the limits of both liberal theory and Dworkin's theory to account for the rights of asylum seekers and refugees, other than as exceptions to the law. To conclude, we turn to some ethical arguments which take the focus off the rights of asylum seekers and instead highlight the needs of the political community and the responsibility of states. This may have the effect of forcing a commitment to the rights of asylum seekers.

---

[167] Dworkin, *Law's Empire*, p. 209.
[168] See Allan, 'Justice and Fairness in Law's Empire' at 66.
[169] Murphy, 'Concepts of Law'. [170] Dworkin, *Justice in Robes*, p. 26. [171] *Ibid.*
[172] Dauvergne has argued that his views are in the same 'communitarian liberal' tradition as Rawls and Walzer. See Dauvergne, 'Amorality and Humanitarianism in Immigration Law'.

Ethical arguments

In his book entitled *The Ethics and Politics of Asylum*,[173] the political scientist Matthew J. Gibney provides some useful tools for critiquing the implications of the exclusion of outsiders from legal systems. Gibney provides a fresh perspective on the matter of inclusion and community, which enables us to move away from the territorial–sovereignty argument to a concern with political institutions as such. This shifts from focusing upon the status of asylum seekers as outsider non-citizens, to focusing upon their needs as disenfranchised persons and the responsibility of the international community.

Gibney makes a more nuanced argument for 'closed' borders.[174] His aim is to determine the limits of the right of states to control entry to their territory. He argues that to allow asylum seekers untrammelled access to refugee status determination procedures by granting a 'right of asylum' would lead to inequality on a global scale by creating inequalities between states, because the 'burden' of asylum would fall inequitably on states (as for example it did in the case of Germany in the early 1990s and as it has on the UK in recent years – see Chapter 5 in this book). He also argues that privileging those who turn up at the border over those who do not is arbitrary from a moral perspective. Moreover, he argues that the moral issues raised by refugeehood do not require more than that the people concerned are provided with a secure new state, not necessarily one of their own choosing. Thus he opposes the idea that refugees can have a moral right to choose their destination.

With respect to his argument about spontaneous refugees and 'choice', there are arguments, based upon empirical evidence, which suggest that the routes that asylum seekers take are based upon a complex set of factors, related to available routes and social factors in some instances. As a special category of 'forced migrants', the notion of 'choice' in this context is in any event a difficult one.[175] There is room in Gibney's

---

[173] Matthew J. Gibney, *The Ethics and Politics of Asylum: Liberal Democracy and the Response to Refugees* (Cambridge University Press, 2004).

[174] Cf. Galloway, 'Liberalism, Globalism and Immigration', who has a modified argument for open borders.

[175] Khalid Koser, 'Strategies, Stories and Smuggling: Inter-regional Asylum Flows and Their Implications for Regional Responses' in Susan Kneebone and Felicity Rawlings-Sanaei (eds.), *New Regionalism and Asylum Seekers: Challenges Ahead* (Oxford: Berghahn Books, 2007), Chapter 2. See Boswell, *The Ethics of Refugee Policy*, who argues the shortcomings of liberal universalism based upon moral agency.

analysis for freedom of choice for those asylum seekers who have no alternative but to flee and who *need* protection. But unless processing of asylum seekers is fair and effective, those needs will not be identified. However, it is not necessary to accept Gibney's views about 'choice' in order to follow the remainder of his argument, which is more concerned with what happens within the border.

Gibney's definition of 'ethical' in this context is 'a moral standard or value' which also takes into account the 'political reality'. He attempts to define normative prescriptions for action that take into account what states could actually do. A concern he expresses in his book is with what is 'politically possible',[176] and how states can be persuaded to respond more ethically (and consequently more generously) to the refugee problem. Gibney develops a 'humanitarian principle', to modify the traditional sovereign state exclusionist argument, by pointing to the responsibility of states to respect the *non-refoulement* principle and to resettle refugees. He argues that states have an obligation to assist refugees when the costs of doing so are low.[177] He says: 'Humanitarianism has no respect for distance; it is owed to all refugees on the basis of need alone.'[178]

Gibney's argument is thus clearly addressed to industrialized states in particular. Their role is explained through the 'harm' principle, which stresses the importance of states as agents in the creation of the refugee problem. As he explains, states are more than a culture or a territory. They are actors and agents in an interconnected global environment.[179] States have a responsibility for asylum seekers when there is a risk of *refoulement* or where there is a causal link between its actions and the reasons for seeking refuge. Gibney advocates that states should respond by more generous resettlement of refugees, as a means of sharing the burden in a global crisis.

Gibney develops two powerful critiques which are useful for assessing the legal implications discussed above. First, he offers insights into the territorial–sovereignty argument. He is concerned that arguments that are used to exclude people on the basis of control of territory should not be overstated. This is partly because the moral claim to such territory is often contested.[180] However, he recognizes that a territorial nexus may

---

[176] Gibney, *The Ethics and Politics of Asylum*, p. 17.   [177] *Ibid.*, p. 231.
[178] *Ibid.*, p. 240.   [179] See the discussion in the Introduction to this volume.
[180] Gibney, *The Ethics and Politics of Asylum*, pp. 39–40. John A. Scanlan and Otis T. Kent, 'The Force of Moral Arguments for a Just Immigration Policy in a Hobbesian Universe: The Contemporary American Example' in Mark Gibney (ed.), *Open Borders?*,

74 REFUGEES, ASYLUM SEEKERS AND THE RULE OF LAW

be relevant to create a proximate relationship or causal link, so as to engage the *non-refoulement* obligation and the harm principle. Under his 'harm principle', physical proximity is but one way in which a causal relation can arise.

Secondly, the ideas of community and membership are more important reasons, in Gibney's view, for including or excluding people from a territory. However, the model of community membership that he develops is based upon the idea of a 'political culture', rather than one based on culture as such (as, for example, Walzer's views might suggest). He is concerned that 'exclusionary inclusion' on the basis of culture and ethnicity should not be overstated as a reason for membership.[181] Rather, he emphasizes the political nature of the state's institutions, through the bonds of membership. He recognizes that these institutions or bonds, in turn, may not be completely independent of cultural and ethnic ties. Thus his concern is with protecting the interests of voting citizens *because* this is a means of preserving the important political institutions of a state. He considers that states are only justified in restricting the entry of non-citizens in order to protect the institutions and values of the liberal democratic welfare state.[182] Importantly, he analyses this concept of political community as a collective extension of the individual's right to self-determination.[183]

In the field of international refugee law, it is often stressed that protection under the Refugee Convention is a surrogate for the bond of 'trust, loyalty and protection' which has broken down between the citizen and her/his state.[184] Shacknove argues that the basic needs of refugees include 'liberty of political participation', in addition to physical security.[185] Gibney's argument develops this idea of political participation, which could also be used to argue for the application of principles of procedural fairness for refugees and asylum seekers. It is potentially a more inclusive view, which contrasts with that of John A. Scanlan and Otis T. Kent and others who privilege citizens per se against outsiders because of their status. Scanlan and Kent said that: 'universal

---

pp. 61–107 argue that a defensive concept of state is embedded in nations which have acquired territory through force.

[181] Gibney, *The Ethics and Politics of Asylum*, p. 43.   [182] *Ibid.*, p. 195.

[183] *Ibid.*, p. 26. Contrast Boswell, *The Ethics of Refugee Policy*, who argues for 'ontological communitarianism' as a 'more plausible account of moral agency and motivation' (p. 6).

[184] Andrew Shacknove, 'Who is a Refugee?' (1985) 95 *Ethics* 274.   [185] *Ibid.* at 280.

THE RULE OF LAW AND THE ROLE OF LAW 75

moral principles must be reducible to the interest of citizens'.[186] For them the ethical equals the interests of citizens.

Thus Gibney enables us to move away from the territorial–sovereignty argument to a concern with political institutions as such and the responsibility of states in this contested area.

Part five: conclusions

In this chapter we canvassed the notion of formal and substantive versions of the rule of law, and the effect that this may have on an understanding of how a legal system operates. We also considered Ronald Dworkin's idea of 'law as integrity' as a comparator and framework, as it contains a concept of an integrated rule of law, reflecting the operation of a legal system which is focused upon the 'community'. These ideas have implications for the role that judges can play in protecting the rights of refugees, and for the role of the executive and the legislature in defining policy and the rights of refugees in this context. Apart from foreshadowing particular concerns about how legislative power is exercised, we highlighted the important role of legislation in bringing international law into national legal systems. This is how states accept the responsibilities to which Gibney pointed in the previous section (and which were explained in the Introduction to this book). Finally, we looked at political and ethical explanations for the 'exclusionary inclusive' characterization of asylum seekers and refugees in our legal systems. We saw that ethical arguments, which recognize the status of refugees in international law, lead to a more inclusive view.

In relation to the rule of law, we saw that there are two main versions: first, the positivist view based upon the idea of authority; and secondly, the substantive view of law, which focuses upon rights. Within these versions of the rule of law, there are overlapping views about the distinction between law and morality, or between law and politics. Turning to the adjudicative role of judges, we saw that the two versions of the rule of law lead to different justifications for such a role in relation to statutory interpretation and the doctrine of judicial review, which have a great practical impact on refugee rights. We also discovered that, despite the fact that both versions of the rule of law support the idea of equality or neutrality and of procedural fairness for all persons, that it is the

[186] Scanlan and Kent, 'The Force of Moral Arguments for a Just Immigration Policy in a Hobbesian Universe', p. 77.

status of asylum seekers and refugees under state laws which leads to their exclusion from access to the territory or legal system of the state.

In Part four, we turned to political theory for guidance, but found that under both communitarian liberalism and Dworkin's view there is little to reassure us about the role of law in the absence of an independent judiciary committed to the protection of the rights of refugees and asylum seekers. While Dworkin's concept of an integrated rule of law provides a clearer explanation for the operation of a legal system which is potentially inclusive of refugee rights, it is unclear whether it avoids altogether the 'exclusionary inclusive' characterization of asylum seekers and refugees in our legal systems. As a number of commentators have suggested, whatever theory of law is appealed to, protection of rights requires a strong cultural ethic which, in turn, depends upon 'a shared political ideal' amongst citizens and officials about the value of such rights.[187] But that culture or 'community' cannot exist unless states accept their responsibility under international law to protect the rights of asylum seekers and refugees, and unless their legal systems operate to protect rather than to frustrate the exercise of such rights.

Despite the possible limitations of Dworkin's concept of 'community', his ideas about norms or values and how a legal system operates provide a useful framework for discussion and analysis. Thus, in this book, Dworkin's model of 'law as integrity' is used as a foil to respond to the following questions (see Chapter 6) which elucidate the operation of legal systems:

- Is there a coherent legislative principle? Of what significance is the method and extent of incorporation of the Refugee Convention and related international law and human rights instruments into the legislation of the national legal system? Are differences in the constitutional and legislative frameworks significant?
- Of what significance are differences in the nature and structure of decision making at the administrative level? And of adjudicative structures for decision making (including opportunities for appeal/ review) – are they determinative of 'rights-respecting' legal systems?
- How integral is the adjudicative process? What values underpin judicial reasoning? Are the courts deferential to executive policy in their approach to refugee law? Of what significance are differences in

---

[187] Tamanaha, 'A Concise Guide to the Rule of Law', p. 13.

the constitutional and the human rights framework for the adjudicative role?

- What are the limits of the integrity principle? How are refugees and asylum seekers defined by the legal system, and what forms of status and rights are granted by the state? That is, are refugees and asylum seekers defined as full members of the communities in which they seek protection?

We turn now to the rule of law experiences of the individual jurisdictions in relation to refugees and asylum seekers.

2

Asylum and the Rule of Law in Canada:
Hearing the Other (Side)

AUDREY MACKLIN

The first part of this chapter provides an historical overview of the Canadian asylum process. The second part explores how international and constitutional law structures shapes and constrains asylum law in Canada. The next two sections discuss elements of the asylum regime through an enlarged conception of the right to be heard. In its traditional and limited iteration (audi alteram partem, or 'hear the other side'), this right is familiar to any student of administrative law in the common law world. A somewhat figurative concept of the right to be heard is used here in order to consider different points in Canadian legal and geographical space where the asylum seeker's audibility is enabled or muted. In particular, attention is drawn to the limits imposed by conventional legal doctrine on what will be, or can be, heard from the other side of a cultural divide, a hearing room, or a border. The conclusion contemplates a separate but related dialogue that has emerged recently, partly in response to the obfuscating noise and troubling silences in the existing regime.

Part one: the asylum seeker in the Canadian legal system

Canada is a settler society par excellence. Almost 20 per cent of the population is foreign-born, putting it right behind Australia as a country of immigration in empirical terms.[1] Canada is also a country of immigration in the normative sense; official discourse celebrates immigration as constitutive of the nation. The image of Canada as an especially welcoming haven for refugees and asylum seekers fits well within this narrative. Indeed, the United Nations High Commissioner

---

[1] Statistics Canada, '2006 Census: Immigration, citizenship, language, mobility and migration', *The Daily* (4 December 2007), p. 1.

78

ASYLUM AND THE RULE OF LAW IN CANADA 79

for Refugees (UNHCR) awarded the Nansen Medal to the Canadian people in 1986 in recognition of Canada's 'outstanding services in supporting refugee causes'.[2]

In light of this image, it seems mildly surprising that Canada was slow to subscribe to the international refugee regime. It was notoriously hostile to Jews fleeing Nazi Germany, and even after the holocaust, remained dilatory and parsimonious in its refugee admissions. It did not sign the 1951 Convention relating to the Status of Refugees (Refugee Convention)[3] until 1969, claiming that accession would impede management of its immigration programme, especially deportation.

The Immigration and Refugee Protection Act 2001 (IRPA)[4] and the Immigration and Refugee Protection Regulations (IRP Regulations)[5] were enacted within months of 11 September 2001 (9/11), although the statute was drafted well before the attacks on the World Trade Center and the Pentagon. Part 2 of IRPA defines the scope of protection, establishes grounds of ineligibility, and adumbrates the process from arrival at a port of entry, to adjudication of the refugee claim, to judicial review, and finally to the removal of unsuccessful claimants.

Refugee protection extends to the following persons:

- A person determined to be a UN Convention refugee;[6]
- A person who faces a substantial risk of torture within the meaning of Article 1 of the Convention Against Torture (CAT);[7]

---

[2] UNHCR, 'The Nansen Refugee Award Flash Presentation', www.unhcr.org/cgi-bin/texis/vtx/events?id=3fb359bd4 (accessed 8 November 2007).

[3] Convention relating to the Status of Refugees, Geneva, 28 July 1951, in force 22 April 1954, 1989 UNTS 137.

[4] Immigration and Refugee Protection Act 2001 (Canada) (IRPA). Editor's note: in 2002 this Act replaced the Immigration Act 1976. The new legislation was controversial and the bills which introduced the changes were widely debated – for Bill C-31 (2000) see UNHCR, 'Comments on Bill C-31' (Submission to the House of Commons Standing Committee on Citizenship and Immigration, July 11, 2000). After a change of government in late 2000, this Bill was replaced by Bill C-11 (2001). The latter bill, which became IRPA, is discussed in: Donald Galloway, 'Criminality and State Protection: Structural Tensions in Canadian Refugee Law' in Susan Kneebone (ed.), *The Refugees Convention 50 Years On: Globalisation and International Law* (Aldershot, UK: Ashgate, 2003), Chapter 5, pp. 111–116. The passage of the legislation is discussed below on pp. 101–4.

[5] Governor General in Council, 'Regulations Amending the Immigration and Refugee Protection Regulations' (14 April 2004) 138 *Canada Gazette* 1.

[6] IRPA, s. 96.

[7] Convention Against Torture and Other Cruel Inhuman or Degrading Treatment or Punishment, New York, 10 December 1984, in force 26 June 1987, UN Doc. A/39/51 (1984), 1465 UNTS 85; IRPA s. 97(1)(a) (CAT).

80　REFUGEES, ASYLUM SEEKERS AND THE RULE OF LAW

- A person who faces a risk to life, or of cruel and unusual treatment, or who risks punishment that is not faced generally by other individuals in that country, is not the result of lawful sanctions, and is not caused by the country's inability to supply adequate health care.[8]

A person may lodge a refugee claim at a land, air or sea port of entry. Canada imposes entry visa requirements on most 'refugee-producing countries' and denies visas to anyone deemed likely to claim asylum. Therefore, the asylum seeker typically lacks the requisite visa entitling entry to Canada and is therefore presumptively inadmissible to Canada.[9] The immigration officer (a government employee) will issue a conditional removal order that comes into effect if and when the refugee application is rejected for ineligibility or after further examination of the merits of the claim. If a non-citizen enters Canada with a visa (student, tourist, temporary worker, etc.), he or she may apply inland at an immigration office for refugee protection and no removal order will be issued as long as the visa remains valid.

At the time the asylum claim is made, the immigration officer may enquire into the basis for the refugee claim, and the officer's notes will be admissible at the refugee hearing. The immigration officer must then determine the asylum seeker's eligibility for referral to the Refugee Protection Division (RPD) of the Immigration and Refugee Board (IRB). The grounds for ineligibility include the following:

- Already recognized as a refugee in Canada or another country to which the claimant can be sent;[10]
- Refugee claim previously rejected or found ineligible in Canada;[11]
- Asylum seeker inadmissible for reasons of security, 'violation of human or international rights' [sic], serious criminality, or organized criminality;[12]
- Arrived from a designated safe third country.[13]

---

[8] IRPA, s. 97(1)(b). Editor's note: this provision has been criticized by commentators on the basis that it provides less than the absolute protection of CAT, Art. 3. Note also that this provision picks up the standards of the Universal Declaration of Human Rights, Paris, 10 December 1948, GA Res. 217 A (III), UN Doc. A/810 (UDHR), Art. 3; International Covenant on Civil and Political Rights, New York, 16 December 1966, in force 23 March 1976, UN Doc. A/6316 (1966), 999 UNTS 171 (ICCPR), Art. 6(1) (the right to life); UDHR Art. 5 and ICCPR Art. 7 (freedom from torture and 'cruel, inhuman or degrading treatment or punishment').

[9] IRPA, s. 41.　　[10] *Ibid.*, s. 101(1)(d).　　[11] *Ibid.*, s. 101(1)(c).

[12] *Ibid.*, ss. 101(1)(f), 101(2).　　[13] *Ibid.*, s. 101(1)(e).

The USA is the only country designated as a safe third country. Pursuant to the Canada-US Safe Third Country Agreement,[14] refugee claimants who arrive at the Canadian border from the USA will be deflected back to the USA to make asylum claims unless they are unaccompanied minors, or have relatives residing legally in Canada.[15] If an immigration officer does not determine eligibility within three days, the claim is automatically referred to the RPD. Where inadmissibility due to security or criminality is at issue, or where the person is the subject of extradition proceedings, referral of the asylum claim is suspended until the resolution of the admissibility or extradition matter.

An eligible asylum seeker will receive a Personal Information Form (PIF), which must be completed in English or French and submitted to the IRB within twenty-eight days. The PIF consists of a long form questionnaire that asks about the asylum seeker's personal history, and requires elaborating in a written narrative the reasons for seeking refugee protection. The asylum seeker may retain legal counsel. In Ontario, British Columbia and Quebec, state-funded legal aid is available, although the rates are considered so low in Quebec that many refugee lawyers no longer accept legal aid clients. Canada detains relatively few asylum seekers prior to their hearings, although the grounds upon which detention is legally permissible were expanded under the 2001 IRPA. Once they submit their PIFs, asylum seekers may work, and may obtain social assistance and limited public health insurance.

Where asylum seekers arrive as a family, each family member must complete a separate PIF and must establish a separate basis for asylum. In other words, a child does not automatically receive refugee status because their parent meets the definition. In practice, the claims of a family are usually processed and heard together, and there is a marked tendency to prioritize the refugee claim of an adult male family member as the 'principal claimant'.

Once the PIF is received by the IRB, the claim is scheduled for a hearing. If the claim fits the profile of claims with high acceptance rates, the claim may be scheduled for an expedited process. If the expedited process does not result in a positive recommendation, or the claim does not fit the profile, it will be scheduled for a full hearing before a single

---

[14] Agreement Between the Government of Canada and the Government of the United States of America for Cooperation in the Examination of Refugee Status Claims from Nationals of Third Countries, 5 December 2002, in force 29 December 2004.

[15] For a detailed discussion, see Part Four [Keeping the Asylum Seeker out of Ear shot].

82   REFUGEES, ASYLUM SEEKERS AND THE RULE OF LAW

member of the Refugee Protection Division of the IRB. The IRB is an independent tribunal established by the executive in 1989 as a response to the *Singh* v. *Canada (Minister of Employment and Immigration)* *(Singh)*[16] decision of the Supreme Court of Canada. The member may be assisted at the hearing by a Refugee Protection Officer (RPO) – a civil servant. Legal counsel or non-legally trained consultants may represent the claimant by posing questions and offering submissions. The hearing is supposed to be inquisitorial and non-adversarial. In rare cases, usually those involving exclusion of the claimant under Article 1F of the Refugee Convention, a representative of the Minister of Citizenship and Immigration will participate by opposing the refugee claim, thus converting the hearing into an overtly adversarial process.

The member may render a decision orally at the conclusion of the hearing, or may reserve judgement. Reasons are required for all negative decisions, and for positive decisions on request. The acceptance rate has fluctuated since the IRB was established in 1989, and an overall acceptance rate masks meaningful variations between countries of origin, types of claims, and individual decision makers. Having said that, it should be noted that the acceptance rate sank to 40 per cent in 2004.[17] By 2006, the acceptance rate had rebounded to 47 per cent, where it had hovered for several years prior to the period 2002–5.[18] (The drop coincided with the general rise in anti-refugee animus following 9/11, but the correlation remains a hypothesis.)

If the claim is accepted, the asylum seeker may obtain permanent resident status and eventually citizenship. If the claim is rejected, the asylum seeker has fifteen days to apply for leave to seek judicial review before the Federal Court of Canada.[19] The grounds of review include error of law, breach of natural justice, or findings of fact made in a 'perverse or capricious manner or without regard to the evidence

---

[16] [1985] 1 SCR 177. *Singh* is discussed at pp. 85–89.

[17] Canadian Council for Refugees, 'Immigration and Refugee Board Statistics 2006', Email Correspondence, 16 March 2007, copy on file with author.

[18] Approximately 41% of claims were rejected, and the remaining 12% were either abandoned, withdrawn or otherwise resolved. Canadian Council for Refugees, 'Immigration and Refugee Board Statistics'. Editor's note: compare the 2002 refugee recognition rate of 55% reported by the UNHCR – this figure includes resettled refugees. See 'Introduction: Refugees and Asylum Seekers in the International Context – Rights and Realities' in this volume.

[19] IRPA, s. 72. The Minister of Citizenship and Immigration is notified of all decisions and, in principle, can seek judicial review of positive decisions, but this rarely happens outside of exclusion cases (IRPA, s. 73).

ASYLUM AND THE RULE OF LAW IN CANADA   83

before it'.[20] In 2001, about 63 per cent of unsuccessful refugee claimants applied for leave to seek judicial review. The Federal Court granted leave in about 12 per cent of the applications, and set aside about 12 per cent of those judicially reviewed.[21] Successful judicial review results in remittance of the case back to the tribunal for rehearing. A decision of the Federal Court may only be appealed to the Federal Court of Appeal if the Federal Court judge certifies a question of general importance arising from the judicial review.

A conditional removal order against a rejected asylum seeker comes into force fifteen days after the negative decision, which coincides with the period for seeking leave for judicial review of a rejected claim. The asylum seeker will also receive notice of her/his entitlement to apply for a Pre-Removal Risk Assessment (PRRA), which is a last-minute evaluation conducted when the individual is 'removal ready'. An asylum seeker who is ineligible for referral to the IRB because of making a prior unsuccessful claim, or who is inadmissible on grounds of security or criminality, may also apply for a PRRA. The PRRA is evaluated according to the same criteria as a protection claim, except that it is conducted in writing by an immigration officer rather than in person by an independent decision maker. Rejected claimants can only raise new evidence or evidence not reasonably available at the time of the hearing before the IRB.[22] Successful PRRA applicants who are inadmissible on grounds of criminality or security are protected from removal but cannot acquire permanent resident status. Moreover, the Minister of Citizenship and Immigration retains discretion to *refoule* a refugee who, in her/his opinion, poses a danger to the public or to national security.[23]

Apart from the refugee protection regime, any non-citizen (including a failed asylum seeker) may seek an exemption from the requirements of IRPA by applying for humanitarian and compassionate consideration.[24] This ministerial discretion is delegated to a senior immigration officer, and is structured by voluminous guidelines. In general, necessary but not sufficient conditions for a successful application for humanitarian and compassionate discretion to remain in Canada is evidence of economic establishment and unusual hardship that would result from removal. The consequences of removal are generally regarded as the province

---

[20] Federal Court Act, s. 18.1(3).
[21] See John Frecker, *Immigration and Refugee Legal Aid Cost Drivers* (Canada: Department of Justice, 2002), p. 90.
[22] IRPA, s. 113(a).   [23] IRPA, s. 115(2).   [24] IRPA, s. 25.

84 REFUGEES, ASYLUM SEEKERS AND THE RULE OF LAW

of refugee determination and are thus irrelevant to a humanitarian and compassionate determination in respect of a failed asylum seeker.

Part two: the right to be heard

The Latin maxim audi alteram partem literally means 'hear the other side', but it has come to encompass a wide array of procedural rules that address prior notification and disclosure, the conduct of the hearing itself, and the provision of reasons afterwards.[25]

At least two types of normative claims are made in support of a right to be heard. The first is instrumental: gathering evidence and argument from a person about whom a decision will be made is likely to produce better and more accurate outcomes, and such decisions are more likely to be accepted as legitimate (even if adverse). The second is deontological: respect for the dignity of individuals militates in favour of enabling them to participate in a process that will affect their interests. Put simply, listening to what someone has to say about how power will be exercised over them signifies that they matter.

It is important to see that these arguments in favour of the right to be heard also support 'voice' in the form of electoral democracy, which in turn underwrites the doctrine of parliamentary supremacy. This idea of being heard serves the rule of law's ultimate task of constraining arbitrary government in the legislative and in the executive sphere. But, of course, the asylum seeker is formally disenfranchised, and cannot even claim the status of a minority member of the polity.[26] The architecture of the rule of law presupposes a certain equilibration and complementarity between political representation and legal subjectivity. The position of non-citizens as people with no voice in the political realm perforce orients them towards the judicial sphere. Unlike minority citizens, they do not even notionally have the capacity to seek remedies at the polls.[27] At the limit, one can ask whether the rule of law could impose a duty to hear asylum seekers upon a legislator that has chosen to close its ears by closing its border.

---

[25] David Mullan, *Administrative Law: Essentials of Canadian Law* (Toronto: Irwin Law, 2001), p. 232.

[26] Susan Kneebone, 'Natural Justice and Non-Citizens: A Matter of Integrity?' (2002) 26 *Melbourne University Law Review* 355.

[27] This chapter is written from a traditional understanding of politics. For an interesting analysis of politics and immigration from the alien sub-altern ('every other') perspective, see Peter Nyers, 'Abject Cosmopolitanism' (2003) 24 *Third World Quarterly* 1069.

There are other ways in which the right to be heard poses specific challenges in the asylum context. Consider the myriad possibilities for distortion of the communication between asylum seeker and decision maker. Asylum seekers often speak a different language, necessitating the use of interpreters. Profound differences of culture, class, personal history and political context manifest through unarticulated assumptions and [mis]readings of the Other (which leads to misunderstandings on both sides). Trauma affects people in different ways: silencing them when they need to speak, suppressing what they cannot bear to but must remember, confusing them when they need to display certitude, and so on. Reliance upon the advice of unqualified and/or unethical people may lead some asylum seekers to embellish or prevaricate. On the other side of the equation, the sensitivity and subjective perception of decision-making autonomy (as distinct from formal independence) affects the capacity of decision makers to hear. The combined effect of these factors can muffle, mute and distort the voice of a refugee in need of protection, and lead to her/him being heard as someone merely mimicking the voice of a refugee. Realistically, no feasible administrative process intended to determine refugee status can fully mitigate the multiple sources of static interference that affect the audibility of the asylum seeker.

The legal doctrine of audi alteram partem does not capture all of these nuances. However, it is this larger question of what it means for an asylum seeker to be heard that offers a link between the rule of law in its political and legal dimensions.

Part three: the audibility of the asylum seeker in Canadian law

The legal soundscape

The current refugee determination system in Canada owes its origin to the 1985 landmark decision of Justice Wilson in Singh. Prior to Singh, it was possible for an asylum seeker's claim to be rejected without an opportunity to appear in person before the decision maker or to see all the evidence relied upon by the decision maker. Singh was one of the first cases decided under the 1982 Canadian Charter of Rights and Freedoms ('Charter').[28] The majority of the Court had little trouble

---

[28] Technically, the Court was unanimous on the result, but split 3–3 on whether the decision should be based on the Canadian Bill of Rights (a statutory human rights statute) or on the constitutionally entrenched Charter of Rights and Freedoms.

86   REFUGEES, ASYLUM SEEKERS AND THE RULE OF LAW

concluding that the legislative scheme was sufficiently comprehensive to exclude the common law principle of natural justice. Instead they turned to the 'fundamental justice' provision in s. 7 of the Charter to fill the gap.[29]

Wilson, speaking for the majority, quickly moved to the question of whether the extant process violated s. 7 of the Charter, which states as follows:

> Everyone has the right to life, liberty and security of the person, and the right not to be deprived thereof, except in accordance with fundamental justice.[30]

In order to determine the content of the asylum seekers' constitutional rights, the Court had to consider first whether asylum seekers, *qua* non-citizens, were included in the term 'everyone'. It also considered whether a 'life, liberty or security' interest was implicated by a process for determining whether the removal of a person from Canada would expose her/him to a serious risk of persecution in another country, and if so, whether the deprivation accorded with principles of fundamental justice.

Wilson's reasoning disclosed a series of moves that manage to counterpoise the universalist impulse of a post-World War II human rights instrument with the positivist strain in Canadian common law jurisprudence. On the question of whether 'everyone' includes asylum seekers, Wilson wrote that the term is broad enough to encompass 'every human being who is physically present in Canada and by virtue of such presence amenable to Canadian law'.[31] While sufficient to resolve the application of s. 7 to asylum seekers in Canada, the dictum leaves dangling the issue of whether the Charter applies extraterritorially to the conduct of Canadian officials abroad who act under authority of Canadian law – in visa posts, on the high seas, in interrogation rooms, or on the battlefield.[32] Does the rule of law follow the exercise of power, or does it stop at the border?

The government advanced two arguments in support of the proposition that the Canadian refugee determination process did not

---

[29] Kneebone, 'Natural Justice and Non-Citizens'.
[30] *Canadian Charter of Rights and Freedoms*, s. 7.   [31] *Singh* [1985] 1 SCR 177 at para. 47.
[32] Examples where these issues might arise include the processing of immigration applications in offices abroad, the participation of Canadian officials in the interrogation of Canadian citizens detained in foreign prisons, and the conduct of Canadian troops in Afghanistan.

ASYLUM AND THE RULE OF LAW IN CANADA 87

implicate the Canadian state in any infringement of the life, liberty or security of an asylum seeker. The first relied on the the claim that rights to life, liberty and security of person protected by the Charter concerned conduct by Canada, not by foreign governments. Persecution, if perpetrated at all, would be at the hands of another state, and so the denial of the s. 7 rights could not be attributed to Canada. Whereas the judgment defers on the extraterritorial reach of the Charter, Wilson's response to this argument implicitly confirms the role of the Charter in constraining otherwise lawful conduct by state actors within Canada where such actions facilitate extraterritorial violations of fundamental rights to life and liberty. Wilson said:

> There may be some merit in counsel's submission that closing off the avenues of escape provided by the Act does not per se deprive a Convention refugee of the right to life or to liberty. It may result in his being deprived of life or liberty by others, but it is not certain that this will happen.
>
> I cannot, however, accept the submission of counsel for the Minister that the denial of the rights possessed by a Convention refugee under the Act does not constitute a deprivation of his security of the person.
>
> For purposes of the present appeal it is not necessary, in my opinion, to consider whether such an expansive approach to 'security of the person' in s. 7 of the Charter should be taken. It seems to me that even if one adopts the narrow approach advocated by counsel for the Minister, 'security of the person' must encompass freedom from the threat of physical punishment or suffering as well as freedom from such punishment itself. I note particularly that a Convention refugee has the right under s. 55 of the Act not to '. . . be removed from Canada to a country where his life or freedom would be threatened . . .'. In my view, the denial of such a right must amount to a deprivation of security of the person within the meaning of s. 7.[33]

The second argument invoked the traditional common law dichotomy of right versus privilege as the determinant of procedural entitlements. Since immigration is not a right, but rather a privilege extended by the state, asylum seekers as non-citizens possess no right to any particular procedural protections in the exercise of the state's sovereign discretion. Wilson firmly rejected this formalist, state-centric perspective in favour of an inquiry into the impact of expulsion on the asylum seeker as individual:

---

[33] *Singh* [1985] 1 SCR 177 at paras. 45–7.

88 REFUGEES, ASYLUM SEEKERS AND THE RULE OF LAW

> Given the potential consequences for the appellants of a denial of that status if they are in fact persons with a 'well-founded fear of persecution', it seems to me unthinkable that the Charter would not apply to entitle them to fundamental justice in the adjudication of their status.[34]

At the same time, Wilson ultimately relied on the statutory basis for asylum. Her assessment of the impact of a negative refugee determination presupposed that 'if the appellants had been found to be Convention refugees as defined in s. 2(1) of the Immigration Act, 1976 they would have been entitled as a matter of law to the incidents of that status provided for in the Act'.[35] The existence of a statutory right did not require the Court to consider whether asylum itself is a human right protected by the Charter. The articulation of refugee status as a statutory right (predicated on meeting the UN refugee definition)[36] also facilitated more vigorous judicial scrutiny than a challenge to the vague wording or explicit grants of executive discretion involved in humanitarian and compassionate applications and decisions to expel refugees on grounds of criminality or security. In these respects, resolution of the *Singh* case did not test the judiciary's fidelity to parliamentary supremacy and executive authority.

Having established a deprivation of a right to security of person, the Court then considered whether the existing procedure was consistent with the principles of fundamental justice. Wilson ruled that fundamental justice included, at a minimum, the common law principles of procedural fairness. The existing process failed to accord the claimants an opportunity to know the case against them, because evidence relied upon by the decision maker was not disclosed to the claimants. It did not let them respond to the case against them, or state their own case insofar as a claim could be rejected, without an oral hearing before the decision maker. Wilson concluded that: 'I am of the view that where a serious issue of credibility is involved, fundamental justice requires that credibility be determined on the basis of an oral hearing'.[37]

The final stage in a Charter analysis considers whether, under s. 1, a violation of a Charter right or freedom is a 'reasonable limit' that is 'demonstrably justified in a free and democratic society'. The judgment in *Singh* pre-dates the Supreme Court's articulation of the test under s. 1, and so the Court's analysis is fairly perfunctory. However, Wilson expressed a pointed lack of sympathy for the government's contention

---

[34] *Ibid.* at para. 52.   [35] *Ibid.*   [36] Refugee Convention, Art. 1A(2).
[37] *Singh* [1985] 1 SCR 177 at para. 59.

ASYLUM AND THE RULE OF LAW IN CANADA   89

that the administrative and financial burden of providing an oral hearing to every refugee claimant would be unreasonably onerous. Not only had the government failed to provide empirical evidence in support of its claim, but Wilson expressed scepticism that a utilitarian cost–benefit analysis could suffice to justify a denial of fundamental justice:

> Certainly the guarantees of the Charter would be illusory if they could be ignored because it was administratively convenient to do so. No doubt considerable time and money can be saved by adopting administrative procedures which ignore the principles of fundamental justice but such an argument, in my view, misses the point of the exercise under s. 1. The principles of natural justice and procedural fairness which have long been espoused by our courts, and the constitutional entrenchment of the principles of fundamental justice in s. 7, implicitly recognize that a balance of administrative convenience does not override the need to adhere to these principles.[38]

The *Singh* decision made an oral hearing an indispensable feature of any subsequent refugee determination process. It continues to exert influence over the Canadian asylum process. In particular, the constitutional requirement for an oral hearing at some stage in the process of determining a claim for refugee protection remains unassailable. Whether the Court would have viewed the matter differently in the absence of a constitutional bill of rights is a matter of speculation. Interestingly, in 1999, an illegal migrant named Mavis Baker challenged the procedural and substantive aspects of the exercise of humanitarian and compassionate discretion under various provisions of the Charter, yet the Supreme Court insisted on resolving the case solely through resort to administrative law principles rather than the Charter.[39] The broad wording and legislative silence regarding the interpretation of humanitarian and compassionate discretion arguably facilitated the deployment of the common law fiction of 'supplying the omission of the legislator', but avoiding the Charter also enabled the Court to deflect the issue of whether the Charter imposes limits on the state's power to deport people outside the context of persecution or torture.

---

[38] *Ibid.* at para. 70. While the Supreme Court has never formally resiled from this statement, subsequent jurisprudence indicates greater judicial tolerance for utilitarian balancing under s. 1, even where the evidentiary record is weak.

[39] *Baker v. Canada (Ministry of Citizenship and Immigration)* [1999] 2 SCR 817.

90   REFUGEES, ASYLUM SEEKERS AND THE RULE OF LAW

Subsequent legal judgments and policy shifts have wandered from the spirit, if not the letter, of the Singh decision. In her decision, Wilson calibrated the requirements of fundamental justice for asylum seekers by reference to the consequences of denial of refugee status and subsequent removal. Yet, in a subsequent case involving the deportation of a long-term permanent resident, the Supreme Court of Canada appeared to revive the right/privilege distinction that Wilson rejected as inapt in the Charter era. In *Canada (Minister of Employment and Immigration)* v. *Chiarelli* ('Chiarelli'),[40] the Court effectively denied the appellant's claim under s. 7 of the Charter to various procedural protections prior to deportation by insisting that 'the most fundamental principle of immigration law is that non-citizens do not have an unqualified right to enter or remain in the country. At common law an alien has no right to enter or remain in the country.'[41] This principle was cited, inter alia, in defence of a process that denied a permanent resident an opportunity to give evidence about the consequences of deportation from Canada.[42] It is routinely quoted with approval any time that the rights of non-citizens in relation to removal is raised; neither Chiarelli itself nor subsequent cases reflect upon Justice Wilson's expression of doubt about the legitimacy of the stark, state-centric predicates of the right/privilege distinction in the migration context.

The judicial combination of Singh and Chiarelli has produced a modified binary, whereby non-citizens who apprehend persecution, torture or death if deported are eligible for the protection of s. 7 of the Charter, while other non-citizens do not. In practice, this means that courts will consider whether the removal of asylum seekers to face possible persecution, the exposure of foreign fugitives to a risk of the death penalty abroad, or deportation of security detainees who face a substantial risk of torture, deprives these non-citizens of security of the person in accordance with fundamental justice. Other non-citizens who may be long-term residents, such as permanent residents convicted of criminal offences or undocumented migrants, must seek their recourse under statute, as inflected by the common law.[43]

The post-9/11 securitization of immigration has dangerously eroded the Charter protection available to non-citizens at risk of torture,

---

[40] [1992] 1 SCR 711.   [41] Chiarelli [1992] 1 SCR 711 at p. 733.

[42] Mr Chiarelli was a long-term permanent resident of Canada who faced removal to Italy, his country of nationality, on the basis of organized criminality.

[43] See *Baker* v. *Canada* [1999] 2 SCR 817.

including refugees. The Supreme Court of Canada's *Suresh* v. *Canada (Minister of Citizenship and Immigration)* (*Suresh*)[44] judgment concerned a Sri Lankan refugee deemed a security threat to Canada on account of his alleged association with the Liberation Tigers of Tamil Eelam (LTTE) as a fundraiser. Although the case was heard by the Supreme Court of Canada before 9/11, the judgment was delivered after the attacks. The Court ruled that, in general, s. 7 of the Charter prohibited expelling a non-citizen to a place where he or she would face a substantial risk of torture, except in exceptional circumstances. The Court refused to attribute the general rule to the binding force of customary international law, or even to Article 3 of the CAT (which specifically prohibits deportation to torture), and pointedly refused to articulate what exceptional circumstances would permit handing over a person to face torture:

> Insofar as Canada is unable to deport a person where there are substantial grounds to believe he or she would be tortured on return, this is not because Article 3 of the CAT directly constrains the actions of the Canadian government, but because the fundamental justice balance under s. 7 of the *Charter* generally precludes deportation to torture when applied on a case-by-case basis. We may predict that it will rarely be struck in favour of expulsion where there is a serious risk of torture. However, as the matter is one of balance, precise prediction is elusive. The ambit of an exceptional discretion to deport to torture, if any, must await future cases [emphasis in original].[45]

The Court has faced considerable criticism for even notionally allowing an exception to the prohibition on torture. The exception is not predicated on an instrumental calculus about the alleged utility of torture (as in the oft-cited 'ticking bomb' scenario), but rather on the availability of deportation as a remedial option available for non-citizens (as opposed to citizens) who pose a danger to national security.

The Supreme Court of Canada's 'hesitant embrace'[46] of international law in *Suresh* did not encompass the prohibition on return to torture as a peremptory norm of international law. The Court arguably revealed a lapse in fidelity to the rule of law that courts in the UK and the European

---

[44] [2002] 1 SCR 3.   [45] *Ibid.* at para. 78 [emphasis in original].
[46] Jutta Brunnée and Stephen Toope, 'A Hesitant Embrace: Baker and the Application of International Law by Canadian Courts' in David Dyzenhaus (ed.), *The Unity of Public Law* (Oxford: Hart Publishing, 2004), pp. 375–89.

Court of Human Rights have managed to resist so far.[47] As with all Supreme Court of Canada decisions regarding the power of the state to expel non-citizens, the Court in *Suresh* studiously avoided any arguments regarding the inequality of citizens versus non-citizens. The reasons for this seem obvious enough: the deportability of non-citizens is the definitive legal distinction between the citizen and the alien. At the same time, the Court's willingness to contemplate – even hypothetically – that individual non-citizens might, under the right circumstances, be justifiably rendered to torture, veers dangerously close to denying to non-citizens the essential humanity that underwrites not only a constitutional guarantee of equality, but even a less robust equality presupposed by the rule of law.

The *Suresh* decision must be situated against the general treatment of international law within the Canadian legal order.[48] As a general proposition, international treaties and conventions are not binding in domestic courts unless incorporated by statute. However, a common law canon of construction directs that 'Parliament is not presumed to legislate in breach of a treaty or in a manner inconsistent with the comity of nations and the established rules of international law.'[49] More recently, the Supreme Court of Canada amplified the role of international human rights norms as relevant considerations in the exercise of discretion. In *Baker* v. *Canada (Minister of Citizenship and Immigration) (Baker)*,[50] a majority of the Supreme Court of Canada invoked the Convention on the Rights of the Child,[51] a ratified but unincorporated convention, as a source of the obligation on an immigration officer to take into account the best interests of Mavis Baker's children in Canada in giving a decision about whether to extend humanitarian and compassionate consideration to Mavis Baker. The Court quoted with approval the principle that, to the extent possible, statutes ought to

---

[47] *Chahal* v. *UK* (1996) 23 EHRR 413 (15 November 1996); the European Court of Human Rights' absolute prohibition on expulsion to a substantial risk of torture under Art. 3 of the European Convention on Human Rights is being relitigated before the European Court of Human Rights in *Ramzy* v. *The Netherlands*, No. 25424/05 (judgment pending). See Chapter 5 in this volume.

[48] See generally, Jutta Brunnée and Stephen Toope, 'A Hesitant Embrace', pp. 375–389 and Audrey Macklin, 'The State of Law's Borders and the Law of States' Borders' in Dyzenhaus (ed.), *The Unity of Public Law*, (Oxford: Hart Publishing, 2004), pp. 173–199.

[49] *Daniels* v. *R* [1968] SCR 517 at 541.   [50]   [1999] 2 SCR 817.

[51] Convention on the Rights of the Child, New York, 20 November 1989, in force 2 September 1990, UN Doc. A/44/49, 44 UN GAOR Supp. (No. 49) at 167.

ASYLUM AND THE RULE OF LAW IN CANADA 93

be interpreted consistently with the values and principles enshrined in international law.[52]

The audibility of the asylum seeker in law

Canada enjoys a favourable reputation for its relatively liberal interpretation of most elements of the refugee definition. In 1993, the Supreme Court of Canada issued the decision in *Canada (Attorney-General) v. Ward (Ward).*[53] The judgment discloses the influence of the scholarship of James Hathaway, and of comparative jurisprudence. In return, *Ward* has also been cited extensively in other jurisdictions, particularly in the common law world. *Ward* resolved several controversial interpretive issues with respect to agents of persecution, unwillingness or inability to protect, burdens of proof in relation to state protection, the definition of a particular social group, the scope of political opinion, and dual nationality.[54] In 1998, *Pushpanathan v. Canada (Minister of Citizenship and Immigration)*[55] rejected an interpretation of the exclusion clause in the Refugee Convention Article 1F that would exclude from refugee protection an asylum seeker convicted of a criminal offence in Canada.

The courts have not been the sole promoters of progressive interpretation of the refugee definition. The IRB's 1993 Gender Guidelines (revised 1996),[56] have been hailed and emulated worldwide for their gender-sensitive interpretation of the refugee definition.[57] The Guidelines confirm that forms of harm inflicted exclusively or mainly on women and girls (rape, female genital mutilation, forced abortion, sex trafficking, etc.) constitute persecution; that feminism or refusal to abide by imposed religious rules might constitute a political opinion or (non)religious

---

[52] *Baker* [1999] 2 SCR 817 at para. 70. Editor's note: See the discussion of principles of statutory interpretation in Chapter 1 in this volume.

[53] [1993] 2 SCR 689.

[54] Audrey Macklin, 'Attorney–General v Ward: A Review Essay' (1994) 6 *International Journal of Refugee Law* 362.

[55] [1998] 1 SCR 982.

[56] Canadian Immigration and Refugee Board, *Guidelines on Women Refugee Claimants Fearing Gender-Related Persecution* (Ottawa: Immigration and Refugee Board, 1993 (updated 1996)).

[57] Heaven Crawley, *Refugees and Gender: Law and Process* (Bristol: Jordans Publishing Ltd, 2001), p. 13; Nicole LaViolette, 'Gender-Related Refugee Claims: Expanding the Scope of the Canadian Guidelines' (2007) 19 *International Journal of Refugee Law* 169 at 178.

94   REFUGEES, ASYLUM SEEKERS AND THE RULE OF LAW

belief; and that a particular social group may be defined by reference to gender or sexual orientation. The IRB also issued Guidelines on Civil War,[58] which clarified that a civilian need not be personally targeted for persecution, as long as one is identified as a member of an ethnic, religious, national or particular social group that is generally at risk of persecution.

These examples validate Canada's reputation for adopting relatively flexible interpretations of the elements of the refugee definition. That is to say, the Canadian jurisprudence and administrative guidelines incorporate the lessons of feminism on the ways that public power can be marshalled to perpetuate private oppression, and have recognized how civil war and 'failed states' have replaced communism as the triggering conditions for flight.[59] An evolving understanding of the nature and scope of international human rights reverberates in the meaning ascribed to persecution and grounds of persecution.[60] Cast in the language of audibility, Canadian refugee law lends a sympathetic doctrinal ear to the narratives of refugee claimants – once the story is heard and if it is believed.

It is these latter preconditions that are preoccupying. Canadian refugee law cannot be accused of deafness to the suffering of asylum seekers. Rather, the declining numbers of asylum seekers entering Canada's refugee determination process and the declining acceptance rate for asylum seekers in Canada suggests that asylum seekers are increasingly kept out of earshot (so they cannot be heard) and decreasingly believed (so that, if heard, they are deemed non-credible). In other words, it is not the 'law' determining who falls within the refugee definition, but rather those who apply it (administrative decision makers of the IRB) and those who control access to the system (the government) who determine, in these two ways, whether and how an asylum seeker will be heard.

The policy makers' motivation in preventing the access of asylum seekers to the refugee determination system is not difficult to fathom. If the number of asylum seekers exceeds whatever level is considered politically palatable, and the independence of the judiciary means that

---

[58] Immigration and Refugee Board, *Civilian Non-Combatants Fearing Persecution in Civil War Situations: Guidelines Issued by the Chairperson Pursuant to Section 65(3) of the Immigration Act* (Ottawa: Immigration and Refugee Board, 1996), www.cisr-irb.gc.ca/en/references/policy/guidelines/civil_e.htm (accessed 3 March 2008).

[59] See 'Introduction: Refugees and Asylum Seekers in the International Context – Rights and Realities' in this volume.

[60] See Chapter 1 in this volume.

the interpretation of the refugee definition cannot be controlled, preventing access to the refugee determination system offers a means of managing numbers. As for the decision makers, the credibility of the asylum seeker seems to be the determinative factor in the vast majority of refugee claims. A jurisdiction may create doctrinal openings to recognize refugee status that other jurisdictions do not, but if the decision makers reject asylum seekers on grounds of credibility, the doctrinal doors are never reached, much less opened. It may seem anomalous that institutionalized scepticism about the credibility of asylum seekers could coexist with a relatively liberal approach to the substance of the refugee definition, but the norms guiding decision makers emerge not only from legal texts, but indirectly from political and institutional sources. Moreover, institutions do not operate on the basis of a singular rationality emanating from a directing mind; and divergent currents may operate simultaneously at different levels of a bureaucratic hierarchy or in different offices.

It is now useful to consider in more detail some of the ways in which the audibility of asylum seekers themselves (as opposed to their narratives) is regulated.

Who is listening?

The rule of law's promise that one will be heard presupposes a listener capable of comprehending and synthesizing what is heard within the terms of the listeners' legal mandate. In other words, it assumes a competent decision maker. The chief tasks of a member of the IRB's Refugee Protection Division consists of eliciting and attending to information, sifting relevant from irrelevant data, determining credibility in accordance with principled criteria, understanding the law, and applying the law to the facts. Members need not be lawyers, and the IRB delivers extensive, sophisticated and ongoing professional training to its members.

The IRB is Canada's largest federal administrative tribunal. At one point in the early 1990s, the IRB had over 200 members in seven cities across the country. At present, the IRB's Refugee Protection Division has 127 members.[61] Virtually from its inception in 1989, pundits, lawyers, opposition politicians and refugee advocates criticized the

---

[61] 'Refugee backlog headed for record high as Tories slow to appoint adjudicators', *Canadian Press*, 8 April 2008, http://canadianpress.google.com/article/ALeqM5iZQAY-wHe3yHqDTUdfK_yeP86PdFQ (accessed 2 May 2008).

96   REFUGEES, ASYLUM SEEKERS AND THE RULE OF LAW

appointment process as little more than an opportunity for the government to reward the party faithful and repay political debts.[62] They charged that competence was sacrificed at the altar of political patronage, with the result that the overall quality of IRB decision makers was markedly worse than it would be under a system of purely merit-based appointment. Successive governments have promised to neutralize the appointment and reappointment process, and move to a more merit-based system.[63] There is no lack of alternative models of appointment and reappointment and, while some governments have behaved more egregiously than others, no government thus far has demonstrated the political will to entirely cease bestowing IRB appointments for reasons other than skill, experience and qualifications.[64]

Not all appointments are based on patronage, and not all patronage appointees are incompetent, but there can be little doubt that the overall level of competence is lower than what might be achieved from a purely merit-based system. Since the IRB is an independent tribunal, members are not employees of the Department of Citizenship and Immigration Canada, but rather are appointed by the Cabinet for fixed terms, usually ranging from two to five years. During the term of appointment, members enjoy virtually unassailable security of tenure (except for extreme cases of personal misconduct);[65] they cannot be instructed to interpret or apply the refugee definition in a certain manner, or raise or lower acceptance rates. Rumours of political interference in particularly controversial decisions emerge, but rarely. After all, the institutional autonomy of the IRB enables politicians to deflect direct criticism of decisions by pointing to the tribunals' independence from government influence.

Nevertheless, this protection of decision-making independence is compromised by the fact that reappointment decisions are ultimately

---

[62] See e.g. Peter Showler, *Refugee Sandwich* (Montreal: McGill-Queen's Press, 2006), pp. 225–6.

[63] See, e.g., Immigration and Refugee Board of Canada, 'Minister Sgro Announces Reform of the Appointment Process for Immigration and Refugee Board Members', Press Release, Ottawa, 16 March 2004.

[64] Macleans.ca, 'Refugee Board in Flux: With its Chairman Departing, Critics Suggest the IRB is Moving Backward', 28 February 2007, www.macleans.ca/article.jsp?content= 20070228_101241_7772 (accessed 3 March 2008).

[65] Incidents that have led to suspension include attempting to extract sex or money in exchange for a favourable decision. For an example, see: Ctv.ca, 'Refugee judge charged with breach of trust', 12 October 2006, www.ctv.ca/servlet/ArticleNews/print/CTVNews/ 20061012/Refugee_judge_061012/20061012/?hub=TorontoHome&subhub=PrintStory (accessed 3 March 2008).

ASYLUM AND THE RULE OF LAW IN CANADA   97

made by Cabinet, and the assessment of the Chair and managers within the IRB about the actual performance of a given member is widely believed not to play a determinative role. Political connections can still matter more than demonstrated [in]competence, even at the reappointment stage.

Incompetence can manifest itself in a number of ways. It may affect the ability to analyse facts in a legal context, to distinguish legitimate from illegitimate inferences, or to articulate coherent reasons for a decision. Incompetence may operate in tandem with bad faith or burnout, and may include failure to interact with claimants in a sensitive and respectful manner, lack of attention to the impact of culture, gender, language and trauma, as well as disregard of the asylum seeker's fear of the hearing room. Now that hearing panels consist of a single member rather than two, the opportunities to mask or compensate for the incompetence of one member with the competence of the other have largely disappeared. Figuratively speaking, incompetent members are hearing-impaired. One cannot be certain whether they are listening, what they are actually hearing, or what analytical or attitudinal limitations might distort reception.

Making oneself heard

Up until 2003, a typical refugee hearing unfolded as follows. The asylum seeker would swear an oath or affirm the truth of their testimony. He or she would then swear or affirm that the contents of their Personal Information Form were true and correct. The decision maker then may or may not indicate specific areas of concern or ambiguity for counsel to focus upon in examination. Counsel for the asylum seeker would begin by posing questions to the claimant to enable her/him to recount the significant events leading up to the decision to seek asylum. If present, a refugee protection officer (RPO) – a civil servant employed by the IRB to assist the decision maker – might ask additional questions or explore terrain that the lawyer did not address. The decision maker might also pose questions directly to the claimant. Where the asylum seeker was unrepresented by counsel, the usual protocol was for the RPO to commence questioning, followed by the decision maker. Although these were the typical patterns, variations would often arise: many hearings were conducted without an RPO; sometimes decision makers posed questions as they arose (rather than waiting until the end); or decision makers with only a few, specific queries would go first. These departures

98   REFUGEES, ASYLUM SEEKERS AND THE RULE OF LAW

from routine would happen with the consent of the claimant's counsel, and the frequency would depend on the decision maker, the RPO and the counsel involved.

In 2003, the Chair of the IRB issued guidelines instituting what became known as 'reverse-order questioning':

> In a claim for refugee protection, the standard practice will be for the RPO to start questioning the claimant. If there is no RPO participating in the hearing, the member will begin, followed by counsel for the claimant. Beginning the hearing in this way allows the claimant to quickly understand what evidence the member needs from the claimant in order for the claimant to prove his or her case.
>
> The member may vary the order of questioning in exceptional circumstances. For example, a severely disturbed claimant or a very young child might feel too intimidated by an unfamiliar examiner to be able to understand and properly answer questions. In such circumstances, the member could decide that it would be better for counsel for the claimant to start the questioning. A party who believes that exceptional circumstances exist must make an application to change the order of questioning before the hearing. The application has to be made according to the RPD Rules.[66]

In the five years preceding the introduction of these guidelines, the IRB was wrestling with a steadily increasing number of claims per year, and a growing backlog of refugee claims awaiting a hearing. The expectation was that reverse-order questions would expedite hearings 'by dispensing with the often lengthy and unfocused examination-in-chief of claimants by their counsel',[67] a characterization that appears to have been accepted at face value by the Federal Court of Appeal in *Canada (Minister of Citizenship and Immigration)* v. *Thamotharem* (*Thamotharem* (FCA),[68] described below. Unsurprisingly, the guidelines have not been withdrawn or amended, even though the number of refugee claims has dropped precipitously in recent years. The IRB has not disclosed any evidence to establish that reverse-order questioning has actually reduced the length of hearings.

---

[66] Immigration and Refugee Board, *Concerning Preparation and Conduct of a Hearing in the Refugee Protection Division: Guidelines Issued by the Chairperson Pursuant to Section 159(1)(h) of the Immigration and Refugee Protection Act* (Ottawa: Immigration and Refugee Board, 2003), paras. 19–23.

[67] *Canada (Minister of Citizenship and Immigration)* v. *Thamotharem* 2007 FCA 198, 25 May 2007 (*Thamotharem* (FCA)) at para. 21.

[68] 2007 FCA 198, 25 May 2007.

The guidelines converted what had been a discretionary and consensual practice into a presumptive norm. Soon after their implementation, the guidelines were subject to judicial review before the Federal Court of Canada on two grounds: first, that they violated procedural fairness and, second, that they impermissibly fettered the statutory discretion of decision makers to do anything that 'they consider necessary to provide a full and proper hearing'.[69] In *Thamotharem* (FC),[70] the asylum seeker's challenge failed on the first but succeeded on the second argument. On appeal, the Federal Court of Appeal sided with the government on both grounds.[71] For our present purposes, the focus is upon the procedural fairness argument. The Federal Court of Appeal adopted the reasoning of the lower court on this issue and added a few supplementary remarks.

The applicant, Thamotharem, and the intervener, Canadian Council for Refugees, advanced several interrelated arguments against reverse-order questioning. First, the high stakes of refugee determination warrant a correspondingly high degree of procedural protection. Secondly, refugee hearings are quasi-judicial processes, and their resemblance to a judicial hearing justify a similar model of questioning. The implication is that the one who bears the burden of proof is entitled to frame his or her case by commencing with examination in chief.[72] Thirdly, certain specific and distinctive features of refugee claimants and the refugee determination context militate against the fairness of reverse-order questioning. These factors were summarized by the Federal Court of Appeal as:

> The vulnerability and anxiety of many claimants, as a result of: their inability to communicate except through an interpreter; their cultural backgrounds; the importance for them of the RPD's ultimate decision; and the psychological effects of the harrowing events experienced in their country of origin.[73]

The government responded that, unlike judicial proceedings, refugee hearings are modelled by statute as non-adversarial (insofar as no party formally opposes the refugee claim),[74] inquisitorial and relatively informal.

---

[69] IRPA, s. 165.   [70] 2006 FC 16, 6 January 2006.
[71] *Thamotharem* (FCA) 2007 FCA 198, 25 May 2007; *Thamotharem* (FC) 2006 FC 16, 6 January 2006.
[72] *Thamotharem* (FCA) 2007 FCA 198, 25 May 2007 at para. 41.   [73] *Ibid.* at para. 36.
[74] In exceptional cases, where the government alleges that the asylum seeker is excluded from refugee protection under Art. 1F of the Refugee Convention, or where it seeks to

100   REFUGEES, ASYLUM SEEKERS AND THE RULE OF LAW

The Federal Court and the Federal Court of Appeal attached considerable weight to both the formal adversarial nature of the refugee hearing and to the informal, non-adversarial and inquisitorial aspects of the hearing, despite acknowledging the 'often times aggressive and probing nature of the questioning conducted at hearings'.[75] Ironically, the Federal Court of Appeal validated the image of a non-adversarial process depicted in the statute while simultaneously adverting to the practice of counsel-led examination questioning as a 'tactical advantage'.[76] It is difficult to discern over whom one might obtain a tactical advantage if there is no adversary. Moreover, the Court of Appeal allowed that this tactical advantage might be 'particularly significant' in light of the aforementioned vulnerability and anxiety of many claimants. It is not obvious why the Court of Appeal depicted the practice of counsel-led questioning as a tactical advantage, instead of a corrective directed at mitigating the factors that constrict asylum seekers' voices and impede their audibility. After all, according to the Federal Court, 'many, if not most, refugee claimants are vulnerable and as a result have difficulty testifying effectively'.[77]

The reasoning of both the Federal Court and the Court of Appeal vacillated between acknowledging the unique vulnerability of 'many, if not most' asylum seekers and the de facto adversarial quality of many refugee hearings, on the one hand, while insisting, on the other, that vulnerable claimants and hostile RPOs or decision makers are rare exceptions. These contradictions are never resolved; the judges simply choose the latter depiction over the former. The result is that 'overly aggressive and badgering' questioning by decision makers can be addressed by seeking judicial review on grounds of bias. As already mentioned, exceptionally vulnerable claimants may be granted an exemption from reverse-order questioning. The identification and separation of 'exceptionally vulnerable' asylum seekers (for whom reverse-order questioning would be unfair) from the pool of merely 'vulnerable' asylum seekers (for whom reverse-order questioning is unproblematic) is ostensibly discernable in advance of the hearing and demonstrated in counsel's written application submitted beforehand. Presumably, proof of exceptional vulnerability would be revealed by a medical or psychological report. The notion that

---

vacate or cease refugee protection, a Minister's Representative will participate and the hearing becomes formally adversarial.

[75] *Thamotharem* (FC) 2006 FC 16, 6 January 2006 at para. 75.

[76] *Thamothamrem* (FCA) 2007 FCA 198, 25 May 2007 at para. 36.   [77] *Ibid.* at para. 90.

asylum seekers can be assigned to one of two categories of vulnerability for the purpose of deciding the order of questioning displays a certain bureaucratic rationality that articulates nicely with a legal propensity for binary categories, but seems incompatible with the original objective of creating a legal space in which the asylum seeker can be heard as a singular and unique individual.[78]

Beyond the merits of judicial reasoning in *Thamotharem* one might plausibly contend that any violation of procedural fairness does not reside in an inherent unfairness of reverse-order questioning per se, but rather on its unilateral imposition on the asylum seeker. If asylum seekers and their counsel consent to reverse-order questioning, there is no principled reason to oppose it. Consent will most often be forthcoming where counsel (based on past experience) has confidence in the competence, integrity and sensitivity of the decision maker and/or the RPO. (Of course, there may be valid reasons why counsel wishes to proceed first even where such confidence exists.) Where hearings are truly conducted in a non-adversarial and fair manner, reverse-order questioning is less likely to be resisted and may actually prove an expeditious, effective and satisfactory means of being heard. In circumstances where consent would not be granted, the imposition of reverse-order questioning compromises any putative efficiency gains, as counsel must invest time in applying for an exemption, or must spend additional hearing time trying to rescue the asylum seeker and her/his narrative from the damaging impact of the RPO or decision maker's mode of questioning.

The Supreme Court of Canada declined to grant Thamotharem leave to appeal, leaving the judgment of the Federal Court of Appeal as the final word on the practice.

Is anyone listening?

The government proposed legislation in 2000 that has since become the Immigration and Refugee Protection Act (IRPA). The refugee determination process in the IRPA differed from its predecessor in two important and interrelated ways. First, the number of decision makers assigned to adjudicate a given asylum claim was reduced from two to one.[79]

---

[78] Donald Galloway, 'Proof and Narrative: Reproducing the Facts in Refugee Cases' (unpublished manuscript on file with author), pp. 26–8.

[79] IRPA, s. 163.

102   REFUGEES, ASYLUM SEEKERS AND THE RULE OF LAW

Secondly, a new appeal tribunal (the Refugee Appeal Division) was introduced in the legislation.[80] The IRPA provides that either a claimant or the Minister may appeal against a decision of the RPD to the Refugee Appeal Division on a question of law, fact, or mixed law and fact.[81] The Refugee Appeal Division was designed to conduct a paper review and to either confirm the RPD's decision, substitute its opinion for that of the RPD, or return the case to the RPD for rehearing.

The move to a single decision maker would clearly confer cost savings on the government. However, critics worried that without a reformed appointment mechanism, the reduction would deprive asylum seekers of the chance that at least one of the two decision makers would be competent. However, these critics were also assuaged by the introduction of the Refugee Appeal Division. They had long advocated for the introduction of a merit-based appeal from the first-level decision, partly as a corrective to the deficiencies in first-level decisions and partly because of the restricted access to judicial review by the Federal Court. In effect, the move to a single decision maker was viewed as a trade-off for an internal merit-based appeal.

In late 2001, IRPA was passed by the Canadian Parliament, shortly after 9/11. However, not all provisions of the new statute were proclaimed in force at the same time. Staggered implementation of a statute is usually justified by a need to give government departments time to adequately prepare for the implementation of a new system. In the case of IRPA, the reduction to single decision maker hearings was immediate. Although the IRB invested considerable time and effort in devising a model for the Refugee Appeal Division, the government did not proclaim in force the sections of IRPA that created the Refugee Appeal Division. As of 2008, the provisions were not proclaimed in force, although they remain in the text of the IRPA. Successive governments have confirmed that the Refugee Appeal Division is not being implemented.[82] Refugee advocates who accepted single-member panels in exchange for a merit-based appeal came to realize that they had been short-changed.

From a rule of law perspective, the persistent refusal of the executive to proclaim in force entire segments of legislation passed by a democratically elected parliament is worrisome. At the same time, pursuing a public law remedy (such as mandamus) compelling the executive to act seems futile as a practical matter (though perhaps of some symbolic

---

[80] *Ibid.*, ss. 110, 111.   [81] *Ibid.*   [82] Showler, *Refugee Sandwich*, pp. 226–7.

ASYLUM AND THE RULE OF LAW IN CANADA   103

value); the likely outcome would surely be that the government would simply repeal the provisions establishing the Refugee Appeal Division. It thus remains that the only recourse available to a rejected asylum seeker to directly challenge a negative decision is judicial review before the Federal Court. Access to the Federal Court is limited by various logistical factors, including short deadlines and cost, but also by two major legal hurdles. First, judicial review is not an appeal on the merits, does not permit the Federal Court to substitute its opinion for that of the original decision maker, and is confined to the following grounds:

> 18.1(4) The Federal Court may grant relief under subsection (3) if it is satisfied that the federal board, commission or other tribunal
>
> (a) acted without jurisdiction, acted beyond its jurisdiction or refused to exercise its jurisdiction;
> (b) failed to observe a principle of natural justice, procedural fairness or other procedure that it was required by law to observe;
> (c) erred in law in making a decision or an order, whether or not the error appears on the face of the record;
> (d) based its decision or order on an erroneous finding of fact that it made in a perverse or capricious manner or without regard for the material before it;
> (e) acted, or failed to act, by reason of fraud or perjured evidence;
> (f) acted in any other way that was contrary to law.[83]

Secondly, asylum seekers must obtain leave of the Federal Court in order to access judicial review. An application for leave is filed in writing, and decided by a judge in writing and without reasons. A leave decision cannot be appealed.[84]

Most observers believe that the Federal Court seldom grants leave to rejected asylum seekers, and that dramatic variations in grant rates exist between individual judges. According to a 2000 report by the Inter-American Commission on Human Rights, using statistics proffered by the Canadian Government, it was disclosed that about 10 per cent of asylum seekers who seek judicial review are granted leave and 40 per cent of those decisions are set aside by the Federal Court on review.[85] This works

---

[83] Federal Courts Act, RSC, 1985, c. F-7.   [84] IRPA, s. 72(2)(e).

[85] Inter-American Commission on Human Rights, *Report on the Situation of Human Rights of Asylum Seekers within the Canadian Refugee Determination System*, 2000, para. 83, www.cidh.org/countryrep/canada2000en/table-of-contents.htm (accessed 3 March 2008). Interestingly, the 2000 figures show that about 75% (or one-third of all finalized claims) of those who received a negative decision sought review. In 2001 the figure in this category was 63%. In 2001 the set-aside rate on review was much lower – only 12% were set aside.

104   REFUGEES, ASYLUM SEEKERS AND THE RULE OF LAW

out at a success rate of 4 per cent for the original pool who applied for judicial review. Based on statistics published on the Federal Court website, a rough estimate of the leave rate for 2006 would be 14 per cent.[86]

Despite the low rates for granting judicial review, the relatively large numbers of asylum claims finalized each year (over 35,000 in 2004–5),[87] in tandem with a declining acceptance rate before the IRB, meant that around 55 per cent of the Federal Court's workload in 2006 consisted of disposing of applications for judicial review and judicial reviews of rejected refugee claims. About 23 per cent of actual hearings concerned judicial review of rejected asylum claims.[88]

Viewed against this statistical landscape, the most plausible motive for requiring leave to seek judicial review is 'docket control' (controlled access). Without an infusion of additional resources, the Federal Court would simply be overwhelmed if it could not restrict institutional access to it by failed asylum seekers. In other words, the very concerns of administrative efficiency and cost that Justice Wilson disparaged as putative justifications for a denial of fundamental justice in the form of an oral hearing before an administrative tribunal appear to exert considerable force when applied to judicial review. In fairness, the courts have departed considerably from *Singh*'s scepticism of utilitarian considerations, and routinely regard with sympathy even speculative and unsupported cost–benefit analyses advanced by governments in defense of rights-constraining practices. Indeed, the Federal Court of Appeal's decision in *Thamotharem* (FCA) is a recent example.

One of the foundational tenets of the rule of law is the guarantee of access to an independent and impartial court (Dicey's so-called 'ordinary courts')[89] to challenge the legality of a decision affecting fundamental rights: the individual's complaint that the executive exceeded the bounds of its legal mandate deserves to be heard. The use of a leave requirement to constrict that access, however compelling the administrative exigencies animating it, directly and incontrovertibly

---

[86] Federal Court, 'Activity Summary: January 1 to December 31 2006', 2006, http://cas-ncr-nter03.cas-satj.gc.ca/portal/page/portal/fc_cf_en/Statistics_dec06 (accessed 3 March 2008).

[87] Immigration and Refugee Board, *Performance Report 2004–5*, p. 22, www.tbs-sct.gc.ca/rma/dpr1/04–05/IRB-CISR/IRB-CISRd45_e.pdf (accessed 3 March 2008).

[88] Calculation based on data referred to in note 87 above. In addition to immigration matters, the jurisdiction of the Federal Court includes admiralty, aboriginal law, other aspects of Crown litigation, citizenship and intellectual property.

[89] Albert Venn Dicey, *Introduction to the Study of The Law of the Constitution*, 10th edn. (London: Macmillan, 1959). See the discussion in Chapter 1 in this volume.

ASYLUM AND THE RULE OF LAW IN CANADA 105

breaches that fundamental principle. The Federal Court refuses to listen to some 85–90 per cent of asylum seekers who seek its attention, and provides no explanation or recourse.[90] Seen in this light, the virtues of a Refugee Appeal Division appear even more obvious, and the disrespect for the rule of law evinced by the refusal to proclaim it in force even more glaring. A Refugee Appeal Division would not be as independent as a court, although it seems plausible to suggest that a genuine appeal on the merits could mitigate the sting of the leave requirement. Thus, at least *someone*, hopefully with specialized expertise and competence, would undertake to review the initial decision.

The leave requirement has never been justified on a principled basis. More specifically, it would be untenable to contend that the rule of law does not apply to asylum seekers, or that anything about the current system provides a satisfactory alternative to, or substitute for, judicial review for those who do not obtain leave. That said, there does not appear to have been any attempt to challenge the judicial leave requirement as a contravention of the rule of law.

Part four: keeping the asylum seeker out of earshot

The general trend of Supreme Court of Canada jurisprudence over the past twenty years has been towards an increasing regard for the rights and interests of asylum seekers and migrants. There have been, of course, notable setbacks as well. Nevertheless, the Court has proved willing to use both the Charter and 'unwritten constitutional principles'[91] embedded in the rule of law to establish that asylum seekers are protected under the Charter, that international law is relevant to the interpretation of Canadian statutes and constitution, and that the refugee definition should be interpreted in a relatively liberal fashion.

With the expansion of asylum seekers' legal entitlements at and inside the Canadian border, came the logical (if pernicious) reaction of the state. As the audibility of asylum seekers in Canadian law was amplified within Canadian territory, the government redoubled its efforts to keep asylum seekers out of legal earshot. The basic strategy is to make it impossible for prospective asylum seekers to travel lawfully to Canada. Familiar non-entrée mechanisms include requiring visas from citizens of 'refugee-producing' countries and then denying visas to anyone deemed likely to make a refugee claim; imposing liability on air and marine

---

[90] Federal Court, 'Activity Summary'.   [91] *Provincial Judges Reference* [1997] 3 SCR 3.

106 REFUGEES, ASYLUM SEEKERS AND THE RULE OF LAW

carriers who transport undocumented or improperly documented migrants; and deputizing private transportation companies as delegates of Citizenship and Immigration Canada. Canada also posts visa officers at foreign airports to check passenger documentation on planes bound for Canada. Most recently, Canada charged a US humanitarian worker with smuggling (an offence under IRPA that carries a maximum life sentence) for transporting twelve Haitian asylum seekers to the USA–Canada border.[92] Far from engaging in a clandestine commercial smuggling operation, the woman was an NGO volunteer who had notified Canadian Border Services Agency of her arrival in order to facilitate processing of the asylum seekers. Although the charges were dropped after public outcry in Canada, the government pointedly refused to clarify the scope of the smuggling law, and appears intent on retaining the threat of smuggling charges as an intimidation tactic to deter those who, for humanitarian reasons, assist asylum seekers in reaching Canada.

One assumption driving non-entrée policies is that Canadian legal protection does not stretch beyond Canada's territorial border to reach asylum seekers. Thus, exercises of state power outside Canadian territory – whether at visa offices abroad or at Heathrow Airport – are de jure or de facto immune from judicial review. The legality of deflecting asylum seekers stranded on the high seas was challenged and found not to breach the Refugee Convention by the US Supreme Court in *Sale* v. *Haitian Centers Council, Inc.*[93] It exposed a gaping escape hatch for states wishing to evade their obligations under the Refugee Convention: the state's obligations begin at the frontier, but there is nothing in law to stop the state from preventing the asylum seeker from reaching the frontier. In other words, the rule of law is regarded as a national enterprise that does not extend beyond territorial borders, rather than as a global or transnational project that might limit the capacity of individual states to frustrate the ability of individuals to access the protection that those very states had undertaken to provide.

The efforts of states to evade legal accountability for deflecting asylum seekers has been largely successful. As long as asylum seekers remains outside the border (or the territorial waters) of the state, the legal system

---

[92] Sidhartha Banerjee, 'Grandmother Charged with Human Smuggling', *The Daily Gleaner*, 9 October 2007, p. A8; The Refugee Lawyers Association of Ontario, 'Drop Charges Against Humanitarian Worker, Demand Refugee Lawyers', Press Release, Toronto, 28 September 2007.

[93] 509 US 155 (1993).

ASYLUM AND THE RULE OF LAW IN CANADA 107

remains deaf to their entreaties. Given this background, the as yet unfinished narrative of the Canada-US Safe Third Country Agreement emerges as a remarkable exception.

Modelled on the Dublin Convention (now the Dublin II Regulation)[94], the Canada-US Safe Third Country Agreement requires the first country of arrival to determine the asylum claim in accordance with the relevant domestic legislation. Canada-bound asylum seekers who arrive at the Canadian border via the USA are deflected back to the USA, and vice versa. The agreement contains a few exceptions, most notably for unaccompanied children and those with relatives in the destination country.[95]

Governments cite various related rationales in support of safe third country agreements. First, these agreements are intended to prevent 'asylum-shopping', whereby asylum seekers attempt to exercise a measure of choice over the destination state. Secondly, they purport to encourage equitable sharing of the responsibility or burden of receiving refugees among states, rather than allowing a situation where a disproportionate number of asylum seekers lodge claims in states with relatively more generous benefits and acceptance rates. Thirdly, governments sometimes claim that such agreements enhance states' ability to manage asylum processing in an 'orderly' fashion. A subtext lurking close to the surface is a belief that many or most asylum claims are fraudulent, and that genuine refugees would gratefully and immediately seek protection in the first country they reached. The analogy is sometimes made to a drowning man grabbing the first lifeboat that comes along.

The history of the Canada-US Safe Third Country Agreement reveals that Canada had been lobbying the USA for an agreement of this type since the mid-1990s. The reason was simple: around 30–40 per cent of asylum seekers in Canada entered via a land border with the USA.[96] In 2004, the year before the Canada-US Safe Third Country Agreement entered into force, about 13,000 asylum seekers entered Canada from the USA.[97] During the same period, around 200 asylum seekers entered the USA from Canada.[98]

---

[94] *Council Regulation (EC) No 343/2003 Establishing the Criteria and Mechanisms for Determining the Member State Responsible for Examining an Asylum Application Lodged in one of the Member States by a Third-Country National* (Dublin II Regulation), Brussels, 18 February 2003, in force 1 September 2003.

[95] IRP Regulations, s. 159.5.

[96] François Crépeau and Estibalitz Jimenez, 'Foreigners and the Right to Justice After 9/11' (2004) 27 *International Journal of Law and Psychiatry* 609 at 613.

[97] *Ibid.*   [98] *Ibid.*

108   REFUGEES, ASYLUM SEEKERS AND THE RULE OF LAW

Consistent with other non-entrée mechanisms, a safe third country agreement with the USA would advance Canada's policy of reducing the number of people claiming asylum in Canada. Of course, the obverse of this proposition is that it would increase the number of people claiming asylum in the USA. This explains why Canada failed in its bid to secure an agreement with the USA in the late 1990s.

After 9/11, the political landscape changed and policing the border became a central policy focus for the USA. The USA and Canada entered into a thirty-point Smart Border Action Plan[99] that involved coordinating, harmonizing and collaborating on various policies and practices governing the movement of goods and people across the Canada–USA border. As with many aspects of US–Canadian relations, the USA held a distinct advantage in securing terms that advanced its interests, given that the size of its population and economy dwarf those of Canada. Nevertheless, negotiations surrounding the Action Plan opened up an opportunity for Canada to revive the safe third country agreement, and Canada succeeded in including it in a package that was ostensibly motivated by security objectives.

Of course, linking a refugee deflection scheme to security concerns raises an obvious question for Americans: if asylum seekers and refugees are 'risky', how could an agreement that would result in a net increase of asylum seekers in the USA advance US security interests? This paradox was exposed in the following exchange between George Gekas, Chair of the House Subcommittee on Immigration, Border Security and Claims, and Kelly Ryan of the US Department of State, about the benefits of the Agreement from the perspective of the USA:

> Mr GEKAS: The staff has prepared one excellent question, I think. Explain how this safe third country agreement would prevent terrorists from coming to the USA from Canada? We will take an hour for your explanation. What is the theory?
>
> Ms RYAN: We don't, and we have never tied this particular agreement to the counterterrorism measures included in the 30-point action plan. This agreement is designed to make a regular process of asylum seekers.
>
> Mr GEKAS: But, you say not directly. But most of you agree that real action toward this agreement was taken after September the 11th

---

[99] *Smart Border Declaration and Associated 30-Point Action Plan to Enhance the Security of Our Shared Border While Facilitating the Legitimate Flow of People and Goods*, 12 December 2001, Canada-US.

ASYLUM AND THE RULE OF LAW IN CANADA 109

meaning, by implication, that this could be another step taken to prevent unsafe border crossing.

Ms RYAN: Negotiation of this proposal was undertaken after September 11th, and at the request of the Government of Canada as part of the 30-point action plan. We think it should be viewed in that context. But it does not directly affect US security . . . So we view this as an important agreement in the context of the overall 30 points that Canada wants and that we are willing to agree to as a trade-off for the other important counterterrorism measures.[100]

The Canada-US Safe Third Country Agreement was duly signed and proclaimed into law in both countries. It entered into force on 29 December 2004. Measured in terms of Canada's objectives, the agreement has been a success, as the number of refugee claimants entering Canada from the USA has declined both in absolute terms and as a proportion of the total number of asylum seekers in Canada. The following statistics compiled by Citizenship and Immigration Canada in its review of the Agreement's first year of operation tell the story:

Land border claims in 2004 and 2005[101]

Year	Total claims	Claims at land border	Land border claims as percentage of total claims
2004	25,521	8,896	34.8%
2005	19,735	4,033	20.4%

As soon as the Canada-US Safe Third Country Agreement entered into force, the Canadian Council for Refugees, the Canadian Council of Churches, and Amnesty International (the NGOs) began working out strategies to challenge its validity under Canadian law. They located a Colombian asylum seeker in the USA ('John Doe'), who was refused

---

[100] House of Representatives, *United States And Canada Safe Third Country Agreement Hearing Before the Subcommittee on Immigration, Border Security, and Claims of the Committee on the Judiciary*, One Hundred Seventh Congress, Second Session, 16 October 2002, pp. 60–1.

[101] Citizenship and Immigration Canada, 'A Partnership for Protection: Year One Review', November 2006, Table 2, www.cic.gc.ca/english/department/laws-policy/partnership/chapter4.asp (accessed 2 May 2008). Virtually all states of the Global North have witnessed a decline in numbers of asylum seekers since 2001. Restrictive policies by destination states may account for part of the decline, along with shifts in the location and duration of refugee-producing conflicts: UNHCR, *The State of the World's Refugees 2006* (Geneva: UNHCR, 2007), pp. 15–17, www.unhcr.org/publ/PUBL/4444afc50.pdf (accessed 2 May 2008).

110   REFUGEES, ASYLUM SEEKERS AND THE RULE OF LAW

protection in the USA because he failed to apply for asylum within a one-year filing deadline. Had he approached the Canadian border to make a claim for refugee status, he would have been deflected back to the USA and subjected to removal without consideration of his asylum claim. On the first anniversary of the agreement, the NGOs and John Doe filed a judicial review application challenging the legality of the Canada-US Safe Third Country Agreement on two grounds. First, the agreement was ultra vires the legislation purporting to authorize it and, secondly, the agreement violated the Canadian Charter of Rights and Freedoms. Specifically, the applicants alleged that the agreement affected the rights of asylum seekers under s. 7 of the Charter to 'life, liberty, and security of the person, and the right not be deprived thereof, except in accordance with fundamental justice', and their right to equality under s.15 of the Charter.

In late 2007, Justice Phelan of the Federal Court ruled in favour of the applicants.[102] For reasons independent of the legal merits of the challenge, almost everyone was surprised by the decision. The Federal Court has a reputation (rightly or wrongly) for being deferential to government, and the fact that the case put the USA under a human rights microscope did not enhance expectations of a favourable outcome for the applicants.[103]

Before addressing the merits of the application, Phelan considered whether the NGOs were entitled to public interest standing. The issue was particularly salient because a leading case from the Supreme Court of Canada had denied public interest standing to the Canadian Council of Churches in a factually similar context.[104] Phelan recognized that NGOs often serve as the 'voice' of asylum seekers who are physically or psychologically unable to speak before the court. These organizations:

---

[102] *Canadian Council for Refugees, Canadian Council of Churches, Amnesty International and John Doe* v. *The Queen* 2007 FC 1262 (29 November 2007) (*CCR et al.* v. *The Queen*).

[103] Shortly before Phelan J rendered his judgment, the Supreme Court of Canada denied leave to hear the appeal of two US army deserters claiming to be conscientious objectors to the war in Iraq. The men failed at their review hearing, on judicial review to the Federal Court and a subsequent appeal to the Federal Court of Appeal. See *Jeremy Hinzman et al.* v. *Canada (Minister of Citizenship and Immigration)* [2006] FCJ No. 521; *Brandon David Hughey* v. *Canada (Minister of Citizenship and Immigration)* 2006 FC 421, leave to appeal dismissed by Supreme Court of Canada, 15 November 2007.

[104] *Canada Council of Churches* v. *Canada (Minister of Employment and Immigration)* [1992] 1 SCR 236.

ASYLUM AND THE RULE OF LAW IN CANADA   111

[B]ring resources and arguments which assist the Court in identifying and considering the relevant issues. They also act or substitute for the unidentified applicants who are unable, for both physical or psychological reasons, to undertake the daunting task of challenging the government . . . I note that although John Doe came forward as a litigant, he was represented by these organizations and did not seek separate representation. It is noteworthy that John Doe was hiding in the United States, unable to secure a reconsideration of his claim there, and feared exposure by arriving at the Canadian border only to be returned to the United States for deportation to Colombia.[105]

Turning to the merits of the application, resolution of both the common law argument (ultra vires) and the Charter claim (violation of ss. 7 and 15) turned on the determination of the same question of law/fact: do the policies and practices of the US asylum regime comply with Article 33 of the Refugee Convention (*non-refoulement* to persecution) and Article 3 of the CAT (non-removal to substantial risk of torture)?

Under the legislative scheme authorizing the Canada-US Safe Third Country Agreement, refugee claimants are ineligible to have their claim referred to the Refugee Protection Division of the IRB if they arrive from a safe third country.[106] The Governor in Council (Cabinet) is delegated authority to designate a safe third country by regulation (which it did in the present case).[107] The factors to be considered in this designation include the country's 'policies and practices with respect to claims under the Refugee Convention and with respect to obligations under the Convention Against Torture'.[108] In addition, Cabinet 'must ensure the continuing review of [these] factors . . . with respect to each designated country'.[109]

The applicants argued that Cabinet exceeded its statutory authority by designating the USA a safe third country when US policy and practice did not adequately protect asylum seekers from *refoulement* to persecution or to torture. Therefore, the designation of the USA as a safe third country was ultra vires. Moreover, the government had failed to fulfil its statutory duty to review the USA's ongoing compliance with the Refugee Convention and the CAT.

The government urged Phelan to assume a deferential stance towards the exercise of Cabinet's regulation-making power. Phelan resisted: 'I cannot agree with the Respondent's position that so long as [Cabinet]

---

[105] *CCR et al.* v. *The Queen* 2007 FC 1262 (29 November 2007) at paras. 51–2.
[106] IRPA, s. 101(1)(e).   [107] *Ibid.*, s. 102(1)(a)(b)(c); IRP Regulations, s. 159.3.
[108] *Ibid.*, s. 102(2)(b).   [109] *Ibid.*, s. 102(3).

112   REFUGEES, ASYLUM SEEKERS AND THE RULE OF LAW

has acted in good faith and for no improper purpose, the Court has no role to play in assessing whether the Regulation is valid'.[110] He went on to specifically reject the position that compliance with the prohibition against *refoulement* to persecution or torture should be regarded as a more or less unreviewable matter of Cabinet's subjective opinion:

> In my view, the issue is whether the conditions for passing the Regulation have been met on an objective basis. The conditions are framed in terms of legal criteria and address the matter in absolute terms of compliance with international law; *not* in terms of [Cabinet's] opinion or reasonable belief in such compliance. As outlined further, the designating country either does or does not comply with international law, and if it does not, Parliament has not given the [Cabinet] the power to enter into a [Safe Third Country Agreement] or to enact a regulation doing so [emphasis in original].[111]

Through a conventional rule of law lens, one might understand this passage as a classic insistence by the judiciary that the executive is equally subject to the dictates of legality. The court will not capitulate to the executive's attempt to define the limits of its own power by conceding that Cabinet has unfettered authority to determine whether mandatory prerequisites to the exercise of its regulation-making power have been met.

Cast in terms of the audibility of the asylum seeker, the rejection of Cabinet's subjective opinion as determinative of US compliance with international law can be understood as a refusal to allow the executive to silence the asylum seeker through an epistemological claim rooted in political power. In other words, the Court did not accept that the status of the Members of Cabinet, as the most powerful members of the government, endows them with a tacit entitlement to deem the USA to be in compliance, based on the bare assertion of a subjective opinion. In so doing, Phelan retained the capacity to listen to the impact of the US regime on that most powerless of legal subjects, the asylum seeker.

Phelan was not unaware of the highly politicized context of the agreement, and implicitly pre-empted the objection that an unelected judge was venturing beyond its appropriate role into a zone of politics properly reserved for elected officials. Phelan tackled this concern by pointing out that judicial review of a statutory prerequisite by an independent judiciary on an objective standard can also insulate political

---

[110] *CCR et al.* v. *The Queen* 2007 FC 1262 (29 November 2007) at para. 58.
[111] *Ibid.* at para. 60 [emphasis in original].

ASYLUM AND THE RULE OF LAW IN CANADA   113

actors from criticism that they might otherwise encounter from the public and other governments:

> It is reasonable to postulate that this objective analysis by a court avoids the diplomatic and other government-to-government consequences of a finding of non-compliance, but it does not lessen the responsibility imposed on the Court.
>
> While the determination of whether to designate another state, or to revoke the designation upon subsequent reviews, particularly one with whom Canada has a close relationship, may be politically charged, the role of the Court is to assess the regulation and compliance from a legal perspective.[112]

Determining US compliance with its international legal obligations came down to a battle of the experts. The applicants filed expert affidavits from ten legal academics, refugee lawyers, and directors of NGO refugee programmes.[113] The government filed three expert affidavits in response, two from law professors and one from the Director of Policy Development and International Protection from Citizenship and Immigration Canada.[114]

Evidence introduced to demonstrate the [non]compliance of US policy and practice focused on the following aspects of the US asylum regime:

- Comparison with UK and European experience with safe third country agreements and the assessment by one country of compliance by another. The objective of this evidence was to establish existing international norms and to place the USA in a comparative context.[115]
- One-year filing deadline for asylum seekers in the USA, subject to proof of changed or exceptional circumstances; where the asylum claim is barred by the one-year deadline, claimants may receive protection from removal ('withholding') only if they demonstrate that persecution or torture is 'more likely than not'.[116]

---

[112] *Ibid.* at paras. 84–5.

[113] The Applicants' expert affidavits were sworn by: Eleanor Acer (Human Rights First); Professors Susan Akram, Deborah Anker, James Hathaway and Karen Musalo; Victoria Neilson (Immigration Equality); Hadat Nazemi (lawyer – evidence deemed inadmissible); Professors Jaya Ramji-Nogales, Andrew Schoenholtz and Philip Schrag; Morton Sklar (World Organization for Human Rights); Steve Watt (American Civil Liberties Union).

[114] The experts for the government were Professor Kay Hailbronner, Professor David Martin and Bruce Scoffield.

[115] *CCR et al.* v. *The Queen* 2007 FC 1262 (29 November 2007) at paras. 110–137.

[116] *Ibid.* at para. 144. See discussion in Chapter 3 in this volume.

114   REFUGEES, ASYLUM SEEKERS AND THE RULE OF LAW

- Categorical exclusion from protection for criminality and terrorism, with no defence for those who provide 'material support' to terrorists under duress.[117]
- Inconsistent interpretation of 'persecution' in US asylum law and inadequate recognition of gender-based asylum claims.[118]
- Standards for credibility determination.[119]
- Detention and access to counsel.[120]
- Interpretation and application of the CAT.[121]

Phelan applied an intermediate standard of review of 'reasonableness',[122] meaning that he asked whether, based on the evidence in relation to each of these elements, it was reasonable for Cabinet to conclude that the USA complies with Article 33 of the Refugee Convention and Article 3 of CAT. In evaluating the evidence of the various experts, Phelan preferred the evidence of the applicants' experts over that of the government where the testimony conflicted. He recognized that the experts on either side might be said to 'speak for or have constituencies', and therefore may 'lean in a direction more favourably to the constituency'.[123] However, he found the applicants' experts 'more credible, both in terms of their expertise and the sufficiency, directness and logic of their reports and their cross examination thereon', and more 'objective and dispassionate in their analysis and report'.[124] The Court did not actually agree that the USA had failed to comply with its international obligations in respect of each alleged deficiency raised by the applicants. However, Phelan did make several important and critical findings regarding the US asylum regime.

---

[117] *Ibid.* at para. 165.   [118] *Ibid.* at paras. 197–216.
[119] *Ibid.* at paras. 217–227.   [120] *Ibid.* at paras. 228–236.   [121] *Ibid.* at paras. 241–262.
[122] Editor's note: Under Canadian law, an administrative decision can be judicially reviewed on three standards of reasonableness: correctness, reasonableness and patent unreasonableness. The least amount of deference for a decision is applied to the correctness standard and the most deference is applied to the patently unreasonable standard. It is quite difficult to prove patent unreasonableness, as the decision must be obviously unreasonable on the face of the tribunal's reasons, either in relation to a question of law or facts. On the other hand, a decision will be unreasonable if it is slightly more difficult, or not so obvious, to find a defect within it (see Mullan, *Administrative Law*, p. 74). In the case of *Dunsmuir* v. *Her Majesty the Queen in Right of the Province of New Brunswick as represented by Board of Management* 2008 SCC 9, the Supreme Court acknowledged the ambiguities and confusion generated by the different standards, and held that there should only be two standards of review: correctness and reasonableness.
[123] *CCR et al.* v. *The Queen* 2007 FC 1262 (29 November 2007) at para. 108.
[124] *Ibid.* at para. 108.

ASYLUM AND THE RULE OF LAW IN CANADA 115

The comparison with the UK and European practice enabled the Court to draw up preliminary standards by which to assess compliance. It concluded, inter alia, that there is a presumption of compliance by a third country (in this case the USA) which the applicants were obliged to rebut; that the focus of the assessment must be on the functional question of whether the third country protects against *refoulement*, not whether the protection confers refugee status; and that there is a rebuttable presumption that differences in legal interpretation of the refugee definition or of the CAT signify differences in treatment.

With respect to the one-year filing deadline for asylum seekers in the USA, Phelan concluded that 'the weight of the expert evidence is that the higher standard for withholding combined with the one-year bar may put some refugees returned to the USA [under the agreement] in danger of *refoulement*. This creates a real risk.'[125] Phelan found that the rule as applied in the USA is inconsistent with the CAT and the Refugee Convention.

The evidence regarding the exclusion from asylum for terrorism indicated that the provision was extremely broad in its application and harsh in its impact. For instance, the nature of the political turmoil in Colombia put ordinary civilians at risk of being coerced at gunpoint by insurgent and terrorist groups into providing food, shelter or money. Even the government's expert, Professor David Martin, conceded that '[a]s applied in the refugee setting, this is no doubt a severe provision, pressing the outer boundaries of the leeway provided to States by the Convention in applying the security-based exclusions provisions'.[126] After reviewing the expert opinions on this provision, Phelan commented critically on Cabinet's apparent indifference to the impact of the exclusion provisions:

> It is difficult to imagine how [Cabinet] could have reasonably concluded that the US complies with the Refugee Convention when the law allows the exclusion of claimants who *involuntarily* provided material support to terrorist groups. The terrorist exclusions are extremely harsh, and cast a wide net which will catch many who never posed a threat. In returning claimants to the US under these circumstances, the weight of the evidence is that Canada is exposing refugees to a serious risk of *refoulement* and torture which is contrary to the applicable Articles of the Refugee Convention and CAT [emphasis added].[127]

On the other hand, the Court did not find the criminality exclusions similarly problematic.

---

[125] *Ibid.* at para. 154.   [126] *Ibid.* at para. 171.   [127] *Ibid.* at para. 191 [emphasis added].

116   REFUGEES, ASYLUM SEEKERS AND THE RULE OF LAW

Phelan next considered arguments based on ambiguities, inconsistencies and uncertainty in the interpretation of the refugee definition, particularly with respect to the meaning of persecution, the scope of 'particular social group', and gender-based asylum claims. Here, Phelan found that the state of flux around gender claims based on domestic violence, and the inconsistency in the acceptability of 'mixed motives' for persecution, created real risks of *refoulement* of refugees from the USA, in violation of the Refugee Convention.[128]

After reviewing evidence of detention of asylum seekers and access to counsel, Phelan did not view the critiques as sufficient to undermine the reasonableness of Cabinet's designation of the USA as a safe third country, but he did remark that 'these issues in combination with more clear contradictions with Convention provisions call the reasonableness of [Cabinet's] determination into question'.[129]

At various stages of the analysis, Phelan compared US policy and practice to the Canadian regime, with the results typically favouring the latter. However, there is one passage where Phelan arguably provided a more favourable depiction of Canadian law than it merits, and this concerns *refoulement* to torture.

As discussed above, the Supreme Court of Canada in the case of *Suresh* did not unequivocally ban return to torture, though it did caution against reliance on diplomatic assurances and reserved return in 'exceptional circumstances' that it declined to enumerate. Sounding somewhat like an apologist for the Supreme Court of Canada, Phelan explained that:

> Because courts are generally loath to make unequivocal statements beyond that which is necessary to decide a case, the Supreme Court went on to speculate that there might someday in some unforeseen circumstance be an 'exceptional circumstance' justifying departure from this norm. This is hardly an approval of *refoulement* to torture. It is evident that Article 3 of CAT is an absolute bar against removal to torture. That prohibition is also part of Canadian law. Canada will not remove a person who is likely to face death or torture.[130]

Unlike Canada, the USA does formally impose an absolute bar on removal to a reasonable likelihood of torture, although it accepts that diplomatic assurances may be adequate to ensure that torture will not ensue.

Here, Phelan invoked the recent experience of Canadian citizen Maher Arar as evidence that US practice does not comply with its legal

---

[128] *Ibid.* at paras. 205–6, 214–216.   [129] *Ibid.* at para. 238.
[130] *Ibid.* at paras. 257–58 (citations omitted).

ASYLUM AND THE RULE OF LAW IN CANADA 117

obligations. The USA wrongly suspected Mr Arar of terrorist connections (based on false and misleading information supplied by Canadian officials). While Mr Arar was changing planes in New York in 2002, US officials seized him and rendered him to Syria, where he was detained for a year and tortured.[131] While careful to acknowledge that the case before him was not that of Mr Arar, Phelan took judicial notice of the findings of the report of the Commission of Inquiry into the Actions of Canadian Officials in Relation to Maher Arar,[132] and concluded that this 'real life example' of extraordinary rendition to torture is 'more credible than the [government's] evidence' that the United States complies with Article 3 of CAT.[133]

Based on his findings regarding the one-year filing deadline, the terrorism exclusion, the inconsistent interpretation of the refugee definition, actual non-compliance with the CAT, and the aggravating effect of detention without access to counsel, Phelan concluded that Cabinet acted unreasonably in designating the USA as a safe third country. Obviously, Phelan was not ruling that the USA systematically or routinely violates the Refugee Convention and the CAT, but rather that the existing regime (which continues to evolve since 2004) creates reasonable risks of such violations. The USA is not a safe third country. Therefore, the designating regulation was ultra vires.

In addition, Phelan found that Cabinet had failed to comply with its statutory obligation to ensure a continuing review of the USA's compliance with the conditions precedent to its designation as a safe third country. While the legislation does not establish a time frame for review, it emerged that the Minister of Citizenship and Immigration 'has not established a review process nor has it reported to [Cabinet]'[134] in the three years since the agreement went into effect.

Having reached the conclusion that the Canada-US Safe Third Country Agreement was effectively ultra vires on non-constitutional grounds, it was not necessary for Phelan to proceed to a Charter analysis. He did so anyway, although the reasoning is relatively spare.

Given the Supreme Court of Canada's judgment in *Singh*, Phelan had little difficulty in determining that asylum seekers' rights under s. 7

---

[131] Commission of Inquiry into the Actions of Canadian Officials in Relation to Maher Arar, *Report of the Events Relating to Maher Arar* (Ottawa: Public Works and Government Services Canada, 2006), p. 149. Mr Arar's ordeal became the focus of public outcry and led to a public inquiry into the incident.
[132] *Ibid.*   [133] *CCR et al.* v. *The Queen* 2007 FC 1262 (29 November 2007) at para. 262.
[134] *Ibid.* at para. 270.

118   REFUGEES, ASYLUM SEEKERS AND THE RULE OF LAW

of the Charter are put at risk when Canada deflects them to the USA in circumstances where the USA is not compliant with CAT and the Refugee Convention. The issue became whether this deprivation accords with fundamental justice. Rather than consider whether *non-refoulement* is itself a principle of fundamental justice (thereby inviting a reiteration of the ultra vires analysis regarding US non-compliance), Phelan focused on whether the Canadian immigration officer's lack of discretion to allow the entry of an asylum seeker who did not fit one of the agreement's narrow exceptions led to arbitrary results in violation of the principles of fundamental justice.

While Article 6 of the Canada-US Safe Third Country Agreement actually authorizes either Party to exercise its discretion to examine a refugee claim if it determines 'that it is in the public interest to do so', the Canadian government decided only to apply the discretion to categories of asylum seekers, not on a case-by-case basis. After comparing US and UK practice, Phelan turned to the question of whether fundamental justice requires individualized consideration of exceptional factors warranting exemption from the application of the agreement. Drawing on constitutional jurisprudence regarding the automatic detention of persons found not guilty by reason of insanity, Phelan ruled that individualized attention is indeed necessary, particularly because of the risk of non-compliance by the USA with the right of *non-refoulement* to persecution or torture. He said: 'Some discretion in the hands of the front line immigration official would protect refugees who would otherwise be exposed to risk of contravention of Arts. 33 and 3 of the Conventions or who for other individual circumstances should not be returned to the US.'[135] The Court declined to consider whether discretion would assume the same constitutional significance were the USA indeed a safe third country.

Another dimension of arbitrariness to which Phelan alluded is the fact that the agreement applies only to asylum seekers arriving by land. Asylum seekers who travel by air directly from the USA are not subject to the agreement and may lodge their asylum claims in Canada. Not only did this distinction trouble Phelan in terms of arbitrariness, it also raises concern about discrimination under s. 15 of the Charter. Phelan struggled with the framework for an equality analysis developed by the Supreme Court of Canada. He was troubled not only by the differential

---

[135] *Ibid.* at para. 310.

impact of the agreement on those who arrive by land versus by air, but also by the specific disadvantage faced by women and 'people from countries which are likely to produce the type of claim which the US may reject'. John Doe, a Colombian, was one such person. Phelan determined that the designation of the USA as a safe third country discriminates both against those who arrive by land rather than by air and, within the category of those arriving by land, against women and persons whose country of origin renders them vulnerable to rejection.

One of the striking features of the Federal Court's judgment in *CCR et al. v. The Queen* is that the 'heavy lifting' is done by the doctrine of ultra vires, not by the Canadian Charter of Rights and Freedoms. In other words, basic principles of the rule of law proved adequate to the normative task of judicial review. The capacity of the rule of law to rise to the task was enabled by the fact that the IRPA provisions explicitly embedded international human rights norms into the conditions precedent for the exercise of executive authority.[136] However, a crucial contribution of Phelan's methodology was his insistence that Cabinet be held accountable on an objective standard of reasonableness to the designation of the USA as a safe third country. The facts of this case brought into direct confrontation two dimensions of the rule of law: first, the considerable deference extended by courts to the exercise of statutory powers by Cabinet; and, second, the responsibility of the courts to safeguard the human rights of those subject to state action. In response, the Federal Court chose an objective rather than subjective standard of review to the exercise of Cabinet authority. It applied a standard of reasonableness which represents an intermediate level of scrutiny between 'correctness' and 'patent unreasonableness'.[137]

The government has sought and obtained leave to appeal against the decision of the Federal Court to the Federal Court of Appeal. There is little doubt that whatever the outcome of the appeal, the losing side will seek leave to appeal to the Supreme Court of Canada. In the interim, the Federal Court of Appeal has granted the government a stay on the enforcement of the remedy ordered by the Federal Court; namely the suspension of the Canada-US Safe Third Country Agreement.

---

[136] In contrast, *Baker* [1999] 2 SCR 817 involved a statutory grant of discretion that articulated no criteria, and so the Supreme Court of Canada had to reach for the Convention on the Rights of the Child, New York, 20 November 1989, in force 2 September 1990, UN Doc. A/44/49, 44 UN GAOR Supp. (No. 49) at 167 on its own initiative.

[137] See note 122 above.

Part five: conclusions

Is the rule of law a national project, in which asylum seekers have a tenuous and territorially circumscribed claim to a voice? Or is it a non-territorial concept that ascribes to each person subject to state authority an entitlement to be heard fully and fairly? The place of the asylum seeker in Canadian law tests these questions about the rule of law. The more that international and supranational law becomes enmeshed with domestic law, whether via common law interpretive techniques, statute, or an entrenched bill of rights, the greater the potential for generating an idea of the rule of a law in a given state as the local instantiation of a global normativity. At the same time, the apparent need to 'domesticate' norms derived from non-national legal orders speaks to a persistent tethering of the rule of law to a conventional notion of state sovereignty.

If one moves beyond the conventional legal order and attends to interactions beyond state institutions, one can even hear evidence of dialogue between asylum seekers and communities within that state, thus challenging traditional assumptions about the rule of law. Since the early 1980s, a few Canadian churches have offered sanctuary to rejected asylum seekers and others facing deportation. Although reliable statistics are difficult to obtain, the number of sanctuary incidents over the past twenty-five years numbers around fifty.[138] In all but one case, immigration authorities have respected sanctuary and have declined to enter the church in order to apprehend the individual or family who has sought refuge.[139] Usually immigration authorities quietly arrive at a negotiated resolution, which sometimes involves the exercise of humanitarian and compassionate discretion, or an orchestrated departure from Canada with an assurance of permission to re-enter, or a permanent departure from Canada. The length of time that individuals spend in sanctuary before a settlement is reached has grown longer over

---

[138] Randy Lippert, *Sanctuary, Sovereignty and Sacrifice: Canadian Sanctuary, Power and Law* (Vancouver: UBC Press, 2005), pp. 15–17. Lippert identifies 36 sanctuary incidents between 1983 and 2003.

[139] The exception was Algerian Mohamed Cherfi, who was apprehended from a Quebec City church in March 2004. He was deported to the USA, the country of last arrival before Canada. Ironically, Cherfi made a successful asylum claim in the USA. For a thoughtful and provocative analysis of the case, see Peter Nyers, 'Taking Rights, Mediating Wrongs: Disagreements over the Political Agency of Non-Status Refugees', in Jef Huysmans, Andrew Dobson and Raia Prokhovnik (eds.), *The Politics of Protection: Sites of Insecurity and Political Agency* (London: Routledge, 2006), pp. 48–67.

the years, possibly as a governmental tactic to wear down the individual and the church's resolve. Nevertheless, sanctuary has proved remarkably successful as a means of resisting an asylum regime that many criticize as flawed. One of the distinctive features of sanctuary in Canada is that it is not clandestine; churches deliberately expend their moral capital to publicize and preclude what they view as a potential injustice. In recent years, much of the critique has focused on the failure of the government to implement the Refugee Appeal Division.

Opponents of sanctuary sometimes describe the practice as a form of civil disobedience that flouts the rule of law by obstructing the enforcement of lawfully issued deportation orders. Sanctuary providers and their defenders counter that they are upholding the rule of law by protecting refugees from a government that has ignored its own legislative undertaking to provide a necessary appeal on the merits, and from a refugee regime that does not fulfil Canada's domestic and international legal obligation of *non-refoulement*.

Even as the asylum seekers' claim to be heard (in the fullest sense) challenges the limited horizons of a state-based conception of the rule of law, it also catalyses new sites within the state where the rule of law can be contested and claimed outside the institutional confines of the legislature, the executive and the courtroom.

The Federal Court of Appeal in *Canadian Council for Refugees* v. *Canada*, 2008 FCA 229, 27 June 2008 allowed the government's appeal. It rejected Justice Phelan's holding that the legislation made compliance with the principle of *non-refoulement* and the CAT conditions precedent to the lawful designation of a third country as 'safe'. The Canadian Council for Refugees has sought leave to appeal the decision to the Supreme Court of Canada.

3

Refugees, Asylum and the Rule of Law in the USA

STEPHEN H. LEGOMSKY

As other chapters of this book illustrate, forced migration is a worldwide phenomenon. It is played out in source countries, receiving countries, and third countries in all the inhabited regions of the planet. The differing policies of the major receiving countries reflect a mixture of historical, cultural, political, ethnic, linguistic, economic and other variables that are not always easy to identify. Like the other chapters of this book, this chapter on the USA's experience will consider the implications of one jurisdiction's refugee and asylum practices for the principle of the rule of law.

Part one provides core background information on US refugee and asylum law and policy. It summarizes the history of the US refugee protection system, the current legislative framework, the asylum adjudication structure, the basic substantive criteria for refugee or asylum status, and related domestic and international mechanisms for providing humanitarian protection in the USA.

Part two, the heart of the chapter, explores the compatibility of US refugee and asylum practices with the principle of the rule of law. After an introductory explanation of the way in which the term rule of law is being used here, that section will examine five settings in which US refugee and asylum practices raise significant rule of law concerns. They include perceived abuses of the asylum system by applicants, but they also include the array of legal and practical barriers to accessing the asylum system, inadequate scrutiny by particular adjudicators, threats to the adjudicators' decisional independence, and US deviations from its international legal obligations.

Part one: refugee and asylum law and practice in the USA

Reading the description that follows, one will notice immediately that the US Congress has spelled out the legal regime governing refugees and asylum in extraordinary detail, in contrast to the parliamentary democracies that are the subject of the other chapters of this book. Parliaments have generally preferred to legislate in broader terms and to delegate far more discretion to their respective governments to work out the details of their refugee and asylum policies.

In the analogous context of immigration regulation it seems that this is no accident. The difference in degree of legislative detail stems from fundamental differences in the way that the US presidential system and the Westminster systems approach separation of powers.[1] Unlike the USA, where the President and the Congress are independently elected, the Westminster system is one in which the composition of Parliament ultimately determines who the Prime Minister and the other members of the Cabinet will be. That reality, combined with the much tighter party discipline typical of the parliamentary democracies, substantially increases the likelihood – though admittedly does not guarantee – that the Parliament and the Cabinet will agree on policy direction and implementation. Under those circumstances, it is not surprising that parliaments would be much more willing than the US Congress to delegate vast discretionary authority to the government rather than assert more policy-making authority itself. Moreover, it might be that the collective accountability of the Cabinet in the Westminster model, compared with the more heavily hierarchical presidential model in the USA, leaves parliaments with more confidence in delegating a broader discretion to the government.[2]

The historical and constitutional basis for refugee protection

In the USA, the refugee protection system has been incorporated into the general scheme for regulating immigration, in various ways that are explored in this chapter. For that reason, the constitutional basis for refugee protection is the same as that of immigration control. In the US federal system, the Supreme Court has long made clear that the Constitution assigns the regulation of immigration exclusively to the national government.[3] The reasons for federal exclusivity stem both from the need for uniformity in admission criteria and from the foreign

---

[1] Stephen H. Legomsky, *Immigration and the Judiciary: Law and Politics in Britain and America* (Oxford University Press, 1987), pp. 259–260.

[2] *Ibid.*

[3] See the landmark cases of *Henderson* v. *Mayor of City of New York*, 92 US (2 Otto) 259 (1875) and *Chy Lung* v. *Freeman*, 92 US (2 Otto) 275 (1876).

124   REFUGEES, ASYLUM SEEKERS AND THE RULE OF LAW

relations problems that would arise if each of the individual states were able to formulate its own immigration policies unilaterally.

Although the USA has been a safe haven for political and religious dissidents since the colonial era, the story of modern American refugee policy did not begin until the lead-up to World War II. Despite the warning signs that were starting to appear in Germany, President Herbert Hoover in 1932 declared: 'With the growth of democracy in foreign countries, political persecution has largely ceased. There is no longer a necessity for the USA to provide an asylum for those persecuted because of conscience.'[4] And even as evidence of the persecution of German Jews began to mount and refugees began to request protection from the USA, American public opinion staunchly opposed their admission: as late as April 1939, some 83 per cent of the American people were opposed to admitting Jewish refugees.[5] Among the reasons for the resistance were the Depression and the accompanying fear of competition for jobs, a fear that the refugees would hold subversive political views, and anti-Semitism. Eventually a few thousand refugees were admitted before the USA's entry into the war, and many more were admitted during and immediately after the war.[6] As was the case elsewhere, more general displaced person legislation was enacted in 1948.[7]

The USA has never ratified the 1951 Refugee Convention.[8] That omission is of little consequence today, however, because in 1968 the USA ratified the 1967 Refugee Protocol,[9] thus binding itself derivatively to the Refugee Convention. At any rate, even before 1968, the USA was admitting thousands of refugees from communist countries. The legal mechanisms employed for that purpose included a series of ad hoc statutes and the government's creative use of a statutory device oddly named 'parole',[10] which then permitted the Attorney General to

---

[4] (1932) 9 *Interpreter Releases* at 261.

[5] Robert A. Divine, *American Immigration Policy, 1924–1952* (New Haven, CT: Yale University Press, 1957), pp. 96–99. See also Bill Ong Hing, 'No Place for Angels: In Reaction to Kevin Johnson' (2000) *University of Illinois Law Review* 559 at 590–591.

[6] See Divine, *American Immigration Policy*, pp. 102–104.

[7] Act of 25 June 1948, ch. 647, 62 Stat. 1009.

[8] Convention relating to the Status of Refugees, Geneva, 28 July 1951, in force 22 April 1954, 1989 UNTS 137.

[9] Protocol relating to the Status of Refugees, New York, 31 January 1967, in force 4 October 1967, 19 UNTS 6223, 6257.

[10] The term 'parole' is more familiarly used to denote one's early release from criminal incarceration, but in 8 USC s. 1182(d)(5)(A) Congress used the term more broadly to

REFUGEES, ASYLUM AND THE RULE OF LAW IN THE USA 125

allow a person to enter US territory temporarily for humanitarian reasons.[11] There was also a 1965 statute under which up to 6 per cent of the general immigrant visas could be allocated to those who were fleeing persecution in either a 'communist-dominated' country or a country in the Middle East.[12]

As the practical limitations of these legal mechanisms became evident, pressure mounted for a more comprehensive US refugee policy. The Refugee Act of 1980, passed mainly to incorporate US obligations under the 1967 Protocol into US domestic law, provided such a scheme.[13] That Act amended the Immigration and Nationality Act[14] in several important ways. It laid out the first US statutory definition of 'refugee', generally tracking the definition contained in the Refugee Convention as expanded by the 1967 Protocol.[15] It created a programme for the permanent resettlement of refugees from overseas. It added a specific provision for granting asylum to refugees who arrived at US shores on their own. It added a *non-refoulement* provision, as required by the Convention and Protocol. And it declared that, with limited exceptions, these provisions were to be the exclusive means of admitting refugees to the USA.[16] These practices remain in place today and are discussed below.

Even after enactment of the generic provisions of the Refugee Act of 1980, and continuing until a few years after the end of the Cold War, US refugee policy was famously preoccupied with communism. Refugees from communist countries were liberally admitted, while refugees from other totalitarian regimes enjoyed only rare success.[17]

---

describe the government's grant of permission to a non-citizen to enter US territory for special compassionate reasons.

[11] Charlotte Moore, *Review of US Refugee Resettlement Programs and Policies* (Washington DC: US Government Printing Office, 1980), pp. 7–11. See also James L. Carlin, 'Significant Refugee Crises Since World War II and the Response of the International Community' (1982) *Michigan Yearbook of International Legal Studies* 3 at 7–9.

[12] Pub. L. 89–236, s. 3, 79 Stat. 911 at 913 (3 October 1965).

[13] Pub. L. 96–212, 94 Stat. 102 (17 March 1980).   [14] 8 USC ss. 1101 et seq.

[15] See *The substantive criteria for refugee status* section below.

[16] 8 USC ss. 1101(a)(42), 1157, 1158, 1182(d)(5)(B), 1251(b)(3).

[17] See Gil Loescher and John A. Scanlan, *Calculated Kindness: Refugees and America's Half-Open Door 1945–Present* (New York: Free Press, 1986); Elizabeth Hull, *Without Justice For All: The Constitutional Rights of Aliens* (Westport, CT: Greenwood Press, 1985).

126   REFUGEES, ASYLUM SEEKERS AND THE RULE OF LAW

The legislative framework

The USA operates by far the largest offshore permanent resettlement programme for refugees in the world.[18] Established by the Refugee Act of 1980, the details of this overseas refugee admission programme appear in the Immigration and Nationality Act.[19] Before the start of each fiscal year, the President, after consulting with Congress, makes an annual determination of the maximum number of overseas refugees who will be admitted in the coming year, and sets sub-ceilings for particular regions or countries. The Secretary of Homeland Security then decides how many refugees to admit, within the Presidential limits. Those who are found to meet the refugee definition (the same definition that governs asylum, as discussed later) and who are not 'firmly resettled' elsewhere are then admitted on the basis of published priorities that change from time to time. Common factors include the urgency of the person's plight, the location of close family members, and various foreign policy factors.[20] The numbers dropped dramatically after 11 September 2001 (9/11) but since then have crept back slowly.[21] They now average approximately 50,000 annual admissions under this offshore refugee resettlement programme.[22]

Admission of a refugee ordinarily permits the refugee's spouse and minor unmarried children to enter as well.[23] Refugee status can be terminated if the Secretary of Homeland Security later finds that the

---

[18] For current statistics on the size of the US offshore permanent resettlement programme, see Bureau of Population, Refugees, and Migration, 'US Refugee Program News', Volume 4, Issue 1, *US Department of State*, 24 April 2006, www.state.gov/g/prm/rls/65215. htm (accessed 16 March 2008). Many other countries offer temporary asylum to greater numbers of refugees, at least on a per capita basis and in some instances even in absolute terms. See US Committee for Refugees and Immigrants, 'Statistics', *World Refugee Survey 2007*, www.refugees.org/article.aspx?id=1941&subm=179&area=Investigate (accessed 16 March 2008), Table 12.

[19] 8 USC s. 1157.

[20] For a more detailed description of the process, see US Department of State, US Department of Homeland Security and US Department of Health and Human Services, *Proposed Refugee Admissions for Fiscal Year 2008, Report to the Congress* (Washington DC: Government Printing Office, 2007).

[21] Swetha Sridharan, 'Material Support to Terrorism: Consequences for Refugees and Asylum Seekers in the United States', *Migration Fundamentals*, January 2008, www. migrationinformation.org/Feature/display.cfm?id=671 (accessed 16 March 2008).

[22] US Department of State, US Department of Homeland Security and US Department of Health and Human Services, *Proposed Refugee Admissions for Fiscal Year 2008*.

[23] 8 USC s. 1157(c)(2).

REFUGEES, ASYLUM AND THE RULE OF LAW IN THE USA 127

person did not meet the refugee requirements at the time of the original admission.[24] A refugee whose status has not been terminated, however, may adjust to permanent resident status one year after admission.[25]

Other provisions of US law allow those who arrive spontaneously to apply for asylum or *non-refoulement* or both. Unlike in Australia,[26] the admission of offshore refugees has no effect on the number admitted in the asylum programme, and vice versa. In the USA, asylum is available to those who meet the refugee definition, do not fall within any of the various criminal and national security exclusions,[27] and receive the favourable exercise of administrative discretion.[28] Once granted, asylum permits the person to remain in the USA as an asylee and, one year later, to adjust to permanent resident status.[29] Similar treatment is provided for the asylee's spouse and minor unmarried children.[30] As is roughly the case under Article 1C(5) of the Refugee Convention, however, asylee status can be terminated if the Secretary of Homeland Security concludes that the person no longer meets the refugee requirements, either because of changed personal circumstances or because of changed country conditions.[31]

Finally, to implement US *non-refoulement* obligations under the Refugee Convention, Congress has created a remedy called 'withholding of removal' for certain refugees who fail to receive asylum for any of various reasons discussed below. This statutory remedy avoids return to the country of persecution but does not result in permanent admission to the USA; forced return to a third country remains possible. In addition, there is no provision for the family members of those refugees who receive the withholding remedy but not asylum.[32]

As elaborated below, these provisions represent almost the entirety of Congress's effort to implement US obligations under the Refugee Convention. Other provisions of the Convention for the most part have not yet been implemented. Since the government has steadfastly maintained that the Convention is not self-executing, there is no domestic enforcement mechanism in the USA for the non-implemented

---

[24] 8 USC s. 1157(c)(4).   [25] 8 USC s. 1159(a).

[26] See Susan Kneebone, 'The Australian Story: Asylum Seekers Outside the Law', Chapter 4 in this volume.

[27] E.g. asylum seekers must not have provided 'material support to terrorism': 8 USC ss. 1158(b)(2)(A)(v), 1182(a)(3)(B)(iv)(VI). See Sridharan, 'Material Support to Terrorism'.

[28] 8 USC s. 1158.   [29] 8 USC s. 1159(b).   [30] 8 USC s. 1158(b)(3).

[31] 8 USC s. 1158(c)(2).   [32] 8 USC s. 1231(b)(3).

provisions. The resulting problems are taken up in the section entitled 'The rule of international law' later in the chapter.[33]

The administrative and adjudicative structures

The institutions and procedures for deciding applications for onshore refugee protection vary depending on the setting, though for the most part they are the same for asylum as for withholding of removal (*non-refoulement*). Indeed, an application for asylum is automatically treated as encompassing an alternative application for withholding in the event that asylum is denied.[34] One important qualification is that an asylum application, unlike an application for withholding, must be filed within one year after the person's arrival in the USA.[35] The process is largely spelled out in various administrative agency regulations rather than in the statute.

If a person has been placed in removal proceedings, either upon arrival at a port of entry or in the interior, he or she may apply for asylum or withholding of removal, or both, in those proceedings. The application is decided by an immigration judge, who performs a quasi-judicial function.[36] The immigration judges are part of the Executive Office for Immigration Review, which is in the Department of Justice.[37] In the case of asylum, the person must demonstrate that he or she is a refugee and that none of the exclusions apply.[38] If the person proves both elements, then the immigration judge has discretion about whether to grant asylum.[39] In the case of withholding, there is no discretion to exercise; if the person is eligible, protection must be granted.[40] In the case of arrivals at the border, there is a special 'expedited removal' procedure for individuals who either lack valid entry documents (most arriving asylum seekers) or are suspected of fraud. Under that procedure, the substantive standards for both remedies are the same, but an asylum officer at the border first screens the person to determine whether he or she has at least

---

[33] Some related remedies, including temporary protected status and relief under the Convention Against Torture (CAT), are summarized in the *Other avenues of humanitarian relief* section below.

[34] 8 CFR s. 208.3(b) (2006).

[35] 8 USC s. 1158(a)(2)(B) (subject to exceptions). See generally the *Impediments to access* section below, at p. 144.

[36] 8 CFR s. 208.4(b)(3) (2006).   [37] 8 CFR s. 1003.10 (2006).

[38] See *The rule of international law* (the exclusion clauses) section below.

[39] 8 USC s. 1158(b)(1)(A).   [40] 8 USC s. 1231(b)(3).

a 'credible fear of persecution'.[41] If so, the person then enters the regular asylum process described above; if not, the person may request a cursory review by an immigration judge.

A person who is not in removal proceedings (regular or expedited) may file an asylum application with US Citizenship and Immigration Services (USCIS), which is in the Department of Homeland Security (DHS).[42] (Until 2002, the asylum applications were filed with the now defunct Immigration and Naturalization Service, which was within the Department of Justice.) The substantive standards are the same as in cases before the immigration judges. The person is interviewed by a specially trained 'asylum officer', who either grants asylum or refers the case to an immigration judge for removal proceedings. In the latter case, the person may renew the asylum application de novo before the immigration judge in the same manner as described above.

Because it is part of the decision whether to order removal, the decision of the immigration judge either granting or denying asylum or withholding is appealable as of right to the Board of Immigration Appeals (BIA), by either the applicant or the government.[43] (The vast majority of the appeals are brought by the applicants.) The BIA, like the immigration judges, is located in the Department of Justice.[44] Its members perform only adjudicative functions. They review de novo on matters of law and discretion. On questions of fact, they may reverse only if the findings are 'clearly erroneous'.[45] As a result of controversial 'streamlining', inaugurated in 2002, many BIA decisions are by single members, and many of those are 'affirmances without opinion' (AWOs). These simply contain one-paragraph boilerplate explanations confirming that the decision of the immigration judge is found to be correct. A significant minority of BIA decisions are still rendered by three-member panels,[46] and occasionally the full Board decides cases *en banc*. There has been a lively recent debate over the quality of the BIA decisions and over the independence of its members from the Attorney General, as discussed in Part two. Responding to criticisms from courts, government officials and scholars, the Attorney General recently ordered a study of the quality of the immigration judge and BIA decisions and the professionalism of their conduct. As a result of that study,

---

[41] 8 USC s. 1225(b)(1)(B)(v). [42] 8 CFR s. 208.4(b)(2) (2006).
[43] 8 CFR s. 1003.1(b)(1–3) (2006). [44] 8 CFR s. 1003.1(a)(1) (2006).
[45] 8 CFR s. 1003.1(d)(3) (2006). [46] 8 CFR s. 1003.1(e)(4–6) (2006).

130   REFUGEES, ASYLUM SEEKERS AND THE RULE OF LAW

several reforms are being instituted, including regular performance reviews of immigration judges and BIA members.[47]

In deciding appeals, the BIA may designate selected decisions as precedents that will bind the immigration judges and the DHS.[48] Moreover, courts defer to 'reasonable' or 'permissible' BIA interpretations of the statute.[49] In these ways, the BIA influences the development of immigration law generally, and asylum law in particular.

Judicial review of asylum denials is normally available. The general rule is that a BIA decision ordering removal (the usual consequence of the BIA denying asylum and withholding) is reviewable, as of right, in the US Court of Appeals that serves the territory in which the hearing before the immigration judge took place.[50] By way of exception, a decision denying asylum on the ground that the application was filed more than one year after arrival is generally not reviewable.[51] Importantly too, expedited removal orders – even those involving asylum denials – are not subject to judicial review.[52]

One difficult issue has been suspensory effect. Under current law, a stay of removal pending judicial review is no longer automatic; the applicant must request it.[53] In deciding whether to stay removal during the many months that judicial review can take, courts usually peruse the record cursorily to assess the likelihood of eventual success.

Since the 2002 BIA reforms noted above, there has been a spectacular increase in petitions for judicial review of removal orders generally, and asylum denials in particular. The vast bulk have been concentrated in two circuits – the Second (covering New York and most of New England) and the Ninth (covering most of the western USA). In those courts the dramatic influx of cases has caused havoc and long delays.[54] Because most other removal orders have been effectively insulated from

---

[47] See generally (2006) 83 *Interpreter Releases* 1725–1728.
[48] 8 CFR s. 1003.1(g) (2006).
[49] *Chevron USA, Inc. v. Natural Resources Defense Council*, 467 US 837 (1984).
[50] 8 USC s. 1252(b)(2).   [51] 8 USC s. 1158(a)(3).   [52] 8 USC s. 1252(a)(2)(A).
[53] 8 USC s. 1252(b)(3)(B).
[54] For the statistics and some thoughtful analysis of the reasons for the influx (and in particular the link to the BIA reforms), see John R.B. Palmer, 'The Nature and Causes of the Immigration Surge in the Federal Courts of Appeals: A Preliminary Analysis' (2006–7) 51 *New York Law School Law Review* 13; John R.B. Palmer, Stephen W. Yale-Loehr and Elizabeth Cronin, 'Why Are So Many People Challenging Board of Immigration Appeals Decisions in Federal Court? An Empirical Analysis of the Recent Surge in Petitions for Review' (2005) 20 *Georgetown Immigration Law Journal* 1.

REFUGEES, ASYLUM AND THE RULE OF LAW IN THE USA 131

judicial review, the surge in petitions for review of removal orders comprises mostly asylum denials.

In recent years a new controversy has erupted over the dramatically different rates at which the various adjudicators grant asylum applications. A sophisticated empirical study published in 2007 showed that, even for asylum applicants from the same country, the probability of success hinges heavily on which asylum officer, which immigration judge, or which court of appeals decides the case.[55]

Importantly, the procedures described in this subsection are subject to one critical caveat: increasingly, refugees encounter obstacles in getting access to them. The barriers that Congress and the government have erected, and the implications of those barriers for the principle of the rule of law, are synthesized in the *Impediments to access* section.

The substantive criteria for refugee status

The US Congress has enacted legislation intended to implement two of the critical provisions of the Refugee Convention – the definition of 'refugee' and the prohibition on *refoulement*. In contrast, however, the USA has never incorporated any of the other Refugee Convention provisions into domestic law. Because the USA regards the Convention as not self-executing, that omission is important. The implications are more fully described in *The rule of international law* section.

In words very close to those of the Refugee Convention definition of 'refugee',[56] the US statute defines 'refugee' so as to require 'persecution or a well-founded fear of persecution on account of race, religion, nationality, membership in a particular social group, or political opinion', whether or not the person is outside his or her country of nationality or habitual residence.[57] As will be noted later, this definition goes further than the Convention requires, both by including internally displaced persons (IDPs) and by permitting an individual to attain

---

[55] Ramji-Nogales et al., 'Refugee Roulette: Disparities in Asylum Adjudication' (2007) 60 *Stanford Law Review* 295 (showing disparities among asylum officers, among immigration judges, and among courts of appeals). See also Peter J. Levinson, 'The Façade of Quasi-Judicial Independence in Immigration Appellate Adjudications' (2004) 9 *Bender's Immigration Bulletin* 1154 (exposing differences among BIA members). For a discussion of why consistency matters in adjudication, what forces influence the likely degree of consistency in a given adjudicative context, and what policy responses are advisable, see Stephen H. Legomsky, 'Learning to Live with Unequal Justice: Asylum and the Limits to Consistency' (2007) 60 *Stanford Law Review* 413.
[56] Refugee Convention, Art. 1A(2). [57] 8 USC s. 1101(a)(42)(A,B).

132   REFUGEES, ASYLUM SEEKERS AND THE RULE OF LAW

refugee status solely on the basis of past persecution even without a fear of future persecution.

Both the BIA and the courts have adjudicated a wide variety of substantive refugee eligibility issues, and their precedent decisions remain an important source of US refugee law. Two of the issues are considered separately in the context of US compliance with its international legal obligations – the standard of proof one must meet to establish the requisite probability of persecution, and the scope of the many affirmative exclusion clauses. A few other key substantive issues will be considered in this subsection; these issues have been selected primarily because they have arisen in many other jurisdictions as well.

Of the five persecution grounds recognized by both the US and Refugee Convention definitions, none is more amorphous than the 'social group' ground. Until very recently, the leading test in the USA and around the world has been the formulation laid out by the BIA in *Matter of Acosta (Acosta)*.[58] The Board in that case defined a social group as a group in which membership is 'immutable', a term the Board used broadly to embrace not only characteristics that are literally unchangeable, but also characteristics that the members 'should not be required to change because [they are] fundamental to their individual identities or consciences'. Applying that test, the BIA and the US courts have recognized a broad range of social groups.[59]

In *Matter of RA (RA)*,[60] however, the Board hinted at significant change. The claimant sought asylum based on domestic violence and argued that the relevant social group comprised Guatemalan women involved with men who believe in male domination of women. Holding that the claimed group was not a social group, the Board suggested that immutability, while necessary, is not enough. Also relevant, the Board said, is 'whether anyone in Guatemala perceives this group to exist in any form whatsoever'. Remarkably, the Board added that her claim failed for the additional reason that 'she has not shown that women are expected by society to be abused, or that there are any adverse societal

---

[58] 19 I & N Dec. 211 (BIA 1985).

[59] E.g. *Matter of Toboso-Alfonso*, 20 I & N Dec. 819 (BIA 1990) (homosexuals); *Fatin* v. *INS*, 12 F 3d 1233 (3rd Cir. 1993) (women, though claim failed for other reasons); *Jie Lin* v. *Ashcroft*, 377 F 3d 1014 (9th Cir. 2004) (family members); *Matter of Kasinga*, 21 I & N Dec. 357 (BIA 1996) (women of a particular tribe who objected to female genital mutilation).

[60] 22 I & N Dec. 906 (BIA 1999), vacated by the Attorney General and remanded for reconsideration after finalization of still pending proposed asylum rules.

consequences to women or their husbands if the women are not abused'.[61]

Following up on that theme, the BIA in January 2007 decided *Matter of AME & JGU (AME)*.[62] There the BIA appears to have held that a social group requires not only immutability, but also both social visibility; and 'particularity' – that is, the definition of the group cannot be too subjective or amorphous. The Board proceeded to hold that wealthy Guatemalans could not be a social group, even though the group was assumed to be immutable, because there was no evidence that society would recognize them as a group and because wealth, being a matter of degree, is too amorphous. The specific result aside, the case leaves the *Acosta* immutability test in doubt. Given the application of similar reasoning in *RA*, the *AME* decision also leaves the future of domestic violence asylum claims uncertain.

The US courts, taking a clear cue from Congress, have been highly supportive of asylum claims, principally from China, that allege fear of forced abortion or sterilization for violating the country's one-child policy. In an unusual move, Congress amended the refugee definition in 1996 to add specific language declaring forced abortion or sterilization, or persecution for refusal to undergo abortion or sterilization, to be persecution on account of political opinion.[63] The courts have interpreted this signal broadly, granting asylum in cases of past involuntary abortion or sterilization (that is, without a showing of a future threat),[64] and in cases in which the claimant can establish a threat only to his or her spouse.[65] Success in these cases is not guaranteed, however, as the courts have also recently denied claims on the basis that forced abortions and sterilizations have become less frequent in China and, therefore, that the fear of persecution is not well founded.[66]

Finally, the US courts have generally recognized claims by non-state actors, an issue that has arisen with particular frequency in the contexts of domestic violence (where claimants have encountered other obstacles, as just discussed) and violent threats from guerrilla forces. The Justice Department, in a proposed regulation that still has not been

---

[61] *Ibid.* at 918–919.   [62] 24 I & N Dec. 69 (BIA 2007).   [63] 8 USC s. 1101(a)(42).

[64] *Matter of CYZ*, 21 I & N Dec. 915 (BIA 1997).

[65] *Qu* v. *Gonzales*, 399 F 3d 1195 (9th Cir. 2005); *Matter of YTL*, 23 I & N Dec. 601 (BIA 2003).

[66] E.g. *Yong Hao Chen* v. *INS*, 195 F 3d 198 (4th Cir. 1999).

134   REFUGEES, ASYLUM SEEKERS AND THE RULE OF LAW

finalized as of this writing, says the persecutor must be either the government or 'a person or group that government is unable or unwilling to control'.[67] In theory, that formulation should cover all private actors. It is *only* in cases where the government is either unable or unwilling to control the persecutor that the feared persecution could ever occur; that is, if the government is both willing and able to control the persecutor, then presumably it will do so and no persecution need be feared. But the proposed regulation makes clear that the literal interpretation was not intended. It lists numerous factors that relate to whether the government of the persecution country has made a good faith effort to control the private actor. If the proposed regulation is ultimately finalized, therefore, the precise limits on non-state-actor asylum claims will require guidance from the BIA and the courts.

Other avenues of humanitarian relief

The law of the USA supplies several distinct remedies for non-citizens who are in need of humanitarian protection. Some are rooted in international human rights agreements; others are solely a matter of domestic law. Some are in widespread use; others are invoked only sparingly.

International human rights instruments

The USA is a party to some of the major international human rights agreements (for example, the International Covenant on Civil and Political Rights,[68] the Convention Against Torture (CAT),[69] and the Convention for the Elimination of All Forms of Racial Discrimination)[70] but not to others (for example, the International Covenant on Economic, Social, and Cultural Rights,[71] the Convention for the

---

[67] 65 Fed. Reg. at 76597 (7 December 2000), proposing to amend 8 CFR s. 208.15(a).

[68] International Covenant on Civil and Political Rights, New York, 16 December 1966, in force 23 March 1976, UN Doc. A/6316 (1966), 999 UNTS 171.

[69] Convention Against Torture and Other Cruel Inhuman or Degrading Treatment or Punishment, New York, 10 December 1984, in force 26 June 1987, UN Doc. A/39/51 (1984), 1465 UNTS 85.

[70] International Convention on the Elimination of All Forms of Racial Discrimination, New York, 21 December 1965, in force 4 January 1969, UN Doc. A/6014 (1966), 660 UNTS 195.

[71] International Covenant on Economic, Social and Cultural Rights, New York, 16 December 1966, in force 3 January 1976, UN Doc. A/6316 (1966), 99 UNTS 3.

Elimination of Discrimination Against Women,[72] and the Convention on the Rights of the Child).[73] Even when the USA does ratify a human rights convention, it typically adds substantial reservations, understandings or declarations. In addition, it tends to regard most human rights agreements as non-self-executing and does not always enact legislation implementing all the provisions of those agreements, thus leaving many of the convention obligations unenforceable in US courts. At the regional level, US law recognizes nothing remotely analogous to Article 3 of the European Convention of Human Rights (ECHR),[74] which the European Court of Human Rights has interpreted as prohibiting *refoulement* to countries where there is a 'real risk' of 'torture or ... inhuman or degrading treatment or punishment'.[75]

It is now possible in the USA to claim protection under the CAT. The US Senate ratified the CAT in 1990,[76] albeit with a long list of reservations, understandings and declarations that narrow its reach considerably. Only in the past ten years has the CAT attained significance in the USA, principally because until 1998 Congress had enacted no domestic legislation to implement it.[77] With this legislation and the corresponding administrative regulation now in place,[78] the CAT today is part of every US refugee advocate's strategic arsenal.

The CAT provision on *non-refoulement*, Article 3(1), is the most relevant here. It says: 'No State Party shall expel, return (*refouler*) or extradite a person to another State where there are substantial grounds for believing that he would be in danger of being subjected to torture.' Unlike the analogous *non-refoulement* provision of the Refugee

---

[72] Convention on the Elimination of All Forms of Discrimination against Women, New York, 18 December 1979, in force 3 September 1981, UN Doc. A/34/46, 34 UN GAOR Supp. (No. 46) at 193.

[73] Convention on the Rights of the Child, New York, 20 November 1989, in force 2 September 1990, UN Doc. A/44/49, 44 UN GAOR Supp. (No. 49) at 167.

[74] European Convention for the Protection of Human Rights and Fundamental Freedoms and its protocols, Rome, 4 November 1950, in force 3 September 1953, ETS 5, 213 UNTS 221 (ECHR).

[75] See *Soering* v. *UK* (1989) 11 EHRR 439 (European Court of Human Rights). See also Maria O'Sullivan, 'The Intersection between the International, the Regional and the Domestic: Seeking Asylum in the United Kingdom', Chapter 5.

[76] See 136 Cong. Rec. S17491–92 (27 October 1990).

[77] See Foreign Affairs Reform and Restructuring Act 1998, Pub. L. No. 105–277, 112 Stat. 2681, Div. G, 22 USC s. 2242 (21 October 1998).

[78] 4 Fed. Reg. 8478 (19 February 1999).

136   REFUGEES, ASYLUM SEEKERS AND THE RULE OF LAW

Convention, the CAT prohibition on *refoulement* is not subject to any exceptions for criminality, national security, or the like.[79]

Article 3(1) of CAT thus promises hope for some people who, for various reasons, are unable to procure *non-refoulement* under the Refugee Convention. Some are individuals who cannot satisfy the substantive criteria for asylum because the harm they fear is not persecution or because the persecution is not on account of any of the five protected grounds. Personal grudges, torture to extract information, and perhaps certain gender-related cruelties are among the possibilities. Others who might benefit from the CAT but not the Refugee Convention are, as mentioned above, individuals who fall within the Refugee Convention disqualifications for criminal or national security reasons.

Conversely, there are situations in which a claim under the Refugee Convention will succeed even though a CAT claim will not. Not all persecution rises to the level of torture. Moreover, as noted earlier, in the USA past persecution – even without a threat of future persecution – is a basis for asylum but not CAT relief. Claims based on non-governmental persecution are also cognizable in the USA, but CAT claims require some element of government acquiescence.[80]

The procedures for filing and adjudicating CAT claims are almost exactly the same as the procedures for asylum and withholding of removal claims based on persecution.[81] The most important procedural difference stems from the absence of exclusion clauses in the CAT. Under the US regulations, individuals who are ineligible for persecution-based relief because of crime, national security, or other positive disqualifications, but immune from return by CAT, receive a form of relief called 'deferral of removal' rather than the usual remedy of 'withholding of removal'. Both CAT-based remedies bar the person's return to the country in which there is a danger of torture, but for 'deferral' the regulations make it procedurally simpler to terminate relief when circumstances change.[82]

Domestic remedies

Temporary protected status   The remedies discussed up to this point have all been for the purpose of avoiding individualized danger – either

---

[79] See 64 Fed. Reg. 8478, 8481 (19 February 1999) (view of former INS); *Matter of HMV*, 22 I & N Dec. 256, at 258 (BIA 1998) (dictum).

[80] CAT, Art. 1(1).   [81] 8 CFR ss. 208.16(c), 208.17, 208.18 (2006).

[82] 8 CFR s. 208.17 (2006).

REFUGEES, ASYLUM AND THE RULE OF LAW IN THE USA 137

persecution or torture. The person who simply fears being caught in the crossfire of an armed conflict or who is fleeing natural catastrophe requires some alternative form of protection. Like many other refugee-receiving countries, the USA grants temporary protection in some such circumstances.

In the USA, two principal vehicles historically supplied that relief on an ad hoc basis. Non-citizens who have not yet entered the USA may, at the discretion of the Attorney General, be 'paroled' into the country.[83] Many years ago, various Attorneys General invoked that authority on a blanket basis to admit groups of people fleeing armed conflict in particular countries.[84] In 1996, Congress expressly prohibited that use of the parole provision.[85] As a result, the government today has no clearly available statutory authority to bring into the USA a group of people who face dangers other than persecution or torture.

As for those who have already entered the USA, either unlawfully or as lawful temporary visitors, the statute provided no obvious form of relief until 1990. The government had to be inventive. It devised a remedy known as 'extended voluntary departure' (EVD). EVD was granted on a blanket basis, typically to nationals of a particular war-torn country, though usually limited to those who had already entered the USA by the date of the EVD announcement or some other date. The grant would typically be renewed if the danger had not sufficiently subsided by the initial expiration date.[86]

Ad hoc responses to specific crises had the advantage of flexibility. But they had clear disadvantages as well – the absence of clear eligibility standards, the resultant political biases in the decisions whether to grant them, inadequate procedural safeguards, and the insecure status of the recipients. There was also a nagging separation of powers question about whether the authority to grant EVD should require Congress's approval.

In 1990 Congress therefore established a new programme to grant 'temporary protected status' (TPS) to certain individuals who could not safely return home. The Secretary of Homeland Security, after

---

[83] 8 USC s. 1182 (d)(5).

[84] See US Congressional Research Service, *Review of US Refugee Resettlement Programs and Policies* (Washington DC: Government Printing Office, 1980), pp. 7–11.

[85] See Illegal Immigration Reform and Immigrant Responsibility Act of 1996, Pub. L. 104–208, 110 Stat. 3009, Div. C (30 Sept. 1996), s. 602(a). The limitation now appears in 8 USC s. 1182(d)(5)(B).

[86] For the details, including a list of countries whose nationals have benefited from EVD, see (1987) 64 *Interpreter Releases* 1093.

138   REFUGEES, ASYLUM SEEKERS AND THE RULE OF LAW

consulting with 'appropriate' government agencies, may designate a
foreign state or part of a foreign state under any of three circumstances:

1. There is an ongoing armed conflict that would pose a serious threat
   to the personal safety of the state's nationals if they were returned
   there.
2. An environmental disaster has substantially but temporarily dis-
   rupted living conditions, and the state has requested designation
   because it cannot adequately handle the return of its nationals.
3. '[E]xtraordinary and temporary conditions' prevent safe return, and
   permitting the state's nationals to remain temporarily in the USA
   would not be contrary to the national interest.

The Secretary specifies the time period, of between six and eighteen
months, for which the designation will remain in force. There is periodic
review of the conditions in the designated countries, resulting sometimes in extensions of those designations and sometimes in their early
termination. There is no judicial review of the Secretary's decision
whether to designate a particular state or whether to terminate or extend
a designation. Once a country is designated for TPS, its nationals then
file individual applications. Eligibility requirements include continuous
physical presence in the USA since the effective date of the designation,
continuous residence since a date specified by the Secretary of Homeland Security, admissibility as an immigrant (with some exclusion
grounds automatically excepted and some others waivable in the exercise of discretion), registration with DHS within a specified time, and
the absence of certain criminal and other disqualifications. The main
benefit of TPS is that, while it is in effect, the beneficiary may not be
removed and may work.[87]

From its inception until the present, the USA has designated fifteen
different states (and Kosovo) for TPS eligibility. As was true of EVD,
relief under TPS has typically been limited to people who arrived in the
USA before the designation date.[88]

Other forms of discretionary relief   The US immigration laws list
many grounds on which non-citizens who have not yet been admitted
are 'inadmissible', and separate grounds on which non-citizens who

---

[87] These and other details appear in 8 USC s. 1254.
[88] See Charles Gordon et al., *Immigration Law and Procedure* (New York: Matthew Bender,
2006), s. 33.08[2].

REFUGEES, ASYLUM AND THE RULE OF LAW IN THE USA 139

have been admitted are 'deportable'. The two sets of grounds differ slightly, but both encompass a wide range of conduct related to crime, violation of the immigration laws, national security, public health, and the economy.[89] The government may institute 'removal' proceedings against individuals who are believed to fall within any of those grounds. But the laws do not require the removal of everyone who is inadmissible or deportable. The statute and the regulations together authorize several forms of discretionary relief. In part, these relief provisions reflect the realities that removal has potentially severe consequences and that, while many of the deportability grounds entail serious misconduct, others do not. The relief provisions also reflect the philosophy that even serious misconduct must be weighed against other factors, such as long-term residence, or an unusual degree of hardship, or the likelihood of persecution or torture in a foreign country. Asylum and *non-refoulement* for Convention refugees and relief under the CAT, already discussed above, are among the defences that may be asserted in removal proceedings.

Some of the other humanitarian remedies, while not frequently requested by refugees, deserve a brief mention here. They include the prosecutorial discretion not to institute proceedings in the first place;[90] a pair of remedies now collectively known as 'cancellation of removal', typically invoked either by lawful permanent residents who have been convicted of crimes or by undocumented immigrants who have lived in the USA for ten years or more and whose removals would cause 'exceptional and extremely unusual hardship' to specified citizen or permanent resident family members;[91] 'registry', which benefits certain immigrants who have resided in the USA since 1972;[92] occasional one-off legalization programmes for persons who were out of status but met specified conditions, normally including residence or physical presence in the USA since a specified date;[93] and 'private bills' passed by Congress

---

[89] See generally 8 USC ss. 1182(a) (inadmissibility) and 1227 (deportability).

[90] In the USA this remedy is known as 'deferred action'. Technically, deferred action simply puts the case on the back-burner, where it could be resuscitated at any time. In practice, however, the relief is usually permanent. Its availability was first publicized by attorney Leon Wildes, who used it on behalf of his client, John Lennon. See Leon Wildes, 'The Nonpriority Program of the Immigration and Naturalization Service Goes Public: The Litigative Use of the Freedom of Information Act' (1976) 14 *San Diego Law Review* 42. The current details appear in (2000) 77 *Interpreter Releases* 1673–1685.

[91] 8 USC s. 1229b.   [92] 8 USC s. 1259.

[93] By far the most ambitious (as of this writing) was a collection of three legalization provisions enacted in 1986. Ultimately, 2.7 million undocumented immigrants received

140   REFUGEES, ASYLUM SEEKERS AND THE RULE OF LAW

to grant relief, usually in the form of lawful permanent residence, to named individuals.[94]

Part two: the rule of law

The expression 'Rule of Law' has long held different meanings for different people. In this chapter the term will be used to capture the culture of obedience by both private individuals and government officials to duly established laws.

In that narrow sense, rule of law is now at the heart of the refugee and asylum debate in the USA. This section will consider five refugee and asylum contexts in which adherence to the rule of law has occupied centre stage. The first, the perceived abuse and manipulation of the asylum system by applicants, is routinely emphasized by immigration restrictionists. The other four are typically asserted by immigrant and refugee advocates, though some of these are also invoked for more policy-neutral reasons by judges and others who simply value and insist on competent legal work by government actors and a degree of scrutiny that assures fidelity to the legislative will. These latter examples relate, respectively, to the network of legal and practical barriers to accessing the asylum system; the careless or shoddy work of particular adjudicators; the threats to judicial and other decisional independence; and US compliance with its international legal obligations.

Perceived abuse of the asylum system

In the USA, the asylum process is part and parcel of the regulation of immigration. This is true in four senses. Formally, the Refugee Act of

---

permanent residence under these programs. See US Immigration and Naturalization Service, *1994 Statistical Yearbook* (Washington DC: Government Printing Office, 1994), Table 4, p. 32. This programme was followed by much smaller legalization plans for Nicaraguans and Cubans in 1997, see Pub. L. 105–100, Title 202, 111 Stat. 2160, 2193 (19 November 1997) (NACARA), and Haitians in 1998, see Pub. L. 105–277, Div. A, section 101(h), Title IX, 112 Stat. 2681 (2 November 1998). At the time of writing, Congress is actively considering a new legalization programme.

[94] Once quite popular, private immigration bills today are rare, both because of potential corruption and unfair influence and because the other remedies described above have been thought to reduce the need for them. See generally Ryan Quinn and Stephen Yale-Loehr, 'Private Immigration Bills: An Overview' (2004) 9 *Bender's Immigration Bulletin* 1147; Robert Hopper and Juan P. Osuna, 'Remedies of Last Resort: Private Bills and Deferred Action' (June 1997) *Immigration Briefings* 1.

1980, which created the original version of today's asylum system, is an amendment to the Immigration and Nationality Act, which continues to govern immigration. Analytically, asylum seekers are non-US citizens who hope to enter and remain in the USA by demonstrating that they meet the definition of 'refugee', just as other non-citizens seek to enter and remain on the basis of family ties, or employment skills, or other valued attributes. However, asylum seekers are different from most of the others. While the distinction between forced and voluntary migration can sometimes be fine, their migration is said to be 'forced', or 'involuntary'. But their non-US nationalities and their entry objectives make them the subjects of immigration policy. Functionally, refugees and asylum seekers face many of the same cultural challenges, have many of the same desires, and wrestle with some of the same government officials and institutions, as other non-citizens. And in terms of perception, many members of the public associate the asylum process with illegal immigration. Those who think of asylum in that way – in both the public and the private sector – worry about asylum seekers abusing or manipulating the system in the same way that they worry about other non-citizens entering the country clandestinely, overstaying their visas, or otherwise violating the immigration laws.

To contextualize the link between asylum abuse and the rule of law, therefore, it is necessary to situate the issue within the broader setting of illegal immigration. As in many European countries and elsewhere around the world, illegal immigration has come to dominate most of the US debates over immigration. The concern is not trivial. While a precise count of the undocumented population in the USA is impossible, a leading demographer produced an estimate of 11 million as of March 2005, with average net annual increases of 500,000.[95]

The actual economic impact of undocumented immigrants remains elusive. As for the labour market, they both take jobs and create jobs, the latter by consuming goods and services and by sustaining marginal enterprises that also employ US workers. Some fear that, by working at low wages in unskilled labour, they adversely affect the wages or working conditions of American workers. As for fiscal impact, undocumented immigrants use government-provided services such as highways, schools and hospitals, and are eligible for emergency medical services. At the same time, however, they are ineligible for almost all other forms of

---

[95] Jeffrey S. Passel, *Estimates of the Size and Characteristics of the Undocumented Population* (Washington DC: Pew Hispanic Trust, 2005).

142   REFUGEES, ASYLUM SEEKERS AND THE RULE OF LAW

public assistance and they pay taxes – federal and state income taxes, sales taxes, gasoline taxes and, indirectly when they rent housing, property taxes. They also pay into the old age social security system but are ineligible to receive benefits when they retire. The fiscal impact, therefore, remains highly uncertain.

Much of the objection to illegal immigration, however, is non-economic. Many Americans simply resent large-scale violations of law by outsiders. Violations of border laws are especially resented because the ethic with which Americans have grown up is that the nation has a right to decide who may enter and remain in US territory and who may not. Illegal immigration denies that fundamental sovereign right.[96] Moreover, the underground subcultures in which many undocumented migrants are forced to live their daily lives generate civil rights problems that some fear will grow worse with time. Indeed, it might well be that sometimes unconscious, and usually unstated, concerns over the rule of law account for much of the public's visceral reaction against what restrictionists and elements of the American press frequently deride as 'amnesty'.[97]

As little consensus as there is about the magnitude of the impact of illegal immigration, there is even less consensus about the policy responses. The historical, current and possible future options span a wide range. Part of the congressional response has been the traditional remedy of deportation (now called removal) proceedings for those who enter or remain unlawfully.[98] Certain violations can destroy a person's eligibility for discretionary relief from removal.[99] More recently, the emphasis has shifted to increased use of the criminal justice system in cases of illegal entry,[100] prioritizing law enforcement (more Border Patrol officers, more and sturdier border fences, more sophisticated

---

[96] *Chae Chan Ping* v. *United States*, 130 US 581 (1889). This was the first case declaring the federal immigration power inherent in 'sovereignty'.

[97] The term seems misplaced, since the only versions of this strategy that Congress has considered would entail imposing stiff fines as a condition for receiving permission to remain. The elements of punishment and amnesty seem hard to reconcile. For that reason, proponents of such relief prefer the term 'legalization'.

[98] See 8 USC s. 1227(a) (listing the various deportability grounds).

[99] E.g. 8 USC ss. 1158(d)(6), 1182(a)(9)(B), 1229a(b)(7), 1229c(c).

[100] This point has been the subject of much recent literature. See, generally, Stephen H. Legomsky, 'The New Path of Immigration Law: Asymmetric Incorporation of Criminal Justice Norms' (2007) 64 *Washington & Lee Law Review* 469; Teresa A. Miller, 'Blurring the Boundaries between Immigration and Crime Control after September 11' (2005) 25 *Boston College Third World Law Review* 81.

REFUGEES, ASYLUM AND THE RULE OF LAW IN THE USA 143

border enforcement technology),[101] greater use of federal–state collaborative enforcement projects,[102] a growing list of city and town ordinances that punish employers and landlords of immigrants believed to be unlawfully present,[103] private vigilantes such as the 'Minutemen', who arm themselves and 'patrol' the border,[104] punishment of employers who knowingly hire unauthorized workers,[105] and other enforcement measures. While many of the initiatives have been directed specifically at illegal immigration, others – particularly those spawned by the attacks of 11 September 2001 – have been driven chiefly by concerns about terrorism. The latter include a range of strategies related to intelligence gathering, detention, visa issuance, tightening of substantive criteria for admission, and truncation of procedural safeguards in removal proceedings.[106]

Others urge positive tacks. Free trade and other programmes designed to stimulate the economies of major immigration source countries are favoured by many.[107] At the time of writing this, there is fierce debate over whether to allow some portion of the current undocumented population to legalize their immigration status over time, as almost

[101] E.g. Illegal Immigration Reform and Immigrant Responsibility Act of 1996, Pub. L. 104–208, 110 Stat. 3009, Div. C (30 September 1996), s. 101; USA PATRIOT Act of 2001, Pub. L. 107–56, 115 Stat. 272 (26 October 26, 2001), ss. 402,403; Intelligence and Terrorism Prevention Act of 2004, Pub. L. 108–458, 118 Stat. 3638 (17 December 2004), Title V and ss. 7206–15; REAL ID Act of 2005, Pub. L. 109–13, 119 Stat. 231, Div. B (11 May 2005), s. 102.

[102] See 8 USC s. 1357(g).

[103] Most of these ordinances have been patterned after the one enacted by Hazleton, Pennsylvania in 2006. See City of Hazleton Ord. 2006–18 (September 2006). Some have challenged their constitutionality on preemption grounds, arguing either that the ordinances conflict with federal measures or that Congress has occupied the field. See, e.g., Huyen Pham, 'The Inherent Flaws in the Inherent Authority Position: Why Inviting Local Enforcement of the Immigration Laws Violates the Constitution' (2004) 31 *Florida State University Law Review* 965.

[104] See David Kelly, 'Border Watchers Capture Their Prey – the Media', *Los Angeles Times*, 5 April 2005, p. A1; Editorial, 'Amateurs on the Border', *Chicago Tribune*, 5 April 2005, p. C22.

[105] See 8 USC s. 1324(a). Restrictionists have long criticized the federal government for lax enforcement of the employer sanctions laws, and there are indications that the government has reinvigorated its interior enforcement operations in response.

[106] These are laid out in more detail in Stephen H. Legomsky, *Immigration and Refugee Law and Policy*, 4th edn. (New York: Foundation Press, 2005), Chapter 10.

[107] See, e.g., Report of the Commission for the Study of International Migration and Cooperative Economic Development, *Unauthorized Migration: An Economic Development Response* (Washington DC: Government Printing Office, 1990).

144   REFUGEES, ASYLUM SEEKERS AND THE RULE OF LAW

3 million were permitted to do in 1986.[108] Still others have urged extending the application of labour law protection to undocumented workers and more rigorously enforcing those labour laws that already apply.[109]

Given the long-standing public angst over illegal immigration, it is not surprising that some would view the asylum process chiefly as a law enforcement problem. Nor can it be denied that some finite number of asylum seekers lack reasonably arguable claims and attempt to play the system. But there has always been a great deal of difference of opinion as to how large that number is.[110] There are at least two incentives to manipulate the asylum process. One is the hope that the application will be granted; the other is that certain interim benefits typically attach while the claim is pending.[111] The challenge has been to prevent asylum abuse without negating the exercise of one's right to apply for asylum in cases that might well be meritorious. But if the rule of law is to be taken seriously, and if public antipathy towards asylum is to be overcome, then refugee advocates need to acknowledge and address the public's legitimate concerns over asylum abuse.

Impediments to access

Inherent in the rule of law is both theoretical and practical access to the legal system. If a person is beyond the coverage of the applicable law even as written, or if the law theoretically reaches a particular individual but practical impediments bar access to legal remedies, then the rule of law does little or nothing either to protect the individual or to restrain unlawful government action. Throughout the Western world, these concerns have arisen in recent years with respect to asylum. As Western nations struggle to reconcile refugee protection with national self-interest, they have been tempted to adopt a series of problematic strategies. Some of these reforms are specifically meant to cut off access

---

[108] See United States Immigration and Naturalization Service, *1994 Statistical Yearbook*, Table 4, p. 32.

[109] See, e.g., Jennifer Gordon, *Suburban Sweatshops: The Fight for Immigrant Rights* (Cambridge, MA: Harvard University Press, 2005); Michael J. Wishnie, 'Immigrants and the Right to Petition' (2003) 78 *New York University Law Review* 667.

[110] See, e.g., Ira J. Kurzban, 'Restructuring the Asylum Process' (1981) 19 *San Diego Law Review* 91 at 96.

[111] See David A. Martin, 'Reforming Asylum Adjudication: On Navigating the Coast of Bohemia' (1990) 138 *University of Pennsylvania Law Review* 1247 at 1287–89.

REFUGEES, ASYLUM AND THE RULE OF LAW IN THE USA 145

to the asylum system entirely. Others permit potential asylum applicants to file claims but discourage them from doing so. While the focus of this subsection is on the law of the USA, the trend towards restricting access is worldwide, and the various examples have collectively been the subject of a rich commentary.[112]

Because these strategies have been catalogued more comprehensively elsewhere,[113] it is sufficient simply to list them here. They include filing deadlines; presumptions that certain countries of origin or certain third countries are 'safe'; expedited removal and other accelerated procedures; preventive detention while the asylum claims are pending; criminal prosecutions of asylum seekers for irregular entries; denial of permission to work; punishing individuals and/or their representatives for filing asylum claims later found to be 'frivolous' or 'manifestly unfounded'; pre-inspection at foreign airports; visa requirements combined with sanctions on commercial carriers who permit improperly documented passengers to land; and the interdiction of vessels on the high seas.[114]

That last barrier, however, bears highlighting here because of its widespread usage and because of the parallels between US practice and Australian practice.[115] Interdiction entails the intended asylum nation intercepting vessels suspected of carrying would-be entrants and then either turning the vessels away before they reach the nation's shores or destroying the vessels and returning the passengers to their home countries. From Southeast Asia to Italy to Australia to the USA, countries have resorted to interdiction to prevent influxes of boat people from accessing domestic asylum systems.

In the case of the USA, the best-known interdictions have been those directed at Haitians. Today, US Coast Guard cutters intercept not only Haitian vessels, but also (in smaller numbers) vessels from Cuba, the

---

[112] See, e.g., Kay Hailbronner, 'New Techniques for Rendering Asylum Manageable', in Kay Hailbronner et al. (eds.), *Immigration Controls*, 4 vols. (New York: Berghahn Books, 1998), vol. IV, p. 59; Rosemary Byrne, Gregor Noll and Jens Vested-Hansen (eds.), *New Asylum Countries? Migration Control and Refugee Protection in an Enlarged European Union* (Dordrecht, The Netherlands: Kluwer Law International, 2002); Maryellen Fullerton, 'Failing the Test: Germany Leads Europe in Dismantling Refugee Protection' (2001) 36 *Texas International Law Journal* 231 at 243–250.

[113] Legomsky, *Immigration and Refugee Law and Policy*, pp. 1095–35.

[114] The subjects of detention and criminal prosecution are revisited in *The rule of international law* section, in the context of US obligations under international law.

[115] The Australian practice is explored by Kneebone, Chapter 4 in this volume.

146   REFUGEES, ASYLUM SEEKERS AND THE RULE OF LAW

Dominican Republic, and even China.[116] Recently the USA has been intercepting vessels off the coast of Ecuador and asserting the USA's right to board and destroy vessels on the high seas anywhere in the world.[117] One of the key issues raised by interdiction is what provision is to be made for those interdicted passengers who request asylum or otherwise indicate a fear of persecution. On that issue, the parameters of US interdiction policy have fluctuated over the years. At one time the policy literally entailed no refugee status determination at all, at least for Haitians; all passengers were simply returned to Haiti. That policy, instituted by former President George H. W. Bush and continued for a short period by President Clinton, was challenged in *Sale* v. *Haitian Centers Council, Inc.* (*Sale*).[118] The plaintiffs argued that the return of refugees violated both the US statutory provision prohibiting the *refoulement* of refugees and the corresponding provision, Article 33, of the Refugee Convention. The Supreme Court concluded that neither provision applied on the high seas and therefore upheld the policy of interdicting and returning the Haitians without refugee status determinations. The legal issues and the reactions of various international bodies to the Court's decision are considered briefly below.[119]

Governments have defended interdiction in various ways. At its core, interdiction is a law enforcement measure, intended to discourage illegal entry generally and abuse of the asylum system in particular. Governments say interdiction is an effective response to the increased incidence of human smuggling and human trafficking; that it deters unlawful secondary movements; that it avoids the expense of providing individualized asylum hearings to new arrivals; that it saves lives; and that it avoids the problem of housing new arrivals when there is a mass influx.[120]

But the costs are great. The most obvious is that full and fair refugee status determinations are either literally or practically impossible. Either such determinations are not even theoretically available (as in the policy challenged in *Sale*) or they are held under conditions that make success

---

[116] For the statistics, see US Coast Guard, 'Statistics', *Alien Migrant Interdiction*, www.uscg. mil/hq/g-o/g-opl/amio/AMIO.htm (accessed 16 March 2008).

[117] See Bruce Finley, 'US Takes Border War on the Road', *Denver Post*, 19 December 2004, p. A-01.

[118] 509 US 155 (1993).

[119] See Interdiction on the high seas subsection below.

[120] Stephen H. Legomsky, 'The USA and the Caribbean Interdiction Program' (2006) 18 *International Journal of Refugee Law* 677 at 685.

REFUGEES, ASYLUM AND THE RULE OF LAW IN THE USA 147

highly problematic. They might be made on board the intercepting vessel, but the noise, chaos and lack of privacy preclude thoughtful and candid interviews. Interpreters are seldom available, and counsel is almost never available. Interviews could be held (and, for a time, were held) at the Guantanamo Bay Naval Station, but space limitations brought that programme to a halt. Nearby islands are another possibility and were used for a time, but those arrangements are as tenuous as the willingness of the countries involved to allow use of their territories for that purpose. Again, the lack of counsel is highly problematic.[121]

At the time of writing, the most recent statement of US interdiction policy was the dramatic announcement of President George W. Bush on 25 February 2005: 'I have made it abundantly clear to the Coast Guard that we will turn back any *refugee* that attempts to reach our shore [emphasis added]'.[122] As another commentator has noted, this was the first time a US President had asserted that even refugees could be returned.[123] The Sale decision appears to insulate the present policy from legal challenges in the US domestic courts,[124] but the compatibility of the US practice with international law and its legitimacy in the eyes of the international community remain tenuous.

Substandard adjudication of asylum claims

As restrictionists rail against asylum seekers who file false claims, refugee advocates point to fundamental lapses by the government officials charged with administering and adjudicating the asylum system. While no one doubts that many asylum officers, immigration judges, and BIA members who adjudicate asylum claims – perhaps the majority – carry out their duties with competence and professionalism, there is a growing concern by judges and others over the many adjudicators whose performances fall short of minimum standards.

The most numerous and egregious failings have occurred since the 2002 BIA 'streamlining' reforms that were discussed earlier.[125] But

---

[121] *Ibid.* at 686.
[122] George W. Bush, 'Remarks by the President and Georgian President Saakashvili in Photo Opportunity', Washington, 25 February 2004 (emphasis added).
[123] Andrew I. Schoenholtz, 'Refugee Protection in the United States Post September 11' (2005) 36 *Columbia Human Rights Law Review* 323 at 362. See also Bill Frelick, 'Abundantly Clear: Refoulement' (2005) 19 *Georgetown Immigration Law Journal* 245.
[124] Legomsky, 'USA and Caribbean' at 686–92.
[125] See *The administrative and adjudicative structures* section above.

148   REFUGEES, ASYLUM SEEKERS AND THE RULE OF LAW

serious deficiencies in the adjudicative process had frequently surfaced even before those reforms. Though some of the criticisms extended to deportation adjudication generally rather than to asylum specifically, the asylum cases have generated the lion's share of the problems. In one case, a clearly exasperated Court of Appeals was unusually acerbic:

> The Board's analysis was woefully inadequate, indicating it has not taken to heart *previous judicial criticisms* of its performance in asylum cases [citing seven cases from the same and other circuits]. The elementary principles of administrative law, the rules of logic, and common sense seem to have eluded the Board in this *as in other cases*. We are being blunt, but Holmes once remarked the paradox that it often takes a blunt instrument to penetrate a thick hide [emphasis added].[126]

Another court, also well before the 2002 reforms that drastically reduced the average time available per case, had this to say about the administrative process that it was reviewing:

> The legal quality of the decisions in the case were substandard. [In footnote: The State Department, whose relevant bureau enjoys a name that indicates a human and humanitarian purpose, instead of providing relevant data within its knowledge of the state of affairs in El Salvador, responded with the kind of perfunctory form letter that might be used by a department store dismissing a customer's mistaken complaint of an overcharge.] [Immigration] Judge Nail was unfamiliar with the statutory difference between the statutes on withholding deportation and granting asylum. The Board invented a new standard that was not responsive to the US Supreme Court. The Board failed to address one of the two principal claims made by the petitioner. The whole record is one of a shoddy process. Courts of appeals spend countless hours of consideration on capital cases arising in this country. Here where Congress has provided that a helpless alien does not have to be sent back to face death if he is eligible for asylum, the process as it is revealed in this case is one of haste, carelessness and ineptitude. The State Department, the Board, and the Immigration Service need to improve their standards.[127]

---

[126] *Galina* v. *INS*, 213 F 3d 955 at 958 (7th Cir. 2000) (emphasis added). The court went on to describe one of the Board's many errors as 'a rather astounding lapse of logic'. *Ibid.* at 959.

[127] *Montecino* v. *INS*, 915 F 2d 518 at 521 (9th Cir. 1990). See also *Castro-O'Ryan* v. *United States Dept. of Immigration and Naturalization*, 847 F.2d 1307 at 1310–12 (9th Cir. 1987), where the applicant vividly testified as to several acts of violence and other torture inflicted on him in police custody. The immigration judge, claiming to summarize the testimony, said simply that the applicant 'was taken into custody by individuals of the government and that he was held overnight and that during the time he was held he was questioned and he was mistreated'. The court reversed the decision.

REFUGEES, ASYLUM AND THE RULE OF LAW IN THE USA 149

Since the BIA reforms, and the resulting shrinkage of the time devoted to each case at the administrative level, judicial criticisms have mounted. Here is one court's summary of some of the post-2002 cases:

> In the year ending on the date of the argument, different panels of this court [the US Court of Appeals for the Seventh Circuit] reversed the Board of Immigration Appeals in whole or part in a staggering 40 per cent of the 136 petitions to review the Board that were resolved on the merits. The corresponding figure, for the 82 civil cases during this period in which the United States was the appellee, was 18 per cent. Our criticisms of the Board and of the immigration judges have frequently been severe. E.g., [case names omitted here] 'the [immigration judge's] opinion is riddled with inappropriate and extraneous comments'; 'this very significant mistake suggests that the Board was not aware of the most basic facts of [the petitioner's] case'; 'the procedure that the [immigration judge] employed in this case is an affront to [petitioner's] right to be heard'; the immigration judge's factual conclusion is 'totally unsupported by the record'; the immigration judge's unexplained conclusion is 'hard to take seriously'; 'there is a gaping hole in the reasoning of the Board and the immigration judge'. Other circuits have been as critical. [E.g.] 'the tone, the tenor, the disparagement, and the sarcasm of the [immigration judge] seem more appropriate to a court television show than a federal court proceeding'; the immigration judge's finding is 'grounded solely on speculation and conjecture'; the immigration judge's 'hostile' and 'extraordinarily abusive' conduct toward petitioner 'by itself would require a rejection of his credibility finding'; 'the [immigration judge's] assessment of [petitioner's] credibility was skewed by prejudgment, personal speculation, bias, and conjecture'; 'it is the [immigration judge's] conclusion, not [the petitioner's] testimony, that strains credulity'.
>
> This tension between judicial and administrative adjudicators is not due to judicial hostility to the nation's immigration policies or to a misconception of the proper standard of judicial review of administrative decisions. It is due to the fact that the adjudication of these cases at the administrative level has fallen below the minimum standards of legal justice. Whether this is due to resource constraints or to other circumstances beyond the Board's and the Immigration Court's control, we do not know, though we note that the problem is not of recent origin.[128]

At the end of its opinion, the court delivered one parting shot: 'We are not required to permit [the asylum applicant] to be ground to bits in the bureaucratic mill against the will of Congress.'[129] The following year the same court faulted an immigration judge for 'factual error, bootless

---

[128] *Benslimane* v. *Gonzales*, 430 F 3d 828 at 829–30 (7th Cir. 2005). [129] *Ibid.* at 833.

150   REFUGEES, ASYLUM SEEKERS AND THE RULE OF LAW

speculation, and errors of logic', adding that '[t]hese have been common failings in recent decisions by immigration judges and the Board', further faulting the Board for simply affirming the immigration judge's decision in a 'one-sentence *per curiam* order', and cataloguing still other decisions by several courts that had criticized immigration judges and the Board in scathing language.[130]

In response to these and other criticisms of the immigration judges and the BIA concerning both the quality of their decisions and (in the case of the immigration judges) their verbal abuse of asylum claimants, Attorney General Alberto Gonzales appointed a review team in 2006. The team briefed the Attorney General on its findings (not made public), and the Attorney General then publicly announced twenty-two measures that he hoped would enhance the professionalism and fairness of the process.[131] At the time of writing, the verdict is still out.

The independence of the adjudicators

This chapter earlier outlined the respective roles of the immigration judges and the Board of Immigration Appeals in asylum cases. In 2002 and 2003 the Attorney General took a series of steps that, as has been argued elsewhere,[132] leave the decisional independence of these adjudicative officers in substantial doubt. Furthermore, the erosion of independence in the administrative phase has occurred during a period in which Congress has been chipping away at the jurisdiction of the federal courts to review the resulting removal orders. As elaborated below, the court-stripping legislation has affected only one category of asylum cases, but the category is a substantial one, and to that extent the concern is that the two sets of developments combine in a potentially dangerous way. The interaction of the loss of decisional independence at the administrative level with the elimination of judicial review means that, for the affected cases, there is no point anywhere in the process at which an asylum decision will be either made or reviewed by a body that enjoys decisional independence.

---

[130] *Pramatarev v. Gonzalez*, 454 F 3d 764 at 765 (7th Cir. 2006).
[131] See (2006) 83 *Interpreter Releases* 122; (2006) 83 *Interpreter Releases* 1725–1728.
[132] Stephen H. Legomsky, 'Deportation and the War on Independence' (2006) 91 *Cornell Law Review* 369.

The immigration judges

Immigration judges are appointed by the Attorney General.[133] At one time, they were part of the now defunct Immigration and Naturalization Service (INS), an enforcement agency. In 1983, however, the Justice Department created the Executive Office for Immigration Review (EOIR) which, as noted earlier, is strictly an adjudicative tribunal, and transferred the immigration judges to the EOIR.[134]

In the past several years immigration judges have complained increasingly of Justice Department actions that have pre-empted decisions formerly entrusted to immigration judges.[135] Most of the complaints have concerned actions that replaced individualized immigration judge decisions with general policies of the Justice Department or the policies of law enforcement personnel.[136] Another complaint related to ex parte Justice Department intervention in the outcome of an individual case.[137]

More important in the present context, there is an emerging fear that ruling against the government in a deportation case can be hazardous to one's job. Like other employees in the federal 'excepted service', immigration judges 'may be disciplined for misconduct, including a penalty of removal under appropriate circumstances'.[138] This is reasonable. There has to be some means to terminate the appointment of a government official – even one who performs adjudicative functions –

---

[133] 8 USC s. 1101(b)(4).

[134] See 48 Fed. Reg. 8038, 8056 (25 February 1983). See, generally, Sidney B. Rawitz, 'From Wong Yang Sung to Black Robes' (1980) 65 *Interpreter Releases* 453.

[135] See National Association of Immigration Judges, *An Independent Immigration Court: An Idea Whose Time Has Come* (Washington DC: Government Printing Office, 2002).

[136] Examples of the issues on which general policy decisions have been imposed on immigration judges from above include whether to close a removal hearing to the public and the press for national security reasons; whether the individual may safely be released on bond; whether to discontinue a hearing because of the failure of the former INS to process a critical application in a timely manner; and whether to implement a congressionally mandated contempt power for immigration judges. *Ibid.* at pp. 8–10.

[137] An INS prosecuting official was displeased with the decision of an immigration judge in an individual case. Rather than appeal the decision to the BIA in the usual manner, the INS official made an ex parte telephone call to the Chief Immigration Judge, an administrator who supervises the corps of immigration judges, and persuaded him to order the immigration judge to change his decision. *Ibid.* at p. 18 n. 33; see also Eric Schmitt, 'Two Judges Do Battle in an Immigration Case', *New York Times*, 21 June 2001, p. 20.

[138] Elaine Komis, 'Memorandum from Elaine Komis, EOIR, to Christopher W. Goddard, Washington University School of Law', 16 March 2005, copy with author.

152 REFUGEES, ASYLUM SEEKERS AND THE RULE OF LAW

for affirmative misconduct. Even without misconduct, however, the EOIR now takes the view that it may 'reassign' immigration judges. It says: '[N]ormally, a reassignment to another position, even one involving a different job title, job series, or duties, is a matter of management discretion and is not considered to be disciplinary in nature if there is no loss of pay or grade'.[139]

As discussed more fully below, Attorney General Ashcroft in 2002 officially announced his plans to reduce the size of the BIA by reassigning some of its existing members at some future time. The language of his announcement caught the attention of the immigration judges as well. The Attorney General said:

> Each Board member is a Department of Justice attorney who is appointed by, and may be removed or reassigned by, the Attorney General. *All attorneys* in the Department are excepted employees, subject to *removal* by the Attorney General, *and* may be transferred from and to assignments as necessary to fulfill the Department's mission [emphasis added].[140]

The Attorney General's reference to 'all attorneys' (not just BIA members), coupled with his explicit claim of power not only to reassign but to 'remove' – a term of art that connotes dismissal[141] – implies that immigration judges could similarly be reassigned or even removed at the pleasure of the Attorney General. Nothing in the announcement suggested that removal – much less reassignment – would require a finding of misconduct.

The BIA

The Attorney General created the BIA in 1940.[142] Like the immigration judges, the BIA was moved to EOIR in 1983.[143] Because the BIA has the jurisdiction to review all removal orders issued by immigration judges,[144] and because many immigration judge removal orders follow their rejection of asylum claims, the BIA's decisions play a fundamental role in asylum cases.

As noted earlier, the main effect of the changes introduced by the Attorney General in 2002 and 2003 was to 'streamline' the BIA operations by delegating most of its decisions to single members rather than three-member panels, prohibiting the single members from giving

---

[139] *Ibid.*　[140] 67 Fed. Reg. at 54893 (26 August 2002) (emphasis added).
[141] See Elaine Komis, 'Memorandum'.　[142] 5 Fed. Reg. 3503 (4 September 1940).
[143] 48 Fed. Reg. 8038, 8056 (25 February 1983).　[144] 8 CFR s. 1003.1(b)(3) (2006).

REFUGEES, ASYLUM AND THE RULE OF LAW IN THE USA 153

reasons for their opinions in most cases, and setting mandatory time-lines for the various stages of the appeals. The stated objective was to attack the large backlog of BIA cases.

In the same announcement, however, the Attorney General also declared his intention to reduce the number of authorized BIA member positions from twenty-three to eleven.[145] Six months later the final regulations were published. The Attorney General refused to disclose the specific criteria he would use to select particular members for 'reassignment'.[146]

Approximately one year after the original announcement, Ashcroft announced his decisions.[147] An empirical study by Peter Levinson, a long-time member of the legal staff of the House Judiciary Committee (which houses the subcommittee that considers immigration legisla-tion), showed that those BIA members who most often ruled in favour of the individual and against the government were chosen for reassign-ment.[148] As that study shows, the general criteria previously announced by the Attorney General – integrity, professional competence and tem-perament – could not explain his selections, for those who lost their jobs were among the most senior and the most highly respected of the Board's members.[149]

Perhaps more striking than the permanent effects of these changes was their immediate impact during the one-year interval between the announcement and the actual reassignments. The empirical data con-firm what one would have predicted – that during that interval several BIA members ruled in favour of the government noticeably more often than those same members had done before the original

---

[145] 67 Fed. Reg. 7309 (19 February 2002) (proposed regulation).

[146] He said only that he would consider 'traditional' factors, would exercise his 'discretion', and would take account of 'integrity . . . professional competence, and adjudicatorial temperament'. Seniority would not be a 'presumptive factor': 67 Fed. Reg. 54878 at 54893 (26 August 2002) (final regulation).

[147] Ricardo Aloso-Zaldivar and Jonathan Peterson, 'Five on Immigration Board Asked to Leave', *Los Angeles Times*, 12 March 2003, p. 16.

[148] Levinson, 'The Façade' at 1155–56.

[149] Four of the twenty-three authorized BIA positions were vacant at the time of the original 2002 announcement and three BIA members left voluntarily before the names of the removed members were announced in 2003. It was therefore necessary to remove only five additional members. *Ibid.* at 1155. They included the former Chair of the Board, two former full-time law professors who had taught immigration law, and other experienced and highly respected BIA members with substantial seniority. They were 'reassigned' to lower-level immigration judge positions or to non-adjudicative pos-itions on the EOIR staff. *Ibid.* at 1156–60.

154   REFUGEES, ASYLUM SEEKERS AND THE RULE OF LAW

announcement.[150] Some others who had been among the more favourable to the individual in their pre-announcement rulings continued that pattern after the announcement; but only one of the latter group survived the purge.[151]

In the US administrative context, the Attorney General's actions were highly unusual. Since the creation of the BIA in 1940,[152] the Attorneys General have been an ideologically diverse group. One can assume they held widely varying views on immigration. One can further assume that from time to time a BIA decision must have rankled them. Yet no Attorney General had *ever* removed a member of the BIA,[153] and BIA members had always assumed they could safely render the decisions they felt the evidence and the law required, without fear that displeasing the Attorney General could jeopardize their jobs. Obviously, that assumption is no longer safe.

The same empirical study that highlighted the effects of the BIA reassignments on members' decisional patterns also revealed the Attorney General's broader philosophy of the role of the BIA members. According to the author of the study:

> Until recently [the issuance of the 2002 Final Rule], the regulations relating to the Board clearly affirmed the decisional independence of Board Members in the very first paragraph by stating unequivocally that 'Board Members shall exercise their independent judgment and discretion in the cases coming before the Board.' . . . With the promulgation of the new rule, however, the Board regulations gave top billing to a sentence with a very different emphasis: 'The Board Members shall be attorneys appointed by the Attorney General to act as the Attorney General's delegates in the cases that come before them.' . . . A somewhat diluted version of decisional independence language came much later.[154]

There are striking parallels to a sequence of events that occurred in Australia in 1997. Two women, in separate cases, had applied for asylum based on claims of domestic violence. The legal issue was a close one; courts and tribunals around the world have differed over whether domestic violence can constitute 'being persecuted for reasons of' either 'political opinion' or 'membership of a particular social group', the

---

[150] *Ibid.* at 1159–1160.   [151] *Ibid.*   [152] 5 Fed. Reg. 3503 (4 September 1940).
[153] See Stephen H. Legomsky, 'Forum Choices for the Review of Agency Adjudication: A Study of the Immigration Process' (1986) 71 *Iowa Law Review* 1297 at 1380, n. 488.
[154] Levinson, 'The Façade' at 1161.

REFUGEES, ASYLUM AND THE RULE OF LAW IN THE USA 155

elements required for refugee status in international law.[155] The Australian Department of Immigration and Multicultural Affairs (DIMA) (as it was then called) denied both claims. Both women appealed as of right to the Refugee Review Tribunal (RRT), supposedly an independent tribunal. In each case the RRT member granted the claim.

The Minister for Immigration appoints RRT members for fixed terms. Upon learning the results of these two cases, the then Minister, Philip Ruddock, issued an angry public statement that RRT members 'would not be reappointed if they made decisions that went beyond the law'. His spokesperson publicly repeated that statement the next day. The RRT members' terms are staggered, and the terms of about one-half of the RRT members were due to expire approximately six months later. During those six months, the asylum approval rates by the RRT dropped from 16 per cent in the year preceding the Minister's threats to 2.7 per cent in the month in which the reappointment interviews were held. When the terms of thirty-five RRT members expired six months later, Ruddock refused to renew sixteen of those thirty-five appointments, replacing them with people of his own choosing.[156]

The courts

Historically, Congress has repeatedly voiced its reservations about judicial review of deportation orders and the resulting delays.[157] As noted earlier, the general rule is that an administratively final order of removal is reviewable as of right by petition for review in the Court of Appeals,[158] but subject now to several glaring exceptions. One of the most sweeping exceptions contains a specific proviso preserving judicial

---

[155] Refugee Convention, Art. (1A)(2). Many writers have discussed the application of the Convention to claims based on domestic violence. See, e.g., Deborah E. Anker, *Law of Asylum in the United States*, 3rd edn. (Boston, MA: Refugee Law Center, 1999), pp. 252–66; Heaven Crawley, *Refugees and Gender: Law and Process* (Bristol, UK: Jordans Ltd, 2002); Legomsky, *Immigration and Refugee Law and Policy*, pp. 995–1049; Susan Forbes Martin, *Refugee Women*, 2nd edn. (Lanham, MD: Lexington Books, 2004); Karen Musalo et al., *Refugee Law and Policy: A Comparative and International Approach*, 2nd edn. (Durham, NC: Carolina Academic Press, 2001), pp. 621–698; Pamela Goldberg, 'Women and Refugee Status: A Review Essay' (1995) 7 *International Journal of Refugee Law* 756.

[156] See Stephen H. Legomsky, 'Refugees, Administrative Tribunals, and Real Independence: Dangers Ahead for Australia' (1998) 76 *Washington University Law Quarterly* 243; Kneebone, Chapter 4 in this volume.

[157] See, generally, Gordon et al., *Immigration Law*, s. 104.01[2].   [158] 8 USC s. 1252.

156   REFUGEES, ASYLUM SEEKERS AND THE RULE OF LAW

review of asylum denials.[159] But another does not. It bars judicial review of so-called 'expedited removal' orders (certain removal orders issued after abbreviated administrative procedures).[160] It contains no proviso for judicial review of asylum denials that occur during expedited removal proceedings[161] which, as explained earlier, are the usual procedure for claims filed by arriving asylum seekers at ports of entry.

The discussion to this point illustrates the threats to the job security of immigration judges and BIA members, the two levels of adjudicators in removal cases. Federal judges, of course, enjoy a very high degree of job security; assuming 'good behaviour', they hold office for life and their salaries cannot be reduced.[162] But the decisional independence that this job security brings is of no value in those cases where Congress has foreclosed federal court jurisdiction, as has happened in certain whole categories of deportation cases.

It is submitted that, in this instance, the whole is greater than the sum of its parts. The combination of destroying the decisional independence of the BIA members *and* eliminating judicial review for whole categories of cases means that, for those cases, there is no longer *any* point in the process at which the lawfulness of the immigration judge's asylum denial will be reviewed by anyone with decisional independence. Moreover, if one takes seriously the additional threats to the decisional independence of the immigration judges themselves, then for the affected cases there is no actor with decisional independence at any stage of the process – not at the original hearing of the asylum claim and not at a review stage. Given the potential magnitude of the interests at stake in asylum cases, the absence of decisional independence is a matter of concern.

The link between decisional independence and the rule of law

Incursions into decisional independence can take many forms, including the intervention of a politically accountable official to influence the outcome of an individual case. The element that the developments traced above calls into question is a narrower one, however – a general threat, real or perceived, that a decision which displeases a government

---

[159] E.g. 8 USC s. 1252(a)(2)(B)(ii) (exempting asylum from the bar on judicial review of discretionary decisions).
[160] 8 USC s. 1252(a)(2)(A).
[161] There are exceptions for individuals who are ordered to be removed after having been granted refugee or asylee status, but not for those who wish to challenge the denials of their claims in the first place. 8 USC s. 1252(e)(2).
[162] US Constitution Art. III, s. 1.

official could pose professional risks for the adjudicator. Those risks might include dismissal, reassignment to a less desirable position, nonrenewal of the appointment at the expiration of a fixed term, or loss of compensation.

Because political accountability is the other side of the independence coin, representative democracies do not insist on independence with respect to those governmental functions that most resemble legislation or other policy making. To the contrary, it is more common to insist on some form of political accountability. Only with adjudicative functions is the ideal of decisional independence ordinarily embraced. Admittedly too, the line that separates adjudication from policy making is elusive. But the decisions that immigration judges and BIA members make in asylum cases – and certainly those that reviewing courts make – constitute adjudication under *any* reasonable definition one might devise. Each claim involves a single dispute between two parties – an individual and a government agency. Each case involves the interpretation or application of law, findings of fact based on the evidence in the record, and/or the exercise of a specific statutory discretion. At every stage of the process, each of these decision makers is bound by specific rules. And in each case the procedures are carefully laid out in the statute and regulations. It is hard to think of *any* definition of adjudication that this process would not satisfy.

Consistent with both early English history and the debate in colonial America, the Federalist Papers (78 and 79) identified two complementary theories of judicial independence.[163] One theory, reflecting traditional separation of powers concerns, was that judges would be unable to provide a check on Congress and the executive branch unless the judges enjoyed some degree of independence. The other theory was that judges needed to be independent in order to prevent the other branches from violating individual rights.

Probably the most obvious of the individual rights that decisional independence was designed to protect is procedural fairness. In the words of one judge, 'the independence of the judiciary from political pressures is an essential aspect of justice at any level'.[164] Simply put, we

---

[163] This issue is explored in depth in Legomsky, 'Deportation and the War on Independence' at 385–403. The paragraphs in this subsection are drawn from that article.

[164] J. Clifford Wallace, 'An Essay on Independence of the Judiciary: Independence From What and Why' (2001) 58 *New York University Annual Survey of American Law* 241 at 242.

158 REFUGEES, ASYLUM SEEKERS AND THE RULE OF LAW

want people who perform adjudicative functions to reach their decisions honestly. We want them to base their findings of fact solely on the evidence before them, and we want them to base their legal conclusions solely on their honest interpretations of all the relevant sources of law – not on the basis of which outcome they think the person (or public) who will be reappointing them might prefer.

A second, related, potential consequence of threats to decisional independence is what might be termed 'defensive judging'. The adjudicator who has to worry about staying popular might have a strong incentive to play it safe. Safety, in turn, might entail avoiding controversial rulings that would attract public attention or otherwise displease one's superiors. Granting an asylum claim might well risk doing this.

Third, decisional independence is conceived as a way to protect unpopular individuals, unpopular minorities and unpopular political viewpoints.[165] In any of those circumstances, reliance on the political process is likely to be misplaced. Judges need the freedom to apply the law objectively in the face of a hostile public. When an asylum seeker makes claims about the treatment suffered at the hands of a government closely allied with that of the USA, there is a particular risk of public or governmental disapproval.

Fourth, and more generally, in the USA certain individual liberty and property rights have been thought important enough to protect even from the majoritarian political process. Those rights have been entrenched in a written constitution that courts have exercised the power to interpret. For the courts to perform the interpretation function in a way that will adequately safeguard those rights against transient majoritarian preferences, a judge requires confidence that an unpopular decision will not have adverse personal consequences.[166]

Much of the above could also be said even for non-constitutional questions such as those typically raised by asylum claims. Rights created or preserved by statutes, for example, might well require similar judicial protection from a hostile transient majority or even a powerful interest

---

[165] E.g. Stephen B. Burbank, 'The Architecture of Judicial Independence' (1999) 72 *Southern California Law Review* 315 at 319; Archibald Cox, 'The Independence of the Judiciary: History and Purposes' (1996) 21 *University of Dayton Law Review* 565 at 572–73; Vicki C. Jackson, 'Proconstitutional Behavior, Political Actors, and Independent Courts: A Comment on Geoffrey Stone's Paper' (2004) 2 *International Journal of Constitutional Law* 368 at 369.

[166] See, e.g., Cox, 'The Independence of the Judiciary' at 570–71.

group. Judges who are dependent on the will of the public's representatives seem poorly suited to that task. In the words of one judge who is usually associated with judicial restraint, to protect fundamental rights judges have to be free to rule against government 'without fear of reprisal'.[167]

While implicit in each of the preceding theories, separation of powers can be viewed as a fifth, separate, reason to ensure decisional independence in adjudication. Even when fundamental rights are not at stake and the particular litigants are not unpopular, the judiciary has historically been seen as an important check on the powers exerted by the political branches of government.

Each of these theories of decisional independence is a means of ensuring fidelity to the rule of law. The first of those theories – that decisional independence is an essential ingredient of fair procedure – presents the clearest case. I would suggest that the procedural fairness rationale that lies at the heart of decisional independence is a specific application of the principle that government actors are bound by the rule of law. I mean this in two different senses. In one sense, the requirement of procedural fairness is itself an element of law to which the rule of law principle demands adherence (at least when procedural due process or some more specific, applicable sub-constitutional equivalent, such as a statutorily prescribed procedure, is required). In another sense, even when no specific rule of constitutional or other law requires procedural fairness, fair procedure is the only way to assure governmental compliance with the applicable *substantive* rules. Therefore, to the extent that the absence of decisional independence impairs the fairness of the procedure, it prevents outcomes that comport with the relevant substantive legal principles.

The link seems clearest for questions of law. If we are truly 'a government of laws, and not of men',[168] and if the people's representatives in the legislature have spoken as to those laws, then procedural ingredients that encourage adjudicators to interpret the law in ways that differ from those decreed by the law makers are inherently in conflict with the rule of law. To the extent that the absence of decisional independence encourages that sort of decision making, therefore, it too is at odds with the goal of respecting the rule of law. To be sure, there will always be debate over both the objectives and the permissible

---

[167] Wallace, 'An Essay on Independence of the Judiciary' at 242.
[168] *Marbury* v. *Madison*, 5 US (1 Cranch) 137 at 163 (1803).

methods of interpreting statutes and other legal instruments. Is it the meaning of the written instrument or the actual intentions of the legislators that a court should seek to discover? What relative weights should be placed on the text and other indicia of legislative purpose and intent? These and other questions remain the subject of legitimate debate, and I do not intend to weigh in on that subject here. It seems sufficient to observe that there is *no* respectable statutory interpretation theory under which a judge should interpret a statute or other source of law by asking the question 'Which interpretation is least likely to cost me my job?' If the rule of law means anything, it surely means, at a minimum, that those charged with interpreting the law must do so on the merits, not on the basis of factors so clearly extraneous to the adjudicative function.

Yet many asylum claims turn on questions of fact. Even as to those, the procedural unfairness that decisional independence is capable of generating can undermine the rule of law. A fact finder who bends his/her analysis of the evidence to reach a result more pleasing to his/her superiors thereby reaches an outcome that differs from the one that the legislature has prescribed for the true facts. The same problem occurs when an appellate tribunal, faced with the question of whether the evidence below is sufficient to support the findings of fact, bends the analysis to reach a result that differs from his/her honestly held view of the merits. The rule of law is violated, not just in the technical sense that an appellate court will characterize a finding of fact based on insufficient evidence as an error 'of law' for purposes of review, but in the very real sense that the adjudicator has thereby produced a result precisely contrary to the outcome prescribed by law on the true facts.

The foregoing reasoning assumed procedural fairness as the relevant decisional independence theory and sought to demonstrate that that theory is ultimately rooted in the rule of law. Similar considerations apply to several of the other decisional independence theories described above. The theories based on defensive judging, protection of unpopular individuals (and unpopular minorities and unpopular viewpoints), and protection of fundamental legal rights all rest on the notion that an adjudicator who is encouraged to base a decision on legally irrelevant factors (especially irrelevant *and secret* factors) is unacceptably likely to reach an outcome that differs substantively from the one that the legislature prescribed on the true facts. For that reason, these theories too can be thought of as applications of the rule of law principle.

REFUGEES, ASYLUM AND THE RULE OF LAW IN THE USA 161

The separation of powers theory of decisional independence requires a somewhat different analysis, but ultimately it too implicates the rule of law. Those who worried that an absence of decisional independence would breach separation of powers were concerned not only about good government, but also about the role of the courts in *checking* the unlawful excesses of the legislative and executive branches.

The rule of international law

In some ways, US refugee policy is a model of generosity, offering protections that exceed those required by international law and those offered by most other resettlement states. The US offshore refugee programme[169] provides permanent resettlement for far more overseas refugees than the offshore programmes of all other industrialized countries in the world combined. Moreover, the US statutory 'refugee' definition, applicable to both overseas refugee admissions and asylum,[170] covers not only those who have escaped their countries of persecution but also persons who are internally displaced, as well as those who have suffered past persecution even when there is no well-founded fear of future persecution.[171] The corresponding definition in the Refugee Convention, in contrast, covers neither IDPs nor past persecution.[172]

These commendable policies, which surpass US international legal obligations, must be acknowledged. But no rule of international law allows a state to violate some of its treaty obligations as a quid pro quo for exceeding others. As this subsection will show, US implementation of its obligations under international refugee law has clearly fallen short in several respects and, at least arguably, has done so in still others.

The shortcomings reflect the failings of all three branches of the US federal government. Congress has yet to implement those provisions of the Refugee Convention (and the CAT, as explained below) that it regards as non-self-executing and therefore in need of legislation. The executive branch has sometimes acted as if it believes that 'non-self-executing' means 'non-binding'. And the federal courts have largely deferred to these congressional and executive lapses, sometimes giving written decisions that can only be described as embarrassingly sloppy and confused.[173]

---

[169] 8 USC s. 1157.   [170] 8 USC ss. 1157, 1158(b)(1), respectively.
[171] 8 USC s. 1101(a)(42).   [172] Refugee Convention, Art. 1A(2).
[173] The analysis of the one-year filing deadline for asylum applications, in *Sukwanputra* v. *Gonzales*, 434 F 3d 627, 632 (3rd Cir. 2006), while not necessarily incorrect in its

162 REFUGEES, ASYLUM SEEKERS AND THE RULE OF LAW

This chapter surveys some arguable (and in some instances, fairly clear) US breaches of international refugee law. They are discussed here in two sections, which deal, respectively, with *non-refoulement* of refugees and other Refugee Convention rights.[174]

Interdiction on the high seas

As discussed earlier,[175] since 1981 the USA, in an attempt to prevent Haitian boat people from accessing its asylum system, has interdicted Haitian vessels on the high seas and returned the occupants to Haiti pursuant to a bilateral executive agreement. Although the agreement specified that the USA would not return refugees, President George H. W. Bush issued an Executive Order in 1992 declaring that US *non-refoulement* obligations under the 1967 Protocol do not apply outside US territory.[176] President Clinton continued this policy until 1994.[177] The effect was to repatriate all the intercepted Haitians without any refugee screening.[178] Since 1994 the policy has changed from time to time. On 25 February 2005, President George W. Bush infamously announced his intention to 'turn back any *refugee* that attempts to reach our shore'.[179] The result has been an ineffectual 'shout test' conducted aboard the intercepting vessel for the purpose of identifying any potential asylum seekers.[180]

Article 33(1) of the 1951 Refugee Convention reads:

> No Contracting State shall expel or return (*refouler*) a refugee in any manner whatsoever to the frontiers of territories where his life or freedom would be threatened on account of his race, religion, nationality, membership of a particular social group or political opinion.

The policy of returning interdicted Haitians to Haiti without refugee screening was challenged in the case of *Sale*.[181] Because the Supreme

---

outcome, is riddled with technical errors that reveal fundamental misconceptions of international law generally and international refugee law in particular.

[174] Serious compliance questions also arise with respect to US implementation of the Convention Against Torture. See, generally, Legomsky, *Immigration and Refugee Law and Policy*, pp. 1145–64.

[175] See the *Impediments to Access* section above.

[176] Exec. Order 12807, 57 Fed. Reg. 23133 (24 May 1992).

[177] (1994) 71 *Interpreter Releases* 743–744.

[178] *Sale* v. *Haitian Centers Council, Inc.*, 509 US 155 at 158, 163–64 (1993).

[179] George W. Bush, 'Remarks by the President' (emphasis added). See also Frelick, 'Abundantly Clear' at 245; Schoenholtz, 'Refugee Protection' at 361.

[180] *Ibid.* [181] *Sale* v. *Haitian Centers Council, Inc*, 509 US 155 (1993).

REFUGEES, ASYLUM AND THE RULE OF LAW IN THE USA 163

Court interpreted the Convention as non-self-executing,[182] the only question it addressed was how to interpret the (almost identically worded) US implementing legislation. Recognizing, however, that Congress had passed the statute for the very purpose of conforming US domestic law to US obligations under the Convention, the Court had to construe the Convention as well, as an aid to divining Congress's intentions. By a vote of 8–1 (Justice Blackmun dissenting), the Court construed both the Refugee Convention and the US statute as inoperative on the high seas. It concluded, therefore, that the USA was free to intercept even Convention refugees on the high seas and return them to their countries of persecution. It reached that result despite the absence of limiting language in the Convention, the affirmative presence of the phrase 'in any manner whatsoever', and the absence of any policy explanation as to why the drafters would want to prohibit states from returning refugees from their territories but not prohibit states from returning refugees whom they had intercepted on the high seas.

The Court's interpretation has been severely criticized by scholars, UNHCR, and the Inter-American Commission on Human Rights.[183] Shortly after the Supreme Court decision in Sale, the Executive Committee of UNHCR issued a statement disagreeing with the decision, based on the language, structure and purposes of the 1951 Convention. UNHCR strenuously maintains that Article 33 of the Convention applies on the high seas. Its statement chastised the Supreme Court:

> UNHCR considers the Court's decision a setback to modern international refugee law which has been developing for more than forty years, since the end of World War II. It renders the work of the Office of the High Commissioner in its global refugee protection role more difficult and sets a very unfortunate example.[184]

---

[182] That premise has been questioned. See e.g. Carlos M. Vasquez, 'The 'Self-Executing' Character of the Refugee Protocol's *Non-refoulement* Obligation' (1993) 7 *Georgetown Immigration Law Journal* 39.

[183] James C. Hathaway, *The Rights of Refugees Under International Law* (Cambridge University Press, 2005), pp. 336–339; Legomsky, 'USA and Caribbean' at 686–692.

[184] 'UN High Commissioner for Refugees Responds to US Supreme Court Decision in *Sale v. Haitian Centers Council*' (1993) 32 *International Legal Materials* 1215; accord, Daniel J. Steinbock, 'Interpreting the Refugee Definition' (1998) 45 *UCLA Law Review* 733 at 755–756; cf. Andrew I. Schoenholtz, 'Aiding and Abetting Persecutors: The Seizure and Return of Haitian Refugees in Violation of the UN Refugee Convention and Protocol' (1993) 7 *Georgetown Immigration Law Journal* 67 (arguing for the UNHCR position even before the decision in *Sale*).

164   REFUGEES, ASYLUM SEEKERS AND THE RULE OF LAW

The Inter-American Commission on Human Rights has expressed similar sentiments and has also suggested that the decision in *Sale* violated the American Declaration of the Rights and Duties of Man.[185] Still others have argued that the decision violates the law of the sea,[186] the CAT, and the International Covenant on Civil and Political Rights.[187]

Standard of proof

In *INS* v. *Stevic*,[188] the US Supreme Court interpreted the US *non-refoulement* provision (then called 'withholding of deportation' under domestic law, now 'withholding of removal') as prohibiting *refoulement* only when the applicant could show that persecution was 'more likely than not'. The Convention (and US statutory) language 'life or freedom would be threatened' certainly appears broader. If a doctor informed a patient that the patient had a 30 per cent chance of surviving a disease, it is hard to imagine that the patient would not regard his or her life as being 'threatened'. No international interpretations were cited; indeed, while foreign formulations of the same language vary, all those contemplate a substantially lower standard of proof.[189]

The exclusion clauses

Article 33(2) of the Refugee Convention exempts a state from the prohibition on *refoulement* if a person 'having been convicted by a final judgment of a particularly serious crime, constitutes a danger to the community'. In the USA, the BIA has interpreted the similarly worded US statutory provision[190] to mean that conviction of a particularly

---

[185] See Organization of American States, 'OAS Human Rights Committee Calls Clinton Haitian Interdiction Policy a Violation of International Law', Press Release, 19 March 1993; Louis Henkin et al., *Human Rights* (New York: Foundation Press, 1999), p. 426.

[186] Jon L. Jacobson, 'At-Sea Interception of Alien Migrants: International Law Issues' (1992) 28 *Willamette Law Review* 811.

[187] See Gerald L. Neuman, 'Extraterritorial Violations of Human Rights by the United States' (1994) 9 *American University Journal of International Law and Policy* and *Loyola of Los Angeles International and Comparative Law Journal* 213.

[188] 467 US 407 at 424 (1984).

[189] See Brian Gorlick, 'Common Burdens and Standards: Legal Elements in Assessing Claims to Refugee Status' (2003) 15 *International Journal of Refugee Law* 357. In *INS* v. *Cardoza-Fonseca* 480 US 421 (1987) the Supreme Court adopted a more generous standard of reasonableness for asylum claims. See the legislative framework at p. 126.

[190] Now 8 USC s. 1231(b)(3)(B)(ii).

serious crime conclusively *makes* a person a danger to the community. To *refoule* a refugee, therefore, the government need make no other showing. The US courts have deferred to that BIA determination as 'reasonable'.[191] Moreover, because another US statutory provision makes every 'aggravated felony' for which a five year prison sentence was imposed a 'particularly serious crime',[192] and because the 'aggravated felony' definition has grown to include a vast array of crimes,[193] a great number of common or garden variety offenses now render even genuine refugees vulnerable to *refoulement*. This result seems hard to reconcile with the limited Convention language 'particularly serious crime' and 'danger to the community'.

Similarly, Article 1F of the Refugee Convention excludes a person from all the Convention protections (not just *non-refoulement*) if 'there are serious reasons for considering that . . . he has committed a serious non-political crime outside the country of refuge prior to his admission to that country as a refugee'. The UNHCR Handbook interprets this provision to require that 'the nature of the offense' be balanced against 'the degree of persecution feared'.[194] Rejecting the UNHCR interpretation, the BIA has held that no such balancing is required.[195] The UNHCR Handbook, while not a binding authority, is nonetheless a persuasive authority.

Detention

The Refugee Convention recognizes a host of refugee rights beyond *non-refoulement*; these include restrictions on penalizing refugees for irregular entry; restrictions on discrimination based on race, religion or country of origin; freedom of movement; and freedom of religion. Some such rights extend to all refugees, while others are limited to those refugees who are 'lawfully' within the state's territory or to those who are 'staying' there or to those whose presence is still more durable.[196] Space does not permit a full discussion here, but serious issues of US compliance with those provisions have arisen in several contexts.

---

[191] *Matter of Carballe*, 19 I & N Dec. 357 (BIA 1986); see, e.g., *Ahmetovic* v. *INS*, 62 F 3d 48, at 52–53 (2nd Cir. 1995); *Arauz* v. *Rivkind*, 845 F 2d 271 at 275 (11th Cir. 1988).

[192] 8 USC s. 1231(b)(3)(B). [193] 8 USC s. 1101(a)(43).

[194] United Nations High Commissioner for Refugees, *Handbook on Procedures and Criteria for Determining Refugee Status under the 1951 Convention and the 1967 Protocol relating to the Status of Refugees* (Geneva: UNHCR, 1992) (UNHCR Handbook), para.156.

[195] E.g. *Matter of Garcia-Garrocho*, 19 I & N Dec. 423 (BIA 1986).

[196] See, generally, Hathaway, *The Rights of Refugees*.

166   REFUGEES, ASYLUM SEEKERS AND THE RULE OF LAW

One of the more controversial issues has been the USA's policy of detaining pre-formulated categories of asylum seekers during the sometimes lengthy periods in which their applications are pending. Detention of some asylum seekers is discretionary and individualized, based on whether the person is likely to flee or to endanger the public.[197] Detention of certain other asylum seekers is mandatory and categorical. Those who apply for asylum upon arrival at US ports of entry, for example, must be automatically detained unless and until they can establish a 'credible fear of persecution'; frequently they are detained even after such showings have been made. Haitian boat people who escape interdiction and reach US shores are detained while their asylum applications are pending. For a brief time in 2003, 'Operation Liberty Shield' mandated the detention of asylum seekers from any of thirty-four countries that the President designated as harbouring terrorists.[198]

As a policy matter, the detention of asylum seekers has both pros and cons. On the positive side, the government argues that it eliminates the incentive for manifestly unfounded claims and thereby deters asylum abuse. It can also be a way to ensure that the applicant appears for his/her asylum hearing or interview and does not engage in unlawful activity in the interim. Making detention mandatory rather than discretionary might be thought to reduce the fiscal costs to the government by rendering detention hearings unnecessary. Mandatory detention also avoids false negatives – that is, cases in which a fact finder releases an asylum seeker who seemed unlikely to abscond or to threaten public safety, but where the prediction proves wrong. On the other hand, detention is the classic deprivation of liberty, can lead to psychiatric harm for traumatized refugees, can separate detainees from their families, can produce economic hardship for the detainees and their families, and is expensive. In addition, depending on the venue and confinement conditions, detention can prevent the asylum seeker from obtaining counsel, communicating with counsel, and otherwise preparing or assisting in the preparation of his or her case. For all these reasons, the commentary has generally been highly critical of US asylum detention policy.[199]

---

[197] 8 USC s. 1226(a); 8 CFR s. 236.1(c) (8) (2006).

[198] See Legomsky, *Immigration and Refugee Law and Policy*, pp. 845, 1106–9.

[199] For just a small sampling, see Amnesty International, USA, 'Lost in the Labyrinth: Detention of Asylum Seekers', Report AMR51/51/99, September 1999 (unpublished); Bill Frelick, 'US Detention of Asylum Seekers: What's the Problem? What's the Solution?' (2005) 10 *Bender's Immigration Bulletin* 159; Stephen H. Legomsky, 'The Detention of Aliens: Theories, Rules, and Discretion' (1999) 30 *University of Miami*

A separate question which arises is whether the exercise of the powers of detention is compatible with the USA's international legal obligations, particularly those that arise under the Refugee Convention, including Article 31 of the Convention. Article 26 of the Convention reads: 'Each Contracting State shall accord to refugees lawfully within its territory the right to choose their place of residence and to move freely within its territory, subject to any regulations applicable to aliens generally in the same circumstances.' Issues include whether asylum applicants at ports of entry are 'within [the] territory' of the state for purposes of Article 26; and whether one who appears at the frontier is lawfully exercising a right recognized in international law, as well as US law, and is therefore 'lawfully' within the state's territory. Article 31 of the 1951 Convention, also relevant here, prohibits penalties, on account of their illegal entry or presence, on refugees who, coming directly from a territory where their life or freedom was threatened ... enter or are present in their territory without authorization, provided they present themselves without delay to the authorities and show good cause for their illegal entry or presence.

Issues arise as to the meaning of 'penalties', 'coming directly' and 'without delay'. Article 3 requires the Contracting States to 'apply the provisions of this Convention to refugees without discrimination as to race, religion *or country of origin* [emphasis added]'.[200]

Based mainly on Article 31, UNHCR has roundly condemned the detention of asylum seekers in the absence of exceptional circumstances found after individualized determinations (as distinguished from the use of mandatory detention categories).[201] Under the UNHCR

Inter-American Law Review 531; Margaret H. Taylor, 'Symbolic Detention' (1998) 20 *In Defense of the Alien* 153; Peter H. Schuck, 'INS Detention and Removal: A White Paper' (1997) 11 *Georgetown Immigration Law Journal* 667.

[200] Emphasis added. Analogous prohibitions on discrimination are contained in other international human rights conventions to which the USA is a party. See, e.g., International Covenant on Civil and Political Rights, ratified by the USA in 1972, Arts. 2(1), 3, 4(1), 26; International Convention on the Elimination of All Forms of Racial Discrimination, ratified by the USA in 1994, Arts. 1(1), 2, 5. But see *ibid.* Arts. 1(2), 1(3). The USA is not a party to the American Convention on Human Rights, San José, 22 November 1969, in force 18 July 1978, 1144 UNTS 123, but it is bound by the American Declaration of the Rights and Duties of Man, Bogotá, 2 May 1948, OAS Res. 30, Art. 2 (adopted by Ninth Annual Conference of American States).

[201] See UNHCR, *UNHCR Revised Guidelines on Applicable Criteria and Standards Relating to the Detention of Asylum-Seekers* (Geneva: UNHCR 1999), confirming UNHCR Executive Committee, 'ExCom Conclusion 44 (XXXVII)', (1986) *Detention of Refugees and Asylum-Seekers.*

168   REFUGEES, ASYLUM SEEKERS AND THE RULE OF LAW

ExCom Conclusion and subsequent 1999 Guidelines cited below, an asylum seeker may be detained only if detention is 'necessary' to accomplish one of four things – verify the person's identity; determine the elements on which the person's claim is based; respond to the destruction of travel or identity documents or the use of fraudulent documents to mislead the authorities of the state in which the person applies for asylum; and 'to protect national security and public order'. The last objective, like all the others, may be invoked only when the facts pertaining to the particular individual so require; there must be 'evidence to show that the asylum seeker has criminal antecedents and/or affiliations which are likely to pose a risk to public order or national security'.[202] Even then, detention is subject to a number of other conditions.[203]

UNHCR has responded more specifically to the selective detention of Haitians. A 2002 advisory opinion by the UNHCR regional representative reiterated that 'there must be an individualized analysis of the need to detain a particular individual'. Deterrence, it said, 'is an inappropriate goal and insufficient reason for detention'. Finally, the opinion added, '[t]he detention of asylum seekers based on their national origin' is discriminatory and therefore violates Article 3.[204]

These UNHCR authorities suggest that not only the Haitian detention policy, but also Operation Liberty Shield and the detention of those asylum seekers who are subjected to expedited removal, are incompatible with US obligations under the Convention. In both the latter programmes, decisions are categorical rather than individualized and, in the case of Operation Liberty Shield, the other UNHCR objections – deterrence as an insufficient reason to detain and discrimination based on country of origin – both apply as well.

The Attorney General may well have legal arguments in opposition to those advanced by UNHCR but, as noted earlier, he chose instead to dismiss the UNHCR objections on the grounds that the Convention and Protocol are not self-executing.[205] Again, while a non-self-executing treaty cannot be enforced *in a domestic court*, the government offered no comment concerning US treaty obligations on the *international* plane.

---

[202] See UNHCR, *UNHCR Revised Guidelines*, Guideline 3.
[203] *Ibid.*, Guidelines 4–10.   [204] (2002) 79 *Interpreter Releases* 630 at 635, 636.
[205] See *Matter of DJ*, 23 I & N Dec. 572 at 584–585 n. 8 (Attorney General, 2003).

Criminal prosecutions

Similar concerns have arisen over the more recent practice, in some US attorneys' offices, of bringing criminal prosecutions against asylum seekers based on their irregular entry into the USA. The practice first came to light in South Florida, where 'local attorneys report that some asylum seekers are arrested upon arrival at Miami International Airport while others have been charged after months of immigration detention'.[206] From autumn 2003 until April 2004, the US Attorney's Office in Miami obtained 75–80 such federal indictments.[207]

These practices raise serious policy issues. One asylum authority, Eleanor Acer, commented: 'There's longstanding recognition that sometimes refugees are forced to flee from their persecutors with false documents . . . That's why Raoul Wallenberg is seen as a hero, for giving false passports to Jews fleeing the Holocaust.'[208]

Mindful of the practical barriers that genuine refugees face in obtaining documents during times of urgent flight, the drafters of the Refugee Convention felt it important to include the non-penalty provisions of Article 31. That prohibition, however, is subject to several conditions. One is that the refugees have to have come 'directly from a territory where their life or freedom was threatened'. Given the circuitous routes that refugees are often forced to take, this issue is critical. Another question is what will constitute 'good cause for their illegal entry or presence'. Still another is the meaning of 'without delay'. One British court extended Article 31 to individuals who had applied for asylum within a few days after their arrival in the UK.[209]

Admittedly, the line-drawing required by Article 31 is not easy. Suppose, for example, a person who entered on false documents (or who evaded inspection) is apprehended months later and criminally prosecuted for the irregular entry. If the person then applies for asylum, must prosecution cease? If the asylum claim is ultimately denied, may prosecution then resume? The policy questions are as difficult as the legal questions. On the one hand, a liberal interpretation of Article 31 assures that valid claims are not discouraged by the prospect of criminal

---

[206] Tanya Weinberg, 'Asylum Seekers Face US Charges: Prosecutors Say Dozens Entered Country Illegally', *Sun-Sentinel*, 16 April 2003, p. 1B.
[207] Kathleen Sullivan, 'The Year in Detention Law and Policy: Immigration Detention Developments May 2003–April 2004' (2004) 9 *Bender's Immigration Bulletin* 851.
[208] Weinberg, 'Asylum Seekers Face US Charges', p. 1B.
[209] *R. v. Uxbridge Magistrates' Court, ex parte Adimi* [2001] QB 667.

prosecution. On the other hand, the Convention drafters surely did not intend to give everyone charged with illegal entry the power to stave off criminal charges simply by filing an asylum application. At the time of this writing, the issue remains unsettled.

Part three: conclusions

The principle of the rule of law means different things to different people in different contexts. In the present context of US refugee and asylum practices, this chapter has considered one narrow meaning – compliance with duly enacted laws.

As Part two illustrated, there is reason for concern. On one side of the equation are the inevitable abuses of the asylum system by a certain number of non-citizens who seek better lives in the USA. On the other side of the equation are the rule of law issues engendered by government conduct – both the enactment of laws that make justice inaccessible and full fidelity to those laws that do provide access. Both of the latter behaviours are perhaps similarly inevitable in a system that depends on live, flesh-and-blood human beings to make and execute laws, but with the official imprimatur of government and their more sweeping consequences, they are of particular concern. These behaviours relate to the various laws that pose obstacles to asylum seekers' substantive determinations of their claims; the work habits and performances of particular adjudicators; the loss of many of the adjudicators' decisional independence; and the government's respect for international law.

This chapter does not suggest that the deficiencies are collectively more worrisome in the USA than they are in other major receiving states. Indeed, safeguarding the rights and the needs of refugees and asylum seekers without compromising the integrity of the asylum system is a challenge that reverberates throughout the world. The other chapters of this book amply illustrate that challenge. But from a nation that rightly boasts of its immigrant heritage, its formative history as a haven for political and religious refugees, and its early embrace of fundamental constitutional liberties, one expects the highest standards of compliance with the principle of the rule of law.

4

The Australian Story: Asylum Seekers outside the Law

SUSAN KNEEBONE

Australia achieved international notoriety through its bold handling of the *MV Tampa* incident in August 2001[1] and the subsequent creation of the Pacific Plan, which involved extraterritorial processing of asylum seekers. The Tampa incident and its aftermath is possibly the most vivid illustration in this book of the role of law in developing state refugee policy which is contrary to the spirit of the 1951 Convention relating to the Status of Refugees (Refugee Convention)[2] (if not international law).[3] Effectively, this Plan situated the asylum seekers in a legal limbo outside the Australian legal system and prevented them from seeking asylum in Australia.[4] Importantly, the arrangements for the Plan were achieved through the passage of legislation by compliant legislators.[5]

---

[1] This incident arose from the arrival of the Norwegian-registered container ship, the *MV Tampa*, with a cargo of 433 asylum seekers rescued en route from Indonesia in the waters off Australia's Christmas Island in late August 2001. The majority of these 'boat people' were part of the 'Afghan diaspora' of 2001 when an estimated 900,000 people fled Afghanistan: Farah Farouque and Darren Gray with *The Guardian*, 'The Afghan diaspora', *The Age*, 30 August 2001, p. 2.

[2] Convention relating to the Status of Refugees, Geneva, 28 July 1951, in force 22 April 1954, 1989 UNTS 137.

[3] The legality of the treatment of the asylum seekers is discussed by Tara Magner, 'A Less Than "Pacific" Solution for Asylum Seekers in Australia' (2004) 16 *International Journal of Refugee Law* 53; Chantal Marie-Jeanne Bostock, 'The International Legal Obligations Owed to the Asylum Seekers on the MV Tampa' (2002) 14 *International Journal of Refugee Law* 279. See also Susan Kneebone, 'The Legal and Ethical Implications of Extra-territorial Processing of Asylum Seekers: the "Safe Third Country" Concept' in Jane McAdam (ed.), *Forced Migration, Human Rights and Security* (Oxford: Hart Publishing, 2008), Chapter 5.

[4] See *Ruddock v. Vadarlis* (2001) 110 FCR 491 (*Vadarlis*) reversing *Victorian Council for Civil Liberties Incorporated v. Minister for Immigration* (North J) (2001) 110 FCR 452.

[5] On 26 September 2001 six Acts were passed with bipartisan support including the Migration Amendment (Excision from Migration Zone) Act 2001; Border Protection (Validation and Enforcement Powers) Act 2001 and the Migration Amendment

172   REFUGEES, ASYLUM SEEKERS AND THE RULE OF LAW

This included a law excising parts of Australian territory from the 'migration zone' as defined in the Migration Act 1958 (Cth) (Migration Act).[6] Through the Pacific Plan, Australia successfully denied the asylum seekers access to the national legal system and outsourced its responsibilities under the Refugee Convention.[7] It will be shown in this chapter that the Pacific Plan was the natural outgrowth of restrictive and deterrent policies to refugees which had developed over the previous decade and which demonstrated the power of the executive to drive a legislative agenda to keep asylum seekers apart from the Australian community.

The first part of this chapter describes the history and development of legal responses to refugees and asylum seekers in Australia (including the legislative framework and the constitutional basis of this jurisdiction). It will describe the prodigious use of restrictive legislation by the Australian government to control the tribunals and courts on refugee law issues, including attempts to oust judicial review. Additionally, it describes the strategic use of litigation by the government to challenge perceived 'judicial activism' in refugee status determination.

The second part of the chapter highlights two particular issues to illustrate the attempts to keep asylum seekers outside the legal system. The first is the creation and scope of the mandatory detention system; the second is the incorporation of the Refugee Convention and human rights standards into Australian law. Under that latter heading, the following issues are discussed:

- the scope of the *non-refoulement* obligation in Australian law and interpretation of Article 1E of the Refugee Convention;

(Excision from Migration Zone) (Consequential Provisions) Act 2001. The amendments excised Christmas Island, Ashmore Reef, the Cocos (Keeling) Islands, and offshore sea and resource installations in Australian territory from the 'migration zone' under the Migration Act 1958 (Cth).

[6] The Migration Amendment (Excision from Migration Zone) Act 2001 granted the power to excise further territories through the passing of regulations (delegated legislation). E.g. Migration Amendment Regulations 2002 (No. 4) were subsequently disallowed by the Senate on 19 June 2002; Migration Amendment Regulations 2003 (No. 8) and Statutory Rule 2003 No. 283 disallowed by the Senate on 24 November 2003. This was done in July 2005, when islands off the coasts of the Northern Territory, Western Australia and Queensland were excised: Migration Amendment Regulations 2005 (No. 6) SLI 171. See Moira Coombs, 'Excising Australia: Are we really shrinking?', Research note 5 2005–6, 31 August 2005, www.aph.gov.au/Library/Pubs/RN/2005-06/06rn05.htm (accessed 14 March 2008).

[7] Susan Kneebone, 'The Pacific Plan: The Provision of "Effective Protection"?' (2006) 18 *International Journal of Refugee Law* 696.

THE AUSTRALIAN STORY 173

- interpretation of the cessation clause (Art. 1C(5) of the Refugee Convention) in the context of the temporary protection visa (TPV) regime.

Finally, the third part of the chapter contains a discussion of interpretation of the refugee definition in Article 1A(2) of the Refugee Convention and legislative intervention on its scope. In this context, a comparison is drawn with the position in New Zealand to highlight the importance of interpreting the Refugee Convention as an instrument of human rights protection.

Significantly, of all the jurisdictions surveyed in this book, Australia alone does not have a Bill of Rights or other overriding code of human rights which applies nationally. As the discussion in this chapter illustrates, there are serious concerns about the 'integrity' of its dualist legal system; that is, about the integration of international law norms into the national legal system.

Part one: development of national legal responses to refugees and asylum seekers

In the Australian context there are several features which are particularly important to a discussion of the rights of refugees and asylum seekers in the legal system. First, the Refugee Convention is indirectly incorporated into general migration legislation (the Migration Act), which gives the Minister for Immigration a number of important personal discretionary powers. Secondly, there is a debate (discussed in Part two) about the extent to which such legislation incorporates the provisions of the Refugee Convention. In Australia, obligations arising under international law are perceived as state obligations at the international level rather than as giving rise to individual rights. These features are rooted in the legal history of refugees in Australia.

The 1951 Refugee Convention, which was negotiated in the aftermath of World War II, was intended to deal with the European problem of 1.25 million postwar refugees. However, Australia readily signed up to and actively supported the drafting of the Convention.[8] Although Australia

---

[8] Mary Crock, 'The Refugees Convention at 50: Mid-life Crisis or Terminal Inadequacy? An Australian Perspective', in Susan Kneebone (ed.), *The Refugees Convention 50 Years On: Globalisation and International Law* (Aldershot, UK: Ashgate, 2003), Chapter 3, p. 47. Australia acceded to the Refugee Convention in 1954 and to the Protocol relating to the Status of Refugees, New York, 31 January 1967, in force 4 October 1967, 19 UNTS 6223, 6257 in 1973.

174   REFUGEES, ASYLUM SEEKERS AND THE RULE OF LAW

had resisted European immigration in the period leading up to World War II,[9] preferring instead to focus on creating a nation in the British mould, it received many displaced persons or refugees from Europe in this post-war period.

This very brief summary of Australia's involvement with the post-World War II refugee crisis contains two important themes which have dominated Australia's policy response to refugees. First, largely because of its geographical position, Australia has always been able to manage the inflow of immigrants and refugees to its shores to a much greater extent than other countries which share land borders. This may be a factor in the development of a strong 'culture of control'[10] in relation to 'outsiders'. Secondly, this ability to control inflows has manifested itself in a preference for selecting immigrants and refugees from offshore. The notion that a person might chose to become a member of the Australian community without having been selected by the Australian Government is not tolerated. In Australia, as in the USA,[11] there is an enormous emphasis on 'border control' as a self-evident notion.

Refugees as constitutional 'aliens'

The fact that refugees and asylum seekers were characterized under the Australian legal system as constitutional 'aliens' from an early date is significant. The Constitution of the Commonwealth of Australia ('Constitution') includes two directly relevant heads of power in s. 51 – the 'immigration and emigration' ('migration') power and the 'naturalization and aliens' ('aliens') power.[12] In some early cases, the courts on occasion found that persons who had been 'absorbed' into the community were no longer 'migrants' and could not be removed from Australia under the 'migration' power.[13] The courts then turned to the 'aliens' power to support such decisions.

---

[9] Malcolm Langfield, *More People Imperative: Immigration to Australia 1901–1939* (Canberra: National Archives of Australia, 1999), p. 85.

[10] Katherine Cronin, 'A Culture of Control: an Overview of Immigration Policy Making', in James Jupp and Marie Kabala (eds.), *The Politics of Australian Immigration* (Canberra: AGPS, 1993), Chapter 5.

[11] See Stephen H. Legomsky, 'Refugees, Asylum and the Rule of Law in the USA', Chapter 3 in this volume.

[12] Constitution, s. 51(xix) ('naturalization and aliens'); and (xxvii) ('immigration and emigration').

[13] E.g. *Potter v. Minahan* (1908) 7 CLR 277; *Ex parte Walsh and Johnson ex p Yates* (1925) 37 CLR 36.

THE AUSTRALIAN STORY 175

The key decision was *Koon Wing Lau* v. *Calwell*,[14] in which the validity and application of the War Time Refugees Removal Act 1949 (Cth) was in issue. The question in that case was whether five 'persons of Chinese race who entered Australia during World War II, who were alleged to be war-time refugees' could be removed at the conclusion of the war. The legislation was held to be valid under both the defence[15] and aliens powers, although some members of the court also relied upon the migration power. There was clear unease among a majority of the judges with the notion that absorbed persons could put themselves outside the reach of the constitutional powers. Chief Justice Latham said:

> No person simply by his own act can make himself a member of the community if the community refuses to have him as a member. The Australian community speaks in respect of immigration through the Commonwealth Parliament.[16]

That view, which reflects strong support for the principle of parliamentary sovereignty,[17] has been echoed in recent times. Importantly, this decision was applied in the 1992 decision *Lim* v. *Minister for Immigration*[18] discussed in Part two, when the High Court upheld the validity of the mandatory detention regime introduced by the Australian government at that time.

When the Migration Act was rewritten in 1989, the Preamble stated clearly that it is an Act 'relating to the entry into, and presence in Australia of aliens, and the departure from Australia of aliens and certain other persons'.

In the next section the development of another 'border control' measure which is central to understanding the status of asylum seekers and refugees in the Australian legal system is explained. This is the Humanitarian Program, which distinguishes 'offshore' refugees and 'onshore' asylum seekers.

Development of Australian refugee policy: offshore and onshore refugees

The Humanitarian Program grew directly out of Australia's response to the Indo-China refugee crisis and its experience with the Comprehensive

---

[14] (1949) 80 CLR 533.
[15] Section 51(vi) of the Constitution. *Ibid.*, Latham CJ and Tiernan J.   [16] *Ibid.* at 561.
[17] See discussion in Chapter 1 in this volume at pp. 57–64.
[18] (1992) 176 CLR 1. The Minister's title changes frequently. 'Minister for Immigration' variously covers Minister for Immigration and Citizenship, Minister for Immigration and Multicultural and Indigenous Affairs and Minister for Immigration, Local Government and Ethnic Affairs.

176   REFUGEES, ASYLUM SEEKERS AND THE RULE OF LAW

Plan of Action (CPA)[19] from the mid-1970s to the late 1980s. The 'first wave' of 'boat people' in the late 1970s included asylum seekers from Vietnam.[20] The CPA, designed to stem the flow of these people, had an important role in the development of Australian policy to spontaneous refugee arrivals. It reinforced the trend to selective resettlement, and the distinction between onshore asylum seekers and offshore refugees which persists in Australian refugee policy today.

The next significant wave of 'boat people' coincided with the end of the Cold War and the 1989 Tiananmen Square incident. In reaction to these world events and the consequent leap in onshore claims for asylum in Australia,[21] the Australian Government commenced a programme of reform, of which the 1992 mandatory detention regime was part. The Migration Act was rewritten to provide a system of entry by visas and a distinction between 'citizens' and 'non-citizens' (and, arising from that, between 'lawful' and 'unlawful' non-citizens). Under this legislation, spontaneous asylum seekers who arrive without visas are 'unlawful non-citizens' (and thus subject to mandatory detention), but asylum seekers who arrive with a visa, such as a tourist or student visa, and who subsequently claim asylum, are 'lawful non-citizens'.

Officially recognized in 1996, the Humanitarian Program is one part of Australia's whole Migration Program, which has increased in size from 74,000 to 158,000 since 1996.[22] Until 2003 the number of available places in the Humanitarian Program was capped at 12,000, with 10,000 places notionally allocated for offshore resettlement and 2,000 for onshore asylum seekers.[23] The offshore programme was directed at two categories of persons:

---

[19] International Conference on Indo-Chinese Refugees, Declaration and Comprehensive Plan of Action, Geneva, 13 June 1989, UN Doc. A/CONF. 148/2.

[20] Robert Manne and David Corlett, 'Sending Them Home: Refugees and the New Politics of Indifference' (2004) 13 *Quarterly Essay* 1.

[21] The numbers peaked at 16,248 in 1990–91. 77 per cent were from the People's Republic of China: Department of Immigration and Citizenship, *Fact Sheet 61: Seeking Asylum within Australia* (Canberra: Department of Immigration and Citizenship, 2007).

[22] Jewel Topsfield, 'Refugee Program to Expand by 500', Canberra, 13 May 2008, www.theage.com.au/articles/2008/05/12/1210444339465.html (accessed 14 May 2008). Australia admitted 157,070 migrants in the 2005–6 financial year, a 20 per cent increase on the previous year: Department of Immigration and Citizenship, *Population Flows: Immigration Aspects 2005–06 Edition* (Canberra: Department of Immigration and Citizenship, 2007), www.immi.gov.au/media/publications/statistics/popflows2005–6/index.htm (accessed 12 March 2008).

[23] US Committee for Refugees and Immigrants, 'Country Updates: Australia', *World Refugee Survey*, 2001, www.refugees.org (accessed 6 May 2008). In May 2008 the new

THE AUSTRALIAN STORY 177

- The Refugee component, for those who meet the Refugee Convention definition of a 'refugee';
- The Special Humanitarian (SHP) component, for persons subject to 'substantial discrimination' or human rights abuse.

In most years until the late 1990s, when the outpouring of asylum seekers from Afghanistan 'tested the waters', the offshore programme was roughly shared equally between these two components, and any unmet places were rolled over. In some years (in fact most) the targets were not met. It is important to note that, under this resettlement programme, approximately 50 per cent were refugees within the meaning of the Refugee Convention. Also importantly, the onshore and offshore components of the programme were linked, meaning that the number of places for 'offshore' applicants would be determined by the number of people who had successfully claimed asylum 'onshore'. Because of this, spontaneous asylum seekers have long been maligned in official discourse as 'queue jumpers', and as less deserving than those who are resettled under the offshore programme (only about half of whom are 'refugees').

In the late 1990s, when the CPA seemed to have done its work in stemming the flow of Indo-Chinese arrivals, the crises in the Middle East produced a new challenge. There was a dramatic escalation in the number of boat arrivals in the eighteen-month period leading up to early 2001. The Humanitarian Program was under strain in this period, as the number of onshore asylum seekers far exceeded the 'quota' of 2,000 places. For example, in the year 2001, 3,891 persons were granted refugee status onshore.[24]

The TPV regime, involving the grant of three-year visas, was introduced in 1999.[25] From that point onwards, only 'lawful non-citizens' could acquire a permanent protection visa. The TPV conferred limited rights.[26] For example, it denied the right to family reunion. But, unsurprisingly, it did not have a deterrent effect. Instead whole families

government announced that the Humanitarian Program would be increased by 500 to 13,500 places. See Jewel Topsfield, 'Refugee Program to Expand by 500', Canberra, 13 May 2008, www.theage.com.au/articles/2008/05/12/1210444339465.html (accessed 14 May 2008). The government also announced that it would focus on taking people from Iraq and Karen refugees from Burma (Myanmar).

[24] Department of Immigration and Multicultural and Indigenous Affairs, *Immigration, Population and Citizenship Digest* (Canberra: Department of Immigration and Multicultural and Indigenous Affairs, 2003), p. 32.

[25] See discussion at pp. 210–12 in this chapter.

[26] Kneebone, 'The Pacific Plan' at 719–720.

178   REFUGEES, ASYLUM SEEKERS AND THE RULE OF LAW

started moving from the Middle East. Many of these were intercepted under the Pacific Plan.

Under the Pacific Plan, two new categories of visas which built on the TPV scheme were created for 'secondary movers'. These 'offshore entry persons' were processed under the SHP component of the Humanitarian Program rather than as refugees.[27] At this time, the total number for the programme was increased from 12,000 to 13,000, but the onshore component disappeared, having been rolled into the SHP component.[28] The asylum seekers processed under the Pacific Plan were only eligible for temporary protection visas in accordance with the policy of deterring 'boat people' from coming to Australia.

In summary, there were three deterrent policies introduced in the period leading up to 2001 which were specifically directed at asylum seekers. They were the mandatory detention policy, the linking of the onshore and the offshore 'quotas' under the Humanitarian Program, and the introduction of the TPV regime. Importantly, all three policies were the prelude to the Pacific Plan introduced in 2001 which, as mentioned above, effectively situated asylum seekers in a legal limbo.

Reform of the legal system for refugee status determination: the battle lines are drawn

While the overall policy in relation to refugees was developing in response to external events, onshore the legal system was also being adjusted. During the 1990s, the legal system was the site of many battles as the executive attempted to control its use by refugees and their advocates. There were two significant and interlinked developments which shaped the executive response. The first flowed from the rewriting of the Migration Act in 1989. The second was the High Court decision in *Chan Yee Kin* v. *Minister for Immigration (Chan Yee Kin)*.[29]

The amendments to the Migration Act in 1989 which replaced the old entry permits with a system of control of entry into Australia by visa also gave the Minister for Immigration a substantial amount of personal discretionary powers. Although in practice the ministerial powers are exercised by a delegate, s. 65 of the Act gives discretion to the Minister

---

[27] *Ibid.* at 718–719.
[28] Department of Immigration and Citizenship, *Fact Sheet 60: Australia's Refugee and Humanitarian Program* (Canberra: Department of Immigration and Citizenship, 2007). 7,000 places are allocated for SHP and 6,000 for the Refugee component.
[29] (1989) 169 CLR 379.

THE AUSTRALIAN STORY   179

to be 'satisfied' that a visa should be granted.[30] Thus, while the Liberal–
National Coalition government (*Coalition*) was in power between 1996
and 2007, the battle was personalized, with the Minister at the forefront
of the line drawn between the tribunals and courts on the one hand and
the government on the other.[31] The election of the Rudd Labor Government in late 2007, and the appointment of a new Minister for
Immigration appears to have defused this situation, as the new Minister,
Senator Chris Evans, has signalled his intention to let the courts and
tribunals perform their role without intervention.[32] Thus, what follows
is an important historical account of the role of law in this context.

To understand the tensions that arose within the legal system, it is
necessary to explain the decision-making structures. The new visa system introduced a special 'protection visa' for onshore refugee applicants. In practice such decisions were made in the first instance by the
Minister's delegate. From 1993, the review of adverse decisions could be
sought in the Refugee Review Tribunal (RRT). In theory the RRT is an
independent merits review body which sits in the executive arm of
government.[33] The next level of challenge is by way of judicial review
through the federal court hierarchy.[34] This is a more limited form of
review than merits review, as explained in Chapter 1. The first battle was
between the Minister and the courts over the role of the courts on
judicial review as a result of the *Chan Yee Kin* decision, the first decision
of the High Court on the 'refugee' definition in Article 1A(2) of the
Refugee Convention.

Chan Yee Kin came before the High Court as an application for
judicial review on the sole ground of unreasonableness, and it succeeded. That is, the focus of the decision was upon the reasons that were

---

[30] Migration Act 1958, s. 65(1)(a)(ii) read with s. 65(1)(b). It is read with Schedule 2,
clause 866 of the Regulations to the Act which requires the Minister for Immigration to
be 'satisfied' that the applicant is a person to whom Australia owes protection obligations under the Refugee Convention. This refers to the health and character of an
applicant.

[31] See John McMillan, '*Federal Court v Minister for Immigration*' (1999) 22 *Australian
Institute of Adminstrative Law Forum* 1.

[32] Jewel Topsfield, 'Bigger Say for Courts on Migrants: Ministerial Rulings to be Scaled
Back', *The Age*, 1 March 2008, p. 11.

[33] See Migration Reform Act 1992 (Cth), Part 4A.

[34] During most of the period under discussion, the hierarchy was constituted by the
Federal Court (single judge), Full Court of the Federal Court with the High Court at the
apex. Importantly the High Court's jurisdiction is protected by the Constitution, as
explained below.

180 REFUGEES, ASYLUM SEEKERS AND THE RULE OF LAW

given by the Minister of Immigration's delegate for refusing Mr Chan's application when he said that Mr Chan had not suffered 'persecution' at the hands of the Chinese authorities.[35] Thus the formulation of the 'real chance' of persecution test for which *Chan Yee Kin* is notable, was a secondary focus of the decision. But it was considered to be a liberal interpretation of the Refugee Convention definition.[36] The government was alarmed by the breadth of the decision. In 1992 an amendment to the Migration Act included a restriction in Part 8 of the Act[37] on rights of judicial review from the RRT to the Federal Court (from which appeals lie to the High Court).[38] Importantly, those restrictions, which initially excluded certain grounds of review, such as natural justice and reasonableness, were introduced as a direct response to *Chan Yee Kin*.

The next battle line that appeared was between the Minister and the RRT. The role of the RRT since its inception has been controversial.[39] Although the legislation appeared to confer a merits review function upon the tribunal in terms that were indistinguishable from other tribunals,[40] it soon became clear that the government regarded the RRT differently. In the early days of its operation, the then Minister for Immigration made it apparent that he was unhappy with the way that the tribunal was operating. The Minister chastised the RRT (and the courts) saying:

> The tribunals and courts may well see their role to defend the rights of individual applicants and I do not dispute that tribunals and courts do need to have regard to the rights of individual applicants. However . . . [t]he legislation not only establishes those rights but balances them against budgetary and other wider community interests.[41]

---

[35] Note that at the time of this decision the status of a refugee was referred to in the then s. 6A of the Migration Act – see discussion in the text below at pp. 198–202.
[36] See Part Three below.   [37] Part 8 came into effect on 1 September 1994.
[38] The High Court's judicial review jurisdiction is entrenched by s. 75(v) of the Constitution. This is an important avenue for the protection of rights as the discussion in the text which follows demonstrates.
[39] Susan Kneebone, 'The Refugee Review Tribunal and the Assessment of Credibility: An Inquisitorial Role?' (1998) 5 *Australian Journal of Administrative Law* 78; Susan Kneebone, 'Is the Australian Refugee Review Tribunal "Institutionally" Biased?' in François Crépeau et al. (eds.), *Forced Migration and Global Processes: A view from Forced Migration Studies* (Lanham, MD: Lexington Books, 2006), Chapter 10.
[40] Section 415 of the Migration Act describes the RRT's function to 'exercise all the powers and discretions that are conferred by this Act on the person who made the decision'.
[41] Phillip Ruddock, Minister for Immigration, 'Speech to the 1997 National Administrative Law Forum', Canberra, 1 May 1997; Phillip Ruddock, Minister for Immigration, 'Speech

THE AUSTRALIAN STORY   181

As the RRT battled with the Minister over its role,[42] and the Minister
tried to reign in the courts through Part 8 of the Act, refugees and their
advocates opened up other fronts in the courts to challenge RRT
decisions. At this stage the battle lines were drawn around provisions of
the Migration Act which describe the RRT's functions in very technical
terms.[43] Two provisions in particular were utilized by refugees and their
advocates to attempt to avoid the judicial review restrictions in Part 8
of the Act. For example, s. 420(2) of the Act, a key provision which
describes the RRT's role, states that the Tribunal:

(a) is not bound by technicalities, legal forms or rules of evidence;
(b) must act according to substantial justice and the merits of the case.

Another relevant provision is s. 430 of the Act, which imposes an
obligation to give reasons for decisions in similar terms to other
statutory provisions which apply to administrative decision makers.

Each of these sections generated an enormous amount of litigation as
refugee advocates attempted to use them to avoid the restrictions in Part
8 in their effort to seek review of adverse RRT decisions, and the government in turn appealed against decisions which were not favourable
to its interpretation of the Act. But the battlefield became more
treacherous as a result of tensions within the court hierarchy. In relation
to each provision, conflicting lines of Federal Court decisions resulted,
which were eventually settled on appeal to the High Court. The government was very concerned about the amount of litigation generated in
the Federal Court from RRT decisions, which in 1998 amounted to
around 68 per cent of that court's work.[44]

The High Court decisions over this period display a tendency to defer
to the Minister's discretion and to a strict interpretation of the powers
in the Migration Act. That conclusion is supported by the discussion of

---

to Faculty of Law, University of Sydney', Continuing Legal Education Conference,
Sydney, 6 June 1997.

[42] A consequence of this was an increase in the number of challenges of RRT decisions.
[43] Susan Kneebone, 'Believable Tales: Proving a Well-Founded Fear of Persecution' (2004)
25 *Migration Action* 4.
[44] John McMillan, '*Federal Court* v *Minister for Immigration*' at 19, n. 1 citing ALRC,
'Review of the Federal Civil Justice System, Discussion Paper 62', 1999, 271. Note an
important contrast with the New Zealand situation, where jurisprudence is largely made
at the tribunal level – the New Zealand Refugee Status Appeals Authority (*NZRSAA*).
Judicial review applications challenging NZRSAA decisions have been made in a very
small number of cases – see www.refugee.org.nz/Stats/stats.htm#Table_60 (accessed 29
April 2008).

182   REFUGEES, ASYLUM SEEKERS AND THE RULE OF LAW

the effect of s. 65 of the Migration Act (which granted personal discretion to the Minister on visa applications) in *Minister for Immigration* v. *Eshetu* (*Eshetu*).[45] The legal issue in this case was the meaning of the words 'substantial justice' in s. 420 of the Migration Act. In a number of cases prior to this decision, the Federal Court had read s. 420 as incorporating the natural justice principle, which was one of the grounds excluded on review by the original Part 8 of the Migration Act. The High Court decision in *Eshetu* makes it clear that the RRT's merits function is modified by its legislative context, which includes s. 65. The majority in that case endorsed the conclusion that in Australia the administrative review of refugee cases is ultimately the responsibility of the Minister. This view, which is based on the terms of the Migration Act, permeates recent High Court jurisprudence, as the discussion in Part two of this chapter illustrates.

Similarly, in relation to s. 430, the High Court in *Minister for Immigration* v. *Yusuf* [46] endorsed a very narrow and technical reading of the effect of that provision. As one commentator has said:

> By and large, the High Court struck down the creative efforts of the Federal Court, forcing the judges to find new grounds to critique the decisions being made.[47]

The Minister perceived the Federal Court as too interventionist in not adhering to the spirit of Part 8 of the Act. In 1997,[48] and again in 1998,[49] the government attempted to introduce legislation to tighten Part 8 of the Act. On both occasions, after Senate Committee[50] inquiries which led to views divided upon party lines, and much debate, the Bills were defeated. In 2000 a committee conducting a further enquiry into the operation of Australia's refugee determination process referred to the fact that:

> The weight of evidence and submissions to the Inquiry argued in favour of the need to maintain a judicial review system that has the power to pass judgment on refugee matters under the rule of law.[51]

---

[45] (1999) 162 ALR 577.   [46] (2001) 206 CLR 323.

[47] Crock, 'The Refugees Convention at 50' in Kneebone (ed.), *The Refugees Convention 50 Years On*, p. 75.

[48] Migration Legislation Amendment Bill (No. 5) 1997.

[49] Migration Legislation Amendment (Judicial Review) Bill 1998. Senate Legal and Constitutional Legislation Committee Inquiry into the Migration Legislation Amendment (Judicial Review) Bill 1998, April 1999.

[50] Note that during these periods the Senate was not controlled by the government.

[51] Senate Legal and Constitutional References Committee, *A Sanctuary Under Review: An Examination of Australia's Refugee and Humanitarian Processes* (June 2000), para. 6.78.

THE AUSTRALIAN STORY   183

It noted:

> However, according to [the Department of Immigration], judicial over-sight involving litigation is a resource-intensive review process.[52]

In light of this debate, the committee recommended improvements to the RRT and further research on 'moving to a wholly judicial determination process'. However, this committee did not represent the government's view. Opportunely, the Tampa episode described at the outset of this chapter occurred in August 2001. In lieu of reform and further research, the government secured the passage of the Migration Legislation Amendment (Judicial Review) Bill on 26 September 2001.[53] This legislation repealed Part 8 and replaced it with a broad privative or ouster clause in relation to RRT decisions.

The legislation was passed in the expectation that its constitutionality would be challenged. The next important development was the decision of the High Court in February 2003 in *S157/2002* v. *Commonwealth* (*S157/2002*),[54] which settled the controversy which had raged in the Federal Court since October 2001 over the validity and interpretation of the new privative clause which attempted to oust (or remove) the High Court's judicial review jurisdiction. In *S157/2002*, the High Court determined that the clause was valid, and that it should be interpreted according to ordinary notions of 'jurisdictional error'.[55] In particular, the High Court said that breach of natural justice amounted to jurisdictional error.[56] The way in which the High Court interpreted the privative clause (and the way in which it has been applied in later cases) effectively rendered it useless at preventing the majority of judicial review claims. As a leading Australian administrative law commentator has noted:

> The government appears now to have conceded that the privative clause has failed abjectly as a means of limiting the grounds, and thereby the volume, of judicial review of migration decisions.[57]

---

[52] *Ibid.*   [53] This was one of the six pieces of legislation referred to in note 5 above.
[54] (2003) 211 CLR 476.
[55] The government responded with the Migration Amendment (Judicial Review) Bill 2004 which was defeated in the Senate after referral to the Senate Legal and Constitutional Committee. The Bill sought to include decisions infected by jurisdictional error within the definition of 'privative clause decision'. Subject to changes to provisions in the Bill on time limits, the Committee recommended that the Bill proceed. Senate Legal and Constitutional Affairs Committee, *Inquiry into the Provisions of the Migration Amendment (Judicial Review) Bill 2004*, 17 June 2004.
[56] *S157/2002* v. *Commonwealth* (2003) 211 CLR 476 at 508.
[57] Caron Beaton-Wells, 'Judicial Review of Migration Decisions: Life after S157' (2005) 33 *Federal Law Review* 142 at 173. See also note 61 below.

184　REFUGEES, ASYLUM SEEKERS AND THE RULE OF LAW

The High Court had already made it clear in *Re Minister for Immigration; Ex parte Miah* (*Miah*)[58] that procedural codes contained in the Migration Act did not exclude the rules of natural justice, which at that time was the basis of most challenges to RRT decisions. Predictably, the government responded to Miah with the Migration Legislation Amendment (Procedural Fairness) Act 2002, which in turn led to numerous judicial challenges.[59]

S157/2002 and *Miah* demonstrated the willingness of the High Court to protect procedural rights and to interpret legal doctrine to protect its constitutionally entrenched jurisdiction. The High Court pitted itself in these battles against the executive and parliament. But on other issues concerning the scope of the Minister's powers under the Migration Act the court has been highly deferential. As noted in Parts two and three, the High Court's reasoning on rights issues is somewhat sparse, in contrast, for example, with the situation in New Zealand. This tendency to protect 'form' (including its own jurisdiction) rather than substance (or rights) has been a feature of the High Court's reasoning in the refugee context over the last decade. Curiously, however, the government perceived the courts to be too interventionist and legislated to codify the Refugee Convention definition by enacting s. 91R of the Migration Act,[60] as described in Part three.

Following *S157/2002*, the number of migration matters (which in reality meant refugee matters) being heard in the Federal Court did not decline in the 2002–3 period,[61] nor in 2004.[62] The government's response this time was to move away from a direct attack on legal doctrines to indirect measures to reduce 'unmeritorious litigation'. The Migration Litigation Reform Act 2005 enhanced the role of the Federal Magistrates Court (FMC) created in 2000. As a result of this legislation, the FMC has

---

[58] (2001) 206 CLR 57.

[59] These challenges culminated in the Migration Amendment (Review Provisions) Act 2006. See Caron Beaton-Wells, 'Disclosure of Adverse Information to Applicants under the Migration Act 1958' (2004) 11 *Australian Journal of Administrative Law* 61. Beaton-Wells, 'Judicial Review of Migration Decisions' at 141.

[60] Migration Legislation Amendment Act 2001 (No 6).

[61] Ron Fraser, 'Developments in Administrative Law' (2004) 40 *Australian Institute of Administrative Law Forum* 1 at 5, citing Attorney-General, 'Media Release', 27 October 2003.

[62] Fraser, 'Developments in Administrative Law' at 8, citing Attorney-General, 'Media Release', 22 January 2004.

THE AUSTRALIAN STORY   185

become the 'gateway' to the Federal Court.[63] This legislation imposed strict time limits and gave the FMC power to summarily dispose of proceedings where it is satisfied that there are no reasonable prospects of success.[64] The legislation also prohibits persons, including lawyers and migration agents,[65] from encouraging 'unmeritorious migration litigation', providing for costs orders against such persons in certain cases.

The developments described demonstrate the willingness of the former government to legislate to overturn the effects of decisions which did not conform to its policies of border control and to ignore the findings of committees and inquiries which were designed to reflect the democratic process. The very robust way in which the government used its legislative powers to achieve its policy objectives in this context raises the issue of whether, overall, this power has been used responsibly, or as it is often suggested, as a measure of populism.[66] In essence, in implementing its objectives, the government attempted to keep asylum seekers and their advocates outside the legal system, apart from the community, and away from the public eye.

Part two: asylum seekers outside the rule of law

Detention of 'aliens': Lim and the consequences of the mandatory detention policy

Whereas, in the battles described above, the government demonstrated its willingness to single out asylum seekers (and their advisors) for 'exclusive' and discriminatory measures within the legal system, the discussion in this section shows how the status of asylum seekers as 'aliens' under the Australian Constitution has meant that they can be excluded altogether from access to the legal system. The importance of

---

[63] Federal Court of Australia, *Annual Report 2005–2006* (Canberra: Federal Court of Australia, 2006), p. 19. Under this legislation the FMC was conferred the original jurisdiction of the High Court.

[64] The Act also imposed uniform time limits for applications for review and limited the ability of the courts to grant extensions of time. This had been attempted, unsuccessfully, in the Migration Amendment (Judicial Review) Bill 2004.

[65] Another element of the assault on the rule of law in this context is the marginalization of the role of lawyers through the Migration Agents scheme: *Cunliffe v. Minister for Immigration* (1994) 182 CLR 272. See also Migration Legislation Amendment Bill (No. 2) 1998.

[66] Adrienne Millbank, *The Detention of Boat People* (2000–1) 8 *Current Issues Brief*, www.aph.gov.au/Library/pubs/CIB/2000–01/01cib08.htm (accessed 10 March 2008) concludes with a reference to the right-wing One Nation's electoral success.

the discussion of mandatory detention which follows is that it demonstrates, first, a willingness by the executive to use legislation to achieve policy objectives which conflict with human rights and, secondly, the pattern of legislative responses to unwelcome judicial decisions which was described above. Importantly, mandatory detention is an issue which has increasingly galvanized sections of the community into action in support of refugee rights. The response to mandatory detention demonstrates the transformation of the community's perspective on the rights of asylum seekers and refugees.

The action in *Lim* v. *Minister for Immigration* (*Lim*)[67] was a class action by thirty-six Cambodians who had fled Cambodia and arrived in Australia in 1989 or 1990 during the operation of the CPA.[68] In 1989 the Migration Act was amended to provide a discretionary power for detention of persons arriving by boat suspected of not holding an entry permit. However, in practice, many Cambodian asylum seekers were detained for several years after their vessels had been burnt. The detention system was attended by long delays and many unsuccessful asylum seekers were deported. Meanwhile, a number of Chinese students were granted permanent residence visas in June 1990.[69] At this point, concerns were raised about using deportation as a solution for unsuccessful asylum seekers, due to the risk of *refoulement*.

The plaintiffs in *Lim* had been detained for two years following the rejection of their claims for asylum. They had then successfully sought judicial review and their applications for asylum had been remitted to the Minister. At the same time, they also sought orders that they be released from custody. Two days before the release applications were to be heard, the government brought in legislation to legalize their detention. This 1992 legislation made the detention scheme mandatory rather than discretionary. The legislation, the Migration Reform Act 1992, was challenged on the basis that it usurped the role of the judiciary.[70] The argument was upheld, in part, in the High Court in relation to s. 54R, which attempted to prevent courts from ordering the release of a

---

[67] (1992) 176 CLR 1.

[68] Anthony North and Peace Decle, 'Courts and Immigration Detention: Once a Jolly Swagman etc' (2002) 10 *Australian Journal of Administrative Law* 5.

[69] This was following the Tiananmen Square massacre in the People's Republic of China on 4 May 1989. Note that this was also the context for the *Chan Yee Kin* decision discussed above.

[70] That is, it was argued that it usurped the power of the High Court to grant remedies under Chapter III of the Constitution.

THE AUSTRALIAN STORY 187

'designated person'. The High Court accepted that authority to detain aliens in custody for the purpose of processing, expulsion or deportation was a valid exercise of the 'aliens' power.[71]

It was significant that the asylum seekers were characterized as constitutional 'aliens'. In their joint judgment, Justices Brennan, Deane and Dawson said that their vulnerability to exclusion and deportation came from that 'alien' status.[72] Importantly, the judges applied the *Koon Wing Lau* decision (referred to above) and older authority,[73] in which the courts had referred to both constitutional and common law powers as the basis of the authority to exclude 'strangers'. By analogy, the power to detain for the purpose of deportation was also described as an incident of executive power.[74]

But limits were also set on the exercise of this power. It was described as a purposive power for a system of non-punitive administrative detention, limited to what is 'reasonably necessary'.[75] Relevantly, various judges in *Lim* referred to the large numbers of persons in detention as an apparent justification for the system.

The deterrent rationale of the legislation, which was upheld by the High Court on constitutional grounds, and its 'border control' policy was made clear in the Second Reading speech of the then (Labor Government) Minister for Immigration, Gerry Hand:

> The Government is determined that a clear message be sent that migration to Australia may not be achieved by simply arriving in this country and expecting to be allowed to move into the community.[76]

This statement indicates that the policy had bipartisan support at that time. The fundamental rationale of the system has subsequently been explained as to maintain the 'integrity' of the offshore Humanitarian Migration Program, including the Refugee Program.[77]

---

[71] The 1983 amendments made it clear that the 'aliens' head of power was the basis for this exercise.

[72] *Lim* (1992) 176 CLR 1 at 29; Toohey J at 50 referred to a 'class of non-citizens'. See also *ibid.* McHugh J at 65.

[73] *Robtelmes* v. *Brenan* 1906 (1906) 4 CLR 395.

[74] *Lim* (1992) 176 CLR 1 at 32 per Brennan, Deane and Dawson JJ.

[75] *Lim* (1992) 176 CLR 1 at 32–33 per Brennan, Deane and Dawson JJ; Gaudron J at 57, McHugh J at 71.

[76] Gerry Hand, Minister for Immigration, 'Debates', House of Representatives, 5 May 1992, p. 2,371.

[77] Adrienne Millbank, *The Problem with the 1951 Convention* (Canberra: Department of the Parliamentary Library, 2000–01), Research Paper 5, www.aph.gov.au/library/pubs/rp/ 2000–01/01RP05.htm (accessed 10 March 2008). See further discussion below.

188   REFUGEES, ASYLUM SEEKERS AND THE RULE OF LAW

The effect of *Lim* was to sanction a regime of detention which is mandatory and non-reviewable. This arises from the provisions in the Migration Act which create the powers to support this system.[78] Consequently, the exercise of these powers gave rise to a regime of prolonged and indefinite detention, which led to a number of critical reports and inquiries into the system.[79] These reports criticized, in particular, the prolonged detention of individuals, and its non-reviewable nature, as well as the harsh conditions of detention. Alternatives (such as release into the community on bridging visas) were suggested, but the recommendations fell on deaf ears. In 1997 the management of detention centres was contracted out to private companies.

Following *Lim*, in a number of challenges it was argued that the consequences of detention took the exercise of powers outside the 'reasonably necessary' limits. In one line of cases it was held that the fact that the applicants and their children had suffered psychological damage as a result of their detention did not make the exercise of power a 'punitive administrative detention'.[80] Other decisions confirmed that

---

[78] The critical provisions are ss. 189, 196, and 198 which are contained in Part 2 of the Migration Act dealing with 'Control of arrival and presence of non-citizens'. Division 7 of Part 2, which contains ss. 189 and 196, deals with 'Detention of unlawful non-citizens' – those without visas. Division 8 of Part 2, which contains s. 198, deals with 'Removal of unlawful non-citizens'.

[79] These include Human Rights and Equal Opportunity Commission (*HREOC*) reports: *Summary of Observations following the Inspection of Mainland Detention Facilities 2007* (2008); *Summary of Observations following the Inspection of Mainland Detention Facilities 2006* (2007); Report No. 28, *Report of an Inquiry into Complaints. . . . at the Curtin Immigration Reception and Processing Centre* (2005); *A Report on Visits to Immigration Detention Facilities by the Human Rights Commissioner, 2001* (2002); *Those Who Have Come Across the Seas: Detention of Unauthorised Arrivals* (1998). All HREOC reports are available at www.hreoc.gov.au/Human_RightS/asylum_seekers/index.html (accessed 10 March 2008). See also Philip Flood, *AO Report of Inquiry into Immigration Detention Procedures* (2001); Joint Standing Committee on Foreign Affairs, Defence and Trade, *A Report of Visits to Immigration Detention Centres* (Canberra: Parliament of Australia, June 2001), www.aph.gov.au/house/committee/jfadt/IDCVisits/IDCindex.htm (accessed 10 March 2008); report of Bhagwati J, Regional Advisor for Asia and the Pacific of the United Nations High Commissioner for Human Rights, *Mission to Australia*, (2002); Commonwealth Ombudsman, *Report of an Own Motion Investigation into The Department of Immigration and Multicultural Affairs' Immigration Detention Centres* (Canberra: March 2001), www.comb.gov.au/commonwealth/publish.nsf/AttachmentsByTitle/reports_2001_dima_idc.pdf/$FILE/IDCMarch1.pdf (accessed 10 March 2008); and the collection at Department of Immigration and Citizenship, 'Detention Services', www.immi.gov.au/managing-australias-borders/detention/index.htm (accessed 10 March 2008).

[80] *NAMU of 2002* v. *Secretary, Department of Immigration and Multicultural and Indigenous Affairs* (with corrigendum) [2002] FCA 907; *NAMU of 2002* v. *Secretary, Department of*

THE AUSTRALIAN STORY 189

neither the harsh conditions of detention,[81] nor the fact that the children were detained in contravention of international human rights standards, affected the legality of the detention regime.[82] However, the limits of the 'reasonably necessary' requirement were tested by the situation of stateless people who were theoretically subject to indefinite detention as they were ineligible for a visa and had no country to which they could be removed under the Migration Act. In a significant shift from the original basis of *Lim*, in 2004 the High Court upheld the legality of the detention of this category of persons.[83] The manner in which this was done is a good example of how the Australian courts deal with human rights issues in the absence of an entrenched Bill of Rights, by applying the principles of interpretation referred to in Chapter 1.[84] The discussion in the next section illustrates the role of the courts to provide a link between the national and the international rule of law. However, this is an unpredictable instrument, as the litigation discussed below demonstrates.

Detention and human rights

Although Australia is a party to the major international human rights instruments, very few are directly incorporated into Australian law. In particular the Convention against Torture, and other Cruel, Inhuman or Degrading Treatment or Punishment (CAT),[85] the International Covenant on Civil and Political Rights (ICCPR)[86] and the Convention on

---

Immigration and Multicultural and Indigenous Affairs (with corrigendum) [2002] FCA 908; *NAMU of 2002* v. *Secretary, Department of Immigration and Multicultural and Indigenous Affairs* [2002] FCA 961; *NAMU of 2002* v. *Minister for Immigration and Multicultural and Indigenous Affairs* [2002] FCA 999.

[81] *Behrooz* v. *Secretary, Department of Immigration* (2004) 79 ALD 176.

[82] *Re Woolley and Another; ex parte M276/2003* (2004) 80 ALD 1, confirmed (2004) 225 CLR 1 (High Court, see below).

[83] *Al-Kateb* v. *Godwin* (2004) 219 CLR 562 (discussed in the text below).

[84] These principles and the presumptions of 'consistency' and of 'legality' are explained in Chapter 1 in this volume.

[85] Convention Against Torture and Other Cruel Inhuman or Degrading Treatment or Punishment, New York, 10 December 1984, in force 26 June 1987, UN Doc. A/39/51 (1984), 1465 UNTS 85. Note: the new Labor Government has announced its intention to ratify the Optional Protocol to CAT: ABC News, 'Amnesty Welcomes Move to Sign Treaty Against Torture', 1 March 2008, www.abc.net.au/news/stories/2008/03/01/2177204.htm (accessed 19 May 2008).

[86] International Covenant on Civil and Political Rights, New York, 16 December 1966, in force 23 March 1976, UN Doc. A/6316 (1966), 999 UNTS 171. Ratified by Australia on 13 August 1980. In *Minister for Immigration* v. *Al Masri* (2003) 197 ALR 241, the court

190 REFUGEES, ASYLUM SEEKERS AND THE RULE OF LAW

the Rights of the Child (CROC)[87] are not incorporated. To a limited extent, the 'gap' between domestic and international law is provided by the optional procedures available under the ICCPR and CAT. Each of the conventions provides a complaint or communication procedure to the relevant committee.[88] A number of key cases have been taken to the committees, and a number of complaints against Australia have been made out.[89] For example, in *A v. Australia*,[90] it was found that the system of mandatory detention which was upheld in the *Lim* decision was 'arbitrary' detention in breach of Article 9 of the ICCPR. But such findings are not enforceable against Australia. The national courts therefore play a vital role in ensuring that the rights of persons are protected.

In *Minister for Immigration v. Al Masri (Al Masri)*,[91] the Full Court of the Federal Court applied the presumptions of 'consistency' and 'legality' to interpretation of s. 196 of the Migration Act. That case was concerned with the limits of the power to detain a Palestinian asylum seeker whose application for a protection visa had been rejected and who had requested that he be returned to the Gaza Strip. In fact, his removal was impracticable. In concluding that his continued detention was unlawful, the Federal Court read the Act to conform with Australia's treaty obligations under Article 9 (the right to liberty) of the ICCPR. The court said that because of:

> [T]he nature and subject matter of the ICCPR, the universal recognition of the inherent dignity of the human person . . . as the source from

noted that although the ICCPR is not incorporated into Australian law, it is referred to in Schedule 2 of the Human Rights and Equal Opportunity Commission Act 1996 (Cth).

[87] Convention on the Rights of the Child, New York, 20 November 1989, in force 2 September 1990, UN Doc. A/44/49, 44 UN GAOR Supp. (No. 49) at 167.

[88] See Nick Poynder, '"Mind the Gap"': Seeking Alternative Protection Under the Convention Against Torture and the International Covenant on Civil and Political Rights', in Kneebone (ed.), *The Refugees Convention 50 Years On*, Chapter 7.

[89] As of 20 April 2004 there were 19 communications lodged with CAT from failed asylum seekers but only one was successful (*Elmi* v. *Australia* Communication No. 106/98, UN Doc. No. CAT/C/22/D/120/1998, 25 May 1999): Bayeofsky.com, 'United Nations Human Rights Treaties', 4 April 2008, www.bayefsky.com/docs.php/area/jurisprudence/treaty/cat/opt/0/state/9/node/5/type/all (accessed 7 May 2008); United Nations High Commissioner for Human Rights, 'Statistical Survey of Individual Complaints Dealt With by the Committee against Torture Under the Procedure Governed by Article 22 of the Convention against Torture and Other Cruel, Inhuman or Degrading Treatment or Punishment', 30 April 2004, www.unhchr.ch/html/menu2/8/stat3.htm (accessed 7 May 2008).

[90] *A (name deleted)* v. *Australia* Communication 560/1993, UN Doc. CCPR/C/59/D/560/1993, 30 April 1997. See further below.

[91] (2003) 197 ALR 241.

THE AUSTRALIAN STORY 191

which human rights are derived, and the reference to and relevance of its principles in domestic law gives the ICCPR a special significance in the application of the principle of statutory construction now being considered.[92]

Applying this principle, the court found that s. 196 was subject to an implied limitation that the period of mandatory detention does not extend to a time when there is no real likelihood or prospect in the reasonably foreseeable future of a detained person being removed and thus released from detention.[93] Moreover, the court found that Article 9 of the ICCPR meant that the individual had a right not to be detained in circumstances which are broadly 'unproportional' or unjust. It has been noted that the court reached this decision without expressly stating that there was an ambiguity in the national legislation in accordance with the established principles of interpretation.[94] However, Mr Al Masri's counsel argued that the statutory provisions read together amounted to a failure of the legislature to make an express provision for Mr Al Masri's situation. Clearly this was a case where the court was prepared to apply the ambiguity principle and the principles of interpretation broadly.

However, the victory for human rights was short lived. In the High Court sequel to the decision, *Al-Kateb* v. *Godwin* (*Al-Kateb*),[95] a majority of the High Court said that the provisions were unambiguous and did permit indefinite detention. A majority also accepted that the mandatory detention system sanctioned under the 'aliens' power and the Migration Act could extend to preventing entry into the Australian community. This was consistent with the government's 'border control' policy. The majority judiciously avoided discussing principles of international law or human rights.

The High Court decision in *Al-Kateb* has been described as representing unprecedented deference by the majority to parliament and the executive. It also displays a tendency to read any 'administrative' detention as purposive or valid.[96] Indeed, in a subsequent decision which

---

[92] *Ibid.* at para. 140. [93] *Ibid.* at para. 155.
[94] Glen Cranwell, 'Treaties and Interpretation of Statutes: Two Recent Examples in the Migration Context' (2003) 39 *Australian Institute of Administrative Law Forum* 49 at 53. See Chapter 1 in this volume for a discussion of the presumption which applies in cases of ambiguity.
[95] (2004) 219 CLR 562.
[96] Michael Zagor, 'Uncertainty and Exclusion: Detention and Aliens and the High Court' (2006) 34 *Federal Law Review* 127.

192   REFUGEES, ASYLUM SEEKERS AND THE RULE OF LAW

concerned the validity of the detention of children,[97] some judges questioned the 'reasonably necessary' limit set by *Lim*. Justice McHugh, for example, thought that it was only necessary to show that the detention was 'non-punitive'.[98] *Al-Kateb* is another example of the High Court's 'formalist' reasoning in this context.

Community responses to the mandatory detention regime

The detention issue, including its natural offshoot, the offshore processing of asylum seekers, is an issue which has aroused the sympathy of large sections of the community. An interesting feature of the *Lim* episode was the important role played by pro bono legal advisers who responded generously to the situation.[99] But a key motive of the government at the time was to keep lawyers out of the process.[100] This was carried out by further legislative reform in 1994 in the Migration Legislation Amendment Act 1994 (Cth) which introduced a system of registration for persons giving immigration assistance or making immigration representations.[101]

Mary Crock says that public opinion at the time of *Lim* (1992) displayed 'a sense of ambivalence towards these people'.[102] However, a paper produced in September 2000 for the Parliamentary Library, on 'The Problem with the 1951 Refugee Convention', suggested that 'asylum seekers do not elicit public sympathy in the way that "obvious" (as seen on television) refugees do'.[103] It suggested that reform to the onshore asylum system was likely 'to win the support of at least the general Australian public'.[104] It expressly referred to the 'voting public' and to the then recent success of European anti-immigration right-wing parties.[105] It was further stated that as most asylum seekers are from the Middle East, Asia and Eastern Europe, rather than Western Europe, in the eyes of the Australian public they are 'less welcome'.[106] It was also suggested that parliamentarians are aware of strong public feeling against boat arrivals.[107] In 2000 the detention of refugees was a politicized and divisive issue. However, in 2001 at the time of the Tampa

---

[97] *Re Woolley and Another; ex parte M276/2003* (2004) 225 CLR 1 (High Court).
[98] *Ibid.* at paras. 77–8 per McHugh J.   [99] *Ibid.* at 340–41.
[100] *Ibid.* at 351, citing 'Commonwealth Parliamentary Debates', House of Representatives, 5 May 1992, p. 2372.
[101] Upheld in *Cunliffe v. The Commonwealth* (1994) 182 CLR 272.
[102] Mary Crock, 'Climbing Jacob's Ladder' at 354.
[103] Millbank, *The Problem with the 1951 Convention*, p. 4.   [104] *Ibid.*, p. 5.
[105] *Ibid.*, p. 6.   [106] *Ibid.*, p. 10.   [107] *Ibid.*, p. 6.

THE AUSTRALIAN STORY

episode referred to at the beginning of this chapter, a majority of the Australian people appeared to support the policy.

Subsequently, it is opposition to the system of mandatory detention and its consequences which has galvanized public sympathy to asylum seekers. In the late 1990s, the 'plight of asylum seekers in remote and punitive detention centres [was] rarely far from the front pages of the national papers'.[108] The Pacific Plan referred to at the beginning of this chapter somewhat stymied that trend, as it was difficult – if not impossible – for lawyers and journalists to obtain visas to visit Nauru. Nevertheless, it soon became clear that these asylum seekers were not as 'alien' as the government would have the public believe. Gradually, they were brought to the mainland and assimilated into the Australian community. According to the government's own statistics, of the 1,550 people held under the Pacific Plan, 65.5 per cent were eventually 'resettled' in Australia or New Zealand.[109]

During 2005 the policy of mandatory detention came to public attention again with the discovery of two cases of misuse of power. One involved the detention of a permanent resident, Cornelia Rau, and the other involved the unlawful detention and deportation of an Australian citizen, Vivian Solon. An inquiry provided a new focus on the mandatory detention policy.[110] Concerns about the mental health effects of mandatory detention on long-term detainees[111] and the detention of children were aired.

In May 2005, the Member for Kooyong, Petro Georgiou, undertook to introduce Private Members' Bills which would have effectively ended

---

[108] Crock, 'The Refugees Convention at 50' in Kneebone (ed.), *The Refugees Convention 50 Years On*, Chapter 3 at p. 49.

[109] At its height in February 2002 1,550 people were held under the Pacific Plan: Department of Immigration and Multicultural and Indigenous Affairs, *Fact. Sheet No. 76: Offshore Processing Arrangements* (Canberra: Department of Immigration and Multicultural and Indigenous Affairs, 2007).

[110] Mick Palmer, *Report on Inquiry into the Circumstances of the Immigration Detention of Cornelia Rau* (Canberra: July 2005) (*The Palmer Report*). John McMillan, *Inquiry into the Circumstances of the Immigration Detention of the Vivian Alvarez Matter, report No. 3 of 2005* (Canberra: Commonwealth Ombudsman, 2005).

[111] In *C v. Australia* Communication No. 900/199 UN Doc. CCPR/C/76/D/900/1999 and *Madafferi v. Australia* Communication No. 1011/2002 UN Doc. CCPR/C/81/D/1011/2001, Australia was found to be in violation of Arts. 7 and 10 of the ICCPR by continuing detention after the deterioration of mental health was known to the Department. In *Shafiq v. Australia* CCPR/C/88/D/1324/2004, it was found that mental health problems had resulted from detention – Australia was found to be in breach of Art. 9(1) of the ICCPR ('arbitrary detention').

194   REFUGEES, ASYLUM SEEKERS AND THE RULE OF LAW

indefinite detention of asylum seekers, limited detention to ninety days for new asylum seekers, and provided access to judicial review. Under these measures, families with children would not be detained, and all long-term detainees of twelve months or longer would have been released into the community.[112]

In order to avoid a showdown with its Members, the government introduced its own reforms,[113] including the Migration and Ombudsman Legislation Amendment Act 2005 and Migration Amendment (Detention Arrangements) Act 2005. These Acts have introduced important reforms to the processing of asylum seekers in Australia, including:

- Requiring that the determination of protection visa applications for detained asylum seekers occur within ninety days;[114]
- Introducing the principle that children should only be detained as a measure of last resort;
- Requiring reports by the Department of Immigration to the Commonwealth Ombudsman on persons being held in detention for more than two years.

Commenting on these measures in March 2006, a Senate committee said:

> While recent changes create scope to ameliorate the harshness of the policy . . . [legislative change] is necessary to better reflect Australia's changed attitude, especially towards those who for various reasons cannot be safely returned to their country of origin. It is the role of law to provide procedural safeguard against over-zealous use of executive power and reflect the community's values of humanitarian concern and fairness.[115]

---

[112] The Migration Amendment (Mandatory Detention) Bill 2005 and Migration Amendment (Act of Compassion) Bill 2005 were introduced into the Senate on 16 June 2005. See Senate Legal and Constitutional References Committee, *Administration and operation of the Migration Act 1958* (Canberra: LCRC, March 2006), p. 156, n. 22.

[113] The government's initial response was to introduce a range of new bridging visas including the Removal Pending Bridging Visa.

[114] As of February 2008, in more than 80 per cent of cases the time frame had been met. As at January 2008 there were still 372 cases pending that were over the 90-day limit: Robert Illingworth, 'Answer to the Senate Standing Committee on Legal and Constitutional Affairs', Canberra, 19 February 2008, pp. 87–88, www.aph.gov.au/hansard/senate/commttee/S10636.pdf (accessed 14 March 2008).

[115] Senate Legal and Constitutional References Committee, *Administration and Operation of the Migration Act 1958* (Canberra: LCRC, March 2006), p. 174, para. 5.85.

THE AUSTRALIAN STORY 195

Further attempts to put asylum seekers outside the rule of law

In April 2006, Prime Minister Howard attempted to further extend measures to keep asylum seekers from accessing the Australian legal system with the introduction of the Migration Amendment (Designated Unauthorised Arrivals) Bill 2006. The purpose of this Bill was to introduce new measures that would mean that all unauthorized boat arrivals would be transferred to offshore processing centres (such as Nauru) for assessment of their refugee claims. The Bill went further than all other measures to date. It meant that all unauthorized boat arrivals ('designated unauthorized arrivals') arriving in any Australian territory would come under the Pacific Plan.[116] Moreover, the whole of the Australian mainland coast would be excised territory. But that was not the only legal fiction, or 'Orwellian doublespeak' as one Member of Parliament described it.[117] The Explanatory Memorandum elaborated:

> The Bill will also deem certain air arrivals to be entry by sea so the persons will be subject to the new regime. Persons who travel most of the way to Australia by sea but travel the last leg by air, before entering (on or after 13 April 2006) and who become unlawful on entry, will be taken to have entered Australia by sea. These are basically situations where persons are airlifted into Australia at the end of their sea journey.[118]

The Bill was a response to the decision in March 2006 by the Department of Immigration to grant protection visas to forty-two out of forty-three West Papuans who had travelled by sea from West Papua. The incident had caused strong protests from the Indonesian government, which resulted in the Indonesian government withdrawing its ambassador.[119] The Bill was intended to deter other asylum seekers from making claims which compromised Australia's foreign relationships. Teresa Gambaro MP, Parliamentary Secretary for Immigration and Citizenship, said:

---

[116] Migration Amendment (Designated Unauthorised Arrivals) Bill 2006, Explanatory Memorandum, para. 2.

[117] Peter Andren, 'Migration Amendment (Designated Unauthorised Arrivals) Bill 2006 Second Reading Speech', House of Representatives, Canberra, 8 August 2006.

[118] Migration Amendment (Designated Unauthorised Arrivals) Bill 2006, Explanatory Memorandum, para. 3.

[119] Mike Steketee, 'The Vanstone Wiggle', *The Australian*, 27 May 2006, p. 20, www.theaustralian.news.com.au/story/0,20876,19267397-7583,00.html (accessed 10 March 2008).

196 REFUGEES, ASYLUM SEEKERS AND THE RULE OF LAW

It is necessary to prevent Australia from being used as a staging post for political protests. In other words, this Bill will act to protect Australia's sovereignty, not diminish it.[120]

The negative response to the Bill was dramatic. Ten rebel Coalition Government MPs threatened to cross the floor. There was widespread opposition to the Bill from NGOs and the community. The same groups who had backed the 2005 changes were galvanized into opposition, fuelled by a sense of betrayal at the departure from the spirit of the 2005 changes. Coalition Government MP Petro Georgiou, who was a prime mover behind the 2005 changes which he believed had been 'welcomed by the community at large', referred to the Bill as 'the most profoundly disturbing piece of legislation I have encountered since becoming a Member of Parliament'. Referring to the 2005 reforms, he said:

> Public attitudes shifted. Australians who had once accepted the [mandatory detention] policy as being necessary came to see that it was cruel and wrong.[121]

Another Coalition Government MP, Judi Moylan, referred to Sir Owen Dixon's view that:

> [T]he rule of law is the assumption on which the Australian Constitution rests. The rule of law is a conservative principle. It is the foundation of democracy. It requires, as a minimum, access to judicial review of administrative action, the right to a fair trial, the right to private communications with a lawyer and access to the courts. This Bill removes or diminishes each of those rights.[122]

The debate on the Bill made it clear that the Members were well informed about the Pacific Plan and profoundly disturbed by its effects.

A Senate Committee which was convened to investigate the Bill recommended that the Bill should not proceed. It noted that:

> With the exception of the Department of Immigration and Multicultural Affairs (Department), all of the 136 submissions and witnesses appearing before the committee expressed complete opposition to the Bill.[123]

---

[120] Teresa Gambaro, 'Summing up Speech', House of Representatives, Canberra, 10 August 2006.

[121] Petro Georgiou, 'Debate on the Migration Amendment (Designated Unauthorised Arrivals) Bill', House of Representatives, Canberra, 9 August 2006.

[122] Judi Moylan, 'Debate on the Migration Amendment (Designated Unauthorised Arrivals) Bill', House of Representatives, Canberra, 9 August 2006.

[123] Senate Legal and Constitutional Legislation Committee, *Provisions of the Migration Amendment (Designated Unauthorised Arrivals) Bill 2006* (Canberra: LCLC, June 2006), para. 3.1.

THE AUSTRALIAN STORY 197

Particular concerns that the Senate Report highlighted as 'rule of law' issues were process issues – denial of natural justice, plus the absence of independent merits and judicial review mechanisms.[124] There were concerns that the Ombudsman's new jurisdiction would not extend to Nauru.[125] Concerns were also expressed about the nature and quality of offshore processing.[126]

On 22 June 2006, the Prime Minister said that the Bill would be redrafted and reintroduced. This was not done. Subsequently the then government simply transferred any intercepted asylum seekers who were being held on Christmas Island[127] to Nauru. In March 2007, eighty-three Sri Lankans were transferred to Nauru. They joined eight Burmese asylum seekers held on Nauru since August 2006. The government threatened the asylum seekers with removal to Indonesia and Malaysia. In April 2007, the government entered into a reciprocal agreement with the USA for the exchange of asylum seekers from Nauru with those from the USA processing facility in Guantanamo Bay. There was discussion of a new 'Atlantic Solution'.[128] However, the Howard Coalition Government was defeated in the election in late November 2007 and a new Labor Government took office under the leadership of Kevin Rudd. One of its first steps was to abolish the Pacific Plan and to bring the refugees held on Nauru to Australia.[129]

The above discussion demonstrates how the Australian government has kept asylum seekers apart from the legal system through the mandatory detention system and offshore processing. In the next section we see how this has been further achieved through limited incorporation of international obligations into the national legal system.

---

[124] *Ibid.*, para. 3.13.   [125] *Ibid.*, para. 3.61.   [126] *Ibid.*, paras. 3.140–41.

[127] Christmas Island is part of Australian territory although it has been excised for the 'migration zone' for the purpose of the Migration Act. Nauru is not Australian territory. It is located in the South Pacific, almost midway between Australia and Hawaii.

[128] Those people who were to be sent to the USA under the refugee swap have now come to Australia. Brendan Nicholson, 'Refugee Status Given to Burmese', *The Age*, 10 December 2007, p. 5.

[129] In February 2008 the last of the refugees, a group of 21 Sri Lankans, were granted permanent protection visas and resettled in Australia: Andrea Jackson, 'Last Refugees Bid Farewell to Nauru – Government Closes Book on Howard's Pacific Solution', *The Age*, 6 February 2008, p. 8. See also, Senator Chris Evans, Minister for Immigration, 'Opening Statement to the Senate Standing Committee on Legal and Constitutional Affairs', Canberra, 19 February 2008, p. 22, www.aph.gov.au/hansard/senate/commttee/S10636.pdf (accessed 11 March 2008).

198 REFUGEES, ASYLUM SEEKERS AND THE RULE OF LAW

Incorporation of the Refugee Convention and 'protection obligations' under Australian law

This section of the chapter demonstrates how Australia has incorporated its 'protection obligations' under the Refugee Convention into the national legal system and how they have been interpreted by the courts. Two particular issues are discussed. The first issue is the incorporation, interpretation and application of the *non-refoulement* obligation in Australian law. The second is the effect of the TPV scheme upon the interpretation of the cessation provisions in Article 1C(5) of the Refugee Convention. Particular themes that emerge from this discussion include: obligations towards asylum seekers are interpreted as arising from administrative discretions rather than from human rights; the personal controlling discretion of the Minister; and the strategic and extensive use of litigation by the government. That is, refugee rights are seen as a 'national project', rather than arising under international law.

Incorporation of the Refugee Convention: a 'false but legislatively required step'?

As an international treaty, the Refugee Convention requires express incorporation into Australian law.[130] The issue of incorporation is an important rule of law issue, as it shows the extent to which states respect their international obligations. For example, as the discussion in Part three illustrates, whereas in New Zealand there is greater receptivity to international law and human rights protection, in Australia there is debate over the extent to which the Convention is incorporated. While this debate potentially leaves the way open for broad judicial interpretation, and indeed the Australian High Court has developed some progressive jurisprudence on the refugee definition,[131] it has mostly adopted a very conservative approach to the scope of Australia's 'protection obligations'. Once again there is a preference for form over substance.

The Refugee Convention has been indirectly incorporated into general migration legislation, namely the Migration Act. Prior to 1992 when

---

[130] See Chapter 1 in this volume.

[131] E.g. *Minister for Immigration* v. *Khawar* (2002) 210 CLR 1 (victim of domestic abuse a 'member of a particular social group'). Other more conservative decisions such as *Applicant A* v. *Minister for Immigration* (1997) 190 CLR 225 (member of a 'particular social group' and the 'one-child policy') have clearly influenced international jurisprudence. See further in Part three below.

THE AUSTRALIAN STORY 199

the Act was amended, as described shortly, and before the visa regime was in place, the Refugee Convention was incorporated via s. 6A(1)(c) of the Migration Act, which referred to a person having the 'status of a refugee'. Under this process it was necessary to establish refugee status in separate proceedings before a quasi-independent body, and then to apply for an entry permit.[132] Importantly, s. 4(1) of the legislation at this time expressly incorporated the whole of the definition in Article 1 of the Refugee Convention.[133]

The pivotal section in the Migration Act is currently s. 36 which now states:

There is a class of visas to be known as protection visas.

A criterion for a protection visa is that the applicant for the visa is a non-citizen *to whom the Minister is satisfied* that Australia has protection obligations under the Refugees Convention [sic] [emphasis added].[134]

It can be seen that the current provision stresses both the Minister's discretion (as does s. 65 of the Act)[135] and the status of the person as a refugee. However, it is the discretionary and administrative nature of the decision-making power rather than the substantive rights of the asylum seeker which have largely dominated the jurisprudence which has emerged around Article 1E and Article 1C(5) of the Refugee Convention. In two recent decisions concerning the scope of these provisions, *NAGV & NAGW v. Minister for Immigration (NAGV)*[136] and *Minister for Immigration v. QAAH (QAAH)*,[137] the High Court has described the relationship between the Convention and the Act in very formalistic terms.

---

[132] In *Mayer v. Minister for Immigration* (1985) 157 CLR 290 the High Court held that a decision about refugee status was a 'decision made under an enactment' and therefore judicially reviewable.

[133] The term 'refugee' was defined in s. 4(1) as having 'the same meaning as it has in Art. 1 of the Refugee Convention'. In *Minister for Immigration v. Thiyagarajah* (1998) 80 FCR 543 von Doussa J suggested that under this legislation the issue was 'whether the asylum seeker *had* the status of "refugee" to the satisfaction of the minister'. He suggested that a person might be a refugee for the purpose of the Refugee Convention but not under the terms of the Migration Act. This is an early example of the trend to distinguish refugee rights in national law from the international 'rule of law'.

[134] The emphasised words were added in 2001 by Migration Legislation Amendment Act (no 6) (MLAA No. 6).

[135] Section 65 gives the Minister for Immigration an overriding discretion in relation to all classes of visas.

[136] (2005) 222 CLR 161.   [137] (2006) 231 ALR 340.

200   REFUGEES, ASYLUM SEEKERS AND THE RULE OF LAW

When s. 36 was added to the Migration Act in 1992, it was then in a division of the Act headed 'Refugees'.[138] It is now in a division headed 'Visas for non-citizens'. The majority of the High Court in *NAGV* pointed out that the Explanatory Memorandum to the 1992 amendment stated that its purpose was to make:

> [A] *technical change* in the way applications for protection as a refugee are dealt with. In future claimants will not apply separately for recognition as a refugee and permission to stay in Australia. Both processes will be combined in an application for a protection visa [emphasis in original].[139]

However, that is not the way that s. 36(2) has been read. In recent years (at least since 2001) it has been interpreted as supporting Australia's administrative processes under the Migration Act rather than as protecting the rights of refugees under the Refugee Convention. Whereas, prior to 1992, under s. 6A the issue of refugee status was dealt with separately and in accordance with the established interpretation of Article 1A(2) of the Refugee Convention (as in *Chan Yee Kin*, discussed above), subsequently the majority of justices on the High Court have stressed the *process* rather than the content of Australia's 'protection obligations'. The contrary view of Justice Kirby, as expressed in *QAAH*, is that:

> The purpose behind these reforms was not to limit the incorporation, into Australian municipal law, of Art 1 of the Convention. If anything, the reform had the effect of extending the incorporation, to include additional provisions of the Convention, by broadening the original, limited reference to 'Art 1 of the Refugees Convention' to the more general 'Refugees Convention and Protocol'.[140]

The view that Kirby expressed in *QAAH* about the effect of the 1992 amendment and the meaning of s. 36(2) is consistent with that expressed in previous decisions.[141] In *Chen Shi Hai* it was recognized that the purpose of s. 36(2) is simply to identify persons entitled to protection.

---

[138] I.e. Division 1AA of Part 2. Section 22AA read: 'If the Minister is satisfied that a person is a refugee, the Minister may determine, in writing, that the person is a refugee.' Section 22AA was in issue in *Minister for Immigration and Ethnic Affairs* v. *Wu Shan Liang* (1996) 185 CLR 259. In that case the High Court said that the reasons of administrative decision makers are not to be scrutinised by over-zealous judicial review. This deferential approach was supported by reference to the words of s. 22AA as it then was.

[139] *NAGV* (2005) 222 CLR 161 at para. 41 (emphasis in the original).

[140] (2006) 231 ALR 340 at para. 69, note 57.

[141] *Chen Shi Hai* v. *Minister for Immigration* (2000) 201 CLR 293 (*Chen Shi Hai*) at para. 41 per Gleeson CJ, Gaudron, Gummow and Hayne JJ: *NAGV & NAGW* v. *Minister for Immigration* (2003) 130 FCR 46 at para. 35 per Emmett J.

THE AUSTRALIAN STORY

Arguably the same reasoning applies to the current s. 36(2) – the scope of Australia's protection obligations under international law needs to be considered as a precedent to the exercise of the Minister's discretion.

Despite these clear textual indications, the majority in *NAGV* stressed the procedural effect of the change and said:

> Section 36(2) does not use the term 'refugee'. But the 'protection obligations under [the Convention]' of which it does speak are best understood as a general expression of the precept to which the Convention gives effect. The Convention provides for Contracting States to offer 'surrogate protection' in the place of that of the country of nationality of which, in terms of Art 1A(2), the applicant is unwilling to avail himself. That directs attention to Art 1 and to the definition of the term 'refugee'.[142]

But other than Articles 1A(2) and 33 of the Refugee Convention,[143] it is unclear which other provisions of the Convention are incorporated via s. 36(2). The majority in *NAGV* said:

> Section 36(2) is awkwardly drawn. Australia owes obligations under the Convention to the other Contracting States, as indicated earlier . . . Section 36(2) assumes more than the Convention provides by assuming that obligations are owed thereunder by Contracting States to individuals. Beginning with that *false but legislatively required step*, the appeal turns upon the meaning of the adjectival phrase 'to whom Australia has protection obligations under [the Convention]' [emphasis added].[144]

Although the majority approved the suggestion of a judge in the court below that 'there is a range of requirements imposed upon Contracting States with respect to refugees, some of which can fairly be characterized as "protection obligations"',[145] it is unclear which provisions are included within this expression. The majority expressly mentioned free access to courts of law (Art. 16(1)), temporary admission to refugee seamen (Art. 11), and the measure of religious freedom provided by Article 4, as examples of 'protection obligations',[146] but their emphasis was upon a textual analysis of the Migration Act. Thus recent decisions of the High Court show a change in the focus of interpretation of the nature and scope of Australia's protection obligation, in comparison to the earlier decision of *Chan Yee Kin*, which recognized the role of international human rights law in defining the rights of refugees.

---

[142] *NAGV* (2005) 222 CLR 161 at para. 32.
[143] As to which, see discussion below at pp. 202–7, 218–226.
[144] *NAGV* (2005) 222 CLR 161 at para. 27 (emphasis added).   [145] *Ibid.* at para. 31.
[146] *Ibid.*

202   REFUGEES, ASYLUM SEEKERS AND THE RULE OF LAW

In a separate judgment in *NAGV*, Justice Kirby said he did 'not accept that the Parliament was mistaken (or that it took a "false" step) in [s. 36(2) in] describing the subjects of the Convention as "a non-citizen . . . to whom Australia has protection obligations"'. He continued: 'Obligations may be owed, in international as in Australian law, otherwise than by and to the parties to a binding agreement.'[147] The contrast between this statement and that of the majority, above, makes it clear that the prevailing view is that the treaties to which Australia is a party do not give rise to obligations to individuals whose rights are affected by such treaties.

The recent decision of the High Court in *NAGV* appears to support a very literal approach to interpretation of Australia's protection obligations, which confirms the trend to 'formalism' which had been developing in a decisions in which Article 1E or Article 1C of the Refugee Convention was relevant. These contexts are discussed in turn.

The *non-refoulement* obligation in Australian law: interpretation of Article 1E of the Refugee Convention and complementary protection

This section discusses the incorporation and content of the *non-refoulement* obligation in Australian law. This is an important *international* rule of law issue, as the *non-refoulement* obligation is one of the core obligations owed by Contracting States under the Refugee Convention.[148] Therefore the extent to which Australia respects this obligation is another indication of its respect for international law and the rights of refugees. This section of the chapter contains a discussion of the use of the *non-refoulement* obligation in interpretation of Article 1E of the Refugee Convention. It focuses upon judicial interpretation and how the courts have responded to executive policy. Secondly, the 'complementary' protection scheme provided by s. 417 of the Migration Act is considered. This demonstrates the controlling and personal role of the Minister in the overall scheme of the Migration Act.

Article 1E and Article 33 of the Refugee Convention   In Australia it has generally been accepted that although Article 33 is not specifically

---

[147] *Ibid.* at para. 68. Footnote in original omitted.
[148] See Susan Kneebone, 'Introduction: Refugees and Asylum Seekers in the International Context – Rights and Realities' in this volume.

THE AUSTRALIAN STORY 203

incorporated into the Migration Act, it is the 'mirror image' of the general protection obligations owed under s. 36(2) to persons who come within the refugee definition in Article 1A(2) of the Refugee Convention.[149] The content of Australia's obligations under Article 33 of the Refugee Convention was litigated extensively in a series of cases which began with *Minister for Immigration* v. *Thiyagarajah* (*Thiyagarajah*)[150] in 1998. This line of cases, which was concerned with Article 1E, indirectly introduced the 'safe third country' concept into Australian law as the corollary of the *non-refoulement* principle. It was accepted that in the absence of evidence of *refoulement*, Australia did not owe protection obligations to asylum seekers. In the process of interpretation of the Refugee Convention, Article 1E was sidestepped and ignored. This line of decisions also sanctioned a low standard for implementation of the *non-refoulement* principle (which under international law requires individual assessment in each case).[151] In the *Thiyagarajah* line of cases, Article 33 was applied as the 'engine room' of the Refugee Convention.[152] However, in applying this principle, the courts used a fairly minimal test of safe third country and 'effective protection'.[153]

The words of Article 33 which prohibit *refoulement* 'in any manner whatsoever' suggest an absolute prohibition against *refoulement*, including indirect or 'chain *refoulement*' through a country which is not a party to the Refugee Convention, or which cannot guarantee that it will not *refoule* a person. This interpretation is consistent with the conclusion of the Executive Committee (ExCom) of the United Nations High Commissioner for Refugees (UNHCR) in UNHCR ExCom Conclusion 58, which states that return to a 'safe third country' is impermissible

[149] *Minister for Immigration* v. *Thiyagarajah* (1998) 80 FCR 543 per von Doussa J. See Savitri Taylor, 'The Right to Review in the Australian On-Shore Refugee Status Determination Process: Is It Adequate Procedural Safeguard Against Refoulement?' (1994) 22 *Federal Law Review* 300.
[150] (1998) 80 FCR 543.
[151] Sir Elihu Lauterpacht QC and Daniel Bethlehem, 'The Scope and the Content of the Principle of *Non-Refoulement*' in Erika Feller et al. (eds.), *UNHCR's Global Consultations on International Protection* (Cambridge University Press, 2003).
[152] *Minister for Immigration* v. *Al-Sallal* (1999) 94 FCR 549 at 559.
[153] The issues are discussed more fully in Susan Kneebone, 'Strangers at the Gate: Refugees, Citizenship and Nationality' (2004) 10 *Australian Journal of Human Rights* 33 and Susan Kneebone, 'What We *Have* Done With the Refugees Convention: The Australian Way' in Savitri Taylor (ed.), *Nationality, Refugee Status and State Protection: Explorations of the Gap between Man and Citizen* (Special edition of *Law in Context*, Federation Press, 2005), pp. 83–119.

204   REFUGEES, ASYLUM SEEKERS AND THE RULE OF LAW

if the asylum seeker has no legal status in the country of return or is not guaranteed to be treated in accordance with basic human rights standards.[154] ExCom Conclusion 85 similarly requires that any country to which asylum seekers are sent must observe their human rights, provide an opportunity for them to seek and enjoy asylum, and protect them from *refoulement*.[155] That is, these authorities suggest that Article 33 requires a legally enforceable right to enter a third county, and a guarantee of human rights protection. However the *Thiyagarajah* decision endorsed a lesser standard.

In *Thiyagarajah*, the question was whether Australia owed protection obligations to the applicant, who had been granted refugee status in France, or whether he was excluded from protection by Article 1E of the Refugees Convention (as an exception to Article 1A(2) of the Convention). Many of the subsequent cases concerned asylum seekers from Middle Eastern countries who had passed through or resided temporarily in another country en route to Australia. In many cases it was decided that, as the asylum seeker had 'effective protection' in the third country, they were not owed 'protection obligations' by the Australian government.

In *Thiyagarajah*, the Minister argued that Article 33 of the Convention was the first 'port of call' in considering the application of the Convention and Australia's protection obligations. The Minister's arguments were accepted by the Full Court of the Federal Court. It decided that, as the applicant had 'effective protection' in France as a 'safe third country', it was not strictly necessary to determine the scope of Article 1E.[156] The decision thus established a trend to make Article 33 the centrepiece of analysis and application of the Refugee Convention in Australian courts. It also simultaneously incorporated the safe third country notion into Australian case-law. In *Thiyagarajah*, Justice von Doussa said:

---

[154] UNHCR ExCom, 'Conclusion no. 58 (XL)', (1989) *The Problem of Refugees and Asylum Seekers Who Move in an Irregular Manner from a Country in Which They Have Already Found Protection.*

[155] UNHCR ExCom, 'Conclusion no. 85 (XLIX)', (1998) *International Protection*, para. (q).

[156] It was accepted that an 'exclusive' rather than 'inclusive' approach to interpretation was acceptable. von Doussa J who gave the leading judgment, agreed that if the applicant came within the scope of Art. 1E, there need be no 'separate and antecedent inquiry' as to whether the applicant has a 'well-founded fear' within the meaning of Art. 1A(2). *Thiyagarajah* (1998) 80 FCR 543 at 555.

THE AUSTRALIAN STORY   205

> The expression 'effective protection' . . . means protection which will effectively ensure that there is not a breach of Art 33 if that person happens to be a refugee.[157]

In subsequent decisions, Article 1E simply dropped out of the picture, or received only a cursory reference, even when it was directly relevant.[158]

The issue was further complicated by the passage of the Border Protection Legislation Amendment Act 1999, which appeared to be an attempt to codify the effect of *Thiyagarajah*. This Act amended s. 36 of the Migration Act to provide:

> Australia is taken not to have protection obligations to a non-citizen who has not taken all possible steps to avail himself or herself of a right to enter and reside in, whether temporarily or permanently and however that right arose or is expressed, any country apart from Australia, including countries of which the non-citizen is a national.[159]

But rather than settling the issue, the meaning of the 'right to enter and reside' in s. 36(3) became contentious. Two lines of conflicting decisions very quickly emerged. The first, influenced by the *Thiyagarajah* jurisprudence, considered that s. 36(3) codified the 'effective protection' cases. This line of authority required that the right 'to enter and reside' be assessed as a matter of practical reality and fact. This line of authority was eventually disapproved by the Full Court of the Federal Court in *Minister* v. *Applicant C* (*Applicant C*).[160] In that case it was established that s. 36(3) was intended to refer to a *legally enforceable right to enter and reside in a third country*. The court in that case rejected the argument that s. 36(3) was simply a codification of the *Thiyagarajah* decision, but it did not directly question its reasoning.[161]

The effect of *Applicant C* was to sanction two standards for implementation of the *non-refoulement* principle. First, the higher standard of s. 36(3), which is consistent with the UNHCR ExCom Conclusions 58 and 85, and secondly a lower standard of 'practical reality and fact' for application of s. 36(2).

Following the decision in *Applicant C*, further conflicting jurisprudence emerged. One line of Federal Court decisions either directly

---

[157] *Ibid.* at 562.

[158] E.g. in *Mylvaganam* v. *Refugee Review Tribunal* [2000] FCA 718, although the RRT had made its decision by applying Art. 1E, Merkel J applied the 'effective protection' approach. This trend began with *Rajendran* v. *Minister for Immigration* (1998) 86 FCR 526. See also *Minister for Immigration* v. *Tas* [2000] FCA 1657.

[159] Migration Act, s. 36(3).   [160] [2001] FCA 1332.

[161] See the discussion in Kneebone, 'Strangers at the Gate' at 53–55.

206   REFUGEES, ASYLUM SEEKERS AND THE RULE OF LAW

challenged the correctness of the 'effective protection' analysis in *Thiyagarajah* or accepted its precedential value with qualification.[162] But an opposing view also emerged that the scope of 'protection obligations' under the Migration Act should be determined by the terms of the Act and whether 'effective protection' is available.[163] Further, this view supported the proposition that, in the absence of an obligation not to *refoule* in that sense, no protection obligations arise.

Although the High Court in *NAGV* accepted the argument that 'effective protection' is not relevant to the interpretation of s. 36(2), it did so in such a way as to give primacy to the processes of the Migration Act rather than to the Refugee Convention. In a joint judgment, Chief Justice Gleeson and Justices McHugh, Gummow, Hayne, Callinan and Heydon said that s. 36(2) directs attention to Article 1A(2) of the Refugee Convention.[164] They also accepted that the protection obligations referred to in s. 36(2) could include other Convention obligations, as discussed above.[165] They did not discuss the correctness of the Full Court decision in the *Thiyagarajah* decision but suggested that they were not bound by what was said in that case about the scope of Article 1E of the Refugee Convention.[166] But their views, as explained above, were premised by their understanding of the effect of the Refugee Convention on Australia's protection obligations, describing s. 36(2) as involving a 'false but legislatively required step'. They did not discuss the scope of Article 33 of the Refugee Convention.

In a separate judgment, Justice Kirby agreed with the construction of s. 36(2) of the Migration Act, although he did not accept the view that it involved a 'false but legislatively required step'. Consistent with the views he has expressed on many occasions, Kirby accepted the full extent of Australia's international obligations and the orthodox principles of interpretation discussed in Chapter 1.[167]

This decision, which stressed the administrative and legislative context of refugee decision making in Australia, shows the extent to which the Australian High Court has deferred to the Minister's policies

---

[162] The first line began with *NAGV & NAGW* v. *Minister for Immigration* (2003) 130 FCR 46; FCAFC 144 (27 June 2003).

[163] The line of contrary authority began with *NAEN* v. *Minister for Immigration* [2003] FCA 216 (Sackville J 10 March 2003).

[164] *NAGV* (2005) 222 CLR 161 at para. 32.

[165] *Ibid.* at para. 31 they referred to Arts. 4, 11, and 16 of the Refugee Convention.

[166] *Ibid.* at para. 53.

[167] See Chapter 1 in this volume at pp. 61–4.

THE AUSTRALIAN STORY 207

in recent years, and the extent to which it has strayed from the path first established in *Chan Yee Kin*, which recognized the human rights of refugees. This discussion of *NAGV* presages the Article 1C(5) issue which is discussed shortly. However, before turning to that, we divert for a moment to complete the discussion of the *non-refoulement* principle by looking at how the executive arm of government deals with *refoulement* issues.

Section 417 of the Migration Act and the Minister's 'humanitarian' discretion Whereas the discussion in the previous section described a somewhat ambiguous approach to Article 33 of the Refugee Convention by the courts, in this section we look at the executive's approach to *refoulement*, which is also somewhat ambivalent. Australia does not have an independent system of complementary protection[168] – instead the Coalition Government expressly preferred to retain the Minister's personal discretion to grant relief from *refoulement* under s. 417 to provide for 'flexibility' on a case-by-case basis[169] and for that reason rejected calls for the introduction of an independent scheme. A 2004 report[170] had recommended that the government consider the introduction of such a scheme to ensure that 'Australia no longer relies solely on the Minister's discretionary powers to meet its *non-refoulement* obligations'.[171] In failing to provide for a complementary protection scheme, the Australian legal system is out of step with other receiving countries.[172] The new Minister appears to recognize that this is a problem and is said to be 'favourably disposed'[173] to considering the introduction of a system of complementary protection.

Section 417, the so-called 'safety-net' provision or 'humanitarian' discretion, gives the Minister for Immigration the power to grant a visa

---

[168] 'Complementary protection' means the protection afforded by states to persons who fall outside the definition of a refugee in the Refugee Convention, Art. 1A(2). For an explanation of how complementary protection operates in other jurisdictions, see Jane McAdam, 'Complementary Protection: A Comparative Perspective', in UNHCR Discussion Paper, No. 2 2005, *Complementary Protection*, pp. 5–6.

[169] DIMIA, 'Complementary Protection and Australian Practice', in UNHCR Discussion Paper, No. 2 2005, *Complementary Protection*, p. 7.

[170] Senate Select Committee on Ministerial Discretion in Migration Matters, *Report* (Canberra: March 2004).

[171] *Ibid.*, p. xviii.   [172] McAdam, 'Complementary Protection', pp. 5–6.

[173] Senator Chris Evans, Minister for Immigration, 'Answer to the Senate Standing Committee on Legal and Constitutional Affairs', Canberra, 19 February 2008, p. 23, www.aph.gov.au/hansard/senate/commttee/S10636.pdf (accessed 11 March 2008).

208 REFUGEES, ASYLUM SEEKERS AND THE RULE OF LAW

(substituting 'a more favourable decision') when all other avenues for claiming refugee status under Australian law have failed.[174] In exercising the powers under s. 417, the Minister can take into account the CAT, ICCPR and CROC obligations. Added by the amendment to the Migration Act in 1989, this power was intended to balance inflexible regulations with a general discretion.[175] However, in the late 1990s it was increasingly used in the context of failed asylum cases or applications for protection visas.[176] It has also been used to achieve major policy objectives. For example, in 2003, when the government decided to begin re-processing the applications of people from East Timor who had fled in the early 1990s (and for whom processing of visa applications had been frozen), it rejected the opportunity to create a special visa category, and instead processed each case individually through the use of s. 417.

The number of applications for s. 417 interventions in 'humanitarian' cases has been consistently high. In 2006–7, the department received over 4,000 requests for ministerial intervention.[177] As of February 2008, there were 2,400 requests for intervention being processed by the Department.[178] However the overall success rate on s. 417 applications in 'humanitarian' (mainly refugee) cases has typically been as low as 5.1 per cent.[179] During his term of office, the previous Minister for Immigration, Kevin Andrews, dealt with 1,846 requests for intervention, resulting in 479 intervention acts.[180] Thus the exercise of the s. 417 discretion does not operate as a true 'safety-net'.

---

[174] Section 417(1) gives the Minister the power to substitute for the RRT a decision 'more favourable to the applicant' if he or she 'thinks that it is in the public interest to do so'. In practice, decisions can also be referred to the Minister by the Department of Immigration, or the RRT or by the individual. Subsection 3 states that the power can only be exercised by the Minister 'personally'.

[175] Kerry Carrington, 'Ministerial Discretion in Migration Matters: Contemporary Policy Issues in Historical Context', Parliament of Australia, (2003) 3 *Current Issues Brief.*

[176] From 1996 to the end of 2002 it was used 1,916 times – 1,046 times re RRT decisions and 516 times re MRT decisions: Kerry Carrington, 'Ministerial Discretion in Migration Matters'.

[177] Topsfield, 'Bigger Say for Courts on Migrants', *The Age.*

[178] Peter Hughes, 'Answer to the Senate Standing Committee on Legal and Constitutional Affairs', Canberra, 19 February 2008, p. 71, www.aph.gov.au/hansard/senate/commttee/S10636.pdf (accessed 14 March 2008).

[179] Senate Legal and Constitutional References Committee, *Administration and Operation of the Migration Act 1958* (Canberra: LCRC, 2006), Chapter 4, p. 125.

[180] Illingworth, 'Answer to the Senate Standing Committee on Legal and Constitutional Affairs', p. 56.

THE AUSTRALIAN STORY   209

The use of s. 417 has been the subject of three major inquiries,[181] which have been critical of the lack of accountability and of the way in which the Minister has exercised this discretion, which is non-delegable, 'non-compellable and non-reviewable'.[182] The *Sanctuary Under Review Report* (2000)[183] was prompted by the cases of two failed asylum seekers, Mr Elmi[184] and a Chinese woman who was returned to China when she was eight months pregnant. Once there, she was forcibly aborted, as she was in breach of the 'one-child policy'. The Senate inquiry in 2004 was prompted by allegations of patronage. Increasingly the focus of critics has been upon the procedural aspects of the decision-making process. The lack of transparency which follows from the informal nature of the process[185] and the standardized form of the statements which are required to be made to Parliament are cited as evidence of this problem. It is also evident that the Minister does not personally exercise the discretions, as a team of fifty people assists the Minister. Applications are first vetted by an officer of the Department, and those which come within the guidelines[186] which

---

[181] Senate Legal and Constitutional References Committee, *A Sanctuary Under Review: An Examination of Australia's Refugee and Humanitarian Processes* (Canberra: Commonwealth of Australia, June 2000); Senate Select Committee on Ministerial Discretion in Migration Matters, *Report*; Senate Legal and Constitutional References Committee, *Administration and Operation of the Migration Act 1958*.

[182] Subsection 7 states that the Minister 'does not have a duty to consider whether to exercise the power under subsection (1) . . . whether . . . requested to do so by the applicant . . . or in any other circumstances'.

[183] Senate Legal and Constitutional References Committee, *A Sanctuary Under Review*, Chapter 8.

[184] Mr Elmi was a Somali asylum seeker who made a claim for refugee status, based on his membership of a minority clan which had a well-documented history of persecution from the dominant clan in Mogadishu. His claim was rejected on the basis that any harm he faced upon return to Somalia would be because of the generalized situation of civil war rather than for any Convention reason. He had unsuccessfully sought review of his case by the High Court, and he had been refused humanitarian entry by the Minister for Immigration under s. 417 of the Migration Act. The circumstances of his removal are described in Poynder, 'Mind the Gap', pp. 189–190. In *Elmi v. Australia* (Communication No. 106/98, UN Doc. No. CAT/C/22/D/120/1998, 25 May 1999) UNCAT rejected Australia's argument that CAT did not apply. The circumstances of his removal are considered in Mary Crock, 'A Sanctuary Under Review: Where To From Here for Australia's Refugee and Humanitarian Program?' (2000) 23 *UNSW Law Journal* 246 at 261–264. See also Senate Legal and Constitutional References Committee, *A Sanctuary Under Review*, Chapter 7, 'The Case of Mr SE'.

[185] E.g. the woman *refouled* to China made repeated verbal requests: Carrington, 'Ministerial Discretion in Migration Matters'.

[186] Note the guidelines were amended in 2005 following the 2004 inquiry to include consideration of Australia's obligations under CAT, ICCPT and CROC.

210   REFUGEES, ASYLUM SEEKERS AND THE RULE OF LAW

have been prepared for the exercise of the s. 417 discretion are passed on to the Minister for personal consideration.

The 2006 Committee noted that the government had chosen to ignore the recommendations of the previous inquiries.[187] It concluded that:

> If at the end of the day the Government intends to honour Australia's obligations under international treaties and conventions such as CAT, CROC and ICCPR, then it would make sense to provide for it upfront, rather than giving it to the Minister involved.[188]

Despite the findings of these independent inquiries, there has been no real change in the process, although the new Minister has signalled his intention to scale back the use of his discretionary powers in the future, stating that he is 'uncomfortable . . . playing God'.[189] The use of s. 417 thus demonstrates a rule of law under strain – when normal democratic processes (inquiries and reports) have been ignored, and where normal procedural protections do not apply. Moreover, there would appear to be breaches of the international standard of *non-refoulement*.

Article 1C(5) and the TPV scheme

As explained above, a deterrent aspect of Australia's refugee policy which singled out spontaneous onshore asylum seekers was introduced in 1999. This was the Temporary Protection Visa (TPV) regime under which refugees received temporary protection through the grant of three-year visas.[190] In this section, the discussion of incorporation of Australia's obligations under the Refugee Convention is continued by explaining how the issue played out through the application of Article 1C(5) to TPV holders. We see how the High Court interpreted the government's powers under the Migration Act according to the government's views, and thus put Australian jurisprudence out of line with international interpretation of the Refugee Convention. First, it is necessary to explain the operation of the TPV scheme.

---

[187] Senate Legal and Constitutional References Committee, *Administration and Operation of the Migration Act 1958*, para. 4.118.

[188] *Ibid.*, para. 4.119 – however, it agreed that some ministerial flexibility is required.

[189] Topsfield, 'Bigger Say for Courts on Migrants', *The Age*. The Immigration Minister has commissioned a report on the use of discretionary powers: Senator Evans, 'Answer to the Senate Standing Committee on Legal and Constitutional Affairs', p. 22. In May 2008, further controversy emerged over the fact that the new Minister had intervened in only a few cases since taking office – see Refugee Council of Australia, 'Controversy Highlights Need to Reform Refugee Determination System', Press Release, 13 May 2008.

[190] On 13 May 2008, the new government announced its intention to end the TPV scheme – see Refugee Council of Australia, 'Ending Temporary Protection: Another Step in Vital Reforms', Press Release, 13 May 2008.

THE AUSTRALIAN STORY

The TPV scheme Initially, TPV holders could apply for a Permanent Protection Visa (PPV) after thirty months of being granted a TPV. However, the TPV system was further amended in September 2001 to preclude an application for a PPV if the person had resided in a country of first asylum en route to Australia for seven days or more (the 'seven days rule' – although the Minister had the power to waive this in the public interest, and in fact often did). These laws were applied retrospectively to those who had not applied for a PPV by 27 September 2001. Thus TPV holders who had not spent seven days in a country where they could have sought protection and who applied before 27 September 2001 could access the PPV scheme, but others could not.

The earliest of the TPVs began to expire in November 2002. The government acted by extending the visas en masse by the creation of a new visa, Temporary Protection (Class XC).[191] Throughout 2003, the government 'froze' the processing of applications by Iraqi asylum seekers. It then lifted the freeze in April 2004. These measures were linked to changing country conditions at that time. As at September 2004 it was estimated that there were about 9,000 people living in Australia on temporary protection, of whom about 2,787 had been processed.[192]

Under the TPV scheme, holders had the right to work and to receive Medicare, but there was no right to family reunion and no right to re-enter Australia if the visa holder departed. In comparison to other persons resettled in Australia (under the Humanitarian Program for example) they did not have access to:

- orientation assistance, including information about essential services;
- accommodation support and provision of basic household items;
- English language tuition;
- community support programmes.

In the absence of government services, this group of people were forced to rely upon the community for support, especially from refugee advocate and church groups, many of whom became outspoken critics of the government's policy.

TPV holders were thus denied many of the rights guaranteed by the Refugee Convention to refugees 'lawfully staying' in Australia. These include the right to housing (Art. 21), public relief (Art. 23), social

---

[191] This was introduced in November 2002. See Migration Regulations 1994, Schedule 1, Regulation 2.08F and Item 1403.
[192] Peter Mares, *The Financial Review*, 29 September 2004, p. 8.

212   REFUGEES, ASYLUM SEEKERS AND THE RULE OF LAW

security (Art. 24), and travel documents (Art. 28). This is consistent with a view of the limited incorporation of Australia's obligations under the Refugee Convention.

As a result of pressure from community groups and NGOs, the government announced new measures in August 2004 for TPV holders, which included access to visas in the general migration programme. In reality, only a handful of TPV holders were eligible for these visas. Pressure also came from within the ranks of government. In May 2005 the group of MPs, led by Petro Georgiou, who secured alterations to the mandatory detention regimes also secured assurances about the TPV processing regime. The government made a commitment that all remaining TPVs which had reached the thirty-month mark would be processed by 31 October 2005. During 2006–7, 332 new TPVs were granted.[193] In 2007, about 1,000 people remained on TPVs.[194] Upon taking office, the new Minister for Immigration, Senator Chris Evans, stated that he was 'committed to ending' the TPV regime.[195] In the budget presented by the new government in May 2008, the TPV was finally abolished.[196]

Returning to April 2004, when the government began to reprocess the TPVs, a new issue arose. This was the application of Article 1C(5) of the Refugee Convention – the 'ceased circumstances' clause.

Article 1C(5) of the Refugee Convention[197]   The issue that arose in relation to TPV holders and Article 1C(5) of the Refugee Convention was a practical one – whether, in applying for a PPV, such persons were required to re-establish de novo that they met the requirements of the Convention definition (the government's view) or whether, as recognized refugees (as a result of the grant of a TPV), they remained so

---

[193] Department of Immigration and Citizenship, *Annual Report 2006–7* (Canberra: Department of Immigration and Citizenship, 2007), Table 40, www.immi.gov.au/about/reports/annual/2006–07/html/outcome1/output1_2_2.htm#table40 (accessed 13 March 2008).

[194] US Committee for Refugees and Immigrants, 'Country Report: Australia 2007', *World Refugee Survey*, www.refugees.org/countryreports.aspx?id=1981 (accessed 13 March 2008).

[195] Senator Evans, 'Answer to the Senate Standing Committee on Legal and Constitutional Affairs', p. 55.

[196] Refugee Council of Australia, 'Ending Temporary Protection: Another Step in Vital Reforms', Press Release, 13 May 2008.

[197] This section draws upon Emily Hay and Susan Kneebone, 'Refugee Status in Australia and the Cessation Provisions: *QAAH of 2004* v. *MIMIA*' (2006) 31 *Alternative Law Journal* 147.

THE AUSTRALIAN STORY 213

unless the government could prove that circumstances had changed so as to activate cessation (the position of refugee advocates). As we shall see, the government's view prevailed.

Once again, the issue was fought out in the Federal Court, with conflicting lines of authority being developed before it was settled by the High Court in favour of the government's view. This decision demonstrates that the High Court is willing to accept an approach to refugee protection which is inconsistent with international jurisprudence and UNHCR recommendations. The episode also demonstrates Australia's opportunism as an international actor in the formulation of refugee policy, as initially Australia had supported the formulation of UNHCR standards, as explained below.

Iraq and Afghanistan have been two major source countries of refugee influx in the period since the introduction of TPVs. Subsequent events in both countries have led to many claims for PPVs being refused by the Minister. In the cases of *NBGM* v. *Minister for Immigration* (*NGBM*)[198] and *QAAH*[199] the applicants were both male Afghanis of Hazara ethnicity and Shi'a religious affiliation. Both were recognized as refugees and granted a TPV, which was subsequently extended, but were later refused PPVs by the Immigration Department and the RRT. The RRT stated in both cases that the circumstances of the persecution had ceased because the Taliban was no longer a governing authority and was not a viable political force, despite ongoing 'security problems'.

In the Federal Court decisions in *NBGM* and *QAAH* there were two different approaches taken. One view (the majority of the Full Court in *QAAH*) acknowledged that a comparison of Article 1A(2) and Article 1C(5) shows that the Refugee Convention involves a two-stage process; namely recognition as a refugee and proof of cessation. The majority in *QAAH* thought that this separation between the two processes was acknowledged by the statutory scheme of the Migration Act (s. 36(2)), which focuses upon a grant of a visa. Following that point, the majority introduced a second distinction between recognition as a refugee in international law and the grant of protection under national law. As Justice Wilcox said in the Full Court in *QAAH*, the fact of recognition as a refugee in international law is 'indefinite', whereas the grant of protection under national law is 'limited'.[200]

---

[198] (2006) 231 ALR 380.   [199] (2005) 145 FCR 363.
[200] *Ibid.* at para. 83.

214   REFUGEES, ASYLUM SEEKERS AND THE RULE OF LAW

In the High Court decision in *QAAH*, Justice Kirby, in dissent, pointed
out that recognition:

> can only lapse in accordance with one of the cessation grounds set out in
> Art 1C. *Protection*, on the other hand, may lapse in accordance with the
> provisions of the Act. Because they are distinct processes, the lapse of
> *protection* does not necessarily have any causal effect on a person's *rec-
> ognition* as a refugee. A person may remain 'recognized' as a refugee
> notwithstanding the periodic lapse of a protection visa. In this sense, the
> Act does nothing more than establish a system of temporary *protec-
> tion*. The periodicity of Australia's protection regime cannot be used to
> infer the existence of a regime of temporary *recognition* [emphasis in
> original].[201]

As Kirby acknowledged later in his judgment in *QAAH*,[202] this argument picks up the UNHCR view that recognition by a state of refugee
status is a 'declaratory' act.[203]

The Minister argued that a de novo hearing was required on an application for a PPV because the *wording* of s. 36(2) required the Minister to
be 'satisfied' that the person was owed protection obligations at the time
of the granting of the visa.[204] That is, the Minister's argument stressed
the terms and effect of the Migration Act. The Minister also perceived
the relationship between Article 1A(2) and Article 1C(5) of the Refugee
Convention in different terms. On this point, the view of Justice Emmett
in *NBGM* was influential, namely that the two Articles should be construed as 'having some symmetry in their effect'.[205] He said that the
underlying rationale of the Convention is that:

> So long as the relevant well-founded fear exists, such that a person is
> unable or unwilling to avail himself or herself of the protection of the
> country of his or her nationality, he or she will be permitted to remain in
> the Contracting State.[206]

He then stated that protection obligations continue only for so long as a
person meets the criteria of Article 1A(2). This view, which is contrary
to established authority, prevailed in the High Court.

---

[201] *QAAH* (2006) 231 ALR 340 at para. 71.   [202] *Ibid.* at para. 96.

[203] UNHCR, *Handbook on Procedures and Criteria for Determining Refugee Status* (Geneva:
1979, re-edited 1992) (UNHCR Handbook), para. 28.

[204] This was the view expressed in the dissenting judgment of Lander J in the Full Court in
QAAH v. *Minister for Immigration* (2005) 145 FCR 363.

[205] *NBGM* [2004] FCA 1373 (25 October 2004) at para. 37.   [206] *Ibid.* at para. 39.

THE AUSTRALIAN STORY 215

In *QAAH*, the High Court took their views about incorporation of the Refugees Convention even further than they had in *NAGV*. The majority said:

> The relevant law of Australia is found in the Act and in the Regulations under it. It is Australian principles of statutory interpretation which must be applied to the Act and the Regulations. One of those principles is s. 15AA(1) of the *Acts Interpretation Act* 1901 (Cth)[207] . . . The Convention has not been enacted as part of the law of Australia, unlike, for example, the Hague Rules and the Warsaw Convention. Section 36 of the Act is the only section (apart from the interpretation section, s. 5) which refers in terms to the Convention. That does not mean that thereby the whole of it is enacted into Australian law.
>
> Hence, by reason of . . . the *Acts Interpretation Act*, the Convention may be considered . . . Further, Australian courts will endeavour to adopt a construction of the Act and the Regulations, if that construction is available, which conforms to the Convention [emphasis in original].[208]

A stated purpose of the temporary protection regime in Australia is to consider, upon application for further protection, 'whether the situation in the home country has changed and the TPV holder is no longer in fear of persecution'.[209] This, in itself, may be in breach of the UNHCR Handbook and Guidelines, which warn against periodic review of status.[210]

The High Court in *QAAH* accepted that the TPV scheme operates as a measure of border control. This view is reflected by the majority in the High Court in *QAAH* when it said:

> Section 36, like the Convention itself, is not concerned with permanent residence in Australia or any other asylum country, or indeed entitlements to residence for any particular period at all.[211]

---

[207] Section 15AA(1) provides: 'In the interpretation of a provision of an Act, a construction that would promote the purpose or object underlying the Act (whether that purpose or object is expressly stated in the Act or not) shall be preferred to a construction that would not promote that purpose or object.' (This is the original footnote in this passage).

[208] *QAAH* (2006) 231 ALR 340 at para. 34.

[209] Department of Immigration and Multicultural and Indigenous Affairs, *Fact Sheet No. 68: Temporary Protection Visa Holders Applying for Further Protection* (Canberra: Department of Immigration and Multicultural and Indigenous Affairs, 2003).

[210] UNHCR, 'Guidelines on International Protection: Cessation of Refugee Status Under Article 1C(5) and (6)', HCR/GIP/03/03, 10 February 2003, para. 3; UNHCR Handbook, para. 135.

[211] *QAAH* (2006) 231 ALR 340 at para. 36.

216 REFUGEES, ASYLUM SEEKERS AND THE RULE OF LAW

Another aspect of the *QAAH* decision demonstrates both the gap between the approach of the Australian High Court and international jurisprudence, and the opportunism of the Australian government on the international stage. This refers to the standard of proof required by Article 1C(5), which simply refers to particular circumstances having 'ceased to exist'.

One formulation of this standard is that it requires proof of 'substantial, effective and durable' change. This was endorsed by the Australian government in its contribution to the UNHCR's Expert Roundtable Series and was further defined as:

- Substantial, in the sense that the power structure under which persecution was deemed a real possibility no longer exists;
- Effective, in the sense that they exist in fact, rather than simply promise, and reflect a genuine ability and willingness on the part of the home country's authorities to protect the refugee;
- Durable, rather than transitory shifts which last only a few weeks or months.[212]

The 'substantial, effective and durable' test is consistent with UNHCR Guidelines and the views of other state parties to the Refugee Convention. However, Justice Emmett in *NBGM* said that this expression does not constitute a legal test, as these words do not appear in the Convention. Emmett said that there should be strict adherence to the actual language of the Convention.[213] By contrast, in *QAAH*, the majority in the Full Federal Court considered that the 'substantial, effective and durable' formulation is mandated by the text of the Convention. They explained that this does not mean that it is a legal test, but that it is a helpful guide to determine the level of change that has occurred. This view was accepted by Justice Allsop in *NGBM*.[214] This higher threshold of what constitutes 'ceased circumstances' places a heavier burden on the state.

Emmett's refusal in *NBGM* to endorse the 'substantial, effective and durable' formulation reflects his approach, which defers to the national or domestic legislation without reference to international guidelines. However, it should be noted that the Department of Immigration approved

---

[212] Department of Immigration and Multicultural Affairs, Refugee and Humanitarian Division, 'The Cessation Clauses (Article 1C): An Australian Perspective', paper delivered to the UNHCR's Expert Roundtable Series, October 2001, p. 8.
[213] *NBGM* [2004] FCA 1373 at para. 44.   [214] *NBGM* [2006] FCAFC 60 at para. 172.

this formulation in its paper for the UNHCR's Expert Roundtable Series, as already discussed. The majority of the High Court accepted Emmett's view as consistent with the Australian administrative processes. While nominally supporting UN guidelines on the application of the provision, in practice Australia's approach is in direct contrast to the cautious process of consultation undertaken by the UNHCR when considering cessation. Yet Australia's paper for the UNHCR's Expert Roundtable Series in 2001 endorsed the cautious and restrictive approach to Article 1C(5) articulated by the UNHCR's Handbook and Executive Committee Conclusions. Of particular importance are statements in the paper to the effect that, once determined to be a refugee, that status is retained 'unless and until' circumstances arise in which cessation can be brought into effect,[215] and a recognition that the burden of proof should be on the authorities to show substantial, effective and durable change.[216] Subsequently, however, as has been explained, the Australian government took a different approach. This was facilitated by the serendipitous coincidence between the TPV regime and Article 1C(5). Once away from the international stage, the Australian Government was unsupportive of the UNHCR. In *QAAH*, Kirby commented critically upon the fact that UNHCR's requested participation in the hearing was confined to written submissions.[217]

Part three: interpretation of the refugee definition and legislative intervention – an Australia/New Zealand comparison

In Part two we examined the limited incorporation of the Refugee Convention into Australian law and the debate that this has generated. In particular, we examined how this has led to restrictive application of the *non-refoulement* principle and the cessation clause (Art. 1C(5)) in Australian law. We saw that the meaning of 'protection obligations' referred to in s. 36(2) of the Migration Act is interpreted as arising from administrative discretions as part of the 'national project' rather than as international human rights protection. Section 36(2) has been described as containing a 'false but legislatively required step'.[218]

---

[215] Department of Immigration and Multicultural Affairs, 'The Cessation Clauses (Article 1C)', p. 8.
[216] *Ibid.*, pp. 16–17.   [217] *QAAH* (2006) 231 ALR 340 at para. 77.
[218] *NAGV* (2005) 222 CLR 161 at para. 27.

218   REFUGEES, ASYLUM SEEKERS AND THE RULE OF LAW

In this part we consider the interpretation of aspects of the refugee definition in Article 1A(2) of the Convention;[219] namely the phrases 'being persecuted' and 'for reasons of', and make some comparison with the New Zealand approach in order to demonstrate the difference that the use of a human rights approach to interpretation can make to the outcome. We will see that the human rights approach to interpretation of the refugee definition (as explained in Chapter 1), which was always muted in Australia, has been overtaken by a codification of these aspects of the definition, added by legislation in 2001 in response to perceived 'activism' by the courts.

The comparison also demonstrates that the New Zealand Refugee Status Appeals Authority (NZRSAA), which is an independent merits review tribunal,[220] has developed a coherent jurisprudence on these issues, which is difficult to compare with that of the Australian courts, which are performing a more limited judicial review function. This difference in institutions, coupled with the human rights focus of the New Zealand legislation, provides us with a clear example of how the rule of law operates in this context in each jurisdiction.

'Being persecuted'

It is now well established that the phrase 'being persecuted', which is the core of the definition of a 'refugee' in Article 1A(2), takes its meaning from the human rights framework. In New Zealand this is the case, whereas Australia's jurisprudence in terms of recognition of human rights is described as a 'patchwork'.[221] A number of key decisions of the NZRSAA, which contain detailed analyses of human rights violations, are regarded as leading international cases on the meaning of 'being

---

[219] A refugee is defined in Art. 1A(2) as a person who: '. . . owing to well-founded fear of being persecuted for reasons of race, religion, nationality, membership of a particular social group or political opinion, is outside the country of his nationality and is unable or, owing to such fear, is unwilling to avail himself of the protection of that country; or who, not having a nationality and being outside the country of his former habitual residence . . . is unable or, owing to such fear, is unwilling to return to it.'

[220] Immigration Amendment Act 1999 (NZ) inserted Part 6A into the Immigration Act 1987. Previously the NZRSAA had operated under Terms of Reference. See www.nzrefugeeappeals.govt.nz (accessed 8 May 2008).

[221] Michelle Foster, *International Refugee Law and Socio-Economic Rights: Refuge from Deprivation* (Cambridge University Press, 2007), at p. 28 describes Australia's approach as 'patchwork' and points out the lack of clear guidance from the superior courts.

THE AUSTRALIAN STORY 219

persecuted' on the basis of gender,[222] or by non-state actors.[223] It is important to note that in New Zealand there is no debate about the extent of incorporation of the Refugee Convention, as in Australia. Indeed the RSAA is required 'to act in a manner that is consistent with New Zealand's obligations under the Refugee Convention',[224] the text of which is set out in a schedule to the Act.

In Australia the importance of human rights in defining 'being persecuted' is less clear. Prior to the insertion of s. 91R into the Migration Act in 2001,[225] there was High Court authority to the effect that fundamental human rights are relevant to understanding its meaning. In *Chan Yee Kin*, several members of the High Court specifically defined 'being persecuted' as involving a breach of human rights. Chief Justice Mason commented:

> The denial of fundamental rights or freedoms otherwise enjoyed by nationals of the country concerned may constitute such harm, although I would not wish to express an opinion on the question whether *any* deprivation of a freedom traditionally guaranteed in a democratic society would constitute persecution if undertaken for a Convention reason [emphasis in original].[226]

In subsequent Australian decisions, the tendency was for only the dissenting judges to discuss human rights,[227] although in many cases the High Court made it clear that a person was 'being persecuted' when denied basic freedoms and human rights.[228] As one commentator has remarked, while not explicitly adopting a human rights approach, decision makers, particularly at the tribunal level, have 'displayed a willingness to consider a wide range of human rights abuses as relevant to the question whether a person is at risk of "being persecuted"'.[229]

---

[222] Refugee Appeal No. 71427/99 (16 August 2000), www.refugee.org.nz/Fulltext/71427-99.htm (accessed 19 May 2008).
[223] Refugee Appeal No. 71462/99 (27 September 1999), www.refugee.org.nz/rsaa/text/docs/71462–99.htm (accessed 19 May 2008).
[224] Immigration Act 1987 (NZ), s. 129D.
[225] See p. 178.
[226] *Chan Yee Kin* (1989) 169 CLR 379 at 388. See also Gaudron J at 413, Dawson J at 399, McHugh J at 430 (emphasis in original).
[227] E.g. *Minister for Immigration* v. *Ibrahim* (2000) 204 CLR 1.
[228] *Chen Shi Hai* (2000) 201 CLR 293 at 303.
[229] Foster, *International Refugee Law and Socio-Economic Rights*, p. 118.

220 REFUGEES, ASYLUM SEEKERS AND THE RULE OF LAW

In Australia, since 2001 the Article 1A(2) definition has been modified by s. 91R of the Migration Act, which confines the meaning of 'persecution' to situations where:

- The 'reason' or 'reasons' for persecution (the grounds are left undefined, subject to s. 91S) is/are the 'essential and significant reason' for one of the reasons mentioned in Article 1A(2) (s. 91R(1)(a)) (the 'nexus' requirement).
- The persecution involves 'systematic and discriminatory conduct' (s. 91R(1)(c)).
- The persecution involves 'serious harm to the person' (s. 91R(1)(b)), the meaning of which is set out in s. 91R(2).

Section 91R of the Migration Act thus defines persecution as involving 'systematic and discriminatory conduct' (s. 91R(1)(c)) and 'serious harm to the person' (s. 91R(1)(b)).

The language of 'systematic and discriminatory conduct' was used by Justice McHugh in *Chan Yee Kin*.[230] A few years later, in *Ibrahim*, McHugh expressly moderated his comments in *Chan Yee Kin* in response to his concern that application of the phrase had become formulaic. He expressly emphasized the human rights dimension of the concept of 'being persecuted'. He described persecution as:

> Unjustifiable and discriminatory conduct directed at an individual or group for a Convention reason ... which constitutes an interference with the basic human rights or dignity of that person or persons in the group ... which the country does not authorise or does not stop, and ... which is so oppressive or likely to be repeated or maintained that the person threatened cannot be expected to tolerate it, so that flight from, or refusal to return to that country is the understandable choice of the individual concerned.[231]

Justice Gaudron similarly described persecution by reference to human rights as 'sustained discriminatory conduct'.[232]

Recent High Court authority suggests that application of s. 91R can lead to narrower decisions and a restrictive application of the refugee definition. There is evidence that it has limited the human rights approach to interpretation of the refugee definition.[233] Its effect is to break

---

[230] (1989) 169 CLR 379 at 430.   [231] (2000) 204 CLR 1 at 65.

[232] *Ibid.* at para. 29. See UNHCR Handbook para. 42 which emphasizes the 'tolerability' of the applicant's situation.

[233] Susan Kneebone, 'Bouncing the Ball between the Courts and the Legislature: What is the Score on Refugee Issues?' in Tom Davis (ed.), *Human Rights 2003: The Year in*

THE AUSTRALIAN STORY 221

up the Convention definition into separate parts which works against a 'holistic' view of the facts and definition.

The High Court decision in *VBAO* v. *Minister for Immigration* (*VBAO*),[234] which concerned the interpretation of the phrase 'threat to ... life or liberty' in s. 91R(2)(a) and the application of the 'real chance' test, is a relevant example. The issue in that case was whether threats that a person had received in their country of origin amounted to 'serious harm' for the purpose of s. 91R(2)(a). The RRT clearly considered that the evidence did not establish such harm. The Federal Magistrate had applied the legislation literally and concluded that such acts came within the meaning of the provision. In rejecting the Federal Magistrate's construction, Justice Gummow noted in a brief judgment that the intention of the legislature in enacting s. 91R was to limit the interpretation of the Refugee Convention to the 'level of harm accepted by the parties to the Convention to constitute persecution'.[235] Therefore, he concluded, given the potentially expansionary effect of including threats as instances of 'serious harm', a more restrictive interpretation should be applied.

The High Court in *VBAO* said that the starting point for defining persecution is the legislation, but practice in the Australian courts and tribunals is inconsistent.[236] Further, although there is often an absence of express reference to human rights, they may be in the background of the decision maker's mind. For example, in *SZDTM* v. *Minister for Immigration*,[237] the judge on judicial review found that the RRT had applied s. 91R too literally and had ignored the 'racial basis' of the attacks upon an Indonesian woman of Chinese ethnic origin. However, in the same case, the judge upheld the RRT decision to reject her claim on the basis of persecution for her Christian faith, as she had not demonstrated 'systematic and discriminatory conduct'. While that analysis undermines the established human rights approach to persecution on the basis of religion,[238] set out in *M93 of 2004* v. *Minister for Immigration*,[239] the Federal Magistrate

---

Review (Melbourne: Castan Centre for Human Rights Law, Monash University, 2004), pp. 135–178.

[234] (2006) 231 ALR 544.

[235] *Ibid.* at 546 (quoting the Explanatory Memorandum to the legislation that introduced s. 91R). Note: the background to the legislation is discussed at pp. 178–85 above.

[236] Kneebone, 'Bouncing the Ball between the Courts and the Legislature', pp. 145–46.

[237] [2006] FCA 188 (Bennett J).

[238] *Wang* v. *Minister for Immigration* (2001) 62 ALD 373.   [239] [2006] FMCA 252.

222   REFUGEES, ASYLUM SEEKERS AND THE RULE OF LAW

accepted that 'serious harm' could be constituted by a denial of the right to education, a fundamental human right.

The effect of s. 91R appears to be to mask the explicit articulation of the human rights framework.[240] This is illustrated by the decision of Justice Merkel in *VTAO* v. *Minister for Immigration* (*VTAO*),[241] which considered the issue of whether a person was being persecuted as a member of a particular social group 'by reason of' a Convention ground. The issues in this case were not dissimilar to the those in the decision of *Chen Shi Hai*, in which it was decided that a 'black child' born to a couple contrary to China's one-child policy, who was denied basic rights to education, food and health, was a member of a 'social group'. In *VTAO*, Merkel said that 'serious harm' required evidence of discriminatory conduct. He said that the tribunal had failed to consider whether the discriminatory treatment ('the harms and disabilities' that parents of such children suffer)[242] over time resulted in them becoming a particular social group.

It is clear that the legislation has added another layer of complexity to the interpretation of the refugee definition and that the role of human rights is unclear. This, in turn, may lead to future inconsistency with international jurisprudence.

'By reasons of' – the 'nexus' requirement

Another point of difference between the Australian and New Zealand approach to interpretation of the Refugee Convention definition is in the application of the causation or nexus test. In requiring a well-founded fear of being persecuted 'for reasons of' race, religion, nationality, membership of a particular social group or political opinion, the refugee definition needs a causal link between the risk of being persecuted and the ground upon which refugee status is claimed. The Convention does not define the causation standard, but in Australia s. 91R has attempted to do this (the 'essential and significant reason'). This has further restricted the interpretation of the refugee definition in Australia and reduced the opportunity for a human rights analysis, in comparison with New Zealand.

The need for a causal link has given rise to several issues. One issue is how to resolve the situation where there is more than one motive for

---

[240] Kneebone, 'Bouncing the Ball between the Courts and the Legislature', pp. 145–46.
[241] [2004] FCA 927.   [242] *Ibid.* at para. 34.

'persecution'. In particular, how is the situation to be resolved where there are 'mixed' motives only some (or one) of which are linked to Convention grounds? A related issue is as to the level of causation which is required to make the link. Is it possible to apply the causation standards from other areas of the law, for example, the 'but for' test from tort law? Another issue that has arisen in cases involving non-state actors is the question of whether the intention of the persecutor is relevant in making that link. Flowing from that is an approach which focuses upon the predicament of the persecuted rather than the intention either of the persecutor or of the country of origin.[243] This approach is applied in New Zealand.[244]

The jurisprudence of the Australian courts on the nexus issue is predictably more complex. Prior to the 2001 amendment, the courts recognized that there are often mixed motives for persecution and declined to impose a strict 'but for' test. In *Chen Shi Hai*, the High Court accepted a statement of Justice French at first instance when he said that:

> Motivation connecting persecution to the relevant attribute is sufficient. Persecution may be carried out coolly, efficiently and with no element of personal animus directed at its objects. There are too many examples of inhuman indifference of which governments are sometimes capable . . . The attribution of subjectively flavoured states . . . to governments and institutions risks a fictitious personification of the abstract and the impersonal.[245]

The Australian courts have recognized that there are often multiple motives for persecution by governments or their agents. In *Chen Shi Hai*, the High Court described the need for a nexus as a 'common thread' that links the persecution and the grounds. But, in that case, the High Court declined to lay down a prescriptive approach to causation, such as by way of a 'but for' test.

The decision in *Minister for Immigration* v. *Sarrazola*[246] is another relevant example of how causation issues were considered in Australia

---

[243] See Foster, *International Refugee Law and Socio-Economic Rights*, pp. 246–86 for a detailed discussion of these issues.

[244] Refugee Appeal No. 72635/01 (6 September 2002), www.refugee.org.nz/Fulltext/72635–01.htm (accessed 19 May 2008); Refugee Appeal No. 74665/03 (7 July 2004), www.refugee.org.nz/Fulltext/74665–03.html (accessed 19 May 2008).

[245] (2000) 201 CLR 293 at 304.

[246] (1999) 95 FCR 517; *Sarrazola No. 2* (2001) 107 FCR 184. The history of this litigation is discussed by Alex de Costa, 'Assessing the Cause and Effect of Persecution in Australian Refugee Law: Sarrazola, Khawar and the Migration Legislation Amendment Act (No. 6) 2001 (Cth)' (2002) 30 *Federal Law Review* 534.

224 REFUGEES, ASYLUM SEEKERS AND THE RULE OF LAW

prior to 2001. In that case, the applicant claimed that her family was targeted by thugs who sought to extort protection money from her. She claimed that this arose from her deceased brother's criminal activities. The RRT applied a 'motivation' test and found that the persecution was for a 'private' reason, namely money, and thus that the applicant was not entitled to refugee status. The Full Court of the Federal Court disagreed and found that the family could be described as a social group, and thus that she was targeted because of her membership of that group.[247] A second Full Court upheld this decision, on the basis that the question to be asked by the RRT was whether 'the family unit considered to be a social group is *publicly* recognized as being set apart as such [emphasis added]'.[248] It considered that the RRT had erred by considering whether the *particular* family was differentiated in the Colombian community by reason of its fame or notoriety.

This decision was followed in other cases[249] and applied in two extortion cases. In *Rajaratnam* v. *Minister for Immigration*[250] it was applied to a Tamil harassed by the Sri Lankan army, and in *Ramirez* v. *Minister for Immigration*[251] to a person harassed by Colombian guerillas.[252]

The Australian government was unsettled by these decisions and that of the High Court in *Minister for Immigration* v. *Khawar* (*Khawar*),[253] in which it was held that a married woman from Pakistan who claimed that she was the victim of serious and prolonged abuse by her husband, and that the police in Pakistan refused to enforce the law against such violence or otherwise offer her protection, was a 'member of a particular social group'. Section 91R(1)(a), which now requires that an applicant for refugee status in Australia must establish that the Convention ground 'is the essential and significant reason' for 'the persecution' was a response to such perceived 'judicial activism'. This causation standard is arguably more difficult to satisfy than that prescribed by the Convention itself.

Further, in s. 91S, the Australian Government attempted to legislate away the effect of *Sarrazola*, which it regarded as a case involving 'privately' motivated persecution rather than persecution for a 'Convention

---

[247] The Court also dismissed the motivation argument, suggesting that it was unreliable, as motivations often involve mixed purposes.

[248] *Sarrazola No. 2* (2001) 107 FCR 184 at 195 per Merkel J. Emphasis added. Note that *ibid.* at 193 Merkel J stressed Art 16.3 of the UDHR.

[249] *C* v. *MIMA* (Wilcox J) (2000) 59 ALD 643. See also *Mocan* v. *RRT* (1996) 42 ALD 241.

[250] [2000] FCA 111.   [251] [2000] FCA 1000.   [252] See also *Giraldo* [2001] FCA 113.

[253] (2002) 67 ALD 577.

THE AUSTRALIAN STORY 225

reason'. Section 91S states that in claims on the basis of membership of a family group, decision makers are to 'disregard any fear of persecution . . . that any other member . . . of the family has ever experienced, where the reason for the fear' does not come within the refugee definition. The express intention of this legislation is acknowledged in the Explanatory Memorandum to the Bill and in the Bills Digest.[254]

There is evidence that s. 91R(1)(a) has added to the complexity of the application of the causation standard. In some cases it has been read literally to determine whether there is a sole Convention reason for the persecution.[255] On this approach, if there is a non-Convention reason for the harm suffered, the decision maker will reject the application even if there are other Convention reasons.[256] Effectively this means that decision makers are giving greater weight to the non-Convention reasons. For example, in *SZAIZ* v. *Minister for Immigration*,[257] the applicant was a wealthy Hindu businessman from Bangladesh. He claimed that he was persecuted on the basis of his religion and that he was at risk of being extorted for his wealth. The RRT found that while his religion may be a factor, the 'essential and significant reason' for the extortion was the wealth of the applicant. The decision was upheld on review.

By contrast, in other cases, decision makers have suggested that s. 91R(1)(a) assists in sifting essential and non-essential reasons for harm. In *SZFZN* v. *Minister for Immigration*,[258] it was found on review that the RRT had failed to evaluate the significance of the harm that the homosexual applicant feared in India. The Federal Magistrate said:

---

[254] Commonwealth of Australia, Department of the Parliamentary Library, Information and Research Services, Bills Digest No. 552001–02, *Migration Legislation Amendment Bill (No. 6) 2001*, 18 September 2001.

[255] E.g. *MZXDQ* v. *Minister for Immigration* [2006] FCA 1632 – journalist applicant from the Ukraine at risk of persecution due only to the motivation of revenge of individuals affected by his actions – no need to consider his membership of a social group.

[256] E.g. *VXAJ* v. *Minister for Immigration* (2006) 234 ALR 381 – trafficked woman at risk because of debt rather than for broader risk of harm; *SZEGA* v. *Minister for Immigration* [2006] FCA 1286 – harm arising from disapproved marriage rather than as members of a social group; *M93 of 2004* v. *Minister for Immigration* [2006] FMCA 252 – RRT said 'persecution' motivated by financial reasons rather than as member of a social group (overturned on review); *SZDQ* v. *Minister for Immigration* [2005] FMCA 415 – photographer feared persecution from the police because of 'rogue' officers rather than political opinion; *SZAIX* v. *Minister for Immigration* [2006] FCA 3 – rape for reasons of revenge not Convention reason.

[257] [2004] FMCA 22 (Raphael J).   [258] [2006] FMCA 1153.

226   REFUGEES, ASYLUM SEEKERS AND THE RULE OF LAW

> I do not consider that the words 'essential and significant' allow a Tribunal to ignore the real or essential underlying Convention reason for a person's conduct. In my opinion, the provision should be applied upon an understanding of normal legal concepts of causation attaching to the phrase 'by reason of'. It provides a gloss requiring disregard of concurrent or contributory Convention causes of persecution if they can be characterised as inessential or insignificant.
>
> In the present case, however, nothing in the Tribunal's reasons suggests that it characterised as inessential or insignificant the underlying anti-homosexual element which, upon the evidence accepted by the Tribunal, appears to explain the friend's father's conduct. In my opinion, it would not have been open to it to do so.[259]

Thus it is unclear whether the nexus test introduced by s. 91R(1)(a) has added anything to the general law.

Part four: conclusions

This chapter has shown the extraordinary and persistent lengths to which the Australian Government has gone to keep asylum seekers beyond the reach of the rule of law. This includes the policies of mandatory detention, excising Australian territory and introducing offshore processing, the introduction of the TPV scheme with the consequent denial of rights, and attempts to deny asylum seekers and their advocates access to the legal system, while at the same time the government has itself used litigation to achieve its policy objectives. It illustrates the significant role of one national legal system in shaping national responses to asylum seekers and refugees in disregard of the international rule of law.

The use of legislation to achieve its agenda is another of the hallmarks of the past decade of government policy in this context. This extended to overturning unwelcome judicial rulings, the wide conferral of personal unreviewable discretions in legislation, and legislating to codify the refugee definition in the Refugee Convention. In this way we see that politics intrudes into the legal system.

Such policies were, in part, made possible by the constitutional status of asylum seekers as 'aliens' and by judicial interpretation of the constitutional powers. Over the period surveyed, the High Court has become more formalistic in its reasoning and less sympathetic to the rights of refugees under the Refugee Convention, seemingly in response to the agenda of the government. The executive also attempted to

---

[259] *Ibid.* at paras. 21–2.

control the judiciary, which often responded in a very traditional or positivist way by deferring to parliamentary sovereignty rather than by recognizing the rights of refugees in international law. In particular, this response stems from the manner and limited extent of incorporation of the Refugee Convention 'protection obligations' into Australian law, which reflects the Coalition Government's receptivity to international law.

In the past decade, the Coalition Government has been seemingly unresponsive to the numerous critical reports and inquiries into its policies, resulting from normal democratic processes. Importantly, it was its own rebel members and the broader community which brought many of these issues to a head in opposing mandatory detention and the TPV scheme.

In this context, the executive has equated 'integrity' with border control. To a large extent, this flows from the government's view of international relationships and its obligations under the Refugee Convention. International law has been seen in a very 'positivist' way as involving relations between states. The Migration Act has been interpreted in that light. Thus the reference to 'protection' obligations in s. 36(2) is read as a 'false but legislatively required step' to reflect the role of the executive under international law in acceding to the Convention. Unsurprisingly, arguments about administrative convenience have prevailed in interpreting the nature of obligations under the Convention incorporated into Australian law.

Australia has also shown that it is prepared to ignore the international jurisprudence which has developed in refugee law. By codifying the Refugee Convention definition, it has watered down a human rights approach to interpretation of the Convention and cast Australian jurisprudence adrift from international refugee law.

Overall it can be queried whether, over the last decade, the Australian government has respected the two key precepts of the international system of refugee protection; namely the right to seek asylum and the right against *refoulement*, and whether it has acted as a responsible Contracting State under the Refugee Convention. However, with the recent change of government, there appear to be signs of hope for more responsible approaches. But the story of this chapter is about the use of a legal system to achieve policy objectives which are at odds with international obligations. The moral of this story is that a rule of law which becomes a 'government of men' is not a good one.

5

The Intersection between the International, the Regional and the Domestic: Seeking Asylum in the UK

MARIA O'SULLIVAN

The UK is a state with strong historical and legal links to the other countries discussed in this book. It has traditionally influenced (and sometimes been influenced by) its common law counterparts and has been particularly prominent historically in developing the concept of law and the rule of law.[1] Against this background, the UK has been struggling, particularly in the last two decades, to adopt asylum law and policies which respect the rule of law, while also conforming to its national interests. Certain aspects of UK asylum law have been quite progressive, such as the interpretation by UK courts of key aspects of the refugee definition.[2] However, in recent years (in line with many other asylum host states), it has sought to restrict the number of asylum seekers entering the country by means of various border control and other deterrent measures. As part of this policy, the UK has introduced restrictive legal terms such as 'safe country of origin' and 'safe third country', accelerated procedures involving limited appeal avenues, and has increasingly pushed for expedited removals of 'failed' asylum

---

[1] See, e.g., the very influential writings of Albert Venn Dicey: such as A. V. Dicey, *Introduction to the Study of the Law of the Constitution*, 10th edn. (London: Macmillan, 1959). Dicey's views are discussed briefly in Susan Kneebone, 'The Rule of Law and the Role of Law: Refugees and Asylum Seekers', Chapter 1 in this volume.

[2] For example, see the purposive, modern interpretation given to 'particular social group' in *R* v. *Immigration Appeal Tribunal, ex parte Shah; Islam and others* v. *Secretary of State for the Home Department* [1999] 2 All ER 545 (HL). This was described by Guy Goodwin-Gill as 'a significant contribution to the development of international refugee law' which would serve as a model in other jurisdictions: see Guy Goodwin-Gill, 'Judicial Reasoning and "Social Group" after Islam and Shah' (1999) 11 *International Journal of Refugee Law* 537. See also Colin Harvey in 'Refugees, Asylum Seekers, the Rule of Law and Human Rights' in David Dyzenhaus (ed.), *The Unity of Public Law* (Oxford: Hart Publishing, 2004), p. 206.

THE INTERSECTION BETWEEN THE INTERNATIONAL   229

seekers.[3] In recent years it has also expressed particular concern over the handling of asylum in the context of national security.[4]

Although there are similarities between the restrictive responses of the UK and that of other common law countries discussed in this book, there are a number of important differences. One significant difference is the existence of close legal and political links between the UK and Europe – both in relation to the influence of the European Convention of Human Rights (ECHR)[5] and the UK's role in the harmonization of asylum by the European Union (EU).[6] This, however, is a relationship beset with contradictions. On the one hand, the UK's move to greater engagement with the EU on asylum matters via harmonization of laws and procedures has arguably resulted in some advances in UK refugee law.[7] However, at the same time, the introduction by the UK of certain restrictive asylum principles, such as 'safe third country of origin', have had their origins in EU fora.[8] Additionally, despite incorporating the ECHR into domestic law in 1998, the UK has since sought to resile from important ECHR rights in relation to national security.

The relationship between the UK and Europe is at the intersection of international, regional and domestic law, and raises some important rule of law issues. For instance, how has the UK's engagement with the

---

[3] Other deterrence measures include the use of detention, voucher systems and involuntary dispersal. One particular issue has been the so-called 'enforced destitution' of asylum seekers in the UK. See Rryszard Cholewinski, 'Enforced Destitution of Asylum Seekers in the United Kingdom: The Denial of Fundamental Human Rights' (1998) 10 *International Journal of Refugee Law* 462.

[4] See, in particular, the discussion in relation to Canada in Chapter 2 in this volume at pp. 105–19.

[5] European Convention for the Protection of Human Rights and Fundamental Freedoms and its protocols, Rome, 4 November 1950, in force 3 September 1953, ETS 5, 213 UNTS 221 (*ECHR*).

[6] The EU currently consists of 25 Member States: see http://europa.eu/ (accessed 18 April 2008).

[7] Discussed further below in *The EU Qualification Directive and the UK*.

[8] E.g. Ministers of the Member States of the European Communities responsible for Immigration, Resolution on a Harmonized Approach to Questions concerning Host Third Countries (London, 30 November and 1 December 1992), www.unhcr.bg/euro_docs/en/_28_%20host_third%20en.pdf (accessed 22 April 2008). See also discussion by Cathryn Costello, 'The Asylum Procedures Directive and the Proliferation of Safe Country Practices: Deterrence, Deflection and the Dismantling of International Protection?' (2005) 7 *European Journal of Migration and Law* 35 at 50; Susan Kneebone, 'The Legal and Ethical Implications of Extraterritorial Processing of Asylum Seekers: The "Safe Third Country" Concept' in Jane McAdam (ed.), *Forced Migration, Human Rights and Security* (Oxford: Hart Publishing, 2008), Chapter 5.

230   REFUGEES, ASYLUM SEEKERS AND THE RULE OF LAW

EU affected its asylum policy and law? What role will international refugee law play within this regionalized system? What does this say about the operation of the rule of law in the UK? In analysing these issues from a rule of law perspective, this chapter will discuss the importance of the European Court of Human Rights on asylum decision making in the UK and address the role of EU harmonization in providing consistency in refugee law decision making and some of the dangers that this may pose in terms of the further development of international refugee law standards.

The first part of the chapter provides an historical overview of UK asylum law and policy and the current legal framework. It describes key aspects of the UK asylum system, such as incorporation of the 1951 Convention relating to the Status of Refugees (*Refugee Convention*)[9] and the 1967 Protocol relating to the Status of Refugees (*Refugee Protocol*)[10], incorporation of the ECHR via the UK Human Rights Act 1998, transposition of EU Asylum Directives and the institutions and procedure for refugee status determination. The second part explores how international law intersects with UK domestic law. Particular focus will be placed on the influence of the ECHR and EU asylum law on UK domestic law. In relation to the ECHR, the discussion in this chapter will analyse the way in which the UK has attempted to evade aspects of the prohibition of torture in Article 3,[11] particularly the attempt by the UK to overturn the European Court of Human Rights decision in *Chahal* v. *UK* (*Chahal*).[12] This discussion highlights the tension between the interests of states in protecting their citizens against national security threats and the nature of Article 3 as an absolute right. In relation to the EU, the discussion will focus on the EU Qualification Directive,[13] which was transposed into UK law in 2006.[14] In order to analyse the rule of law

---

[9] Convention relating to the Status of Refugees, Geneva, 28 July 1951, in force 22 April 1954, 1989 UNTS 137 (*Refugee Convention*).

[10] Protocol relating to the Status of Refugees, New York, 31 January 1967, in force 4 October 1967, 19 UNTS 6223, 6257 (*Refugee Protocol*).

[11] ECHR, Art. 3 provides that 'No one shall be subjected to torture or to inhuman or degrading treatment or punishment'.

[12] (1996) 23 EHRR 413.

[13] Council Directive 2004/83/EC of 29 April 2004 on minimum standards for the qualification and status of third-country nationals or stateless persons as refugees or as persons who otherwise need international protection and the content of the protection granted, OJ 2004 No. L 304/12, 30 September 2004 (*Qualification Directive*).

[14] 'Transposition' refers to the process whereby EU Member States are required to incorporate the particular EU Asylum Directive into national law. E.g. the transposition

THE INTERSECTION BETWEEN THE INTERNATIONAL   231

implications arising from the latter, the discussion will focus upon the provisions relating to cessation and revocation of refugee status. The conclusion discusses the implications of European regional developments for both UK domestic law and the development of international refugee law more broadly. In doing so, it is concluded that, while the development of harmonized EU asylum directives are beneficial in terms of ensuring consistency across EU jurisdictions, the inconsistencies between the directives and international refugee law are of great concern.

Part one: context – a brief history of asylum law and policy in the UK

UK governments have at various times attested to the UK's proud tradition of asylum.[15] However, this version of history is disputed. According to Dallal Stevens:

> Sometimes viewed with scepticism or fear, sometimes accepted grudgingly, always perceived as alien, asylum seekers to the British Isles have, throughout history, faced an uncertain welcome.[16]

As Stevens notes, although the UK 'has sought for decades to proclaim its great tradition of asylum', the treatment of refugees during World Wars I and II was 'undoubtedly problematic'.[17] This is echoed by Gina Clayton, who states that '[e]very history of immigration shows that in Britain each new group of arrivals has been regarded with suspicion and hostility'.[18]

---

provision of the Qualification Directive (Art. 38) requires states to 'bring into force the laws, regulations and administrative provisions necessary to comply with this Directive before 10 October 2006'. States are required to at least incorporate the 'minimum standards' set out in the Directives, but theoretically are permitted to pass national laws which implement more 'favourable standards' so long as they are compatible with the Directive – see Qualification Directive, Art. 3. The Directive came into force in the UK on 9 October 2006 and was transposed into UK law via the Refugee or Person in Need of International Protection (Qualification) Regulations 2006, and amendments to the UK Immigration Rules.

[15] E.g. The Home Office has stated 'The United Kingdom has a proud tradition of providing a place of safety for genuine refugees': Home Office, 'Asylum', www.bia. homeoffice.gov.uk/asylum/ (accessed 30 March 2008).

[16] Dallal Stevens, *UK Asylum Law and Policy: Historical and Contemporary Perspectives* (London: Sweet and Maxwell, 2004), p. 31.

[17] Ibid., p. 68.

[18] Gina Clayton, *Textbook on Immigration and Asylum Law*, 2nd edn. (Oxford University Press, 2006), p. 5.

232   REFUGEES, ASYLUM SEEKERS AND THE RULE OF LAW

However, the UK has, during various periods in recent history, accepted quite substantial numbers of refugees. For instance, during the 1950s the UK accepted over 21,000 refugees from Hungary,[19] and during the 1960s and 1970s it also accepted groups of refugees from Kenya, Uganda, Chile and Vietnam.[20] But the policies adopted by the UK governments during these periods were problematic. For instance, in certain cases the UK only agreed to take refugees who had connections with the UK.[21] During the 1980s, public debate and UK government policy was influenced quite significantly by high numbers of asylum applications from Tamils from Sri Lanka.[22] For instance, after a controversial attempt by the Home Secretary to remove a number of Sri Lankan asylum seekers who had arrived at Heathrow airport in 1987 without valid visas, the UK passed the Immigration Carriers Liability Act 1987, which provided for the fining of carriers who transported undocumented passengers.[23] Indeed, Dallal Stevens identifies the arrival of the Tamil asylum seekers as the period in UK political history when the:

> discourse surrounding refugees altered markedly ... Thereafter it became the norm to describe asylum seekers as 'manifestly bogus', 'economic migrants' or even 'liars, cheats and queue jumpers', as one MP [Member of Parliament] described the Tamils.[24]

The seeds of public discontent and increasing government concern over asylum which began in the 1980s continued and intensified during the 1990s, which was dominated by debates over the acceptance of refugees from the Former Yugoslavia. Initially, the UK adopted a very restrictive approach to these refugees, and agreed to accept only a small number of refugees relative to other European asylum host states. It returned many of the asylum seekers to other EU countries, such as Germany.[25]

---

[19] See Joanne van Selm-Thorburn, 'Exceptional Leave to Remain in the United Kingdom' in *Refugee Protection in Europe: Lessons of the Yugoslav Crisis* (The Hague: Martinus Nijhoff Publishers, 1998), pp. 215–16. The fact that the UK accepted such a large number of refugees may be explained by the fact that the Hungarian refugees received what Stevens has described as 'massive public sympathy' (Stevens, *UK Asylum Law and Policy*, p. 72).

[20] Stevens, *UK Asylum Law and Policy*, pp. 76–91. For instance, Stevens notes that in 1968 large numbers of Asians from East Africa who were fleeing persecution (particularly from Kenya) entered the UK. In fact, Stevens reports that by February 1968, approximately 750 Kenyan Asians were arriving in the UK every day: see Stevens, *UK Asylum Law and Policy*, p. 76. For an excellent discussion of this period, see Tony Kushner and Katharine Knox, *Refugees in an Age of Genocide* (London: Frank Cass, 1999), Chapters 9–11.

[21] See discussion by Stevens, *UK Asylum Law and Policy*, pp. 86–89.   [22] *Ibid.*, pp. 92–93.
[23] *Ibid.*, p. 94.   [24] *Ibid.*, p. 97.   [25] *Ibid.*, pp. 101–102.

THE INTERSECTION BETWEEN THE INTERNATIONAL   233

Although the UK agreed to give temporary protection to some Kosovan refugees in 1999,[26] some commentators have been critical of aspects of the UK response to Former Yugoslavian refugees during this period.[27] In more recent years, UK asylum policy has been marked by similar trends evident in many other industrialized Western countries, such as increasing government and public discontent about asylum policy and the high number of asylum seekers,[28] inflammatory media reporting,[29] and government concerns over delays in decision making,[30] border control and national security.[31] Arguably, some of these trends and concerns have been more marked in the UK. For instance, the UK Government has focused particularly on limiting the number of asylum seekers entering their territory and addressing delays in refugee status decision making. Compared with many other EU countries, the UK has, during various periods, received the largest numbers of asylum applications. For instance, in the year 2002, the number of asylum applications

---

[26] See the Information Centre for Asylum and Refugees (*ICAR*) which notes that the UK Kosovo Humanitarian Evacuation Programme brought a total of 4,346 evacuees to the UK in 1999: ICAR, 'The History of Kosovars in the UK', Navigation Guide, www.icar.org.uk/?lid=307 (accessed 16 April 2008).

[27] E.g. Stevens says 'For a country such as the UK, so openly proud of its asylum record, the handling of the case of the former Yugoslavia is testament to the sharp division which exists between rhetoric and reality': Stevens, *UK Asylum Law and Policy*, p. 103. See also Kushner and Knox, *Refugees in an Age of Genocide*, pp. 361–366. Note, however, that other commentators have highlighted positive aspects of the UK's resettlement of these refugees – see Vaughan Robinson and Caroline Coleman, 'Lessons Learned? A Critical Review of the Government Program to Resettle Bosnian Quota Refugees in the United Kingdom' (2000) 34 *International Migration Review* 1217.

[28] See Matthew J. Gibney, *The Ethics and Politics of Asylum: Liberal Democracy and the Response to Refugees* (Cambridge University Press, 2004), pp. 245–46.

[29] The UK tabloid press has reported on asylum in inflammatory and negative ways (e.g. frequently using terms such as 'bogus' asylum seeker). See, e.g., the extract from a report in *The Sun* newspaper: 'we resent the scroungers, beggars and crooks who are prepared to cross every country in Europe to reach our generous benefits system' (7 March 2001); and the following headlines from the *Daily Express*: 'Asylum: We're Being Invaded' (10 August 2001); 'Asylum Invasion reaches 12,000 a Month' (14 August 2001). The editors of the *Daily Express* and the *Daily Mail* were called to give evidence on this issue to the Joint Committee of Human Rights in 2007: see Stephen Brook, 'Mail and Express Deny Asylum Bias', *The Guardian*, 23 January 2007. However, in a report on press coverage of asylum in the UK, ICAR in 2007 concludes that 'there has been an overall improvement in press coverage of asylum since the Press Complaints Commission (*PCC*) introduced new guidance for journalists': see ICAR, *Reporting Asylum: The UK Press and the Effectiveness of PCC Guidelines*, January 2007, p. 1, www.icar.org.uk/?lid=4775 (accessed 17 April 2008).

[30] See discussion below at pp. 255–7.   [31] See discussion below at pp. 259 and following.

234 REFUGEES, ASYLUM SEEKERS AND THE RULE OF LAW

lodged in the UK reached a high of 84,130.[32] Statistics from the United Nations High Commissioner for Refugees (UNHCR) confirm that the UK received the largest number of asylum seekers of the industrialized countries in 2001 and 2002.[33] As well as leading to both public and governmental concerns, these numbers also put enormous pressure on the decision-making capacities of the UK Home Office and contributed to serious problems with delays in decisions. These problems were later used by the UK Government as justification for the introduction of restrictive asylum measures (such as restrictions in appeal rights and use of 'accelerated' refugee determination procedures).

Significantly, the early 2000s was a period characterized by intense public debate over asylum, which was a significant electoral issue in the 2001 and 2005 UK elections.[34] The then UK Home Secretary, David Blunkett (2001–4), was particularly outspoken about perceived abuses in the asylum system. For instance, during parliamentary debates in 2002, he stated that the asylum system in the UK was 'virtually unworkable' due to the availability of judicial review and '[t]he whole system is riddled with delay, prevarication, and, in some cases, deliberate disruption of the appeals process'.[35] During this period, the UK Government proposed a number of very controversial and highly restrictive measures, including proposals to rewrite the Refugee Convention,[36] to oust judicial review,[37] and to introduce extraterritorial

---

[32] See Home Office, *Asylum Statistics United Kingdom* 2002 (London: Home Office RDSD, 28 August 2003). Since then, asylum applications have dropped significantly. For instance, in 2007 the UK received 23,430 asylum applications: see Home Office, *Asylum Statistics: 4th Quarter 2007 United Kingdom* (London: Home Office RDSD), p. 2.

[33] See UNHCR, *Statistical Yearbook 2002: Trends in Displacement, Protection and Solutions*, July 2004, p. 40, www.unhcr.org/home/STATISTICS/41206f790.pdf (accessed 16 April 2008).

[34] See, e.g., Paul Waugh, 'Election 2001: Migrants – Tories Put Asylum and Refugees at Heart of', *The Independent*, 19 May 2001 which reports that the then Conservative Opposition leader, William Hague, declared in a pre-election speech that Britain had become the 'asylum capital of Europe', and said it should be 'a safe haven, not a soft touch'.

[35] David Blunkett, House of Commons Debates, Vol 384, col 355, 24 April 2002 (D. Blunkett).

[36] See, e.g., Alan Travis, 'Straw Aims to Rewrite Treaty on Refugees', *The Guardian*, 8 June 2000.

[37] The UK Government attempted to introduce an ouster clause into the Asylum and Immigration Treatment of Claimants Bill 2003. This clause was quite wide in that it attempted to prevent judicial scrutiny of all decisions of the Asylum and Immigration Tribunal. The clause was criticized by various legal groups including the Law Society, the Bar Council, the Joint Parliamentary Committee on Human Rights and various senior judges. Ultimately the government decided not to include the clause in the second

processing of asylum claims in North Africa similar to that of the Australian 'Pacific Plan'.[38] For various reasons, however, none of these proposals were implemented and appear (for the moment at least) to have been shelved by the current UK Government.[39]

Most recently, in February 2008, the Home Office very publicly announced that asylum applications were the lowest in fourteen years.[40] The Home Office linked this to the efficiency of border controls.[41] Additionally, the UK is currently grappling with reconciling its asylum laws and policies with terrorism and national security issues.

Part two: the asylum seeker and refugee in the UK legal system

In the UK context there are several features which are particularly significant to a discussion of the role of law in establishing the rights of refugees and asylum seekers in the legal system: the incorporation of the Refugee Convention and ECHR into domestic law; the constitutional and administrative structures in the UK; and procedures for refugee status determination. These issues will be discussed in turn.

---

reading version of the Bill. For an excellent discussion of the issues raised by this attempt, see Richard Rawlings, 'Review, Revenge and Retreat' (2005) 68 *Modern Law Review* 378.

[38] Letter from the then PM Tony Blair to the Greek Presidency of the EC, 10 March 2003, discussed by Stevens, *UK Asylum Law and Policy*, p. 428. Indeed the UK has looked very much to Australia for guidance on refugee policy generally, see e.g. the discussion of Australia's 'Pacific Plan' in Susan Kneebone, 'The Pacific Plan: The Provision of "Effective Protection"?' (2006) 18 *International Journal of Refugee Law* 696.

[39] The then UK Prime Minister Tony Blair resiled from the proposal to amend the Convention in a speech in 2005. However, note that prior to the 2006 General Election, the opposition Conservative Party stated that if elected they would withdraw from both the Refugee Convention and the ECHR: see Nicholas Blake, 'The Impact of the Minimum Standards Directives 2004/83/EC on National Case Law' in International Association of Refugee Law Judges (*IARLJ*), *The Asylum Process and the Rule of Law* (New Delhi: Manak Publications, 2006), p. 47.

[40] See Home Office, 'Lowest Number of Asylum Applications in 14 Years', *News and Updates*, 26 February 2008, www.ind.homeoffice.gov.uk/sitecontent/newsarticles/lowestnumberasylumapps (accessed 28 March 2008).

[41] In a Home Office press release it stated 'Britain's tougher border controls have led to the lowest level of asylum applications in 15 years': Home Office, 'Annual Asylum Applications at a Fifteen Year Low: Record Number of Foreign National Prisoners Removed', Press Release, 20 November 2007, www.ind.homeoffice.gov.uk/sitecontent/newsarticles/annualasylumapplications (accessed 16 April 2008).

236 REFUGEES, ASYLUM SEEKERS AND THE RULE OF LAW

Incorporation of the Refugee Convention into domestic law

The UK is a party to both the Refugee Convention and the Refugee Protocol, having ratified the Convention on 11 March 1954[42] and acceded to the Protocol on 4 September 1968.[43] The UK has a dualist legal system and thus its international legal obligations must be incorporated through statute law.[44] The UK's obligations under the Convention are now explicitly mentioned in UK domestic law, and parts of the Convention have been reflected in the UK Immigration Rules.[45] However, for many years after the UK had signed the Refugee Convention, it was not incorporated into domestic legislation, and asylum was referred to only briefly in the Immigration Rules.[46] A number of commentators have criticized the UK's tardiness in incorporating the Convention.[47]

Thus, it was not until the passing of the Asylum and Immigration Appeals Act 1993 that the UK made reference to the Refugee Convention in statute law.[48] While this was a welcome legal development, what had historically been a problem with an *absence* of asylum legislation quickly grew to one of a *proliferation* of legislation in the 1990s. In the space of only ten years, the UK passed another five major pieces of legislation in quick succession: the Asylum and Immigration Act 1996, the Immigration and Asylum Act 1999, the Nationality Immigration

---

[42] UK Treaty Series No. 039/1954 : Cmd 9171.

[43] UK Treaty Series No. 015/1969 : Cmnd 3906.

[44] See *J.H. Rayner* v. *Department of Trade* [1990] 2 AC 418; *R* v. *Home Secretary, ex parte Brind* [1991] 1 AC 696; *R* v. *Lyons* [2003] 1 AC 976.

[45] For instance, para. 338 of the Immigration Rules provides that: 'All asylum applications will be determined by the Secretary of State in accordance with the Geneva Convention'. Also, a version of Art. 1C of the Refugee Convention is incorporated via para. 339A; parts of Art. 1F are set out in para. 339D, which provides for exclusion from humanitarian protection; and a version of Art. 28 is set out in para. 344A.

[46] For instance, in the 1970s and 1980s, the primary piece of legislation operating in the immigration field was the Immigration Act 1971, and it made no mention of the Convention or its Protocol. The 'soft law' Immigration Rules of 1983 only briefly mentioned the Convention (Rule 16 of the *Statement of Changes in Immigration Rules* (1983), HC 169).

[47] Stevens, *UK Asylum Law and Policy*, pp. 79–80; and Robert Thomas, 'The Impact of Judicial Review on Asylum' (2003) *Public Law* 479, at 480–483, 509.

[48] Section 2 of the 1993 Act, headed 'Primacy of Convention' stated that 'Nothing in the immigration rules (within the meaning of the 1971 [Immigration] Act) shall lay down any practice which would be contrary to the Convention'. Further, the interpretation provisions in s. 1 defined a 'claim for asylum' as a claim by a person that it would be contrary to the UK's obligations under the Refugee Convention for the person to be removed from the UK.

and Asylum Act 2002, the Asylum and Immigration (Treatment of Claimants etc) Act 2004, the Immigration, Asylum and Nationality Act 2006, and associated subordinate legislation. It has also passed immigration legislation which, although not directly focused on asylum, has impacted on asylum matters.[49] Some commentators have noted that these legislative pronouncements were a reaction to the increasing number of immigrants to the UK and public concern over those numbers.[50]

The asylum legislation introduced in the period 1993–2006 set out technical and complex legislative provisions which, for the most part, have attempted to restrict the ability of asylum seekers to apply for asylum in the UK. It is not possible to analyse here the detail of the each legislative change which took place over this period. However, it is significant that, in this period, the various pieces of legislation introduced (and later 'refined') such concepts as 'safe country of origin', 'safe third country', 'fast-track procedure' and 'manifestly unfounded claims', and used these concepts to restrict appeal avenues.[51] Controversially, UK legislation has set out restrictive interpretations of the exclusion provisions in Article 1F[52] and Article 33(2)[53] of the Refugee Convention. For instance, s. 54 of the Immigration and Asylum

---

[49] E.g. The Immigration (Carrier's Liability) Act 1987. The government also recently introduced the Criminal Justice and Immigration Bill 2007 into Parliament – as discussed at p. 260 below.

[50] See, e.g., Will Somerville, 'The Immigration Legacy of Tony Blair', Migration Policy Institute, May 2007, www.migrationinformation.org/Feature/display.cfm?id=600 (accessed 18 April 2008).

[51] For a discussion of the various changes introduced via these Acts, see Stevens, *UK Asylum Law and Policy*, pp. 163–219. An example of the restrictions in appeal avenues is that if the Home Office finds that an applicant is from a safe country of origin as per s. 94(4) Nationality, Immigration and Asylum Act 2002 and that his/her claim is therefore 'clearly unfounded', that applicant may not appeal within the UK, but only from outside the UK: see further discussion of appeal avenues at pp. 252–5 below.

[52] Article 1F of the Refugee Convention provides that the Convention shall not apply to 'any person with respect to whom there are serious reasons for considering that: (a) he has committed a crime against peace, a war crime, or a crime against humanity, as defined in international instruments drawn up to make provision in respect of such crimes; (b) he has committed a serious non-political crime outside the country of refuge prior to his admission to that country as a refugee; (c) he has been guilty of acts contrary to the purposes and principles of the United Nations'.

[53] Article 33(2) of the Refugee Convention sets out an exception to the *non-refoulement* principle set out in Art. 33(1). It provides that the *non-refoulement* principle may not be claimed by a refugee 'whom there are reasonable grounds for regarding as a danger to the security of the country in which he is, or who, having been convicted by a final judgment of a particularly serious crime, constitutes a danger to the community of that country'.

238   REFUGEES, ASYLUM SEEKERS AND THE RULE OF LAW

Act 2006 sets out a statutory interpretation of Article 1F(c) (persons 'guilty of acts contrary to the purposes and principles of the United Nations'). It enlarges the scope of Article 1F(c) by including 'acts of committing, preparing or instigating terrorism (whether or not the acts amount to an actual or inchoate offence)' and acts of 'encouraging or inducing others' to do the same.[54] Likewise, s. 72 of the Nationality, Immigration and Asylum Act 2002 sets out a particular domestic construction of Article 33(2) of the Refugee Convention for the purposes of excluding persons from its protection.[55]

The frequent legislative changes outlined above have usually followed the release of substantial policy papers by the government, where it has introduced new policy 'platforms' on asylum.[56] These policies reflect an approach to asylum policy and planning which is generally patchwork and reactive in nature. Indeed, a number of concerns have been raised by the UK courts and by commentators about the nature of asylum legislation in the UK and the way in which the government has frequently amended the legislation since 1993. For instance, the UK Court of Appeal noted that asylum was 'an area where the law is riddled with obscurities and regularly amended by primary and secondary legislation and by rules'.[57] Commentators such as Robert Thomas and Gina Clayton have raised concerns about the frequent passing of legislation and the technicalities and complexities introduced by each new Act.[58] Indeed, Clayton says that 'haste and lack of consultation have come to characterize the process of legislating on immigration and asylum issues'.[59]

---

[54] Immigration and Asylum Act 2006, s. 54(1).

[55] Section 72 sets out that in the 'construction and application' of Art. 33(2) by providing that a conviction in the UK warranting two years' imprisonment is indicative of a particularly serious crime which creates a presumption of a danger to the community (s. 72(2)). Section 72(3) extends this to comparable crimes and sentences committed overseas and s. 72(4) allows the Secretary of State to specify crimes in the form of an order for which a conviction would be sufficient to raise such a presumption regardless of duration of the sentence.

[56] E.g. in 1998 the government released a White Paper entitled 'Fairer, Faster and Firmer'; in 2002 it released another White Paper 'Secure Borders, Safe Haven: Integration with Diversity in Modern Britain' and in 2005 the 'Five Year Strategy for Asylum and Immigration'. In 2005 the government also announced the 'New Asylum Model', which is discussed below.

[57] *Zenovics* v. *Secretary of State for Home Department* [2002] EWCA Civ 273, para. 33.

[58] Robert Thomas: 'Parliament has legislated for asylum policy on five separate occasions since 1987 with each Act making the law progressively more technical and complex': Thomas, 'The Impact of Judicial Review on Asylum' at 483.

[59] See Clayton, *Textbook*, p. 40.

THE INTERSECTION BETWEEN THE INTERNATIONAL 239

Problems with consultation have included the passing of late amendments and the failure to give adequate notice of proposals to key stakeholders and relevant Parliamentary Committees. For instance, the Home Affairs Committee inquiry into asylum applications, which was dealing with the 2004 Asylum and Immigration (Treatment of Claimants etc) Bill, said the following:

> [W]e have not had the benefit of a draft bill nor — in common with other interested parties – were we given more than a few weeks notice of the proposals even in outline.[60]

In addition to incorporation of the Convention via legislation, key Articles of the Convention are also referred to in various asylum regulations[61] and the current version of the UK Immigration Rules.[62] Although the Immigration Rules are 'soft law' (that is, they are administrative rules which do not have the legal status of legislation), they are binding in that failure to act in accordance with the rules can render a decision appealable.[63] Some commentators have raised concerns with the way in which the Immigration Rules are drafted and passed. Clayton notes that they 'allow considerable scope for individual judgment'[64] and notes that they are made by the Minister subject to the negative resolution procedure and 'are therefore subject only to very limited parliamentary scrutiny'.[65]

The UK's incorporation of the ECHR and EU asylum directives

As stated in the introduction, the UK's role in European regional arrangements and instruments differentiates it from the other common law countries analysed in this book and raises particular rule of law issues relating to the way in which asylum law is harmonized regionally, and its consistency with international refugee law.

---

[60] Home Affairs Committee Inquiry into Asylum Applications, January 2004, No. 218, para. 3, cited in Clayton, *Textbook*, p. 40.

[61] See, e.g., the Refugee and Persons in Need of International Protection (Qualification) Regulations 2006 which set out a construction of the exclusion grounds under Art. 1F(b) of the Refugee Convention.

[62] As discussed above in note 45 (re: Immigration Rules).

[63] See Nationality and Asylum Act 2002, s. 86, which provides that an appeal must be allowed if the decision 'is not in accordance with the law (including the Immigration Rules)', discussed in Clayton, *Textbook*, pp. 31, 259.

[64] See Clayton, *Textbook*, p. 29.   [65] Ibid., p. 31.

240 REFUGEES, ASYLUM SEEKERS AND THE RULE OF LAW

Incorporation of ECHR via the Human Rights Act 1998

The ECHR, and the right of petition to the European Court of Human Rights in Strasbourg, have been important bulwarks against UK law which breaches the human rights of asylum seekers in the UK.[66] Significantly, the ECHR was made part of UK domestic law when the UK passed the Human Rights Act (HRA) in 1998. This Act, which came into force throughout the UK on 2 October 2000, incorporates a range of rights contained in the ECHR.[67] It provides that 'so far as is it possible to do so' both primary and secondary legislation 'must be read and given effect in a way which is compatible with Convention rights',[68] and provides that it is unlawful for a 'public authority'[69] to act in a way which is incompatible with Convention rights.[70] Further, it provides that where a court is satisfied that a provision of primary legislation is incompatible with a Convention right, it may make a 'declaration of incompatibility'.[71] Significantly, in terms of statutory interpretation by the UK judiciary, s. 3 of the HRA provides that courts must interpret both primary and secondary legislation in a way which is compatible with Convention rights.

The HRA does not specifically set out protections for asylum seekers or refugees.[72] However, a number of ECHR provisions have been used by asylum seekers in litigation under the HRA: Article 3 of the ECHR, which prohibits the return of a person where there are substantial grounds for believing that there is a real risk of torture or inhuman

---

[66] For a more detailed discussion of the use of the ECHR by asylum seekers see Nicholas Blake and Raza Husain, *Immigration, Asylum and Human Rights* (Oxford University Press, 2003).

[67] The HRA covers most of the Articles of the ECHR which the UK has ratified: Arts. 2–12 and 14 of the ECHR, Arts. 1–3 of the 1st Protocol to the ECHR and Art. 6 of the 6th Protocol to the ECHR. However, the HRA does not refer to Art. 13 ECHR which provides for an 'effective remedy before a national authority' for 'everyone whose rights and freedoms as set forth in this Convention are violated'.

[68] HRA, s. 3(1).

[69] This is defined in s. 6(3) to include a 'court or tribunal' and 'any person certain of whose functions are functions of a public nature, but does not include either House of Parliament or a person exercising functions in connection with proceedings in Parliament.

[70] HRA, s. 6(1).   [71] *Ibid.*, s. 4(1).

[72] The ECHR itself does not set out protections for asylum seekers or refugees. Protocols 4 and 7 do provide some procedural rights to aliens: Art. 4. of Protocol 4 prohibits collective expulsion of aliens; Art. 1 of Protocol 7 contains certain procedural guarantees against expulsion. However, the UK has not ratified these protocols.

THE INTERSECTION BETWEEN THE INTERNATIONAL 241

and degrading treatment or punishment; Article 5(1)(f) relating to detention;[73] and Article 8, which sets out the right to respect for family life.[74]

It should be noted that the HRA is limited in scope in a number of ways. One limitation is that, unlike the US Bill of Rights, it is not constitutionally entrenched[75] and therefore can be amended, or indeed repealed, by Parliament. Additionally, while s. 6(1) of the HRA makes it unlawful for a public authority to act in a way which is incompatible with an ECHR right, it only allows a court to make a 'declaration of incompatibility' in relation to the legislation which impugns the HRA, it does not empower courts to invalidate or set aside the legislation. Furthermore, s. 6(2) of the HRA reflects the status of parliamentary sovereignty in the UK, by providing that it will not be unlawful for a public authority to act in a way which is incompatible with a Convention right if the public authority was required to act in the particular way by primary legislation.[76]

Although legislation cannot be invalidated if it impugns the HRA, s. 19 of the HRA requires legislation (including subsidiary legislation) to be certified as complying with the ECHR. This has been particularly important during the transposition of the various EU asylum directives into UK law, as it provides a link between the harmonized national asylum standards and European human rights law. For instance, the changes introduced in the UK Regulations and Immigration Rules to transpose the various EU asylum directives are assessed for their compliance with the ECHR, and a statement regarding this compliance

---

[73] ECHR Art. 5(1) provides: 'Everyone has the right to liberty and security of person. No one shall be deprived of his liberty save in the following cases and in accordance with a procedure prescribed by law . . . (f) the lawful arrest or detention of a person to prevent his effecting an unauthorised entry into the country or of a person against whom action is being taken with a view to deportation or extradition'.

[74] ECHR Art. 8(1) 'Everyone has the right to respect for his private and family life, his home and his correspondence'. Article 8(2) then sets out some qualifications to this right.

[75] Although some commentators have noted that it has 'profound constitutional significance': John Wadham, Helen Mountfield, Anna Edmundson and Caoilfhionn Gallagher, *Blackstone's Guide to the Human Rights Act 1998*, 4th edn. (Oxford University Press, 2007), p. v.

[76] Specifically, s. 6(2) HRA provides that the s. 6(1) duty on public authorities does not apply if: '(a) as the result of one or more provisions of primary legislation, the authority could not have acted differently; or (b) in the case of one or more provisions of, or made under, primary legislation which cannot be read or given effect in a way which is compatible with the Convention rights, the authority was acting so as to give effect to or enforce those provisions'.

242 REFUGEES, ASYLUM SEEKERS AND THE RULE OF LAW

is made by the Minister of State for the Home Department in the relevant Explanatory Memoranda to the legislation.[77]

Transposition of EU directives

Somewhat surprisingly for a country that has tended to be hesitant about signing key EU treaties and immigration agreements,[78] the UK has been one of the leaders in the move to harmonize EU asylum laws and procedures.[79] This may spring from the fact that the UK Government has, for many years, been concerned that the UK receives more applications for asylum than most other EU countries[80] and is therefore keen to push towards greater uniformity in laws and standards.

For many years, EU Member States have cooperated in a 'burden-sharing' arrangement, whereby states have signed regulations to determine which Member State will be responsible for examining an asylum application lodged in the EU (the Dublin Convention and from 2003, the Dublin II Regulation).[81] However, this agreement does not set out any harmonized standards in relation to the definition of a refugee or to refugee decision-making procedures, and is generally considered (by both Member States and commentators) to have been of limited success.[82] Thus, in 1999, EU Member States commenced negotiations to establish the 'Common European Asylum System' (CEAS) to harmonize EU asylum law.[83] The CEAS consists of two phases: the first phase is the

---

[77] See, e.g., *Explanatory Memorandum to the Refugee or Person in Need of International Protection (Qualification) Regulations* 2006, No. 2525, para. 6.1, www.opsi.gov.uk/si/em2006/uksiem_20062525_en.pdf (accessed 31 March 2008).

[78] E.g. the UK has not signed the Schengen Agreement, under which EU countries agreed to dismantle internal borders (creating a common external border), thereby allowing passport-free movement between certain European countries.

[79] See, e.g., Clayton, *Textbook*, p. 137: 'In terms of asylum policies, the UK is a key player, not swept unwillingly into European co-operation, but in the forefront of promoting deterrent measures'.

[80] See discussion above pp. 233–4.

[81] The Dublin Convention first came into force on 1 September 1997 for the first twelve signatories (which included the UK). A revised version now applies between most Member States: Council Regulation (EC) No. 343/2003 of 18 February 2003, establishing the criteria and mechanisms for determining the Member State responsible for examining an asylum application lodged in one of the Member States by a third-country national, OJ 2003 No. L 50/1, 1 September 2003 (Dublin II Regulation).

[82] See Stevens, *UK Asylum Law and Policy*, pp. 377, 406–10; Guy S. Goodwin-Gill and Jane McAdam, *The Refugee in International Law*, 3rd edn. (Oxford University Press, 2007), pp. 400–2.

[83] The basic structure of the CEAS and the first phase was defined by the Council of Europe during a meeting in Tampere in October 1999 (the Tampere Conclusions) and

THE INTERSECTION BETWEEN THE INTERNATIONAL   243

harmonization of EU asylum law through the drafting of common minimum standards, and the second aims to achieve 'a higher common standard of protection and greater equality in protection across the EU and to ensure a higher degree of solidarity between EU Member States'.[84] As part of the first phase of the CEAS, EU Member States agreed to a series of asylum 'directives' as part of its attempt to establish a common procedure and uniform status for asylum across the EU. The UK has signed up to a number of these directives and has transposed them into its domestic law. These include: the EU Temporary Protection Directive,[85] the EU Qualification Directive,[86] the EU Procedures Directive[87] and the EU Reception Directive.[88] In addition to these directives, it should also be noted that the EU influences UK domestic law and policy via negotiations (formal or otherwise), recommendations

guidelines for the second phase confirmed by the Hague Program in 2004: for further discussion of the development of the CEAS, see Maria-Teresa Gil-Bazo, 'The Protection of Refugees under the Common European Asylum System: The Establishment of a European Jurisdiction for Asylum Purposes and Compliance with International Refugee and Human Rights Law', Cuadernos Euopeos de Deusto, No. 36/2007, pp. 153–82, available at Social Science Research Network (SSRN) website at www.ssrn.com (accessed 16 April 2008).

[84] See EU, 'Green Paper on the Future Common European Asylum System', Press Release, MEMO/07/229, Brussels, 6 June 2007, http://europa.eu/rapid/pressReleasesAction.do?reference=MEMO/07/229 (accessed 31 March 2008). According to this press release, some proposed measures for the second stage include greater harmonisation of procedures, the drafting of EU-wide guidelines on issues such as gender persecution, and greater efforts to more equitable burden-sharing.

[85] Council Directive 2001/55/EC of 20 July 2001 on minimum standards for giving temporary protection in the event of a mass influx of displaced persons and on measures promoting a balance of efforts between Member States in receiving such persons and bearing the consequences thereof OJ 2001 No. L 212/12, 7 August 2001. This has been transposed into UK law by: the Displaced Persons (Temporary Protection) Regulations 2005, Part 11A Immigration Rules and reliance on existing legislation.

[86] Qualification Directive, see note 13 above.

[87] Council Directive 2005/85/EC of 1 December 2005 on minimum standards on procedures in Member States for granting and withdrawing refugee status OJ 2005, No. L 326/13. This has been transposed into UK law via The Asylum (Procedures) Regulations 2007, amendments to the Immigration Rules, and reliance on existing law. This Directive is controversial as it extends the notions of 'countries of first asylum' and confirms the use of 'accelerated procedures' and 'unfounded applications'.

[88] Council Directive 2003/9/EC of 27 January 2003 laying down minimum standards for the reception of asylum seekers OJ 2003, No. L 31/18. Transposed into UK law via the Asylum seekers (Reception Conditions) Regulations 2005, the Asylum Support (Amendment) Regulations 2005 and changes to the Immigration Rules (see Statement of Changes in Immigration Rule HC 194 – January 2005.

244 REFUGEES, ASYLUM SEEKERS AND THE RULE OF LAW

by the Council of Europe's Parliamentary Assembly and Committee of Ministers, and other 'soft law' measures.[89]

Administrative and constitutional structures

The constitutional structure of the UK has a number of salient features that are relevant to the discussion of asylum and the rule of law. First, the UK (unlike the USA and Australia) does not have a single written constitution. Secondly, the doctrine of parliamentary supremacy means that statute law remains the supreme law. This can raise problems in relation to the interpretation of statutes which incorporate international law. As mentioned earlier, the UK (like the other common law countries discussed in this book) operates a dualist system in relation to international law. The UK courts have adopted the approach that Parliament is presumed to have intended to legislate compatibly with treaties to which the UK is a party.[90] However, there is a countervailing principle that courts may not interpret the Convention in a way which conflicts with national legislation.[91]

The UK judiciary has been instrumental in overseeing the application of asylum law. In *Bugdaycay* v. *Secretary of States for the Home Department*,[92] a key UK asylum case, Lord Bridge, in dicta, noted that decisions affecting the right to life must be subject to the 'most anxious scrutiny' by the courts.[93] Since then, the UK courts have handed down landmark decisions on key asylum issues such as access to judicial review,[94]

---

[89] See, e.g., Parliamentary Assembly of the Council of Europe, 'Recommendation 1624 (2003) on Common Policy on Migration and Asylum', 30 September 2003; Committee of Ministers of the Council of Europe, 'Recommendation R (2005) 6E to Member States on Exclusion from Refugee Status in the Context of Article 1F of the Convention Related to the Status of Refugees', 23 March 2005.

[90] See, e.g., *R* v. *Home Secretary, ex parte Brind* [1991] 1 AC 696.

[91] *R* v. *Lyons* [2003] 1 AC 976, 992E, 995G, 1000: where there is an express and applicable provision of domestic law it is the duty of the courts to apply that, even if this would render the UK in breach of an international treaty or rule of customary international law; see *R (on the application of Pepushi)* v. *Crown Prosecution Service* [2004] EWHC 798 (Admin): where a statute clearly conflicts with the Refugee Convention, the statute prevails, even if this defeats part of the protection of the Convention (see Clayton, *Textbook*, p. 394). Editor's note: this common law principle is consistent with the effect of the HRA s. 6(2) discussed above, which preserves the principle of parliamentary sovereignty.

[92] [1987] AC 514.   [93] *Ibid.* at 531.

[94] See e.g. *M* v. *Home Office* [1994] 1 AC 377 (House of Lords).

THE INTERSECTION BETWEEN THE INTERNATIONAL 245

challenges to the 'safe third country' removals,[95] and removal of asylum seeker support.[96] In doing so, the UK courts have considered 'modern' developments in, and interpretations of, international refugee law. For instance, UK courts routinely refer to the UNHCR Handbook[97] and learned academic commentary[98] when interpreting key aspects of the Convention. They have also drawn quite significantly from jurisprudence in other similar jurisdictions, particularly Australia and Canada.[99]

The UK judiciary has shown its willingness to check executive action in a number of key asylum cases. One illustration of this is the case of *R (on application of Q and others) v. Secretary of State for the Home Department,*[100] involving the implementation of the controversial s. 55 of the Nationality, Immigration and Asylum Act 2002, which provided for the withdrawal of income support from certain asylum seekers.[101] A group of asylum seekers who had been denied support under s. 55 of that Act lodged a court action arguing that the decision was unlawful and breached their human rights under the ECHR. The Court of Appeal held that the imposition by the legislature of a regime which prohibited asylum seekers from working and from receiving support may in some circumstances breach that individual's right not to be subjected to

---

[95] See e.g. *R v. Secretary of State for the Home Department, ex parte Adan, Subaskaran and Aitseguer* [2001] 2 AC 477 (*Adan*) (House of Lords).

[96] *R (on application of Q and others) v. Secretary of State for the Home Department* [2004] QB 36.

[97] See, e.g., *R v. Secretary of State for the Home Department, ex parte Robinson* [1998] QB 929 at 938; *Adan* [2001] 2 AC 477 at 489–491; *R (Sivakumar) v. Secretary of State for the Home Department* [2003] UKHL 14, [2003] 1 WLR 840; *Sepet and Bulbul v. Secretary of State for the Home Department* [2003] UKHL 15; 1 WLR 856 at 864–865. Contrast this with the reluctance of the Australian High Court to consider the UNHCR Handbook or other UNHCR guidelines – see, e.g., discussion of *Minister for Immigration v. QAAH* (2006) 231 ALR 340 in Susan Kneebone, 'The Australian Story: Asylum Seekers Outside the Law', Chapter 4 in this volume at pp. 210–17.

[98] See, e.g., *R (European Roma Rights Centre and others) v. Immigration Officer at Prague Airport and another* [2004] UKHL 55, [2005] 2 WLR 1 at 16, 41.

[99] See, e.g., Ibid., *Secretary of State for the Home Department, ex parte Robinson* [1998] QB 929 at 939–940.

[100] [2004] QB 36.

[101] Section 55(1) of the 2002 Act permitted the Secretary of State and local authorities to refuse support and community care to failed asylum seekers where the Secretary is not satisfied that 'the claim was made as soon as reasonably practicable after the person's arrival in the United Kingdom'. According to the UK Refugee Council, this rule was applied very strictly, with some asylum seekers being denied support even though they claimed asylum shortly after arriving in the UK: see UK Refugee Council, 'High Court Ruling Restores Food and Shelter to Destitute Asylum Seekers', Press Release, 19 February 2003, www.refugeecouncil.org.uk/news/press/2003/february/20030219high. htm (accessed 22 April 2008).

246 REFUGEES, ASYLUM SEEKERS AND THE RULE OF LAW

inhuman or degrading treatment under Article 3 of the ECHR.[102] Further, it held that the system instituted under s. 55 (of refusing support) was not fair or fairly operated.[103] In some cases, members of the judiciary have been openly and highly critical of the actions of the Home Office, pointing to an 'unacceptable disregard by the Home Office of the rule of law'.[104]

However, on the other hand, the judiciary has deferred to the executive in other key decisions. For instance, in the appeal in the important case of *R (Saadi)* v. *Secretary of State for the Home Department*,[105] where the applicants challenged their seven-day detention as part of the 'fast-track' procedure operating at Oakington Detention Centre, the House of Lords adopted a balancing approach to the issues of administrative efficiency and detention, finding that detention at Oakington was reasonable.[106]

---

[102] [2004] QB 36 at 83–84.

[103] [2004] QB 36 at 83–84. Note that the decision of Justice Collins at first instance, who held that the treatment breached Art. 3, was publicly criticized by the then Home Secretary David Blunkett, who stated in an interview with the BBC: 'Frankly, I'm personally fed up with having to deal with a situation where Parliament debates issues and the judges then overturn them. I don't want any mixed messages going out so I am making it absolutely clear today that we don't accept what Justice Collins has said', see *BBC News UK*, 'Blunkett to Fight Asylum Ruling', 20 February 2003, http://news.bbc.co.uk/1/hi/uk/2779343.stm (accessed 18 April 2008).

[104] *R (Karas and Miladinovic)* v. *Secretary of State for the Home Department* [2006] EWHC 747 (Admin) per Munby J: 'What the present case and others like it reveal, in my judgement, is at best an unacceptable disregard by the Home Office of the rule of law, at worst an unacceptable disdain by the Home Office for the rule of law, which is as depressing as it ought to be concerning' (para. 87). See also *R (SK)* v. *Secretary of State for the Home Department* [2008] EWHC 98 (Admin) per Munby J: 'I have to say that the melancholy facts that have been exposed as a result of these proceedings are both shocking and scandalous . . . They are scandalous for what they expose as the seeming inability of that Department to comply not merely with the law but with the very rule of law itself' (para. 2).

[105] *R (on the application of Saadi, Maged, Osman and Mohammed)* v. *Secretary of State for the Home Department* [2002] UKHL 41, [2002] 1 WLR 3131 (House of Lords).

[106] This was a significant decision, as Collins J at first instance had held, in reliance on a right to liberty under Art. 5, that the detention was not lawful. Colin Harvey states that the Court of Appeal judgment demonstrates 'a willingness to defer to the overall objectives of asylum policy and judicial "understanding" of the concerns of public administration', see Harvey, 'Refugees, Asylum Seekers, the Rule of Law and Human Rights' in Dyzenhaus (ed.), *The Unity of Public Law*, p. 212. Interestingly, the European Court of Human Rights upheld the House of Lords decision (by a narrow majority): see *Saadi* v. *United Kingdom*, Application No. 13229/03, European Court of Human Rights (Grand Chamber), 11 July 2006.

THE INTERSECTION BETWEEN THE INTERNATIONAL 247

Certain decisions of the UK courts involving the Human Rights Act 1998 and national security issues have caused particularly strong tensions between the executive and judiciary. For instance, the government was highly critical of the Court of Appeal decision in *S and others v. Secretary of State for the Home Department*.[107] This case involved a group of Afghan asylum seekers who fled from the Taliban in 2000 by hijacking a plane and landing at Stanstead airport in the UK. They lodged applications for asylum in the UK, but these were rejected and they were subject to deportation orders. However, on appeal against their removal, the Asylum and Immigration Tribunal (AIT)[108] found that removal would breach their human rights under Article 3 of the ECHR on the basis that they faced torture or other serious ill-treatment if returned to Afghanistan. The Home Office attempted to avoid this decision by amending its administrative policy on granting leave to such persons – a move which the Court of Appeal held was unlawful. In response to this judgment, the government introduced the Criminal Justice and Immigration Bill in order that it may avoid the obligation to grant leave in such cases in the future.[109] This illustrates that the UK Government is willing to pass legislation to override those court decisions which interfere with its ability to manage its asylum process, particularly in relation to public order and national security issues.

Academic and other commentators seem to differ on the view of the stance of the UK judiciary. Lord Chief Justice Phillips has stated that 'despite the threat of terrorism, the UK courts are not showing the traditional deference to action taken by the executive in the interests of national security'.[110] On the other hand, commentators such as Colin Harvey have stated that, in national security and asylum matters, the judiciary's willingness to defer to executive decision-making is 'particularly marked'.[111] Guy Goodwin-Gill and Jane McAdam state that, in the UK, 'the jurisprudence has tended to fall somewhere along the

---

[107] [2006] EWCA Civ 1157.   [108] Discussed below at pp. 252–3.

[109] *Criminal Justice and Immigration Bill, Regulatory Impact Assessments*, p. 155 at www. justice.gov.uk/docs/regulatory-impact-assessments.pdf (accessed 18 April 2008). This Bill is discussed further at p. 260.

[110] Lord Chief Justice Phillips, Lord Chief Justice of England and Wales, 'Reflections on the Rule of Law America's 400th Anniversary at Jamestown Addresses: Rule of Law Conference: Global Issues and the Rule of Law' (2007) 42 *University of Richmond Law Review* 37 at 39.

[111] Harvey, 'Refugees, Asylum Seekers, the Rule of Law and Human Rights' in Dyzenhaus (ed.), *The Unity of Public Law*, p. 216.

248   REFUGEES, ASYLUM SEEKERS AND THE RULE OF LAW

spectrum between deference and review'.[112] Harvey's view appears to be supported by some case law; for instance, in the decision of *Secretary of State for the Home Department* v. *Rehman* (*Rehman*), heard prior to but decided *after* the attacks of 11 September 2001, the House of Lords gave significant latitude to the Home Secretary in relation to cases involving national security.[113]

Scrutiny of executive action by parliamentary committees, government bodies and NGOs

The UK has several parliamentary and other government bodies which act as an oversight mechanism for asylum law and policy. First, the Joint Parliamentary Committee on Human Rights, which consists of twelve members appointed from both the House of Commons and the House of Lords, does important consultation work on human rights issues, including asylum and refugee matters. It has the power to scrutinize all legislation and can comment on legislation which affects human rights.[114] However, the extent to which the Committee's comments influence the drafting of legislation is limited by governmental procedures. For instance, Clayton states that, on occasions, the Home Office did not reply to the Committee's questions until crucial parliamentary stages had been passed.[115] Further, a significant report by the Committee on the treatment of asylum seekers[116] was largely rejected by the government.[117]

---

[112] Goodwin-Gill and McAdam, *The Refugee in International Law*, p. 536. Note, however, that the authors seem to be talking about the jurisprudence of both the Asylum and Immigration Tribunal and the courts here, not simply the judiciary.

[113] *Rehman* [2001] 3 WLR 877. In *Rehman*, the House of Lords held that the Special Immigration and Asylum Commission should have granted the primary decision maker, i.e. the Home Secretary, considerable discretion with respect to his decision to remove Mr Rehman from the UK on national security grounds.

[114] Joint Parliamentary Committee on Human Rights, www.parliament.uk/parliamentary_committees/joint_committee_on_human_rights.cfm (accessed 18 April 2008).

[115] See Clayton, *Textbook*, p. 40.

[116] Joint Committee on Human Rights, *The Treatment of Asylum Seekers*, Tenth Report of 2006–07, HL Paper 81, HC 60 (London: House of Commons, 30 March 2007), www. publications.parliament.uk/pa/jt200607/jtselect/jtrights/81/81i.pdf (accessed 18 April 2008).

[117] See Joint Committee on Human Rights, *Government Response to the Committee's Tenth Report of this Session: The Treatment of Asylum Seekers*, Seventeenth Report of 2006–7, HL Paper 134, HC 790 (London: House of Commons, 5 July 2007), www.publications. parliament.uk/pa/jt200607/jtselect/jtrights/134/134.pdf (accessed 18 April 2008).

THE INTERSECTION BETWEEN THE INTERNATIONAL   249

Secondly, a number of human rights commissions, such as the Northern Ireland Human Rights Commission[118] and the newly formed British Commission on Human Rights and Equality,[119] operate in the UK. However, these currently do not have explicit terms of reference to examine refugee or asylum seeker matters.

Another important development in terms of oversight is the new Independent Immigration Inspectorate, which was introduced via the UK Borders Act 2007 to oversee the operations of the UK Border and Immigration Agency (BIA) (which is the executive agency of the UK Home Office responsible for immigration control and asylum policy). The Inspectorate is to report to the Secretary of State annually[120] and such reports are to be laid before Parliament.[121] Importantly, in terms of the rule of law, the Borders Act empowers the Chief Inspector to examine consistency of approach within the BIA[122] and to examine the certification of those asylum and human rights claims which have been classed as 'clearly unfounded' pursuant to s. 94 of the Nationality, Immigration and Asylum Act 2002.[123] The Inspectorate will not, however, have the power to intervene in individual cases.[124] In addition to this, a non-governmental commission called the Independent Asylum Commission, funded by various charitable trusts, was established in 2006 after citizens' groups and local NGOs highlighted the need for a comprehensive review of asylum in the UK. It has been conducting public hearings across the UK and released an interim report into asylum in March 2008, which was critical of certain aspects of the UK asylum process.[125]

A strong NGO community exists within the UK, which appears to exert some influence on policy and decision making by the UK Government (although it is obviously difficult to accurately measure

---

[118] Northern Ireland Human Rights Commission, www.nihrc.org (accessed 18 April 2008).
[119] UK Equality and Human Rights Commission, www.equalityhumanrights.com (accessed 18 April 2008).
[120] UK Borders Act 2007, s. 50(1) states that the Chief Inspector shall report in writing to the Secretary of State (i) once a year and (ii) at such other times as requested by the Secretary of State in relation to specified matters.
[121] UK Borders Act 2007, s. 50(2). However, s. 50 (3) allows the Secretary of State to withhold material from the copy laid before Parliament if he thinks publication is 'undesirable for reasons of national security' or 'might jeopardise an individual's safety'.
[122] UK Borders Act 2007, s. 44(2)(a).   [123] *Ibid.*, s. 44(2)(e).
[124] Home Office Policy statement on the Inspectorate, March 2007, at point 7.
[125] For the terms of reference and interim report of the Independent Asylum Commission, see www.independentasylumcommission.org.uk (accessed 18 April 2008).

250 REFUGEES, ASYLUM SEEKERS AND THE RULE OF LAW

'effectiveness' in this context). The UK Refugee Council is particularly active in this area and appears to be quite influential.[126] Organizations such as the Immigration Law Practitioners' Association (ILPA),[127] Justice,[128] Liberty,[129] and Amnesty International,[130] while not solely asylum-focused, regularly make oral and written submissions to government about asylum issues. However, as has been the case with some of the inter-governmental bodies discussed earlier, government has not always consulted properly with NGOs in relation to certain decisions. For instance, when the government introduced significant changes to UK law (such as time-restricted refugee protection permits) via the Immigration Rules in 2006, a number of NGOs noted that, because most of the changes were implemented through the Immigration Rules and policy documents rather than primary legislation, the changes were rushed through and little time was given to consultation.[131]

Refugee status decision making in the UK today

Current refugee status determination practices in the UK appear to have improved somewhat since the 1980s and 1990s, when severe backlogs in the UK Home Office caused long delays in decision making. Today the refugee determination process is characterized by the existence of two streams: on the one hand, a fairly comprehensive decision-making process with in-country appeal rights for most asylum seekers; but, on the other, the existence of 'accelerated' procedures for those applicants deemed to have 'unfounded claims' because they come from a 'safe country of origin' or 'safe third country', and a detained fast-track procedure.

Refugee status determination in the UK

Decisions on refugee status in the UK are taken, in the first instance, by case workers within the Border and Immigration Agency of the Home

---

[126] www.refugeecouncil.org.uk (accessed 18 April 2008).
[127] www.ilpa.org.uk (accessed 18 April 2008).
[128] Justice is the British section of the International Commission of Jurists: see www.justice.org.uk (accessed 18 April 2008).
[129] www.liberty-human-rights.org.uk/ (accessed 18 April 2008).
[130] www.amnesty.org.uk (accessed 18 April 2008).
[131] See London Refugee Economic Action (LORECA), 'LORECA Policy Briefing Series: Impact of Temporary Leave on Refugee's Employability Prospects in London', Briefing 1, October 2006, p. 6, www.loreca.org.uk/downloads/LORECA_Policy_Briefing_1.doc (accessed 2 April 2008).

THE INTERSECTION BETWEEN THE INTERNATIONAL   251

Office.[132] An asylum seeker can make three types of claims in order to remain in the UK: an 'asylum claim' under the Refugee Convention; a claim for humanitarian protection or discretionary leave under complementary protection principles;[133] and/or a 'human rights claim' under the ECHR/ Human Rights Act.[134] Importantly, the UK Home Office operates a 'one-stop', single determination procedure for considering asylum applications, as case workers are instructed to consider the eligibility of an applicant under all three categories (asylum, complementary protection or human rights), even if the claim is only made on one of these grounds.[135] Significantly, in terms of ensuring a level of consistency across the Home Office, the decisions of Home Office case workers are guided not only by relevant legislation and the Immigration Rules but also by detailed 'Asylum Policy Instructions' (Apis) and 'Asylum Policy Guidance'.[136]

[132] The Border and Immigration Agency: www.bia.homeoffice.gov.uk (accessed 19 April 2008). Under legislation, the formal decision whether or not to grant status is taken by a member of the Executive: the Secretary of State for the Home Department.

[133] 'Complementary protection' refers to the protection given by states to persons who fall outside the legal definition of refugee in the Refugee Convention, Art. 1A(2). On this point, see discussion in 'Introduction: Refugees and Asylum Seekers in the International Context – Rights and Realities' in this volume at pp. 28–31 and Chapter 4 at pp. 207–10. Note that the criteria for humanitarian protection are set out in paras. 339C–D of the Immigration Rules. However, discretionary leave is granted outside the Immigration Rules and thus the criteria for this are set out in the Asylum Policy Instructions on Discretionary Leave; see www.bia.homeoffice.gov.uk/sitecontent/documents/policyandlaw/asylumpolicyinstructions/apis/discretionaryleave.pdf?view=Binary (accessed 31 March 2008) (API Discretionary Leave).

[134] A 'human rights claim' is a claim by a person that their removal would be unlawful under s. 6(1) of the HRA as being incompatible with his or her rights under the ECHR: see UK Home Office, 'Asylum Process Guidance', www.ukba.homeoffice.gov.uk/sitecontent/documents/policyandlaw/asylumprocessguidance/consideringanddecidingthe claim/ (accessed 10 April 2008). Note that now there is a significant degree of overlap between complementary protection and 'human rights' claims. However, in relation to torture cases, the ECHR is broader than the humanitarian protection provisions in the Immigration Rules, as the torture provisions under the Immigration Rules only cover prohibited treatment that would occur *in the country of origin.*

[135] See BIA, 'Asylum Process Guidance: Considering the Asylum Claim' at www.bia. homeoffice.gov.uk/sitecontent/documents/policyandlaw/asylumprocessguidance/consider inganddecidingtheclaim/ (accessed 19 April 2008). This single determination procedure is consistent with UNHCR's position (UNHCR, 'Complementary Protection', EC/GC.01/ 18) and the Commission of the EU (Commission of the EU, *A More Efficient Common European Asylum System: The Single Procedure as the Next Step,* COM (2004) 503 Final, 15 July 2004).

[136] The APIs reflect government policy on asylum which Home Office case workers are to follow: see www.bia.homeoffice.gov.uk/sitecontent/documents/policyandlaw/asylumpolicyinstructions/ (accessed 23 May 2008). The Asylum Process Guides are guides

A 'Country-Specific Asylum Policy Team' and the Country of Origin Information Service also provide case workers with guidance and reports on country of origin information.[137] All of the above information is available to the public (without charge) via the Internet.[138] The latter is a welcome initiative in terms of the rule of law, as it has introduced some transparency into the process of asylum decision making in the UK.[139]

In the event that the Home Office finds that the applicant is a refugee, they will be granted refuge status and given a five-year temporary residence permit (called 'limited leave to remain'). Near the end of this term, such applicants may apply for permanent settlement, that is, 'indefinite leave to remain' in the UK. Alternatively, an applicant may be found to be entitled to one of the two forms of complementary protection applicable in the UK: Humanitarian Protection, which entitles the applicant to be granted leave to remain in the UK for a period of five years,[140] or Discretionary Leave under which an applicant will be granted leave to remain for a period of no longer than three years.[141] Those applicants granted complementary protection are able to apply for indefinite leave to remain after meeting specific qualification criteria.[142]

In the event that a person is refused refugee status or complementary protection, he or she may be able to appeal against that decision to the AIT which is empowered to re-examine the merits of the individual's

on asylum procedures; see www.bia.homeoffice.gov.uk/policyandlaw/guidance/asylumprocess/ (accessed 19 April 2008).

[137] For instance, the Home Office produces Operational Guidance Notes (OGNs) on certain countries: see www.bia.homeoffice.gov.uk/sitecontent/documents/policyandlaw/countryspecificasylumpolicyogns/ (accessed 19 April 2008).

[138] See. e.g.. Home Office, 'Country of Origin Information Service', 2008, www.homeoffice.gov.uk/rds/country_reports.html (accessed 19 April 2008).

[139] As Justice Burnton of the UK High Court noted in *R (Salih)* v. *Secretary of State for the Home Department* [2003] EWHC 2273 at para. 45, it is a 'fundamental requirement of the rule of law that the law should be made known'. Editor's note: see the discussion of procedural and substantive views of the rule of law in Chapter 1 of this volume.

[140] Immigration Rules, para. 339E.

[141] See Home Office, 'Asylum Policy Instructions: Discretionary Leave', 9 April 2008, www.bia.homeoffice.gov.uk/sitecontent/documents/policyandlaw/asylumpolicyinstructions/ (accessed 19 April 2008).

[142] Applicants who have completed five years' Humanitarian Protection leave will be eligible to apply for Indefinite Leave to Remain (see Home Office, 'API: Humanitarian Protection', October 2006, para. 9). Applicants with Discretionary Leave status are eligible to apply for Indefinite Leave to remain after either six or ten continuous years of Discretionary Leave (depending on the reason the applicant was granted leave) (see Home Office, 'API: Discretionary Leave').

THE INTERSECTION BETWEEN THE INTERNATIONAL   253

application.[143] If the AIT refuses the application, the applicant may then apply to the High Court for a review of that decision, who can order that the AIT 'reconsider' the case. This process is governed by complex requirements set out in the Nationality, Immigration and Asylum Act 2002[144] and is restricted in a number of ways. For instance, it is subject to extremely short time limits and legal aid is only granted retrospectively (that is, after the review and reconsideration process).[145]

In addition to statutory appeal avenues, applicants may also (in some circumstances) be able to lodge an application for judicial review of certain asylum decisions.[146] Ultimately, applicants may also be able to appeal (with leave) to the House of Lords, and from there, if a case involves the breach of a right under the ECHR, to the European Court of Human Rights in Strasbourg.

Accelerated procedures and limited appeal rights

The above process applies in the majority of asylum applications. However, if an applicant is deemed to come from a 'safe country of origin' or 'safe third country', special procedures will apply. The concept of a 'safe country of origin' is incorporated into UK law via s. 94 of the Nationality, Immigration and Asylum Act 2002, which provides that the Secretary of State can deem a country to be 'safe' and certify claims from that country as 'clearly unfounded'. The consequences for an asylum seeker affected by these provisions is that they will be processed via an 'accelerated procedure' at the Oakington or Harmondsworth 'Immigration Removal' (detention) centres[147] and will not have a right

---

[143] The AIT was created pursuant to the Asylum and Immigration (Treatment of Claimants) Act 2004 and commenced operation on 4 April 2005. It is designed to operate as an independent Appeals Tribunal (it is part of the Department of Constitutional Affairs rather than the Home Office). This is in direct contrast to Australia, where the Refugee Review Tribunal is established under the Migration Act 1958 (Cth) and tribunal members are appointed by the Minister for Immigration (see Chapter 4 in this volume at pp. 178–85. The AIT replaces the Immigration Appellate Authority, which consisted of two tiers: adjudicators and the Immigration Appeal Tribunal. The AIT operates according to an adversarial model: see BIA, 'Asylum Process Guidance: The Appeals Process', www.bia.homeoffice.gov.uk/sitecontent/documents/policyandlaw/asylumprocessguidance/theappealsprocess/ (accessed 19 April 2008).

[144] If so, the applicant will have a right of appeal to the AIT and from there may appeal (if they meet the criteria) to the High Court and House of Lords (see Nationality, Immigration and Asylum Act 2002, ss. 103A–E).

[145] The review and reconsideration process is discussed in detail in Robert Thomas, 'After the Ouster: Review and Reconsideration in a Single Tier Tribunal' (2006) *Public Law* 674.

[146] See Stevens, *UK Asylum Law and Policy*, pp. 316–23.

254   REFUGEES, ASYLUM SEEKERS AND THE RULE OF LAW

of appeal within the UK, only an 'out of country' appeal (that is, the appeals are 'non-suspensive'). The criteria for a 'safe country' is quite broad and ambiguous: s. 94(5) provides that a country can be added to the list where the Secretary of State is satisfied that:

(a) there is *in general* in that State or part no serious risk of persecution of persons entitled to reside in that State or part;
(b) removal to that State or part of persons entitled to reside there will not *in general* contravene the UK's obligations under the Human Rights Convention [emphasis added].[148]

Currently there are twenty-four states listed as 'safe' pursuant to the above section. The list includes states such as Albania, Bolivia, Bosnia-Herzegovina, Mongolia, Kenya (men only), Liberia (men only), India, Kosovo, Nigeria (men only) and Sierra Leone (men only).[149] The notion of a 'safe country of origin' is extremely controversial and NGOs and commentators have disputed both the use of such a category and some of the countries which have been designated as 'safe'.[150] In this context, it is significant that applicants have challenged the categorization of certain countries as 'safe' in UK courts.[151]

Similarly controversial is the notion of a 'safe third country', which, as with 'safe country of origin', also entails restrictions in an applicant's procedural rights. Schedule 3 to the Asylum and Immigration (Treatment of Claimants etc) Act 2004 Act contains three lists of 'safe third countries'. As an example of how these lists work, the first list (which is the one most commonly utilized) consists of twenty-six countries of the European Economic Area. The effect of finding that an applicant has travelled from a 'first list' safe third country is that their asylum claim will not be dealt with in the UK. Rather, they will be removed to the relevant European country for their asylum claim to be dealt with and are unable to lodge an appeal against their removal from the UK.[152]

---

[147] In 2005, the Prisons and Probation Ombudsman for England and Wales published an inquiry into allegations of racism and mistreatment of detainees at Oakington. See www.ppo. gov.uk/download/Stephen_Shaw_report_on_Oakington_IRC.pdf (accessed 19 April 2008).
[148] Section 94(5), emphasis added.
[149] For a full, current list of states see BIA, 'Certification Under Section 94 of the NIA Act 2002', 02 April 2008, www.bia.homeoffice.gov.uk/sitecontent/documents/policyandlaw/ asylumprocessguidance/specialcases/ (accessed 19 April 2008).
[150] See, e.g., Clayton, *Textbook*, p. 405.
[151] See, e.g., *R (Husan)* v. *Secretary of State for the Home Department* [2005] EWHC 189 (Admin) where the High Court declared that the inclusion of Bangladesh as 'safe' under s. 94(4) of the Nationality, Immigration and Asylum Act 2002 was unlawful.

THE INTERSECTION BETWEEN THE INTERNATIONAL   255

It is significant to note, given the discussion in this chapter on the relationship between the UK and the EU, that both the concept of a 'safe country of origin' and 'safe third country' originated in Europe.[153] Indeed, both terms are now explicitly set out in the EU Procedures Directive.[154]

Controversies within the Home Office and the 'New Asylum Model'

A discussion of refugee status determination in the UK would not be complete without mentioning the problems that have arisen in the last decade or so in relation to the Home Office, which has been plagued by controversy and has been the object of both parliamentary and public criticism. One of the most serious problems has been delays in decision making, which for many years caused a large backlog of undecided cases. For instance, in 1991, 72,070 asylum applications were awaiting an initial decision by the Home Office.[155] Although this figure dropped in 1993 to 45,805, it rose again in 1995 to 69,650 applications.[156] The Home Office addressed some of this backlog by conducting a 'clearance' of backlog cases from 1998 to 2001, providing concessions to families in 2003–6,[157] and increasing staffing levels.[158] Recent statistics indicate that there were only 6,900 applications awaiting initial decisions at the end of December 2007.[159]

---

[152] For further information on how these lists operate, see Clayton, *Textbook*, pp. 422–423, 425–426; and the UK Home Office, 'Safe Third Country Cases', February 2007, www.ukba.homeoffice.gov.uk/sitecontent/documents/policyandlaw/asylumpolicyinstructions/apis/safethirdcountrycases (accessed 19 April 2008).

[153] See note 8 above.

[154] EU Procedures Directive, see note 87 above, Arts. 23, 27–36.

[155] Madeline Watson and Philip Danselman, *Asylum Statistics United Kingdom* 1997 (Home Office, 21 May 1998), Summary tables, p. 15, www.homeoffice.gov.uk/rds/pdfs/hosb1498.pdf (accessed 19 April 2008).

[156] Note that the backlog also appears to have been exacerbated by problems with a computerization project and an ill-timed move of the Immigration and Nationality Directorate's headquarters which 'led to a massive bureaucratic breakdown': see Mark Tran and Patrick Barkham, 'Clearing the Asylum Backlog', *The Guardian*, 24 July 2000, www.guardian.co.uk/world/2000/jul/24/qanda.marktran (accessed 1 April 2008). See discussion of this issue by Clayton, *Textbook*, p. 15.

[157] This initiative (known as 'the Family ILR exercise') was announced by the Home Secretary in 2003 and allows certain asylum seeker families who have been in the UK for four or more years to stay. By 31 March 2007, 24,615 cases (main applicants, excluding dependants) had resulted in grants of Indefinite Leave to Remain, with 320 cases still to be decided: see Home Office, *Asylum Statistics United Kingdom 2006*, 3rd edn. (London: Home Office RDSD, 21 August 2007), p. 4.

[158] See Mark Tran and Patrick Barkham, 'Clearing the Asylum Backlog'.

256 REFUGEES, ASYLUM SEEKERS AND THE RULE OF LAW

Criticisms have also been made of the quality of initial decision making by the Home Office. For instance, in 2004 two major reports were released which were critical of the processes utilized in the Home Office. First, a report by the House of Commons Home Affairs Committee[160] raised concerns about the 'poor quality of much initial decision-making by immigration officers and case workers'.[161] Secondly, the National Audit Office released a report which raised particular concerns about the high numbers of asylum applications received in the years 1999–2002, the backlog of cases awaiting an initial decision, and the increasing volume of appeals lodged and approved.[162] Academic commentators have also raised concerns about the decision-making processes of the Home Office.[163]

Measures instituted to address Home Office problems

The government has introduced various measures in an attempt to address some of the identified deficiencies in Home Office decision making. This includes the development of what is called the 'New Asylum Model' (NAM), which has been in operation for all new asylum claims lodged since 5 March 2007. One of the measures introduced as part of this initiative has been the setting of targets and timetables for decision making within the Home Office. For example, the NAM provides that asylum applications should be dealt with, from application to final resolution, within six months. The government also introduced what is referred to as a 'tipping point public performance target', which (using a rather complicated formula) states that:

> The number of failed asylum applicants removed each month exceeds the number of new asylum applicants who, it is predicted, will not be granted leave to remain in the UK, as a result of their asylum application.[164]

---

[159] Home Office, *Asylum Statistics: 4th Quarter 2007 United Kingdom*, p. 3.

[160] The Home Affairs Committee is responsible for examining the expenditure, policy and administration of the Home Office and its associated public bodies: see www.parliament. uk/parliamentary_committees/home_affairs_committee.cfm (accessed 19 April 2008).

[161] Home Affairs Committee, *Second Report 2003–4*, para. 143.

[162] Report by the Comptroller and Auditor-General, HC535, Section 2003–4, 23 June 2004, p. 5.

[163] See, e.g., Stevens, *UK Asylum Law and Policy*, pp. 307–13; Thomas, 'The Impact of Judicial Review on Asylum' at 492–94.

[164] See Home Office, 'Public Performance Target: Removing More Failed Asylum Seekers Than New Anticipated Unfounded Applications', *Statistics for First Quarter 2006* (London: Home Office RDSD), pp. 2–5.

THE INTERSECTION BETWEEN THE INTERNATIONAL   257

Measures to improve the accountability of case determination has also been introduced in the Home office via the 'case owners' structure, whereby one case owner will be appointed to a case at its commencement and will be responsible for it until it is resolved. The UK Refugee Council has welcomed the introduction of the 'case owner' approach, but has highlighted some problems with the process, such as delays in asylum seekers being given legal advice.[165] The European Council of Refugees and Exiles (ECRE) has also highlighted concerns with the model, noting that interviews take place as early as the sixth day after initial screening, which does not give asylum seekers sufficient time to prepare their cases.[166] Other initiatives introduced as part of the NAM which have been welcomed by NGOs include the introduction of an accreditation scheme for Home Office decision makers and the provision of more in-depth training on refugee and human rights law.[167]

Analysis of the above issues from the rule of law perspective

Before discussing the two issues which are the focus of this chapter – the ECHR and the EU Qualification Directive – it is useful to note some of the rule of law implications arising from the above overview of UK asylum law and procedure. The overall picture from the above is that initial decision making by the Home Office has been very problematic. The rapid increase in numbers of asylum applications contributed to long delays in decision making, which, in turn, caused public concern and consequent pressure on government to adopt restrictive measures. In this regard, the use of 'safe country' and 'accelerated' procedures to expedite decision making raises concerns, as they have the potential to result in breaches of the *non-refoulement* principle. The emphasis on expedited decision making, particularly the setting of targets and time limits, illustrates the tension between efficiency and administrative justice. While the introduction of efficiency

---

[165] UK Refugee Council, *Asylum Seekers' Experiences of the New Asylum Model: Findings From a Survey With Clients at Refugee Council One Stop Services* (London: UK Refugee Council, January 2008), pp. 17–18, www.refugeecouncil.org.uk/NR/rdonlyres/92F64E45-864C-4899-A7E4–65C08917AA16/0/NAMmonitoring.pdf (accessed 19 April 2008).

[166] European Council of Refugees and Exiles (*ECRE*), *Country Report 2005*, United Kingdom, August 2006, p. 327, www.ecre.org/files/ECRE%20Country%20Report%202005rev.pdf (accessed 22 April 2008).

[167] Discussed in UNHCR, *Quality Initiative Project: Fourth Report to the Minister* (London: UNHCR, January 2007), p. 7, www.ind.homeoffice.gov.uk/sitecontent/documents/aboutus/reports/unhcrreports/ (accessed 17 April 2008).

258 REFUGEES, ASYLUM SEEKERS AND THE RULE OF LAW

measures is an important way of avoiding delays in decision making, and from that perspective is beneficial to administrative justice,[168] it does pose some dangers for the rule of law in terms of the propensity of such measures to lead to serious legal errors (and, thus, also possible breaches of the *non-refoulement* principle).[169] While there are oversight mechanisms in place in the UK, including the AIT and the judiciary, restrictions on appeals hampers the ability of asylum seekers to utilize those two important protectors of the rule of law.

Finally, the restrictive interpretation of Articles 1F and 33(2) of the Refugee Convention in UK legislation (discussed above) illustrates an important rule of law issue. As noted in Chapter 1 of this book, there is a need for specific legislative incorporation of international human rights law treaties (which arises from the 'legislative principle' of parliamentary sovereignty).[170] However, significant problems arise when domestic legislation restricts international treaty provisions, as is the case with the UK legislation which interprets Articles 1F and 33(2) of the Refugee Convention.[171] In such instances, legislation supposedly 'incorporating' the Convention is, in fact, restricting the operation of the Convention domestically.

Part three: analysis – the intersection between the international, regional and domestic: rule of law implications

As foreshadowed in the introduction to this chapter, in order to highlight some current and important rule of law issues arising in the UK, the focus is on two developments: attempts by the UK government to restrict certain aspects of the ECHR in relation to national security and the UK's transposition of the EU Qualification Directive on asylum. Each issue is discussed in turn.

---

[168] For a discussion of this issue, see Peter Billings, 'Balancing Acts: Six Acts in Search of Equilibrium' (2006) 20 *Journal of Immigration Asylum and Nationality Law* 197.

[169] See Erika Feller in IARLJ, *The Asylum Process and the Rule of Law*, p. 40.

[170] See Chapter 1 in this volume.

[171] UNHCR has criticised both s. 54 and s. 72 in this regard. For instance, it notes that s. 72 and its related Order 'set a threshold for an exception to the *non-refoulement* principle that are not in line with the letter and spirit of the 1951 Convention, and do not meet the criteria as set out in Article 33(2) of the 1951 Convention': UNHCR London, 'Comments on the Nationality, Immigration and Asylum Act 2002 (Specification of Particularly Serious Crimes) Order 2004', November 2004, www.unhcr.org.uk/legal/positions/UNHCR%20Comments/SeriousCrimesOrder2004.htm (accessed 1 April 2008). In relation to s. 54, see UNHCR, *Parliamentary Briefing, Criminal Justice and Immigration Bill*, House of Lords Second Reading, 22 January 2008, p. 3, www.unhcr.org.uk/info/briefings/responding_to_policy/documents/UNHCRBriefingCJIBJan08.pdf (accessed 1 April 2008).

THE INTERSECTION BETWEEN THE INTERNATIONAL 259

The UK and ECHR: national security concerns

National security concerns and the combating of terrorism have featured much more prominently in UK legislation and policy since 11 September 2001 and the UK terrorist attacks of 7 July 2005.[172] In particular, groups within the UK have voiced concerns over 'home grown' terrorists[173] and a perceived link between asylum and terrorism.[174] One particular issue has been the difficulty the UK has faced in balancing their national security concerns with their obligations under human rights law, particularly in relation to the prohibition against torture in Article 3 of the ECHR. As mentioned earlier in this chapter, Article 3 of the ECHR has proved quite significant in protecting the human rights of asylum seekers and refugees in Europe. However, its application to situations where states wish to deport a person from their territory for national security reasons has caused a great deal of controversy. One of the main areas of controversy has been the relevance of national security to the Article 3 question; that is, should any risk of ill-treatment in a person's country of origin be 'balanced' against the perceived threat to national security. The answer to this question, according to the European Court of Human Rights in the landmark case of *Chahal*,[175] is that a State Party to the ECHR cannot deport or extradite a person to a country when there are substantial grounds for believing that he or she faces a real risk of treatment contrary to Article 3. This has been a cause of great concern to the UK Government, who have expressed frustration at its inability to deport suspected terrorists and the implications this has for carrying out its role in protecting UK citizens.[176]

Against this context, the UK has been attempting to resile from certain aspects of Article 3 relating to national security concerns. For

---

[172] See, e.g., the Anti-Terrorism Crime and Security Act 2001; and the Terrorism Act 2006.

[173] See e.g. Robert Winnett, 'Britain "a Soft Touch for Home Grown Terrorists"', *The Daily Telegraph*, 26 February 2008, www.telegraph.co.uk/news/main.jhtml?xml=/news/2008/02/15/nterror115.xml (accessed 19 April 2008).

[174] See the very interesting discussion of this issue in Jef Huysmans, *Nexus Terrorism/Immigration/Asylum/Refuge in Parliamentary Debates in the UK: Commons Debates since 11 September 2001*, Report for ESRC project MIDAS (Migration, Democracy and Security) in the New Security Challenges programme, 2 November 2005, www.midas. bham.ac.uk/researchandpolicy.htm (accessed 19 April 2008).

[175] *Chahal* (1996) 23 EHRR 413.

[176] See, e.g., Brendan Carlin, 'John Reid Calls for Human Rights Law Reform', *The Daily Telegraph*, 17 September 2007, www.telegraph.co.uk/news/main.jhtml?xml=/news/2007/09/17/nreid117.xml (accessed 17 April 2008).

instance, the UK Government has introduced the Criminal Justice and Immigration Bill, which seeks to introduce a new immigration status for certain asylum seekers and other migrants, called 'special immigration status'.[177] This provision was introduced as a means of avoiding the effect of the judgment of the Court of Appeal in what is known as the 'Afghan hijacking' case (*S v. Secretary of State for the Home Department*, which is discussed above).[178] Essentially, this 'special immigration status' may be given to those persons classed as 'foreign criminals'[179] who are liable to be deported but who cannot be removed because of the UK's obligations under the ECHR and Human Rights Act.[180] The Bill is significant in that, if passed, it will restrict the rights of asylum seekers who have been excluded from the Refugee Convention or who have had their refugee status revoked pursuant to UK legislation.[181] The effect of designating a person with this 'special status' is that they will be denied rights which are normally granted to refugees, such as permission to work, ordinary state benefits, leave to remain, and access to family reunion rights. They may also be subject to certain residential restrictions (such as restrictions on where they live, reporting conditions, electronic monitoring and curfews).[182] Not surprisingly, this new status has been criticized by various UK NGOs such as the UK Refugee Council[183] and the Joint Council for the Welfare of Immigrants.[184]

---

[177] See Criminal Justice and Immigration Bill (Vol 1) (amended) as of 13 March 2008, available at www.publications.parliament.uk/pa/ld200708/ldbills/041/2008041a.pdf (accessed 19 April 2008).

[178] See p. 247 above.

[179] Criminal Justice and Immigration Bill, clause 130. Note that the list of crimes is quite wide. For instance, it includes a crime committed in the UK leading to a sentence of imprisonment of two years or more.

[180] Criminal Justice and Immigration Bill, clause 129. The status is also applicable to family members of such individuals.

[181] Criminal Justice and Immigration Bill, clauses 129–133, when read with s. 72 of the Nationality, Immigration and Asylum Act 2002 (which is designed to give domestic effect to Art. 33(2) of the Refugee Convention) and s. 54 Immigration, Asylum and Nationality Act 2006 (which interprets Art. 1F of the Refugee Convention).

[182] Criminal Justice and Immigration Bill, clauses 132–133. See discussion in ILPA, 'Special Immigration Status', Information Sheet, 1 August 2007, www.ilpa.org.uk/infoservice/Info%20sheet%20special%20immigration%20status.pdf (accessed 19 April 2008).

[183] See UK Refugee Council Briefing, 'Special Immigration Status', October 2007, www.refugeecouncil.org.uk (accessed 20 April 2008).

[184] Joint Council for the Welfare of Immigrants, 'Parliamentary Briefing: Clauses 115–122 Special Immigration Status', House of Commons, Second Reading, 8 October 2007, www.jcwi.org.uk/news/jcwi%5B1%5D.cjb.brief.pdf (accessed 20 April 2008).

THE INTERSECTION BETWEEN THE INTERNATIONAL 261

In addition to this, the UK Government has sought to overturn the European Court of Human Rights decision in *Chahal*.[185] In this case, the UK proposed to deport Karamjit Singh Chahal, a Sikh activist, to India on the basis that he had been involved in terrorist activities and posed a risk to the national security of the UK. Mr Chahal applied for asylum but was rejected at first instance and on appeal. He brought his case to the European Court of Human Rights in Strasbourg, arguing that his deportation to India would breach Article 3 of the ECHR.[186] The UK Government argued in response that no real risk of ill-treatment had been established and that, as the reason for the intended deportation was national security, the guarantees afforded by Article 3 were not absolute. In particular, the government argued that the threat posed by an individual to the national security of the Contracting State was a factor to be weighed in the balance when considering Article 3.[187]

In delivering its judgment in *Chahal*, the Strasbourg Court (in a majority judgment of twelve votes to seven) noted that 'it was well aware of the immense difficulties faced by States in modern times in protecting their communities from terrorist violence'[188] but affirmed the absolute nature of the prohibition against torture or inhuman or degrading treatment or punishment, 'irrespective of the victim's conduct'.[189] Thus, the Court held:

> Whenever substantial grounds have been shown for believing that an individual would face a real risk of being subjected to treatment contrary to Article 3 if removed to another State, the responsibility of the Contracting State to safeguard him or her against such treatment is engaged in the event of expulsion.[190]

Significantly, the majority of the Court held that a balancing approach could not be applied to this type of situation:

> In these circumstances, the activities of the individual in question, however undesirable or dangerous, cannot be a material consideration. The protection afforded by Article 3 is thus wider than that provided by Articles 32 and 33 of the United Nations 1951 Convention on the Status of Refugees.[191]

---

[185] Chahal (1996) 23 EHRR 413.   [186] Ibid., at para. 72.
[187] *Ibid.*, para. 76.   [188] *Ibid.*, para. 79.   [189] *Ibid.*, para. 79.   [190] *Ibid.*, para. 80.
[191] *Ibid.*, para. 80. This is because the European Court of Human Rights has held that Art. 3 applies irrespective of the applicant's conduct, whereas Art. 32 of the Refugee Convention permits (in certain circumstances) the expulsion of a refugee on national security or public order grounds and Art. 33(2) provides that the benefit of the *non-refoulement* protection in Art. 33(1) cannot be claimed by certain refugees, for instance, those considered a danger to the security of the country of asylum – see text of Art. 33(2) in note 53 above.

262   REFUGEES, ASYLUM SEEKERS AND THE RULE OF LAW

Additionally, although the UK had attempted to argue that it had received diplomatic assurances by India that Mr Chahal would not be ill-treated, the majority of the Court held that, given the country information on the use of torture in India, those assurances would not 'provide Mr Chahal with an adequate guarantee of safety'.[192]

In contrast, the minority of the Court (seven judges) agreed that national security issues were not a relevant consideration in relation to a risk of ill-treatment *within* the jurisdiction of a Contracting State, but that the position is different when only the *extraterritorial* application of Article 3 is at stake.[193] The Court held that in the latter situation:

> A Contracting State which is contemplating the removal of someone from its jurisdiction to that of another State may legitimately strike a fair balance between, on the one hand, the nature of the threat to its national security interests if the person concerned were to remain and, on the other, the extent of the potential risk of ill-treatment of that person in the State of destination.[194]

Thus, the decision in *Chahal* was significant in that it emphasized the absolute nature of Article 3, and that this protection applies irrespective of the applicant's conduct. In this respect, Article 3 may provide human rights protection for those asylum seekers who may be excluded from the protections of the Convention under Article 1F or Article 33(2).[195] The European Court of Human Rights had already ruled in previous jurisprudence that expulsion by a Contracting State of an asylum seeker may breach Article 3 and therefore engage the responsibility of that State under the Convention.[196] The importance of *Chahal* is that it adds a further layer of protection for those applicants who may be subject to deportation for national security reasons.

The *Chahal* judgment therefore has the effect of preventing the UK from deporting those foreign nationals who are perceived by the UK as

---

[192] *Chahal* (1996) 23 EHRR 413 at para. 105.
[193] The joint, partly-dissenting opinion of Judges Gölcüklü, Matscher, Freeland, Baka, Mifsud Bonnici, Gotchev and Levits, in *Chahal* (1996) 23 EHRR 413 at para. 1 ('*Chahal* dissenting judgment').
[194] *Chahal* dissenting judgment, para. 1.
[195] For the detail of Arts. 1F and 33(2) see notes 52 and 53 above. As commentators have noted, in these respects, Art. 3 has broader application than Arts. 32 and 33 of the Refugee Convention: see Goodwin-Gill and McAdam, *The Refugee in International Law*, p. 311; Blake and Husain, *Immigration, Asylum and Human Rights*, para. 2.4. See also 'Introduction: Refugees and Asylum Seekers in the International Context – Rights and Realities' in this volume at pp. 11–14.
[196] See *Cruz Varas and others* v. *Sweden* Series A, No 201, (1992) 14 EHRR 1.

THE INTERSECTION BETWEEN THE INTERNATIONAL   263

a threat to national security, where there are substantial grounds to show that the applicant will be subjected to treatment in breach of Article 3. Thus, the UK Government has been very critical of the judgment in *Chahal* and has attempted to limit its effect. For instance, the Strasbourg Court's approach to the balancing issue has been questioned by the UK Attorney General, Lord Goldsmith QC,[197] and the former home secretary, John Reid, described the *Chahal* decision as 'outrageously imbalanced'.[198] In 2005 the UK Government attempted to resolve some of these difficulties by negotiating diplomatic assurances (Memoranda of Understanding) with Jordan, Libya and Lebanon, relating to the treatment of returnees, including asylum seekers.[199] This is despite the fact that the European Court of Human Rights raised doubts about the use of such assurances in *Chahal*.[200] At the time, the then Prime Minister, Tony Blair, stated:

> [T]he circumstances of our national security have now self-evidently changed and we believe we can get the necessary assurances from the countries to which we will return the deportees, against their being subject to torture or ill-treatment contrary to Article 3.[201]

Not surprisingly, the use of such assurances in relation to torture has provoked strong criticism from the UN Committee against Torture, the UK Joint Committee on Human Rights and a number of UK NGOs.[202]

Against this context, in 2007 the UK attempted to challenge the *Chahal* judgment by intervening in the European Court of Human Rights case

---

[197] See, e.g., Lord Goldsmith QC who has stated that '[t]here is reason to doubt that this was the correct legal solution': Lord Goldsmith, 'Symposium: Global Constitutionalism: Keynote address' (2007) 59 *Stanford Law Review* 1155 at 1164.

[198] Press Association, 'Human Rights Act Reform Ruled Out', 20 July 2006.

[199] Human Rights Watch, 'Undermining the Torture Ban', *HRW Backgrounders*, November 2006, www.hrw.org/backgrounder/eca/uk1106/4.htm (accessed 1 April 2008).

[200] *Chahal* (1996) 23 EHRR 413 at para. 105.

[201] Tony Blair, 'Prime Minister's Press Conference', 10 Downing Street, 5 August 2005, www.number-10.gov.uk/output/Page8041.asp (accessed 31 March 2008).

[202] See, e.g., Concluding Observations of the Committee against Torture, *Conclusions and Recommendations: United Kingdom of Great Britain and Northern Ireland – Dependent Territories*, 10 December 2004, CAT/C/CR/33/3 para. 4(d); House of Lords, House of Commons, Joint Committee on Human Rights, *Nineteenth Report*, Session 2005–6, para. 131, www.publications.parliament.uk/pa/jt200506/jtselect/jtrights/185/18508.htm (accessed 19 April 2008); UK Refugee Council and others, *Joint Response to the Home Office Consultation on Exclusion or Deportation from the UK on Non-conducive Grounds* (London: UK Refugee Council, August 2005), www.refugee-action.org.uk/campaigns/documents/Response.doc (accessed 19 April 2008).

264 REFUGEES, ASYLUM SEEKERS AND THE RULE OF LAW

of *Saadi* v. *Italy*.[203] This case concerned a Tunisian citizen, resident in Italy, whom the Italian Government regarded as posing a terrorist threat and wanted to deport for reasons of national security. Saadi had been convicted in absentia in Tunisia of terrorist offences, and argued that he faced a serious risk of being tortured if he was returned to Tunisia in breach of Article 3 of the ECHR.[204] Italy attempted to argue that there was no significant risk of torture in this case, as Tunisia had given assurances that the applicant would be treated fairly. The UK hoped to use this case to overturn the ruling on Article 3 in *Chahal* and establish a new principle that, in the case of those suspected of terrorism, the risk of torture in the country they are deported to should be balanced against the risk to national security they pose in the country wishing to deport them.

UK arguments as intervener

In its oral submissions to the European Court of Human Rights, the UK accepted that Article 3 is an absolute prohibition by a Contracting State,[205] but argued that neither the facts in *Saadi* v. *Italy* nor in *Chahal* concerned conduct which came within Article 3 by a *Contracting State*, but the possibility of such conduct by a *non-Contracting State*. It submitted that the reasoning of the majority in *Chahal* is therefore incorrect when it does not allow Contracting States to give any consideration to the safety of persons within their territory. It also noted that the prohibition in *Chahal* is wrong in an expulsion situation, where the degree of risk in the receiving country depended on a speculative assessment. Instead, the true basis of the obligations of a Contracting State to the ECHR are those stated by the European Court of Human Rights in *Soering* v. *UK*;[206] that is, that Article 3 is only relevant in removal

---

[203] Application No. 37201/06. Heard by the Grand Chamber on 11 July 2007. The UK was given permission to intervene as a third party and to make both written and oral submissions. Note that the UK has also been given permission to intervene in the case of *Ramzy* v. *Netherlands* (Application No. 25424/05) but that case has been held up by procedural delays. It is unlikely that the UK will pursue this second case, given the result in *Saadi* v. *Italy*.

[204] He also argued that return would breach Art. 8 ECHR relating to family unity.

[205] Article 3 is a non-derogable right (pursuant to Art. 15(2) ECHR) and it contains no express limitations, as do other ECHR rights.

[206] In *Soering* v. *UK*, Series A, No. 161; (1989) 11 EHRR 439 the European Court of Human rights held that a decision by a Contracting State to extradite a person could breach Art. 3 if the individual concerned faced a real risk of being subjected to torture or to inhuman or degrading treatment in the country to which he or she is to be

THE INTERSECTION BETWEEN THE INTERNATIONAL   265

situations where a Contracting State *knowingly* returns a non-national to another State to face torture.[207] In this respect, the UK modelled its submissions on the dissenting opinion of the European Court of Human Rights in *Chahal*.[208]

In support of its submissions, the UK argued that the nature and scale of threat from terrorism have changed dramatically in the last ten years and that recourse to the criminal law in order to protect citizens from terrorism is no longer sufficient protection. It also referred to the exclusion clauses in the Refugee Convention, arguing that, as protection of that Convention is denied to terrorists, states are entitled under international law to consider their own national security and are entitled to remove non-nationals where there is objective evidence that they pose a threat to national security. In summary, the UK argued that the Court should reconsider its findings in *Chahal* to allow national security considerations to be taken into account in situations where a Contracting State proposes to remove a person to a non-Contracting State. In doing so, the UK submitted that the Court should state explicitly that, in removal cases, a Contracting State's responsibility will not be engaged unless it is proven that it is 'more likely than not' that person will be subject to treatment prohibited by Article 3 if the person is removed. Finally, the government submitted that Contracting States could obtain diplomatic assurances that an applicant would not be subjected to treatment contrary to Article 3.[209]

Judgment of the European Court of Human Rights

The Grand Chamber handed down judgment in this case on 28 February 2008. In an unanimous judgment, it affirmed the approach of the Court in *Chahal*, reiterating that:

> The prohibition of torture and of inhuman or degrading treatment or punishment is absolute, irrespective of the victim's conduct . . . the

---

returned (para. 91). In this case the court held that the extradition would violate Art. 3 ECHR because the individual concerned was likely to face many years on 'death row', which constituted inhuman treatment.

[207] UK, Oral submissions in *Saadi* v. *Italy*, Application No. 37201/06, European Court of Human Rights (Grand Chamber), 11 July 2007, available at www.echr.coe.int/ECHR/EN/Header/Press/Multimedia/Webcasts+of+public+hearings/ (accessed 19 April 2008), summarized in para. 117–23 of judgment of the Grand Chamber.

[208] As discussed in the text to note 193 above.

[209] UK, Oral submissions in *Saadi* v. *Italy*, Application No. 37201/06, European Court of Human Rights (Grand Chamber), summarized in judgment of Grand Chamber, 28 February 2008 at para. 122–23.

266 REFUGEES, ASYLUM SEEKERS AND THE RULE OF LAW

nature of the offence allegedly committed by the applicant is therefore irrelevant for the purposes of Article 3.[210]

On the issue of a 'balancing exercise' in relation to Article 3, the Court further held:

> The Court considers that the argument based on the balancing of the risk of harm if the person is sent back against the dangerousness he or she represents to the community if not sent back is misconceived. The concepts of 'risk' and 'dangerousness' in this context do not lend themselves to a balancing test because they are notions that can only be assessed independently of each other. Either the evidence adduced before the Court reveals that there is a substantial risk if the person is sent back or it does not. The prospect that he may pose a serious threat to the community if not returned does not reduce in any way the degree of risk of ill-treatment that the person may be subject to on return.[211]

The Court rejected the argument by the UK that a distinction must be drawn under Article 3 between treatment inflicted directly by a Contracting State and that which might be inflicted by another state.[212] With regard to the argument by the UK that where an applicant presents a threat to national security, stronger evidence must be adduced to prove that there is a risk of ill-treatment, the Court held that:

> Such an approach is not compatible with the absolute nature of the protection afforded by Article 3 either. It amounts to asserting that, in the absence of evidence meeting a higher standard, protection of national security justifies accepting more readily a risk of ill-treatment for the individual.[213]

Finally, in relation to the use of diplomatic assurances, the Court confirmed the approach taken in *Chahal*, that is, even if diplomatic assurances as to the treatment of an applicant are given, this:

> does not absolve the Court from the obligation to examine whether such assurances provided, in their practical application, a sufficient guarantee that the applicant would be protected against the risk of treatment prohibited by the Convention.[214]

Analysis

The UK's intervention in *Saadi* v. *Italy* highlights a number of rule of law issues. First, it illustrates the importance of having a strong regional

---

[210] *Saadi* v. *Italy*, Application No. 37201/06, European Court of Human Rights (Grand Chamber), Judgment, 28 February 2008 at para. 127 (unreported).
[211] *Ibid.* at para. 139.   [212] *Ibid.* at para. 138.   [213] *Ibid.* at para. 140.
[214] *Ibid.* at para. 148.

THE INTERSECTION BETWEEN THE INTERNATIONAL   267

court to enforce a state's international (or in this case, regional) human rights obligations.[215] This is particularly so, as the UK has not accepted the right of individual petition in relation to either the UN Convention against Torture (CAT)[216] or the International Covenant on Civil and Political Rights (ICCPR)[217] and, even if it did, the recommendations and observations of those committees are not binding.

Secondly, it raises the question of how influential this latest reinforcement of *Chahal* by Strasbourg will be on other jurisdictions, particularly those common law countries discussed in this book. Interestingly, by way of comparison, the Supreme Court of Canada in the case of *Suresh* v. *Canada (Minister of Citizenship and Immigration)*[218] held that the question of deportation to torture *was* 'one of balance'.[219] As Audrey Macklin notes in this book, in taking this approach, the Supreme Court of Canada 'arguably revealed a lapse in fidelity to the rule of law that courts in the UK and the European Court of Human Rights have managed to resist so far'.[220] As the Supreme Court of Canada stated this by way of obiter,[221] it will be interesting to see how influential the Strasbourg decision in *Saadi* v. *Italy* will be on future Canadian case law (and, indeed, on jurisprudence elsewhere).

---

[215] Goodwin-Gill and McAdam also note the influence of Strasbourg in relation to the development of *non-refoulement*, noting the court 'has consistently reinforced the absolute and non-negotiable nature of Art. 3 ECHR50, and has been particularly influential on the domestic and supranational law of the EU Member States': Goodwin-Gill and McAdam, *The Refugee in International Law*, p. 310.

[216] Convention Against Torture and Other Cruel Inhuman or Degrading Treatment or Punishment, New York, 10 December 1984, in force 26 June 1987, UN Doc. A/39/51 (1984), 1465 UNTS 85 (CAT). The UK is party to the CAT (ratifying it on 7 January 1989). However, the UK has not incorporated it into domestic law. It also has not accepted the right of individual communications to the CAT Committee pursuant to Art. 22 of the Convention: see Joint Committee on Human Rights, *Nineteenth Report*, Session 2005–6, paras. 31–2.

[217] International Covenant on Civil and Political Rights, New York, 16 December 1966, in force 23 March 1976, UN Doc. A/6316 (1966), 999 UNTS 171 (ICCPR).

[218] [2002] 1 SCR 3.

[219] The Supreme Court commented that: 'We do not exclude the possibility that in exceptional circumstances, deportation to face torture might be justified . . . We may predict that [the balance] will rarely be struck in favour of expulsion where there is a serious risk of torture. However, as the matter is one of balance, precise prediction is elusive': *Suresh* v. *Canada (Minister of Citizenship and Immigration)* [2002] 1 SCR 3 at para. 78.

[220] Audrey Macklin, Chapter 2 at p. 85 in this volume.

[221] The comment was obiter, as the Court did not rule on the issue, noting instead that 'ambit of an exceptional discretion to deport to torture, if any, must await future cases' (para. 78).

268 REFUGEES, ASYLUM SEEKERS AND THE RULE OF LAW

Thirdly, the issue highlights the importance of international human rights, in addition to regional human rights standards. If the European Court of Human Rights had upheld the arguments of the UK, then presumably the UK would still have been in breach of its international obligations under customary international law and the CAT if it had attempted to deport people in *Chahal*-type situations.[222] Indeed, the UN Committee on Torture has echoed the Strasbourg approach to the issue of balancing.[223]

The EU Qualification Directive and the UK

In this section, the rule of law implications arising from the transposition of the EU Qualification Directive into UK law are discussed, both for the UK itself and also for the future development of international refugee law more broadly.

The EU Qualification Directive

The EU Qualification Directive was settled by EU Member States as part of the creation of a 'Common European Asylum System' (CEAS) and, indeed, it is described in EU documentation as 'one of the four building blocks' of the first stage of that common system.[224] The aim of the Qualification Directive is to harmonize the way in which Member States interpret the definition of both refugee and 'subsidiary' (complementary)

---

[222] Goodwin-Gill and McAdam take this approach, noting that even if *Chahal* were overturned, State Parties would be prevented by Art. 7 of ICCPR, Art. 3 CAT and by customary international law from returning people to such forms of harm: Goodwin-Gill and McAdam, *The Refugee in International Law*, p. 312. Although note that James Hathaway adopts a different view of the status of the prohibition against torture as a rule of customary international law: see discussion in 'Introduction: Refugees and Asylum Seekers in the International Context – Rights and Realities' in this volume at pp. 31–34.

[223] In *Paez v. Sweden* the Committee held that the involvement of a person in terrorist activities is not relevant to a consideration of the risk of torture or ill-treatment: see *Paez v. Sweden*, CAT 39/1996, 28 April 1997. For a discussion of the use of international human rights law in relation to refugees and asylum seekers, see Colin Harvey, 'Regionalism, Human Rights and Forced Migration', in Susan Kneebone and Felicity Rawlings-Sanaei (eds.), *New Regionalism and Asylum Seekers: Challenges Ahead* (Oxford: Berghahn Books, 2007).

[224] EU, 'Entry into Force of European Rules on the Qualification and Status of Persons in Need of International Protection', *EU at the UN*, EC06–307EN, 10 October 2006, www.europa-eu-un.org/home (accessed 20 April 2008).

THE INTERSECTION BETWEEN THE INTERNATIONAL 269

protection status and the rights that are given to beneficiaries on employment, education and family reunification.[225] It must also be noted, however, that a strong motivation behind the Qualification Directive, and indeed the whole CEAS, is to reduce differences in the law and practice of EU Member States and therefore to avoid 'asylum-shopping' (particularly given the limited success of the Dublin Convention, discussed above). Indeed, the need to limit the movement of asylum seekers within the EU is explicitly provided for in Recital 7 in the Qualification Directive, which notes that:

> The approximation of rules on the recognition and content of refugee and subsidiary protection status should help to limit the secondary movements of applicants for asylum between Member States, where such movement is purely caused by differences in legal frameworks.[226]

The Directive was unanimously adopted by Member States on 19 April 2004 and entered into force on 20 October 2004.[227] Despite unanimous support, to date only seven of the twenty-five EU Member States have transposed the Directive into domestic law.[228] However, it is binding on all Member States, even those who have not transposed it, due to the doctrine of the supremacy of EC law, which means that the Qualification Directive is directly applicable in Member States.[229]

The Qualification Directive is regarded as one of the, if not the, most important of the EU directives on asylum. For instance, EC Vice President Franco Frattini, Commissioner for Justice, Freedom and Security, has commented on the importance of this Directive, noting that:

> It guarantees that the protection needs of asylum seekers will be assessed according to the same criteria wherever they make their claim in Europe and that, on the basis of their protection needs, they will be entitled to a consolidated set of rights and benefits in all Member States.[230]

---

[225] See *ibid*.   [226] Qualification Directive, Recital 7.

[227] EU, 'Entry into Force of European Rules on the Qualification and Status of Persons in Need of International Protection', *EU at the UN*, EC06–307EN, 10 October 2006, www.europa-eu-un.org/home (accessed 20 April 2008).

[228] See, e.g., UK, France, Estonia, Lithuania, Austria, Slovenia and Luxembourg. The EU has threatened the other Member States with legal action if they do not transpose the Directive: see 'EU Threatens Legal Action Against 19 EU Governments Over Failure to Implement New Asylum Rules', Associated Press, 10 October 2006.

[229] See Art. 249 Treaty establishing the European Community, discussed in Sionaidh Douglas-Scott, *Constitutional Law of the European Union* (Harlow Pearson Education, 2002), pp. 288–91.

[230] EU, 'Entry Into Force of Key Asylum Law Creating a "Level Playing Field" in Asylum Policies Throughout Europe Hampered by Failure of Timely Transposition by most

270 REFUGEES, ASYLUM SEEKERS AND THE RULE OF LAW

A question arises as to whether the Qualification Directive is in fact consistent with the Refugee Convention, especially given its importance in the CEAS scheme. The Qualification Directive is intended, at least in theory, to follow the Refugee Convention. For instance, Recital 2 of the Directive notes that the CEAS is 'based on the full and inclusive application of the Geneva Convention', Recital 3 provides that 'The Geneva Convention and Protocol provide the cornerstone of the international legal regime for the protection of refugees', and Article 21(1) refers to the principle of *non-refoulement.*[231]

The Directive does appear to set down certain provisions which are consistent with contemporary international refugee law norms and may improve refugee status decisions in some EU Member States. The most significant provision is arguably the introduction of minimum standards for 'subsidiary' protection, which is an important development in both the EU and international refugee law context.[232] Other significant provisions include those which recognize that non-state actors can be actors of persecution or serious harm,[233] and those which establish that the 'best interests of the child' should be a primary consideration for Member States.[234] Some commentators have also pointed to the fact that the Directive introduces a 'widely inclusive definition of membership of a particular social group'.[235]

However, many commentators have also noted that the Directive contains provisions which are inconsistent with international refugee law standards.[236] One example is Article 14(4) of the Directive, which

---

Member States', Press Release, IP/06/1345, 10 October 2006. A number of academic commentators have also noted the importance of the Directive: see Catherine Teitgen-Colly, 'The European Union and Asylum: An Illusion of Protection' (2006) 43 *Common Market Law Review* 1503 at 1504; Helene Lambert, 'The EU Asylum Qualification Directive: Its Impact on the Jurisprudence of the United Kingdom and International Law' (2006) 55 *International and Comparative Law Quarterly*, 161 at 161.

[231] The Charter of Fundamental Rights of the European Union [2000] OJ C/364/1 also states that '[t]he right to asylum shall be guaranteed with due respect for the rules of the Geneva Convention. . . . and the Protocol . . . in accordance with the Treaty establishing the European Community' (Art. 18). Article 19(2) of the EU Charter also sets out the *non-refoulement* principle. Note, however, that the Charter is not yet legally binding.

[232] Qualification Directive, Art. 15. However, the Directive sets out wide exclusion criteria in relation to complementary protection and the rights attaching to complementary protection status are less than that for refugees.

[233] *Ibid.*, Art. 6.   [234] *Ibid.*, Art. 20(5).

[235] Lambert, 'The EU Asylum Qualification Directive' at 169.

[236] See Lambert, 'The EU Asylum Qualification Directive' at 177–182; Teitgen-Colly, 'The European Union and Asylum' at 1556.

THE INTERSECTION BETWEEN THE INTERNATIONAL 271

provides that Member States may revoke, end or refuse to renew a person's refugee status when:

(a) there are reasonable grounds for regarding him or her as a danger to the security of the Member State in which he or she is present;
(b) he or she, having been convicted by a final judgment of a particularly serious crime, constitutes a danger to the community of that Member State.

This appears to be inconsistent with the Refugee Convention in that the Convention does not set out any such revocation grounds. It therefore goes beyond the exclusion criteria set out in Article 1F of the Convention.[237] Indeed, the UNHCR has criticized Article 14(4) on the basis that it substantially modifies the exclusion clauses of the Refugee Convention by adding the exceptions to the *non-refoulement* principle in Article 33(2) of the Convention as a basis for *exclusion* from refugee status. UNHCR note that this is incorrect, as Article 33(2) was not conceived as the basis upon which refugee status could be terminated, but rather as a reason for denying protection.[238] This conclusion by UNHCR is explained by the fact that Article 33(2) is worded as an exception to the *non-refoulement* protection; that is, it relates to the *return* of a refugee to his or her country of origin. It is not stated to affect the *definition* of a refugee set out in Article 1A(2) of the Refugee Convention. Therefore, a finding by a state that the *non-refoulement* protection does not apply to a refugee because of Article 33(2) may permit a state to return that refugee to his or her country of origin, but it leaves the refugee status of that person unchanged (unless the state also successfully applies the exclusion criteria in Article 1F to that person).

Secondly, Article 14 requires Member States to revoke refugee status where the refugee has ceased to be a refugee in accordance with Article 11(1)(e) of the Directive. Article 11(1)(e) of the Directive purports to reflect the Article 1C(5) cessation clause in the Refugee Convention, which provides that the Convention may cease to apply to a refugee if:

> he can no longer, because the circumstances in connection with which he has been recognized as a refugee have ceased to exist, continue to refuse to avail himself of the protection of the country of his nationality.[239]

---

[237] Discussed in note 52 above.
[238] UNHCR, *UNHCR Annotated Comments on the EC Council Directive 2004/83/EC of 29 April 2004*, 28 January 2005, pp. 30–1, www.unhcr.org/cgi-bin/texis/vtx/refworld/rwmain?docid=4200d8354 (accessed 1 April 2008).
[239] See the discussion in Chapter 4 in this volume at pp. 210–17.

272   REFUGEES, ASYLUM SEEKERS AND THE RULE OF LAW

However, Article 1C of the Refugee Convention sets out what is known as the 'compelling reasons' exception to cessation. That is, it states that cessation will not apply to a statutory refugee (a refugee falling under Article 1A(1) of the Convention, that is a pre-1951 refugee) who:

> is able to invoke compelling reasons arising out of previous persecution for refusing to avail himself of the country of nationality/former habitual residence.

This exception is considered to be important because it recognizes that even if a refugee no longer has a well-founded fear of persecution, due to a change in circumstances, if he or she has suffered atrocious forms of persecution then they cannot be expected to return to their country of origin.[240] It is therefore recognized by the UNHCR and academic commentators as reflecting a general humanitarian principle applicable to all Convention refugees (that is, whether pre-1951 or post-1951 refugees).[241] However, neither Article 11(1)(e) of the Qualification Directive nor para. 339A of the UK Immigration Rules includes this 'compelling reasons' exception to cessation. This raises the question of whether the Directive and relevant UK law are consistent with the Refugee Convention.

In assessing the compatibility of the Directive (and relevant UK law) with the Refugee Convention in relation to cessation, it is acknowledged that the text of Article 1C(5) clearly limits the exception to pre-1951 refugees. Thus, Article 11(1)(e) of the Directive and the UK Immigration Rules are not inconsistent with the *literal* wording of the Refugee Convention. However, it is strongly arguable that these provisions are inconsistent with contemporary international refugee law norms. First, many states, both EU countries such as France and Belgium and non-EU countries such as Canada and the USA, have interpreted the exception as applying broadly to *all* refugees.[242] Indeed, UNHCR has consistently

---

[240] See UNHCR Handbook, para. 136: 'It is frequently recognized that a person who – or whose family – has suffered under atrocious forms of persecution should not be expected to repatriate. Even though there may have been a change of regime in his country, this may not always produce a complete change in the attitude of the population, nor, in view of his past experiences, in the mind of the refugee.'

[241] See e.g. UNHCR, *Annotated Comments*, p. 25.

[242] See, e.g., Office Français de Protection des Réfugiés et Apatrides (OFPRA), 'Summary of Cessation', www.ofpra.gouv.fr/index.html?xml_id=263&dtd_id=14 (accessed 1 April 2008); US Code of Federal Regulations, 8 CFR s. 208.13(b)(1)(iii)(A), Immigration and Refugee Protection Act 2001, Canada, s. 108(4). See also discussion in Goodwin-Gill and McAdam, *The Refugee in International Law*, pp. 145–49.

THE INTERSECTION BETWEEN THE INTERNATIONAL 273

argued that the exception reflects a broad humanitarian principle which should be applied to *all* Convention refugees.[243] Secondly, building on the themes discussed in other chapters in this book, given that the Convention has been acknowledged as a 'living instrument' and should therefore be interpreted in accordance with modern developments and interpretation, it is strongly arguable that the compelling reasons exception should apply to not only pre-1951 but to all Convention refugees. As noted in Chapter 1 of this book, Article 31 of the Vienna Convention on the Law of Treaties[244] requires that a treaty be interpreted in 'good faith in accordance with the ordinary meaning to be given to the terms of the treaty in their context and in the light of its object and purpose'. This approach accords with the Preamble of the Refugee Convention, which makes it clear that its object and purpose is to assure to refugees 'the widest possible exercise of ... fundamental rights and freedoms'. It is strongly arguable, therefore, that a good faith implementation of Article 1C(5) requires states to apply the 'compelling reasons' exception to all Convention refugees. Indeed, some commentators have suggested that the exception represents a rule of customary international law.[245]

In addition, it is of concern that Article 14 *requires* Member States to revoke the refugee status of a person who comes within the cessation provisions of Article 11 of the Directive. This mandatory wording is replicated in para. 339A of the UK Immigration Rules, which states that a person's grant of asylum *will* (rather than may) be revoked or not renewed if the Secretary of State is satisfied that cessation has occurred. The fact that decision makers are *required* (rather than *permitted*) to revoke refugee status based on cessation is significant in that the Refugee Convention does not set out any such revocation provision and such a requirement does not leave a decision maker with any discretion to maintain a person's refugee status despite the occurrence of a change in circumstances in the refugee's country of origin. It will be of particular significance to the many EU countries which do not yet systematically apply the Article 1C(5) cessation provisions.[246] The mandatory nature

---

[243] See UNHCR Handbook, para. 136; UNHCR, 'Guidelines on International Protection: Cessation of Refugee Status under Article 1C(5) and (6) of the 1951 Convention relating to the Status of Refugees (the "Ceased Circumstances" Clauses)', HCR/GIP/03/03, 10 February 2003, para. 31; UNHCR *Annotated Comments*, p. 25.

[244] Vienna Convention on the Law of Treaties, Vienna, 23 May 1969, in force 27 January 1980, 1155 UNTS 331.

[245] Goodwin-Gill and McAdam, *The Refugee in International Law*, p. 148.

[246] Currently, only the UK and Germany apply Art. 1C(5) to recognized refugees.

274   REFUGEES, ASYLUM SEEKERS AND THE RULE OF LAW

of Article 14 means that these countries will presumably be required to revoke the refugee status of those persons who come under the Article 11 cessation provisions.[247]

Implications for the rule of law

What are the implications of the above discussion for the rule of law? Do harmonized asylum directives like the EU Qualification Directive bring any benefits to international refuge law in respect to the rule of law? What implications will the regionalized, harmonized standards have for the development of international refugee law more generally? In particular, given that certain provisions of the EU Qualification Directive (and the other EU asylum directives) are inconsistent with the Refugee Convention, how will the harmonized standards affect the interpretation given by non-EU courts to these provisions and how will it affect any future development of customary international law? The responses to these questions are set out below.

Benefits of harmonization from a rule of law perspective

First, it must be acknowledged that transposition by the UK of the EU Qualification Directive (and other EU asylum directives) has resulted in the structuring of executive discretion in certain areas of refugee determination. For instance, the clear incorporation of Article 1C(5) in the Immigration Rules is a positive development in terms of the rule of law, as it provides more certainty (at least in some instances) for decision makers and the judiciary. This is in contrast to Australia, where the lack of incorporation of Article 1C(5) has created great confusion and uncertainty for decision makers and the courts.[248] On the other hand, the fact that many of the transposed provisions in UK law (for example in relation to revocation) set out mandatory requirements poses problems in the context of the rule of law. For instance, the obligatory

---

[247] Although Art. 3 of the Qualification Directive provides that states can maintain more favourable standards than those minimum standards set out in the Directive, Art. 3 also provides that such higher standards must be compatible with the Directive. A state's revocation provision which is phrased only permissively and is not mandatory may not be seen as compatible with the Directive. On the legal issues arising from the introduction or retaining of more favourable standards, see Gil-Bazo, 'The Protection of Refugees', pp. 170–173.

[248] See Kneebone, Chapter 4 in this volume at pp. 210–17.

THE INTERSECTION BETWEEN THE INTERNATIONAL   275

nature of many of the Articles means that executive discretion will not merely be structured, but mandated. Thus, this may not leave decision makers with sufficient discretion to do justice in individual cases.

Secondly, harmonization of asylum law may effect a number of benefits in terms of consistency of standards and decision making. It is widely acknowledged that inconsistencies in refugee status determination are not desirable from either a legal or political perspective. UNHCR has, for instance, highlighted on a number of occasions the importance of a level of uniformity among State Parties in relation to interpretation of the Convention. In its 1996 Report on International Protection it noted:

> The UNHCR has constantly sought to bring about a certain measure of uniformity in the elaboration of eligibility criteria with a view to ensuring that all applicants are treated according to the same standards.[249]

In this regard, the UNHCR has explicitly stated that it supports the harmonization of asylum procedures within the EU.[250] The UK House of Lords has also, in a number of cases, stated that the Refugee Convention should be given a consistent interpretation among the Contracting States in order to provide an effective system of refugee protection.[251]

However, the problem with the EU Qualification Directive is that certain significant inconsistencies exist between the Directive and the Refugee Convention. Thus, one could argue, as a number of other academic commentators have, that the Directive has set out standards which reflect the 'lowest common denominator'.[252]

---

[249] UNHCR, *Report on International Protection*, UN Doc. A/AC.96/527 (1976), para. 30.

[250] Erika Feller, UNCHR Assistant High Commissioner for Refugees, speaking at a meeting of Institute of European Affairs: Jill Donoghue and Johnny Ryan, *Rapporteurs Report*, (Ireland: Institute of European Affairs, 23 July 2006), www.iiea.com/images/managed/news_attachments/erika%20feller%20rep%20eport.pdf (accessed 2 April 2008).

[251] See, e.g., *Adan* [2001] 2 AC 477, where the House of Lords stated that national courts, when faced with 'material disagreement on an issue of interpretation' must resolve it by searching 'untrammelled by notions of national legal culture, for the true autonomous and international meaning of the treaty. And there can only be one true meaning' (*ibid.* at 517). The Lords also stated: 'the Refugee Convention must be given an independent meaning . . . without taking colour from distinctive features of the legal system of any individual contracting state. In principle therefore there can only be one true interpretation of a treaty' (*ibid.* at 516).

[252] See Teitgen-Colly who notes that the Qualification Directive and the other EU asylum directive 'only lay down minimum standards often based on the lowest common denominator': Teitgen-Colly, 'The European Union and Asylum' at 1518.

Oversight by the European Court of Justice

An independent arbiter of the law is a hallmark of the rule of law.[253] Given this, what body will enforce the Directive and arbitrate on it under UK law? How will individual asylum seekers challenge the transposition of the Directive into UK law? It is likely that the European Court of Justice (ECJ) will play an important part in the oversight of implementation of the Qualification Directive.[254] However, some commentators have raised concerns about its likely approach to refugee issues.[255] Indeed, some commentators have raised concerns about this in relation to national security and public law issues. For instance, Maria-Teresa Gil-Bazo notes that:

> The ECJ has consistently ruled that rights are not necessarily absolute and, therefore, that they can usually be subject to restrictions in the general interest as long as those restrictions do not constitute a disproportionate and unreasonable interference in relation to the aim pursued, undermining the very substance of that right. It is, therefore, possible that the ECJ may find that security grounds constitute an interference with the right to be granted protection under the Directive that is compatible with *Community standards* [emphasis in original].[256]

Influence of harmonized standards outside the EU

The Qualification Directive, along with the other EU asylum directives which have been finalized, are not simply significant for the EU. They also represent significant developments for the future development of international refugee law – as they will be transposed and applied by states which also have international obligations under the Refugee Convention and other international human rights law instruments. It will therefore be important to see which obligations prevail in cases of conflict between international law and the EU directives, and how

---

[253] See Chapter 1 in this volume.

[254] The ECJ has jurisdiction to interpret the legal measures adopted on asylum under Art. 68 EC.

[255] For instance Elspeth Guild states that: 'from the Court of Justice's single encounter so far with refugees . . . it has shown itself to be particularly exclusionary-minded and negative about the extension of rights to refugees' (2004) 29 *European Law Review* 198 at 218.

[256] Maria-Teresa Gil-Bazo, 'Refugee Status and Subsidiary Protection under EC Law: The Qualification Directive and the Right to Be Granted Asylum' in Anneliese Baldaccini, Elspeth Guild and Helen Toner (eds.), *Whose Freedom, Security and Justice? EU Immigration and Asylum Law and Policy* (Oxford: Hart, 2007), p. 250 (emphasis in original, footnote omitted).

THE INTERSECTION BETWEEN THE INTERNATIONAL   277

national judiciaries will interpret the directives. In particular, does greater EU engagement by the UK signal a future in which the UK will turn increasingly to the EU rather than its common law counterparts of USA, Canada, Australia and New Zealand? What are the implications of this for the development of international refugee law?

The fact that certain provisions in the Qualification Directive are inconsistent with international refugee law clearly has great importance in the UK and EU, but also has the propensity to influence refugee status decision making in non-EU states. As Ninette Kelley points out:

> Given the size of the EU and the proportion of asylum claims it receives, a further lowering of procedural and interpretative standards could have a significant negative impact on the international refugee protection system for years to come.[257]

A UNHCR representative echoes this point, noting that 'given the standing of the European Union on the world stage, this Directive is likely to have great impact not just in Europe but even beyond'.[258] In particular, one must question whether the EU Directive will be used by the UK and other EU countries to deviate from non-EU interpretations of the Convention and which will therefore fragment the international nature of the Convention.[259]

Against this background, the expansion of the refugee exclusion criteria in Article 14 of the Qualification Directive and the omission of the compelling reasons exception to cessation in Article 11 of the Directive (and transposition by the UK of those EU provisions), are of concern for a number of reasons. First, Article 14 of the Directive and the relevant UK law interpreting that provision are of concern as other commentators have noted:

> Because the clauses express a limitation on an otherwise recognized human right, a significant degree of caution is necessary in the adjudication of

[257] Ninette Kelley, 'International Refugee Protection: Challenges and Opportunities' (2007) 19 *International Journal of Refugee Law* 401 at 429 (footnote excluded).

[258] Michael Kingsley-Nyinah, UNHCR, Evidence to the House of Lords Select Committee on the EU, in House of Lords Select Committee on the European Union, *Defining Refugee Status and Those in Need of International Protection*, Session 2001–2, 28th Report, HL Paper 156, 2002, Minutes of Evidence, 10 April 2002, Q. 86, p. 22, www.publications. parliament.uk/pa/ld200102/ldselect/ldeucom/156/156.pdf (accessed 22 April 2008).

[259] The UNHCR has emphasized the international character of the Convention: see, e.g., UNHCR, *Extraterritorial Effect of the Determination of Refugee Status*, 17 October 1978, No. 12 (XXIX) – 1978, para. (a), www.unhcr.org/cgi-bin/texis/vtx/refworld/rwmain? docid=3ae68c4447 (accessed 10 April 2008).

278 REFUGEES, ASYLUM SEEKERS AND THE RULE OF LAW

exclusion so that deserving persons are not denied the protections of refugee status.[260]

Secondly, the omission of the compelling reasons exception from the Directive and the relevant UK law is of concern because cessation of refugee status is an unsettled area of international refugee law. This is primarily because there has been little state practice of the application of Article 1C(5) to recognized refugees.[261] Accordingly, there is some uncertainty about what should be the precise 'content' of Article 1C(5) and how it should be applied in practice.[262] Thus, the EU Directive and national transposition (particularly the UK example) is likely to be very influential in further development of this area of refugee law on the international level, especially in relation to the formation of a rule of customary international law on the applicability of the compelling reasons exception. As the UK House of Lords EU Committee has noted:

> For a major regional group of countries such as the Union to adopt a regime apparently limiting the scope of the Geneva Convention among themselves would set a most undesirable precedent in the wider international/global context.[263]

Part four: conclusions

The place of asylum seekers and refugees in UK law and policy raises timely questions about the rule of law. The UK has, through a frequently changing legislative framework, deterrence, restrictions in asylum appeal avenues, the use of expedited removals and decision-making targets, sought to attain a 'managed migration' system. As part of this struggle, international refugee law continues to influence UK asylum law and

---

[260] Kate Jastram and Shelley Cavalieri, 'Human Rights in Refugee Tribunals' (2005) 24 *Refugee Survey Quarterly* 6 at 16.

[261] Only Australia and Germany have applied it to date. As to why other states have not utilised the provision, see UNHCR Global Consultations, *Summary Conclusions: Cessation of Refugee Status*, www.unhcr.bg/global_consult/cessation_refugee_status_en.pdf (accessed 19 April 2008).

[262] Joan Fitzpatrick et al., 'Current Issues in Cessation of Refugee Protection is a Subject of Confusion Mixed With Heightened Interest Among States, Refugees and the United Nations High Commissioner for Refugees (UNHCR)', background paper as part of the Global Consultations on International Protection, paras. 1, 59, www.unhcr.org/protect/PROTECTION/3b3889c28.pdf (accessed 20 April 2008).

[263] House of Lords Select Committee on the European Union, *Defining Refugee Status*, para. 54.

policy, but increasingly this influence is coming from the EU rather than the UK's common law counterparts.

Chapter 1 of this book posed the question: Of what significance is the method and extent of incorporation of international law obligations into the legislation of the national legal system? Clearly, incorporation of the ECHR into UK law via the HRA has had profound implications for the rights of asylum seekers and refugees in the UK. The importance of a strong Strasbourg Court is central to the maintenance of the rule of law within the UK in this regard – as illustrated by the recent challenge by the UK to *Chahal*.[264] The fact that the UK has attempted increasingly to engage with the EU on asylum matters but has attempted to resile from key ECHR protections reflects the growing influence of national security issues in UK asylum law and policy.

The formation of harmonized EU asylum law via initiatives such as the EU Qualification Directive is beneficial in terms of bringing a level of consistency amongst refugee status decision making across jurisdictions. In this regard it has the potential to enhance the rule of law in Member States. However, there are significant disadvantages with such harmonization, as seen in the inconsistencies between the Qualification Directive and the Refugee Convention.

In particular, the interpretation in the EU Directive (and the relevant UK law) of the exclusion and cessation provisions of the Refugee Convention are of central significance to the rule of law in the UK, given the UK's increased push to remove more and more asylum applicants as 'failed asylum seekers' from UK territory. As noted in the first part of this chapter, the UK judiciary has constrained unlawful executive action in a number of landmark cases. However, whether the courts will do so in relation to some of the revocation issues, particularly those involving national security, is yet to be seen. In this context, it should be noted that some commentators believe that the courts have tended to defer more to the executive in relation to national security.

The challenge for the development of international refugee law in the future will be the extent to which the European harmonization on asylum complies with rule of law principles, particularly in balancing regional harmonization with respect for international standards. Recently, commentators and bodies such as the International Association for

---

[264] The effectiveness of the European Court of Human Rights is briefly discussed by Harvey, 'Regionalism, Human Rights and Forced Migration', in Kneebone and Rawlings-Sanaei (eds.), *New Regionalism*, pp. 213–216.

280 REFUGEES, ASYLUM SEEKERS AND THE RULE OF LAW

Refugee Law Judges (IARLJ) have emphasized the importance of a 'transnational judicial dialogue' in relation to international refugee law.[265] Although harmonization of refugee law within Europe is to be welcomed in terms of consistency, it is also hoped that this does not simply result in the formation of minimal regional standards, but can also contribute to a broader, transnational development of high-level refugee protection standards.

[265] The IARLJ has established transnational Working Parties in an effort to develop a coherent body of international refugee jurisprudence: see www.iarlj.nl/general/ (accessed 8 April 2008).

6

Conclusions on the Rule of Law

SUSAN KNEEBONE

This book explores national legal responses to issues raised by refugees and asylum seekers and the rule of law. The issue of the rights and status of the asylum seeker in the legal system raises fundamental questions about how to maintain the 'integrity' of the rule of law when it is under challenge, and the role of the state to protect individuals who are not its 'nationals'. The basic argument in this book is that the way that the rule of law operates at the national level in relation to refugees and asylum seekers in the jurisdictions examined is denying them access to their rights under international law.[1] In particular, the twin precepts of refugee protection – the right to seek asylum and the right against *non-refoulement* – are under threat.

A comparison of the five jurisdictions – namely Canada, the USA, Australia, New Zealand and the UK – tells some interesting stories. Although they share a common law heritage, majority language and colonial past, and a tendency to borrow ideas for responses from each other, there are differences in each jurisdiction in the way that the Refugee Convention[2] is received, which influence the precise way in which each legal system responds to issues about asylum seekers and refugees. Yet, despite those differences, there are broadly similar patterns in the response of these receiving countries to asylum seekers and refugees over the last decade.

One common response is to exclude asylum seekers and refugees from access to the legal system. The measures include preventing access to territory (and thus to the legal system) through pre-arrival measures, or by denying access to the legal system through legal fictions such as the 'safe third country' idea. If asylum seekers and refugees manage to

---

[1] See 'Introduction: Refugees and Asylum Seekers in the International Context – Rights and Realities' (Introduction) in this volume.
[2] Convention relating to the Status of Refugees, Geneva, 28 July 1951, in force 22 April 1954, 1989 UNTS 137 (Refugee Convention).

281

282   REFUGEES, ASYLUM SEEKERS AND THE RULE OF LAW

overcome those hurdles, they have difficulty accessing justice, as specific rules plus the standards of adjudication are increasingly aimed at excluding them from participating fully in the process. Furthermore, access to judicial review is restricted in some respect in all jurisdictions (except for New Zealand).[3] Thus the risk of *refoulement* from all these restrictive measures is real.

As Legomsky says, both 'theoretical and practical' access to a legal system is inherent in the rule of law.[4] Yet the responses of the jurisdictions considered in this book demonstrate that the rights due to asylum seekers and refugees under the international rule of law[5] are being denied by national legal systems which owe protection obligations to asylum seekers under international law. This suggests that there are very real concerns about the integrity or coherency of these 'dualist' legal systems that require international law standards to be specifically incorporated into domestic or national law for implementation. In particular, as explained below, there is an interesting story to tell about how each jurisdiction has interpreted and applied the *non-refoulement* obligation in Article 33 of the Refugee Convention and the interrelationship between that obligation and those arising under the Convention Against Torture and Other Cruel Inhuman or Degrading Treatment or Punishment (CAT).[6]

To some extent, the responses can be explained by contextual factors – concerns about the large number of applicants for refugee status (as in the UK and the USA) and concerns about national security issues (as in the UK, Canada and the USA, to a certain extent) have been a driving factor in those jurisdictions. Yet in the Australian situation, there is no apparent evidence for concern on either basis.[7] The Australian response

---

[3] In New Zealand the Judicature Amendment Act 1972 contains an unrestricted right of review, subject to a time limit. Judicial review applications challenging New Zealand Refugee Status Appeals Authority (NZRSAA) decisions have been made in a very small number of cases – see www.refugee.org.nz/Stats/stats.htm#Table_60 (accessed 29 April 2008).

[4] See Chapter 3 in this volume at p. 144

[5] See Introduction in this volume at p. 2 note 6 for an explanation of this term.

[6] Convention Against Torture and Other Cruel Inhuman or Degrading Treatment or Punishment, New York, 10 December 1984, in force 26 June 1987, UN Doc. A/39/51 (1984), 1465 UNTS 85 (CAT).

[7] Chantal Marie-Jeanne Bostock, 'The International Legal Obligations Owed to the Asylum Seekers on the MV Tampa' (2002) 14 *International Journal of Refugee Law* 279 at 293; Susan Kneebone, 'The Pacific Plan: The Provision of "Effective Protection"?' (2006) 18 *International Journal of Refugee Law* 696 at 698, 718; Susan Kneebone and Sharon Pickering, 'Australia, Indonesia and the Pacific Plan' in Susan Kneebone and Felicity Rawlings-Sanaei (eds.), *New Regionalism and Asylum Seekers: Challenges Ahead* (Oxford: Berghahn Books, 2007), Chapter 7, pp. 172–74.

CONCLUSIONS ON THE RULE OF LAW 283

is largely driven by the perceived need to deter spontaneous asylum seekers. It is probably no coincidence that New Zealand, which has the lowest number of refugee applicants (proportionate to its population),[8] also has the fewest symptoms of rule of law 'malaise' (and hence is the least discussed in this book).[9] New Zealand is a model in this respect, and another aspect of its response provides an important lesson.

Within the Pacific region, New Zealand has been an important ally to Australia in refugee matters (albeit, not always uncritically). For example, initially when the Pacific Plan was in operation, New Zealand shared the burden with Australia.[10] By contrast, other 'regional' examples discussed in this book do not provide such positive examples of burden- or responsibility-sharing. For example, the Canada-US Safe Third Country Agreement,[11] which is discussed by Macklin in Chapter 2, was largely shaped by US concerns about border security in the 'post-9/11 political landscape' and was basically concerned to make it impossible for prospective asylum seekers to travel lawfully to Canada.[12] Another commentary on the Canada–USA relationship describes it as a retreat from 'historic protection roles by heightening their law-enforcement priorities and correspondingly diminishing their commitments to civil liberties and refugee protection'.[13]

The UK experience provides yet another example of a regional response. As O'Sullivan explains, the UK is linked to Europe through the European Convention of Human Rights (ECHR)[14] and the UK's role in the harmonization of asylum law by the European Union (EU). However, as she says, this 'is a relationship beset with contradictions'.[15]

---

[8] Dana Krause and Isabel Knott, 'Refugee Determination Processes: A View Across the Tasman' (2002) 27 *Alternative Law Journal* 220 at 221.

[9] See Chapter 4, Part three in this volume.

[10] See Kneebone, 'The Pacific Plan' at 708.

[11] Agreement Between the Government of Canada and the Government of the United States of America for Cooperation in the Examination of Refugee Status Claims from Nationals of Third Countries, 5 December 2002, in force 29 December 2004.

[12] Chapter 2, Part four in this volume at xxxx.

[13] François Crèpeau and Stephen H. Legomsky, 'North American Responses: A Comparative Study of U.S. and Canadian Refugee Policy' in Kneebone and Rawlings-Sanaei (eds.), *New Regionalism*, Chapter 6, p. 137.

[14] European Convention for the Protection of Human Rights and Fundamental Freedoms and its Protocols, Rome, 4 November 1950, in force 3 September 1953, ETS 5, 213 UNTS 221 (ECHR).

[15] Chapter 5 in this volume at p. 229.

284   REFUGEES, ASYLUM SEEKERS AND THE RULE OF LAW

On the one hand, although there is a strengthening of refugee law protection through the ECHR, the UK experience shows that there are issues about consistency between principles of international refugee law and the results of the harmonization process. O'Sullivan describes this process as leading to 'minimal regional standards'.[16]

These regional examples are some indication of how receiving states regard their responsibility towards asylum seekers. Such attitudes are not always conducive to responsibility sharing, but rather are indicative of responsibility shifting.[17] In this way, the receiving states discussed in this book mirror the global response of other industrialized states (see Introduction). The reluctance of industrialized states to see the issues from a global perspective is a hindrance to the solution of the refugee 'problem'.

But the immediate concern of this book is with how national refugee policy is developed, and the subtext that underlies national policy. The rule of law is important for that reason, because it shows how states perceive their responsibilities towards individual asylum seekers and the extent to which they accept their responsibilities under international law. The individual contributors have chosen rule of law issues which highlight both national policy and approaches to international obligations in the particular jurisdiction. A summary of the issues discussed follows.

Part one: chapter highlights

In the case of Canada (Chapter 2 – 'Asylum and the Rule of Law in Canada: Hearing the Other (Side)'), Audrey Macklin discusses the importance of access to the legal system and of hearing what the asylum seeker has to say. This includes a discussion of the importance of conferring procedural fairness. Macklin refers to Canada's respect for international law, and Canada's reputation as a generous supporter of refugees' rights, but laments the way in which, increasingly, asylum seekers are being 'kept out of earshot', both literally and metaphorically. In particular, Macklin highlights the role of the 1982 Canadian Charter of Rights and Freedoms[18] and of the Canada-US Safe Third Country Agreement in relation to the 'audibility' of the asylum seeker.

---

[16] Chapter 5 in this volume at p. 280.

[17] Savitri Taylor, 'The Pacific Solution or a Pacific Nightmare? The Difference Between Burden Shifting and Responsibility Sharing' (2005) 6 *Asian-Pacific Law and Policy Journal* 1.

[18] Canadian Charter of Rights and Freedoms 1982 (Charter).

In relation to the USA, Stephen Legomsky (Chapter 3 – 'Refugees, Asylum and the Rule of Law in the USA') describes the strong criminal justice and law enforcement response to asylum seekers, who are associated with illegal immigration. As with the Australian response, deterrence and border control are driving motivations for refugee law and policy. Legomsky focuses, in particular, upon reforms to the Board of Immigration Appeals (BIA) and problems of independence and 'substandard adjudication' at that level of decision making. Legomsky also points to the USA's somewhat ambivalent approach to international law and to the international rule of law in this context.

The Australian story, as told by Susan Kneebone (Chapter 4 – 'The Australian Story: Asylum Seekers outside the Law'), is one of the executive attempting to keep asylum seekers and refugees (and their advocates) out of the legal system, through the use of legislation and strategic litigation, and attempts to control the judiciary. In the Australian case there is also concern about how a 'dualist' legal system operates because of the particular and limited (and contested) way in which the Refugee Convention is incorporated, in contrast with New Zealand.

The chapter on the UK by Maria O'Sullivan (Chapter 5 – 'The Intersection between the International, the Regional and the Domestic: Seeking Asylum in the UK') discusses the relationship between the UK and Europe, and the EU and its effect on refugee law and policy. As stated above, this relationship has both positive and negative effects on UK refugee law and policy. Thus the response of the UK to international law is conflicted. Moreover, O'Sullivan describes the UK's law and policies as 'patchwork and reactive'.

From these brief summaries, it can be seen that each contributor focuses upon different aspects and levels of the national legal system. It is also apparent that each contributor has an individual view about the meaning of the 'ideal' of the rule of law, but that we share a common concern with its operation at the national level. To structure our conclusions, we have chosen to use Dworkin's model of 'law as integrity' (as explained in Chapter 1) as a foil to respond to the following questions:

- Is there a coherent legislative principle? Of what significance is the method and extent of incorporation of the Refugee Convention and related international law and human rights instruments into the legislation of the national legal system? Are differences in the constitutional and legislative frameworks significant?

286   REFUGEES, ASYLUM SEEKERS AND THE RULE OF LAW

- Of what significance are differences in the nature and structure of decision making at the administrative level? And, of adjudicative structures for decision making (including opportunities for appeal/review) – are they determinative of 'rights-respecting' legal systems?
- How integral is the adjudicative process? Are the courts deferential to executive policy in their approach to refugee law? What values underpin judicial reasoning? Of what significance are differences in the constitutional and the human rights framework for the adjudicative role?
- What are the limits of the integrity principle? How are refugees and asylum seekers defined by the legal system, and what forms of status and rights are granted by the state? That is, are refugees and asylum seekers defined as full members of the communities in which they seek protection?

The structure of the remainder of this chapter is formed by responses to these questions.

Part two: responses to Dworkin's framework

Is there a coherent legislative principle?

One of the issues addressed in this book is whether, in the context of the rights of refugees and asylum seekers, there is a 'coherent legislative principle' in operation. Under Dworkin's theory (as explained in Chapter 1), this is a principle directed at both legislators and at interpreters of legislation. It requires that law makers make morally coherent 'sets of laws', and it requires judges and those who apply legislation to interpret such legislation in accordance with his interpretive theory of law. Dworkin also recognized the adjudicative role of judges and intended that there be coherency between the legislature and the judiciary. His theory is based on the assumed existence of coherent community goals and policies which are moral and fair; that is, 'integrated'.

An alternative description of the idea of a 'coherent legislative principle' is that the legislative power is held as a public trust for achieving 'social goals for the common good'.[19] But there are many examples in this book of the use of legislation to drive executive agendas to keep asylum seekers out of legal systems. In Chapter 1, some concerns about the extensive and sometimes hasty or inappropriate use of legislative powers in this context were foreshadowed, as illustrated by the

---

[19] Dennis J. Galligan, *Law in Modern Society* (Oxford University Press, 2007), p. 258.

CONCLUSIONS ON THE RULE OF LAW 287

discussion in Chapters 4 and 5 of the Australian and UK experiences in particular. The UK's recent actions, characterized by a proliferation of legislation, have been described as a 'panicked response' led by a 'misguided belief in the power of legislation' to deter asylum seekers.[20]

In relation to Canada, Macklin describes the Canadian Government's failure to implement enacted provisions of the legislation which would establish a Refugee Appeal Division (RAD) to hear appeals from the Immigration and Refugee Board (IRB)[21] as a misuse of public trust in the exercise of legislative power. As Macklin explains, in the debate leading to the passage of the legislation, the promise to create the RAD was a significant factor in persuading refugee advocates to accept substantial changes to the IRB.

It is interesting to note that the problem of extensive and hasty use of legislative powers described elsewhere does not appear to be an issue in the USA. As Legomsky explains,[22] the US Congress has spelled out the legal regime governing refugees and asylum in extraordinary detail, in contrast to the parliamentary democracies that are the subject of the other chapters of this book. Indeed, he gives one example, involving the application of China's 'one-child policy', where Congress amended the refugee definition in 1996 to add specific language declaring forced abortion or sterilization, or persecution for refusal to undergo abortion or sterilization, to be persecuted on account of political opinion.[23]

However, Legomsky raises concerns about the conferring of broad legislative discretions upon individual officials, the exercise of which are difficult to challenge, because of their breadth. Parallel concerns were raised in the Australian context, especially in relation to the Migration Act s. 417, which confers the so-called 'safety-net' provision or 'humanitarian' discretion upon the Minister for Immigration as a substitute for a system of complementary protection.[24]

In relation to the coherency of the 'legislative principle', it is of concern to observe that parliaments in the UK and in Australia have legislated, or attempted to legislate, to overturn judicial decisions in this

---

[20] Dallal Stevens, *UK Asylum Law and Policy: Historical and Contemporary Perspectives* (London: Sweet and Maxwell, 2004), p. 219. See Chapter 5 in this volume for a detailed summary of the issues.
[21] Immigration and Refugee Protection Act 2001 ('IRPA'), ss. 110. 111. See Chapter 2 in this volume at pp. 101–5.
[22] Chapter 3 in this volume.   [23] 8 USC s. 1101(a)(42).
[24] Chapter 4 in this volume at pp. 207–10.

288   REFUGEES, ASYLUM SEEKERS AND THE RULE OF LAW

area. It raises the question of which 'community' (under Dworkin's theory) the legislator represents? Or, expressed in terms of the separation of powers, it challenges the independence of the judiciary in relation to these issues, and raises the question of what values, and whose values, are applied in the legal system – matters to which we return below.

The particular issue which is summarized here is the important role of the legislative principle in determining the relationship between national and international law in this context.

Of what significance is the method and extent of incorporation of the Refugee Convention and related international law and human rights instruments into the legislation of the national legal system?

Under the 'dualist' systems of law which operate in all the jurisdictions discussed in this book, there is a need for specific legislative incorporation of the Refugee Convention and related international law and human rights instruments.[25] The extent of incorporation, and indeed the lack of incorporation in some instances (see, in particular, the position in Australia and in the USA), raises the issue of whether there is 'good faith' implementation by a state of its international obligations.[26]

In this context, we considered differences in methods and extent of incorporation of the Refugee Convention and related international law and human rights instruments into the legislation of the national legal system, and whether they, in turn, reflect differences in the constitutional and legislative frameworks. It seems that the method and extent of incorporation of these instruments is significant in explaining differences in responses in the five jurisdictions. Further, these differences in incorporation reflect the respective legislative frameworks.

It is generally accepted that the most important human rights instruments related to the Refugee Convention[27] are the CAT, the

---

[25] Chapter 1 in this volume.

[26] Vienna Convention on the Law of Treaties, Vienna, 23 May 1969, in force 27 January 1980, 1155 UNTS 331 (Vienna Convention), Arts. 26 and 27. Note: this issue was discussed in *R* v. *Immigration Officer at Prague Airport; ex parte European Roma Rights Centre* [2004] UKHL 55; [2005] 2 AC 1 (*European Roma Rights Centre*). The House of Lords determined that there had not been a lack of 'good faith' in that instance. See Guy S. Goodwin-Gill and Jane McAdam, *The Refugee in International Law*, 3rd edn. (Oxford University Press, 2007), pp. 387–388 – this criterion of 'good faith' looks at the practical effects and the proportionality of the response.

[27] Note the debate referred to in the Introduction, p. 2 note 6 about the composition of the 'International Bill of Rights'. James C. Hathaway, *The Rights of Refugees Under*

CONCLUSIONS ON THE RULE OF LAW 289

International Covenant on Civil and Political Rights (ICCPR)[28] and the Convention on the Rights of the Child (CROC).[29] The Introduction explained the significance of the CAT and the ICCPR in relation to the *non-refoulement* principle.[30] The legislative history of incorporation of the Refugee Convention and human rights instruments provides meaningful insights into how refugees are perceived and received in each jurisdiction, and how their rights are defined in national systems.

Apart from the UK, the other jurisdictions had little experience with refugees up until World War II. Surprisingly, the UK, which has the longest recent history of receiving refugees, was the last to legislate to incorporate the Refugee Convention. Today, as O'Sullivan recounts, it is bound by the ECHR through the Human Rights Act 1998 (HRA). Although the CAT is not incorporated in UK law, the HRA incorporates specific ECHR human rights protection. Importantly, as O'Sullivan explains, the ECHR provides a prohibition on torture and of inhuman or degrading treatment or punishment that is absolute, and stronger than the protection against *refoulement* provided by the Refugee Convention.[31] However, other aspects of refugee protection are affected by the UK's relationship with the EU and the harmonization process. As O'Sullivan describes, the protection which the Refugee Convention provides is modified by this process.[32]

International Law (Cambridge University Press, 2005), p. 8 argues that in addition to the Refugee Convention (and the Refugee Protocol), the International Covenant on Civil and Political Rights, New York, 16 December 1966, in force 23 March 1976, UN Doc. A/6316 (1966), 999 UNTS 171 (ICCPR) and the International Covenant on Economic, Social and Cultural Rights, New York, 16 December 1966, in force 3 January 1976, UN Doc. A/6316 (1966), 99 UNTS 3 (ICESCR) comprise the IBR.

[28] ICCPR was ratified by Australia on 13 August 1980. In *Minister for Immigration* v. *Al Masri* (2003) 197 ALR 241, the court noted that although the ICCPR is not incorporated into Australian law, it is referred to in Schedule 2 of the Human Rights and Equal Opportunity Commission Act 1996 (Cth).

[29] Convention on the Rights of the Child, New York, 20 November 1989, in force 2 September 1990, UN Doc. A/44/49, 44 UN GAOR Supp. (No. 49) at 167 (CROC).

[30] Introduction in this volume at pp. 11–14.

[31] *Chahal* v. *UK* (1996) 23 EHRR 413 (15 November 1996) (*Chahal*).

[32] In Chapter 5 in this volume, O'Sullivan describes how the 'compelling reasons' exception in Art. 1C(5) of the Refugee Convention is modified by the Qualification Directive (Council Directive 2004/83/EC of 29 April 2004 on minimum standards for the qualification and status of third-country nationals or stateless persons as refugees or as persons who otherwise need international protection and the content of the protection granted, OJ 2004 No. L 304/12, 30 September 2004).

290 REFUGEES, ASYLUM SEEKERS AND THE RULE OF LAW

The USA, whose first modern experience of a refugee influx[33] was through the infamous St Louis incident in 1939, dealt with refugees in the post-World War II period as 'displaced persons'[34] (as did the other immigrant-receiving countries discussed in this book). Legomsky describes how protection was provided for refugees in a piecemeal way, in response to developments. The 1980 Refugee Act provided a refugee definition and an asylum procedure. The USA also introduced the 'withholding of deportation' procedure to implement the *non-refoulement* obligation in Article 33 of the Refugee Convention. In 1996 an expedited claims procedure requiring proof of a 'credible fear' of persecution was added in response to attacks on the World Trade Center. Additionally, more recently, a separate procedure for claiming protection under the CAT was added.

In fact, the USA has not incorporated the Refugee Convention. However, in 1968 it ratified the Refugee Protocol[35] and other protection mechanisms through legislation. The 1980 Refugee Act was enacted to incorporate the Refugee Protocol.[36] The USA is a party to other major human rights instruments such as the ICCPR and CROC, but tends to regard most human rights agreements as 'non-self-executing' and does not always enact legislation implementing all the provisions of those agreements, thus leaving many of these obligations unenforceable in US courts.[37]

In Canada, the Immigration and Refugee Protection Act 2001 (IRPA) is unique, as it separates refugee protection from general migration issues and incorporates the Refugee Convention and other human rights standards for such protection.[38] In particular, it incorporates the CAT[39] and provides protections which are similar to those in the ICCPR.[40] This Act, which replaced an older Immigration Act,[41] was intended to put refugee rights on a surer footing. In particular, it contains a Pre-Removal Risk Assessment (PRRA) process, which is intended to provide extra protection against *refoulement*.[42] The interaction between the 1982 Charter and the *non-refoulement* principle is discussed extensively by Macklin

---

[33] Another view of history is that the USA was initially a refugee settlement par excellence.
[34] Act of 25 June 1948, ch. 647, 62 Stat. 1009 (1948 Displaced Persons Act).
[35] Protocol relating to the Status of Refugees, New York, 31 January 1967, in force 4 October 1967, 19 UNTS 6223, 6257 (Refugee Protocol).
[36] Chapter 3 in this volume at pp. 123–5.
[37] Chapter 3 in this volume at pp. 134–40.   [38] See Chapter 2 in this volume.
[39] IRPA, s. 97(1)(a).   [40] IRPA, s. 97(1)(b).
[41] See Chapter 2 in this volume, at p. 79 note 4.   [42] IRPA, s. 113(a).

CONCLUSIONS ON THE RULE OF LAW   291

and is summarized below. There is no doubt that the Charter has had the effect of putting human rights on the agenda in Canada. But it is unclear whether it has led to a stronger recognition of international human rights.

In Australia, the history of legislative incorporation of the Refugee Convention shows how the focus of refugee protection has shifted from a concern with refugees and the refugee definition to the administrative process.[43] Recently, the High Court of Australia described the specific provisions in the Migration Act 1958 s. 36(2) as containing a 'false but legislatively necessary step'.[44] In Australia, there is also legislative modification of the definition of a refugee in Article 1A(2) of the Refugee Convention.[45] Although Australia is a party to the major international human rights instruments, very few are directly incorporated into Australian law. In particular the CAT, ICCPR and CROC are not incorporated. Of all the jurisdictions surveyed in this book, Australia alone does not have a Bill of Rights or other overriding code of human rights which applies nationally. As the discussion in Chapter 4 illustrates, there are serious concerns about the 'integrity' of its dualist legal system; that is, about the integration of international law norms into the national legal system. This includes concerns about the application of Article 1C(5) of the Refugee Convention (the 'cessation provision').[46]

The significance of the method and extent of incorporation of the Refugee Convention is demonstrated, in particular, by the comparison between Australia and New Zealand.[47] In New Zealand, Part 6A of the Immigration Act 1987, which came into force in 1999, governs refugee issues. In New Zealand, in comparison to Australia, there is no debate about the extent of incorporation of the Refugee Convention. Indeed the Refugee Status Appeals Authority (RSAA) is required 'to act in a manner that is consistent with New Zealand's obligations under the Refugee Convention',[48] the text of which is set out in a schedule to the Act. Moreover, Articles 32 and 33 of the Refugee Convention have been directly incorporated through s. 129X of the Immigration Act.[49] By contrast, in some of the jurisdictions discussed in this book, there is legislative modification of the exceptions (exclusion provisions) to refugee

---

[43] Chapter 4 in this volume at pp. 198–202.
[44] *NAGV & NAGW* v. *Minister for Immigration* (2005) 222 CLR 161 at para. 27.
[45] Migration Act, s 91R. See Chapter 4, Part three in this volume at pp. 210–17.
[46] See Chapter 4 in this volume [Article 1C(5) and the TPV scheme].
[47] See Chapter 4, Part three in this volume [Part Three].
[48] Immigration Act 1987, s. 129D.   [49] Immigration Act 1987, s 129X.

292   REFUGEES, ASYLUM SEEKERS AND THE RULE OF LAW

protection in Article 1F and Article 33(2)[50] of the Refugee Convention. For example, in the UK and Australia, legislation has set out restrictive interpretations of these exclusions.[51]

Are differences in the constitutional and legislative frameworks significant?

In the UK, which does not have a single written constitution and where immigration powers are sourced back to the prerogative, the 'sovereign right to exclude' aliens[52] as legal doctrine is as much evident as it is in jurisdictions such as Australia and the USA, where there are written constitutions. In those jurisdictions, the rights of asylum seekers as 'alien' non-citizens are governed by general immigration statutes. In the USA, as in Australia, the asylum process is part and parcel of the regulation of immigration, which derives from constitutional powers in respect to aliens. In the UK, these powers are modified, as described above, by its relationship with the EU.

In Canada, the Charter has sometimes provided enhanced protection of common law and other constitutional rights (as in *Singh* v. *Canada (Minister of Employment and Immigration)* (*Singh*)).[53] But as Macklin recounts in Chapter 2, it has not been the sole or consistent source of rights protection in this context.[54]

Thus, while the method of incorporation of the Refugee Convention and related human rights instruments appears to be a significant factor, the constitutional background, whether derived from the prerogative or a specific head of power appears to lead to similar legal doctrine, namely the sovereign right to exclude.

However, differences in the legislative frameworks do appear to be significant, as the Australia–New Zealand comparison demonstrates. In

---

[50] See the discussion of these provisions in Chapter 5 in this volume.
[51] In the USA and Canada, restrictive interpretations of the exclusion clauses have resulted from administrative and judicial decisions. See Chapters 2 and 3 in this volume.
[52] *Musgrove* v. *Toy* [1891] AC 272. Note: 'New Zealand does not have a written constitution. The power to legislate in the immigration and refugee context is a prerogative power stemming from state sovereignty.' (Rodger Haines, 'The Asylum Seeker in the Legal System: NEW ZEALAND', Montreal, 4 September 2006, p. 9, para. 27 (copy on file with the author)).
[53] [1985] 1 SCR 177. *Singh* is discussed in Chapter 2 in this volume at pp. 85–90.
[54] See the discussion in Chapter 2 in this volume of *Canada (Minister of Employment and Immigration)* v. *Chiarelli* [1992] 1 SCR 711 and *Baker* v. *Canada (Ministry of Citizenship and Immigration)* [1999] 2 SCR 817.

CONCLUSIONS ON THE RULE OF LAW 293

Australia, for example, the rights of refugees have been shaped by the legislative rather than the human rights context. In New Zealand, where the legislation provides clearer directions to the Refugee Convention, a human rights approach prevails in the RSAA.[55] In relation to Canada, where the legislation separates refugee protection from general immigration regulation, it is no accident that, as Macklin says:

> The general trend of Supreme Court of Canada jurisprudence over the past twenty years has been toward an increasing regard for the rights and interests of asylum seekers and migrants. There have been, of course, notable setbacks as well. Nevertheless, the Court has proved willing to use both the Charter and 'unwritten constitutional principles'[56] embedded in the rule of law to establish that asylum seekers are protected under the Charter, that international law is relevant to the interpretation of Canadian statutes and constitution, and that the refugee definition should be interpreted in a relatively liberal fashion.[57]

Thus it seems that adherence to the 'legislative principle' is essential in achieving coherency between national and international law.

Nature and structure of decision making

Decision making at the administrative level

When the number of people seeking refuge was small, it was possible to keep decision making within the executive. Other than in Canada, the bulk of initial decisions about refugee status are made within the bureaucracy.[58] As the number of asylum seekers has increased, it has been necessary for the executive to share or to hand over that power to administrative tribunals which have been created in all jurisdictions.

Neutral adjudication at this level is vital for the operation of the rule of law, as explained in Chapter 1,[59] for reasons of both political accountability and for ensuring equal treatment of refugees and asylum seekers

---

[55] Chapter 4, Part three in this volume.
[56] *Provincial Judges Reference* [1997] 3 SCR 3 (original footnote).
[57] Chapter 2, Part four in this volume.
[58] O'Sullivan describes reform at the 'initial' Home Office level. She describes the new Independent Immigration Inspectorate which was introduced via the UK Borders Act 2007 to oversee the operations of the UK Border and Immigration Agency ('BIA'). See Chapter 5 in this volume at pp. 248–50. Additionally the 'New Asylum Model' instituted by the Home Office has a strong focus on efficiency. See Chapter 5 in this volume at pp. 256–7.
[59] Chapter 1 in this volume at pp. 50–2.

within the legal system. It is essential for protection against *refoulement*. Moreover, decisional neutrality as an aspect of the principle of procedural fairness is essential for the same reason. However, as the discussion in this book demonstrates, there are problems with ensuring neutrality and compliance with procedural fairness at this level. Overall, it seems that when it comes to refugees and asylum seekers, governments are compromising the standards of the rule of law for this class of persons. As O'Sullivan expresses it in relation to the UK, there is 'tension between efficiency and administrative justice'.[60] This theme is repeated in other jurisdictions. This is despite differences in models of administrative adjudication in the jurisdictions.

The Canadian Refugee Protection Division (RPD) of the IRB has, for many years, had the most generous outcomes for refugee status and has been perceived to provide a 'Cadillac'[61] model of adjudication. Of all the administrative tribunals in the jurisdictions which were discussed, it has consistently had the highest acceptance rate of refugee claimants. It has a prestigious reputation for the quality of its decisions and of its guidelines on substantive aspects of the Refugee Convention definition, and on practical application of the principles. The RPD, rather than the courts, has played a large role in establishing universal refugee law principles. The Canadian model was a direct result of the Singh decision.[62] Yet this model of fairness has been progressively pared back by successive Canadian governments, as Macklin describes in Chapter 2.[63]

The problems which Macklin describes are not unique to Canada. She details concerns about the transparency of the appointment process and the quality of appointees. Such concerns are echoed by Legomsky in relation to the USA's Board of Immigration Appeals (BIA).[64] It too has struggled to establish its 'credibility' and independence from the Department of Justice in which it is located. Legomsky refers to the giving of 'one-paragraph boilerplate' reasons (or 'affirmances without opinion' (AWOs)) for decisions and 'substandard adjudication' as symptoms of the problems. This is most worrying, as the BIA is an

---

[60] Chapter 5 in this volume.
[61] Crépeau and Legomsky, 'North American Responses' in Kneebone and Rawlings-Sanaei (eds.), *New Regionalism*, p. 141.
[62] [1985] 1 SCR 177. *Singh* is discussed in Chapter 2 in this volume at pp. 85–90.
[63] Chapter 2 in this volume at pp. 85–93.
[64] Chapter 3 in this volume at pp. 128–31, 147–50.

CONCLUSIONS ON THE RULE OF LAW   295

'adjudicative' tribunal, whose decisions establish jurisprudence ('precedent decisions').[65]

As in other jurisdictions, such as the UK and Australia, there is an increasing emphasis on efficiency at this level. This has led to measures to reduce the size of hearing panels and to shorten the length of hearings. Macklin, for example, describes the issue of guidelines in 2003 by the Chair of the IRB instituting what became known as 'reverse-order questioning' aimed at expediting hearings. She describes how the guidelines passed scrutiny by a seemingly deferential Federal Court of Appeal in *Canada (Minister of Citizenship and Immigration)* v. *Thamotharem* (*Thamotharem* (FCA)).[66]

In terms of the outward signs of independence, New Zealand's RSAA is the closest to the Canadian model. Of all the administrative tribunals in the jurisdictions which we discuss, the RSAA is closest to a judicial model and has achieved unusual world standing in terms of the creation of substantive international jurisprudence. Members of the RSAA are appointed by the Governor-General on the advice of the Minister of Immigration and must be barristers and solicitors of the High Court of New Zealand who have held practising certificates for at least five years or who have other equivalent or appropriate experience (whether in New Zealand or overseas).[67] The RSAA has the powers of a Commission of Inquiry under the Commissions of Inquiry Act 1908 and all the provisions of that Act except the provisions relating to costs apply to the RSAA as if it were a Commission of Inquiry. The procedure of the RSAA is in its discretion.[68] However, despite these outward trappings and legislative prescriptions, the RSAA is not immune from the political trend to reduce its role.[69]

In Australia, where in contrast to Canada the courts decided that there was no general obligation to provide an oral hearing to asylum

---

[65] In the USA there is another level of decision making below the BIA which applies to removal proceedings. This refers to the 'quasi-judicial' role of immigration judges who are part of the Executive Office for Immigration Review (EOIR), which is in the Department of Justice: 8 CFR s. 1003.10 (2006). Legomsky also details concerns about political interventions at that level. See Chapter 3 in this volume at pp. 150–56.

[66] 2007 FCA 198, 25 May 2007.   [67] Immigration Act 1987, s. 129N.

[68] Immigration Act 1987, Schedule 3C, Clauses 7 and 8.

[69] An Immigration Bill 2007 tabled in the New Zealand Parliament on 8 August 2007 proposes to disestablish the RSAA and to replace it with an Immigration and Protection Tribunal with an expanded jurisdiction similar to that which applies in Canada under IRPA, s. 96 and s. 97 (information supplied by Rodger Haines QC, at round table, Montreal, 4 September 2006 – see Preface to this volume).

seekers,[70] the Refugee Review Tribunal (RRT) was established as an inquisitorial tribunal in a legal system where there was existing experience with the concept of administrative tribunals and non-judicial merits review. On balance, the RRT has struggled to perform this role and to provide fair hearings.[71] For that reason, many applicants have sought judicial review in the courts. The government, in turn, has consistently attempted to exclude judicial review and to minimize the role of the legal profession in this context.[72]

Currently there are two streams in the refugee determination process in the UK: on the one hand, a fairly comprehensive decision-making process with in-country appeal rights for most asylum seekers (through the Asylum Immigration Tribunal (AIT)); but, on the other, the existence of 'accelerated' procedures apply to those applicants deemed to have 'unfounded claims' because they come from a 'safe country of origin' or 'safe third country', or because they have been in detention. Such applicants only have the right to an 'out of country' appeal.

In the UK there has also been much experimentation with different models of adjudication. The UK's AIT is a new, single-tier tribunal which in 2005 replaced the previous two-tier system.[73] Members of the Tribunal are called Immigration Judges and they may sit in panels of one, two or three. The Tribunal, which is described as an independent judicial body, was created to assist in dealing with severe backlogs in the refugee determination process. If a person is refused refugee status or complementary protection under UK law, he or she may be able to appeal against that decision to the AIT, which is empowered to re-examine the merits of the individual's application.

---

[70] *Zhang* v. *Minister for Immigration* (1993) 45 FCR 384.

[71] Susan Kneebone, 'The Refugee Review Tribunal and the Assessment of Credibility: An Inquisitorial Role?' (1998) 5 *Australian Journal of Administrative Law* 78; Susan Kneebone, 'Is the Australian Refugee Review Tribunal "Institutionally" Biased?' in François Crèpeau et al. (eds.), *Forced Migration and Global Processes: A View from Forced Migration Studies* (Lanham, MD: Lexington Books, 2006), Chapter 10.

[72] Chapter 4 in this volume at pp. 178–85.

[73] The AIT was created pursuant to the Asylum and Immigration (Treatment of Claimants) Act 2004 and commenced operation on 4 April 2005. It is designed to operate as an independent Appeals Tribunal (it is part of the Department of Constitutional Affairs rather than the Home Office). The AIT replaces the Immigration Appellate Authority which consisted of two tiers: adjudicators and the Immigration Appeal Tribunal. The AIT operates according to an adversarial model: See BIA, 'Asylum Process Guidance: The Appeals Process', www.bia.homeoffice.gov.uk/sitecontent/documents/policyandlaw/asylumprocessguidance/theappealsprocess/ (accessed 19 April 2008).

Judicial review

In Chapter 1, the importance of judicial review and the 'adjudicative' role of judges for protecting substantive rights are explained.[74] In Chapter 2, Macklin gives a detailed account of the value of that process in relation to the Canada-US Safe Third Country Agreement.[75] Yet in all jurisdictions (with the exception of New Zealand), there are restrictions on the right to judicial review or appeal from administrative tribunals. Importantly, such restrictions have been put in place in response to increased numbers of applications for asylum at the administrative level. Unfortunately policy makers appear to ignore the clear link between the decline in standards at that level, and the increasing numbers seeking judicial review.[76]

The restrictions on judicial review take various forms, although none are as extensive as Australia's ouster clause, described in Chapter 4.[77] In Australia, the effect of the ouster clause in terms of curbing judicial power was arguably pyrrhic. As a result, the Australian Government introduced further restrictions on access to judicial review and attempted to curtail the role of the legal profession. By contrast, in the UK, the attempt to introduce an ouster clause failed.[78]

In Canada, the restriction takes the form of a leave requirement which operates fairly severely. Macklin explains that effectively only a very small proportion of applicants who seek judicial review do so successfully.[79] In the USA there are some restrictions on judicial review (for example, late filing of the asylum application and expedited removal orders) but no general restrictions.

In the UK, if the AIT refuses the application, the applicant may then apply to the High Court for a review of that decision, who can order that the AIT 'reconsider' the case. This process is governed by requirements set out in the Nationality, Immigration and Asylum Act 2002[80] and is restricted in a number of ways. For instance, it is subject to

---

[74] Chapter 1 in this volume, Part Two at pp. 48–50.
[75] Chapter 2 in this volume, Part Four.   [76] Legomsky, Chapter 3 in this volume.
[77] Chapter 4 in this volume at pp.178–85.
[78] The UK Government attempted to introduce an ouster clause into the Asylum and Immigration Treatment of Claimants Bill 2003. See Chapter 5 in this volume at p. 234 note 37.
[79] Chapter 2 in this volume.
[80] If so, the applicant will have a right of appeal to the AIT and from there may appeal (if they meet the criteria) to the High Court and House of Lords (see Nationality, Immigration and Asylum Act 2002, ss. 103A–E).

298   REFUGEES, ASYLUM SEEKERS AND THE RULE OF LAW

extremely short time limits, and legal aid is only granted retrospectively (that is, after the review and reconsideration process).[81] In addition to statutory appeal avenues, applicants may also (in some circumstances) be able to lodge an application for judicial review of certain asylum decisions.[82] Ultimately, applicants may also be able to appeal (with leave) to the House of Lords and, from there, if a case involves the breach of a right under the ECHR, to the European Court of Human Rights in Strasbourg. Thus, in the UK, the link with Europe potentially provides more avenues of review.

The story of the rule of law is very much played out at the level of judicial review in Australia and the UK. By comparison, in New Zealand and Canada, most substantive decisions are made at the administrative level, and judicial review plays a lesser role. In the case of Canada, leave is required to seek judicial review and it is granted in only a small percentage of cases. The comparative unimportance of judicial review perhaps relates to the quality of RPB decisions. In the case of New Zealand, judicial review also plays a lesser role, possibly as a result of the fact that issues of substantive law are dealt with adequately by the RSAA. But in Australia and the UK, decisions of the courts on judicial review have resulted in undignified exchanges between the executive and the judiciary.[83]

Restrictions on judicial review display a deliberate policy to exclude asylum seekers and refugees from access to the legal system. They are not designed to encourage 'rights-respecting' legal systems, but rather the reverse.

How integral is the adjudicative process? What values underpin judicial reasoning? Are the courts deferential to executive policy in their approach to refugee law?

In Chapter 1, the importance of adjudication (the role of judges) in the legal system was explained by reference to formal (positivist) and substantive versions of the rule of law.[84] Dworkin's theory of 'law as integrity' is concerned with both the 'fit' and the 'value' of legal principles. It was

---

[81] The review and reconsideration process is discussed in detail in Robert Thomas, 'After the Ouster: Review and Reconsideration in a Single Tier Tribunal' (2006) *Public Law* 674–678.

[82] See Stevens, *UK Asylum Law and Policy*, pp. 316–323.

[83] See Kneebone, Chapter 4 in this volume and O'Sullivan, Chapter 5 in this volume at pp. 244–48.

[84] Chapter 1 in this volume, Part two: integrity and adjudication.

CONCLUSIONS ON THE RULE OF LAW   299

argued that a substantive vision of the rule of law can be justified in this context; namely where the rights of refugees and asylum seekers are defined in international law and translated into action in national legal systems. In practice, this requires that the provisions of the Refugee Convention should be interpreted within a human rights framework.[85]

The focus of Dworkin's theory is upon substantive values. He explains that 'law as integrity' asks judges to assume, 'so far as this is possible, that the law is structured by a coherent set of principles about justice and fairness and procedural due process'.[86] He is also concerned with equal protection – which flows from neutral decision making. This interpretive theory of law is based on the assumed existence of community or communal goals and policies which are moral and fair or 'integral'.

In practice, as discussion in this book illustrates, the courts vacillate between deference to the executive and the legislature, and promotion of the values inherent in human rights protection. For example, while courts may support the executive's interpretation of its powers, especially where issues of national security are concerned (as in the case of the UK and Canada),[87] and processes on the one hand (as is the case in Australia, where such interpretations may also provide procedural protection to refugees),[88] there are also many instances where courts uphold substantive values by 'good faith' interpretation of the refugee definition[89] (see the discussion in Chapters 2 and 3).

In Canada, it is well established that the refugee definition should be interpreted in a relatively liberal fashion.[90] The general trend of Supreme Court of Canada jurisprudence over the past twenty years has been towards an increasing regard for the rights and interests of asylum seekers and migrants. In the USA also, the courts have been relatively generous in their interpretation of the refugee definition.[91] In Australia,

---

[85] Michelle Foster, *International Refugee Law and Socio-Economic Rights: Refuge from Deprivation* (Cambridge University Press, 2007), p. 28.

[86] Ronald Dworkin, *Law's Empire* (Cambridge, MA: Belknap Press, 1986), p. 243.

[87] E.g. *S and others* v. *Secretary of State for the Home Department* [2006] EWCA Civ 1157, discussed in Chapter 5 in this volume, and *Suresh* v. *Canada (Minister of Citizenship and Immigration)* [2002] 1 SCR 3 (Suresh), discussed in Chapter 2 in this volume.

[88] E.g. *Re Minister for Immigration; Ex parte Miah* (2001) 206 CLR 57 discussed in Chapter 4 in this volume.

[89] This refers to Art. 31(1) of the Vienna Convention which requires that a treaty 'shall be interpreted in good faith in accordance with the ordinary meaning to be given to the terms of the treaty in their context and in the light of its object and purpose'.

[90] Chapter 2 in this volume.

the picture is more complex. While the High Court of Australia has produced some of the leading international jurisprudence,[92] the role of judges is made more complex by the legislation incorporating the Refugee Convention, as it appears to make the legislative meaning more important than the words of the Convention. In particular, in Australia, the interpretation of the Refugee Convention, Article 1E and Article 1C(5) has produced some inconsistency with the international jurisprudence.[93] Further, in the case of Australia, the comparison with New Zealand demonstrates the difference that results from a human rights approach to interpretation.[94]

Of what significance are differences in the constitutional and the human rights framework for the adjudicative role?

As suggested above, it is difficult to conclude that differences in constitutional frameworks are a significant factor in the way that courts approach these issues – although, as the Australian story reveals, the courts may rely upon such framework to support its decisions.

Another way to approach this issue is to ask whether the Refugee Convention is considered to be the primary instrument of rights protection in the jurisdictions we have considered, or whether the existence of protection under other human rights instruments or under other common law or administrative law principles[95] are also important in the protection of refugees and asylum seekers. This is an important issue because, as was explained in the Introduction, respect for the Refugee Convention is essential for the international regime of refugee protection. There are concerns that respect for it is being eroded indirectly by the application of other human rights instruments, or by minimal interpretation of its obligations, or by the practical application of inappropriate standards of protection. This is an assertion which we can substantiate by considering the application of the fundamental *non-refoulement* principle in the various jurisdictions.

---

[91] Chapter 3 in this volume.

[92] E.g. *Chan Yee Kin* v. *Minister for Immigration* (1989) 169 CLR 379.

[93] See Chapter 4 in this volume at pp. 198–207, 212–17.

[94] Chapter 4 in this volume, Part three.

[95] In Chapter 1 in this volume it was noted that administrative law principles play a large role in rights protection in some jurisdictions. In particular, compliance with procedural fairness is essential. See, in particular, Chapter 2 at Part two, Chapter 3 at pp. 156–61, Chapter 4 at pp. 181–85, Chapter 5 at pp. 257–8.

CONCLUSIONS ON THE RULE OF LAW 301

As was explained in the Introduction to the book, the *non-refoulement* principle is mirrored in other treaties which prohibit torture and cruel, inhuman or degrading treatment or punishment, such as the ICCPR.[96] The *non-refoulement* principle is also affirmed in the CAT,[97] which contains an absolute prohibition against torture. The fact that the *non-refoulement* principle goes beyond Article 33 of the Refugee Convention is evidence towards its status as an implied component of a customary prohibition on torture and cruel, inhuman or degrading treatment or punishment. But, as was explained in the Introduction, this interpretation is disputed.[98] The fact that different standards are set by the Refugee Convention and various human rights instruments leaves them open to individual state interpretation.

There are several issues which have been raised in the various chapters, which illustrate how the *non-refoulement* principle is applied. One such issue is the matter of extraterritorial application of the *non-refoulement* principle. Another is the interrelationship between Article 33 of the Refugee Convention and the CAT or similar standards. A third issue is the application of the standard at the national level.

The debate over the extraterritorial application of the *non-refoulement* principle is one example of state interpretation which appears contrary to the spirit of the Refugee Convention and counter to the possible status of the *non-refoulement* principle as a customary prohibition. In Australia, the UK and the USA, the courts have deferred to the government's interpretation in this respect to determine that the Refugee Convention does not have extraterritorial application.[99] In both Australia (*Ruddock v. Vadarlis (Vadarlis)*),[100] and the USA (*Sale*

---

[96] ICCPR, Art. 7. See Goodwin-Gill and McAdam, *The Refugee in International Law*, p. 209. Note that in New Zealand, ICCPR Arts. 6 and 7 have been incorporated into national law by ss. 8 and 9 of the New Zealand Bill of Rights Act. In *Zaoui v. Attorney-General* [2006] 1 NZLR 289 at paras. 78–93, the obiter view was expressed that these provisions may prevent the removal of a person at risk of death or torture even though that person may not be a Convention refugee. See Rodger Haines, 'National Security and *Non-Refoulement* in New Zealand: Commentary on *Zaoui v. Attorney-General (No 2)*' in Jane McAdam (ed.), *Moving On: Forced Migration and Human Rights* (Oxford: Hart Publishing, 2008), Chapter 3.

[97] CAT, Art. 3. This treaty provides that a person shall not be returned to a place of torture. Goodwin-Gill and McAdam, *The Refugee in International Law*, p. 208.

[98] Introduction to this volume at pp. 11–14.

[99] See *Ibid.*

[100] (2001) 110 FCR 491 reversing *Victorian Council for Civil Liberties Incorporated v. Minister for Immigration* (North J) (2001) 110 FCR 452, discussed briefly in Chapter 4 in this volume.

302 REFUGEES, ASYLUM SEEKERS AND THE RULE OF LAW

v. *Haitian Centers Council, Inc.* (*Sale*)[101] the courts gave primacy to domestic (national) legislation to reach that conclusion.

In *R* v. *Immigration Officer at Prague Airport; ex parte European Roma Rights Centre* (*European Roma Rights Centre*),[102] the House of Lords found that the pre-clearance scheme operated by the UK at Prague Airport did not breach Article 33 of the Refugee Convention. The House of Lords limited its operation to acts at the UK border or from within the UK. In their view, the asylum seekers in the pre-clearance area were not refugees within the meaning of the Refugee Convention Article 1A(2), as they had not left the Czech Republic. The *non-refoulement* principle was defined as applying to rejection at the frontier. But, while the House of Lords found that there was no breach of Article 33, it decided that the scheme was discriminatory, as it was in breach of UK Race Relations Act 1976. Thus the House of Lords also ultimately relied upon national legislation to reach their conclusion.

The application of the CAT provision on *non-refoulement*, Article 3(1), is also relevant in this context. This provision states: 'No State Party shall expel, return (*refouler*) or extradite a person to another State where there are substantial grounds for believing that he would be in danger of being subjected to torture.' Unlike the analogous *non-refoulement* provision of the Refugee Convention, the CAT prohibition on *refoulement* is not subject to any exceptions for criminality or national security, and thus may provide greater protection. In both the USA and Canada, refugee protection can be sought on the basis of the CAT prohibition against torture.

In the Supreme Court of Canada's decision in *Suresh* v. *Canada (Minister of Citizenship and Immigration)* (*Suresh*),[103] the issue was the effect of the CAT on the Canadian Charter. The Court in that case ruled that, in general, s. 7 of the Charter[104] prohibited expelling a non-citizen to a place where he or she would face a substantial risk of torture, except in exceptional circumstances. Macklin points out, however, that the Court stopped short of designating *non-refoulement* as a rule of customary international law, or even of recognizing the absolute nature of the prohibition in Article 3 of the CAT. It also, as Macklin says, 'pointedly

---

[101] 509 US 155 (1993), discussed in Chapter 3 in this volume.
[102] [2004] UKHL 55; [2005] 2 AC 1 discussed in the Introduction to this volume.
[103] [2002] 1 SCR 3.
[104] This is the guarantee of the 'right to life, liberty and security of the person' discussed in the Singh decision [1985] 1 SCR 711. See Chapter 2 in this volume at pp. 85–93.

CONCLUSIONS ON THE RULE OF LAW   303

refused to articulate what exceptional circumstances would permit handing over a person to face torture'. It was clearly a decision which deferred to the executive's power in relation to national security. She comments:

> The Court arguably revealed a lapse in fidelity to the rule of law that courts in the UK and the European Court of Human Rights have managed to resist so far.[105]

In the UK, as O'Sullivan explains in Chapter 5, the prohibition on torture in Article 3 of the ECHR[106] can be the basis for arguing against return to a country when there are substantial grounds for believing that he or she faces a real risk of treatment contrary to Article 3. In the UK it appears that Article 3 of the ECHR provides stronger protection than the Refugee Convention. However, the UK is attempting to limit the prohibition of torture in Article 3 by attempting to overturn the European Court of Human Rights decision in *Chahal* v. *UK* (*Chahal*).[107] As O'Sullivan explains, this action highlights the tension between the interests of states in protecting their citizens against national security threats and the nature of Article 3 as an absolute right. The UK is attempting to argue that a 'balancing' approach should apply, as in the Canadian *Suresh* decision.[108] O'Sullivan describes how, in 2007, the UK attempted to challenge the *Chahal* judgment by intervening in the European Court of Human Rights case of *Saadi* v. *Italy*.[109]

The contrast between the decisions of *Chahal* and *Suresh* illustrate the difference that an external adjudicator can make – in *Chahal*, the standards were set by the European Court of Human Rights. But, in *Suresh*, the Supreme Court of Canada was deferential to the executive's role.

---

[105] Citing *Chahal* (1996) 23 EHRR 413 (15 November 1996) – see Chapter 2 in this volume.

[106] ECHR, Art. 3 provides that 'No one shall be subjected to torture or to inhuman or degrading treatment or punishment'.

[107] (1996) 23 EHRR 413.

[108] The Supreme Court commented that: 'We do not exclude the possibility that in exceptional circumstances, deportation to face torture might be justified . . . We may predict that [the balance] will rarely be struck in favour of expulsion where there is a serious risk of torture. However, as the matter is one of balance, precise prediction is elusive': *Suresh* [2002] 1 SCR 3 at para. 78.

[109] Application No. 37201/06. Heard by the Grand Chamber on 11 July 2007. The UK was given permission to intervene as a third party and to make both written and oral submissions. Note that the UK has also been given permission to intervene in the case of *Ramzy* v. *Netherlands* (Application No. 25424/05) but that case has been held up by procedural delays.

304 REFUGEES, ASYLUM SEEKERS AND THE RULE OF LAW

Finally, in terms of the practical application of the *non-refoulement* standard, the Australian story (the interpretation of Article 1E of the Refugee Convention and the application of s. 417 of the Migration Act) suggests that the standards for application of the *non-refoulement* principle fall short of what is required.[110] In all, it seems that, in application of the *non-refoulement* principle, national laws and national standards are of paramount importance.

What are the limits of the integrity principle?

In Chapter 1, the role of 'the community' and of national boundaries in defining (exclusively) the rights of asylum seekers was discussed. We saw the tendency of legal systems to define refugees and asylum seekers as 'outsiders' and we saw that the notion of territorial–parliamentary–state–sovereignty, which is represented by state borders and national jurisdictions, leads to a legal impasse which reinforces the lack of a legally enforceable right to seek asylum, and the non-extraterritorial application of the right against *refoulement*.[111] We explored the exclusive notion of 'communitarian liberalism' and Walzer's argument[112] that membership in a community is an issue of distributive justice. A practical example of this latter idea appears in Legomsky's discussion of the US perspective of the issue of asylum as one of 'illegal migration', in which outsiders abuse the system to obtain benefits.[113]

In Chapter 1 we also explored possible limits to Dworkin's theory of 'law as integrity', which is based on the assumed existence of coherent community goals and policies which are moral and fair; that is, 'integrated'. Although his theory was not framed with the issues of asylum seekers in mind, it has the potential to be used to exclude 'outsiders', as does communitarian liberalism. We then turned to ethical arguments which move the focus away from the territorial–parliamentary–state–sovereignty impasse to a concern with the responsibilities of states towards refugees and asylum seekers.[114] We saw that, within this

---

[110] Chapter 4 in this volume.
[111] See *Sale*, 509 US 155 (1993); *Vadarlis* (2001) 110 FCR 491; (2001) 110 FCR 452 and *European Roma Rights Centre* [2004] UKHL 55; [2005] 2 AC 1 discussed above.
[112] Michael Walzer, *Spheres of Justice: A Defence of Pluralism and Equality* (Oxford: Basil Blackwell, 1983), pp. 31–63.
[113] Chapter 3 in this volume at pp. 140–4.
[114] Specifically, the views of Matthew J. Gibney, *The Ethics and Politics of Asylum: Liberal Democracy and the Response to Refugees* (Cambridge University Press, 2004).

CONCLUSIONS ON THE RULE OF LAW   305

framework, there is room to recognize the rights and status of refugees and asylum seekers.

The issue of the status granted to refugees and asylum seekers is dealt with in the Refugee Convention. As Jane McAdam has pointed out, the unique feature of the Refugee Convention in comparison to other human rights instruments is that international law requires that the person be granted the status of a refugee.[115] McAdam explains that, whereas the grant of Convention status entitles the person to the full range of Convention rights,[116] 'no comparable status arises from recognition of an individual's protection need under a human rights instrument'.[117] As James Hathaway says: 'Refugee status is a categorical designation that reflects a unique ethical and consequential legal entitlement to make claims on the international community'.[118]

As in the discussion above, we have seen that the Refugee Convention is bypassed in many jurisdictions, where there is an inclination to grant lesser forms of protection to recognized refugees or to deny them rights which the Refugee Convention grants. Increasingly, the status-conferring function of the state is used to marginalize the international system of refugee protection and to diminish the status of refugees and asylum seekers within the community. To conclude this discussion, we consider two sub-questions:

- How are refugees and asylum seekers defined by the legal system, and what forms of status and rights are granted by the state?
- That is, are refugees and asylum seekers defined as full members of the communities in which they seek protection?

In some jurisdictions, such as Australia and the UK, there is a trend to grant what are essentially complementary forms of protection to recognized refugees. By contrast, in Canada, if the asylum claim is accepted, the asylum seeker may obtain permanent resident status and eventually citizenship. While this is not a requirement of the Refugee Convention as such,[119] it accords with the grant of Convention status.

---

[115] Jane McAdam, 'The Refugee Convention as a Rights Blueprint for Persons in Need of International Protection' in McAdam (ed.), *Forced Migration*, Chapter 10, p. 267.
[116] See Introduction to this volume at pp. 6–8.
[117] McAdam, 'The Refugee Convention as a Rights Blueprint' in McAdam (ed.), *Forced Migration* p. 267.
[118] James C. Hathaway, 'Forced Migration Studies: Could We Agree Just to 'Date'?' (2007) 20 *Journal of Refugee Studies* 349 at 352.
[119] Refugee Convention, Art. 34 requires Contracting States 'as far as possible' to 'facilitate the assimilation and naturalization of refugees'.

306   REFUGEES, ASYLUM SEEKERS AND THE RULE OF LAW

Australia's Temporary Protection Visa (TPV) system, which has been used in relation to Article 1(C)(5) of the Refugee Convention (the cessation provision), is mirrored in the UK. In Australia, TPV holders had less social and economic rights than other refugees.[120] In Australia there is currently no formal system of complementary protection available, other than through the Minister's exercise of discretion under the Migration Act 1958 (Cth), s. 417.[121]

In the UK, applicants granted refugee status are given a five-year temporary residence permit (called 'limited leave to remain'). Near the end of this term, applicants may apply for permanent settlement; that is, 'indefinite leave to remain' in the UK. Alternatively, an applicant may be found to be entitled to one of the two forms of complementary protection applicable in the UK: Humanitarian Protection, which entitles the applicant to be granted leave to remain in the UK for a period of five years,[122] or Discretionary Leave, under which an applicant will be granted leave to remain for a period of no longer than three years.[123] Those applicants granted complementary protection are able to apply for indefinite leave to remain after meeting specific qualification criteria.[124]

In the context of national security concerns, the UK Government has introduced the Criminal Justice and Immigration Bill, which seeks to introduce a new immigration status for certain asylum seekers and other migrants, called 'special immigration status'.[125] Essentially, this 'special immigration status' may be given to those persons classed as 'foreign criminals',[126] who are liable to be deported but who cannot be removed

---

[120] Chapter 4 in this volume. Note that in the May budget the Labor Government announced its intention to abolish the TPV scheme, www.minister.immi.gov.au/media/media-releases/2008/ce05-budget-08.htm (accessed 23 May 2008).

[121] Chapter 4 in this volume.   [122] Immigration Rules, para. 339E.

[123] See Home Office, 'Asylum Policy Instructions: Discretionary Leave', 9 April 2008, www.bia.homeoffice.gov.uk/sitecontent/documents/policyandlaw/asylumpolicyinstructions/ (accessed 19 April 2008).

[124] Applicants who have completed five years' Humanitarian Protection leave will be eligible to apply for Indefinite Leave to Remain: see Home Office, 'API: Humanitarian Protection', October 2006, para. 9. Applicants on Discretionary Leave are eligible to apply for Indefinite Leave to remain after completing either six or ten continuous years of Discretionary Leave (depending on the reason the applicant was granted leave): see Home Office, 'API: Discretionary Leave'.

[125] See Criminal Justice and Immigration Bill (Vol 1) (amended) as of 13 March 2008, available at www.publications.parliament.uk/pa/ld200708/ldbills/041/2008041a.pdf (accessed 19 April 2008).

[126] Criminal Justice and Immigration Bill, clause 130.

CONCLUSIONS ON THE RULE OF LAW 307

because of the UK's obligations under the ECHR and Human Rights Act.[127] As O'Sullivan explains, the Bill is significant, as it will restrict the rights of asylum seekers who have been excluded from the Refugee Convention or who have had their refugee status revoked pursuant to UK legislation.[128] The effect of designating a person with this 'special status' is that they will be denied rights which are normally granted to refugees, such as permission to work, ordinary state benefits, leave to remain and access to family reunion rights. They may also be subject to certain residential restrictions (such as restrictions on where they live, reporting conditions, electronic monitoring and curfews).[129] Not surprisingly, this new status has been criticized by various UK NGOs such as the UK Refugee Council[130] and the Joint Council for the Welfare of Immigrants.[131]

In the USA, a person granted asylum is permitted to remain in the USA as an asylee and, one year later, to adjust to permanent resident status.[132] Similar treatment is provided for the asylee's spouse and minor unmarried children.[133] However Article 1(C)(5) of the Refugee Convention can be invoked at the end of this period, and asylee status can be terminated if the Secretary of Homeland Security concludes that the person no longer meets the refugee requirements, either because of changed personal circumstances or because of changed country conditions.[134] As we have seen both in relation to Australia and the UK, there are issues about the way that Article 1(C)(5) is applied in those jurisdictions. It seems that, in these jurisdictions, the granting of refugee status is regarded as a matter of state discretion rather than as a right of the individual.

But what of the broader community and the way that it defines them? Can we be certain that the legal status granted to asylum seekers and refugees reflects the views of the community? As we have seen in a

---

[127] Criminal Justice and Immigration Bill, clause 129.

[128] Criminal Justice and Immigration Bill, clauses 129–133, when read with s. 72 of the Nationality, Immigration and Asylum Act 2002 (which is designed to give domestic effect to Art. 33(2) of the Refugee Convention) and s. 54 Immigration, Asylum and Nationality Act 2006 (which interprets Art. 1F of the Refugee Convention).

[129] Criminal Justice and Immigration Bill, clauses 132–33.

[130] See UK Refugee Council Briefing, 'Special Immigration Status', October 2007, www.refugeecouncil.org.uk (accessed 20 April 2008).

[131] Joint Council for the Welfare of Immigrants, 'Parliamentary Briefing – Clauses 115–122 Special Immigration Status', House of Commons, Second Reading, 8 October 2007, www.jcwi.org.uk/news/jcwi%5B1%5D.cjb.brief.pdf (accessed 20 April 2008).

[132] 8 USC s. 1159(b).   [133] 8 USC s. 1158(b)(3).   [134] 8 USC s. 1158(c)(2).

308 REFUGEES, ASYLUM SEEKERS AND THE RULE OF LAW

number of chapters, the role of civil society and community organizations is vital to asserting their rights in this context. Although governments respond to perceived public disquiet, there is also evidence that civil society and community organizations have played a significant role in shaping responses. In Australia, for example, increasing pressure was exerted upon the Coalition Government in the last few years from within its own ranks, by those who directly represent the views of refugee advocacy groups.[135]

In the UK there is evidence of 'good practice' in terms of dialogue between government and civil society. There are many opportunities for NGOs to lobby on particular issues. There are organizations such as the Refugee Council, which have a particularly strong voice in the debate. The Immigration Law Practitioners' Association is another important network. While it is often difficult for NGOs to achieve direct results in the current context, it is also the case that, through lobbying and strategic litigation, it has been possible to blunt the harsher edges of some government policy in this area.[136]

In Canada, the Canadian Council for Refugees (CCR) is the main advocacy organization. It is an umbrella group of immigrant, refugee and settlement organizations. It advocates on behalf of refugees and, to a lesser extent, other migrants. Other NGO groups from the faith community, legal sector and civil society also advocate on behalf of refugees. The executive consults such groups more or less regularly, and the regulatory process contemplates consultation. However, refugee advocates and NGOs express concerns about how meaningful their participation is. But, as we saw, it was a coalition of NGOs that mounted the successful challenge to the Canada-US Safe Third Country Agreement.

Part three: conclusions

As the discussion in this book has demonstrated, the rule of law is challenged by its application to refugees and asylum seekers at the national level. The summary in this chapter suggests that the executive arm of government is able to implement a restrictive agenda by the use of legislation which does not conform to a 'legislative principle'. The most important indicator of respect for the Refugee Convention is the

---

[135] Chapter 4 in this volume.

[136] E.g. R (on application of Q and others) v. Secretary of State for the Home Department [2004] QB 36 discussed in Chapter 5 in this volume at pp. 245–6.

level of its incorporation into national laws, rather than differences in constitutional frameworks. As we have seen, some jurisdictions do not satisfy this indicator. Another indicator of the malaise of the rule of law is the failure to provide fair and neutral hearings at the administrative level. In this setting, the judiciary has a very difficult task to work coherently with the legislature and to implement the 'integrity' principle.

In the Introduction, the following question was posed: How can coherency between the national and the international rule of law be achieved? In the light of the analysis in this book, the answer seems obvious – only by respecting the rights-granting nature of the Refugee Convention, and by incorporating such rights into national legal systems, and by developing a legal culture which respects such rights. One way in which this culture can be encouraged is by the acceptance of human rights protection at the national level. Rather than viewing refugees and asylum seekers as migrants, the basic rights they are owed under the Convention must be given. These are, in addition to the rights against *refoulement* (Art. 33) and discrimination as to 'race, religion or country of origin' (Art. 3),[137] non-penalization for movement to seek asylum (Art. 31) and free access to courts of law 'on the territory of all Contracting States' (Art. 16(1)). By acknowledging such rights, the right to seek asylum will follow, the risk of *refoulement* will be minimized, and respect for the rule of law will be restored.

---

[137] See also Refugee Convention, Art. 4 – freedom of religion and Art. 8 – exemption from exceptional measures on the ground of nationality.

Appendix

Montreal 4 September 2006
The Asylum Seeker in the Legal System
Project outline issues

- The method and extent of **incorporation of international law obligations** – are they directly or indirectly incorporated into general migration legislation or into a purpose-specific statute? Are all relevant treaty obligations specifically incorporated? Have treaty obligations been modified by legislation?
- Is a distinction made in incorporating legislation between **asylum seekers and refugees**, that is between those who arrive spontaneously and those who come under a resettlement programme? In relation to those who arrive spontaneously, are distinctions made according to the route taken or the method of arrival? Are the international law obligations incorporated equally for all classes of persons?
- Which institution is responsible for the **initial decision** as to status? Does the legislation confer additional discretions or personal residuary powers on an administrative decision maker which qualify the international law obligations?
- What is the **institutional framework for decision making** after the initial decision as to status? That is, is it administrative or adjudicative, judicial or quasi-judicial?
- What are the opportunities for **appeal or judicial review** in this institutional framework? What proportion of initial applications proceed to judicial review? What type of issues are heard on judicial review? What are the outcomes of each category of issue on judicial review?
- What is the response of the **executive government to the outcomes from judicial review**? That is, does it modify previous policy or practices, or increase the restrictiveness of its approach in response to significant judicial determinations?
- What is the **constitutional basis of jurisdiction** in this context? Is that jurisdiction an entrenched/plenary jurisdiction? Is primacy accorded to constitutional rights as distinct from statutory rights in the national legal system?

310

APPENDIX   311

- What is the **human rights framework** in the relevant jurisdiction – its role and effect? Are the rights of asylum seekers in international law mirrored in such a framework?
- Is there specific legislative incorporation of the basic *non-refoulement* principle? At what stage of the proceedings is the *non-refoulement* principle considered? What standard is applied? Is there a special procedure in relation to removals which considers the *refoulement* issue?
- How has a 'safe third country' concept been incorporated into the legal system: through judicial interpretation or specific legislation? What standards are applied to determine whether a country is indeed 'safe'?
- Approaches to the **interpretation of national legislation in the light of international law obligations** and human rights provisions – use of principles of interpretation or external guidance? For example, in relation to non-entrée and detention practices, what standards are applied?
- Approaches to interpretation of the **refugee definition** in the Refugees Convention – what **standard of proof** is applied to the refugee definition, how are **exclusion clauses** in the Refugees Convention interpreted? What is the approach to the issue of persecution by **non-state agents**?
- What are the **outcomes** of a successful application for asylum – that is, what is the **status and standard of protection** granted? Can the asylum seeker transit from that status to nationality or citizenship? That is, where does the asylum seeker sit in the hierarchy of membership of the community? What social and economic rights attach to the status conferred? That is, are asylum seekers receiving 'effective protection'?
- What role do **refugee advocates and NGOs** have in the formation of policy? Does the executive arm of government consult such groups regularly? Are the views of those groups taken into account?
- The reactions of executive government – are they justified in terms of **public policy/public opinion**? What evidence do governments rely upon in support of their actions?

BIBLIOGRAPHY

Aleinikoff, T. A., 'State Centred Refugee Law: From Resettlement to Containment', *Michigan Journal of International Law*, 14 (1992), 120.

Allan, James, Fried, Charles and Dworkin, Ronald, '"The Supreme Court Phalanx": An Exchange' (6 December 2007) 54 *New York Review of Books*, 19 (2007).

Allan, T.R.S., 'Justice and Fairness in Law's Empire', *Cambridge Law Journal*, 52 (1993), 64.

Law Liberty and Justice: The Legal Foundations of British Constitutionalism (Oxford: Clarendon Press, 1993).

Anker, D., *Law of Asylum in the United States*, 3rd edition (Boston, MA: Refugee Law Center, 1999).

Anker, D., Fitzpatrick J. and Shacknove, A., 'Crisis and Cure: A Reply to Hathaway/ Neve and Schuck', *Harvard Human Rights Journal*, 11 (1998), 295.

Baldaccini, Annelise, Guild, Elspeth and Toner, Helen (eds.), *Whose Freedom, Security and Justice? EU Immigration and Asylum Law and Policy* (Oxford: Hart, 2007).

Balkin, R., 'International Law and Domestic Law' in S. Blay (ed.), *Public International Law: An Australian Perspective* (Melbourne: Oxford University Press, 1997), Chapter 5.

Barnett, L., 'Global Governance and the Evolution of the International Refugee Regime', *International Journal of Refugee Law*, 14 (2002), 238.

Barutciski, M., 'A Critical View on UNHCR's Mandate Dilemmas', *International Journal of Refugee Law*, 14 (2002), 365.

'Disclosure of Adverse Information to Applicants under the Migration Act 1958' 11 *Australian Journal of Administrative Law*, 61 (2004).

Bayne, Peter, 'The Common Law Basis of Judicial Review' 67 *Australian Law Journal*, 781 (1993).

Beaton-Wells, C., 'Disclosure of Adverse Information to Applicants under the Migration Act 1958, 11' *Australian Journal of Administrative Law*, 61, (2004).

'Judicial Review of Migration Decisions: Life after S157', *Federal Law Review*, 33 (2005), 142.

Beatty, D. M., *The Ultimate Rule of Law* (Oxford University Press, 2004).

Betts, A., 'Towards a Mediterranean Solution? Implications for the Region of Origin', *International Journal of Refugee Law*, 18 (2006), 652.

Betts, A. and Durieux, J.-F., 'Convention Plus As a Norm-Setting Exercise', *Journal of Refugee Studies*, 20 (2007), 1.

Billings, P., 'Balancing Acts: Six Acts in Search of Equilibrium', *Journal of Immigration Asylum and Nationality Law*, 20 (2006), 197.

Bix, B., 'Legal Positivism' in M. Golding and W. Edmundson (eds.), *The Blackwell Guide to the Philosophy of Law and Legal Theory* (London: Blackwell, 2005), Chapter 2.

Blake, N., 'The Impact of the Minimum Standards Directives 2004/83/EC on National Case Law' in International Association of Refugee Law Judges (IARLJ) (eds.), *The Asylum Process and the Rule of Law* (New Delhi: Manak Publications, 2006).

Blake, N. and Husain, R., *Immigration, Asylum and Human Rights* (Oxford University Press, 2003).

Bosniak, L., *The Citizen and the Alien: Dilemmas of Contemporary Membership* (Princeton, NJ: Princeton University Press, 2006).

Bostock, C. M.-J., 'The International Legal Obligations Owed to the Asylum Seekers on the MV Tampa', *International Journal of Refugee Law*, 14 (2002), 279.

Boswell, C., *The Ethics of Refugee Policy* (Aldershot, UK: Ashgate Publishing, 2005).

Brennan, G., 'Limits on the Use of Judges', *Federal Law Review*, 9 (1978), 1.

'The Purpose and Scope of Judicial Review' in M. Taggart (ed.), *Judicial Review of Administrative Action in the 1980s: Problems and Prospects* (Auckland: Oxford University Press and Legal Research Foundation Inc, 1986), pp. 18–35.

'The Impact of a Bill of Rights on the Role of the Judiciary: An Australian Response' in Phillip Alston (ed.), *Towards an Australian Bill of Rights* (Canberra: Centre for International and Public Law and HREOC, 1994).

'Extra-Judicial Notes', *Australian Bar Review*, 17 (1998), 9.

Brunnée, J. and Toope, S., 'A Hesitant Embrace: Baker and the Application of International Law by Canadian Courts' in D. Dyzenhaus (ed.), *The Unity of Public Law* (Oxford: Hart Publishing, 2004).

Burbank, S. B., 'The Architecture of Judicial Independence', *Southern California Law Review*, 72 (1999), 315.

Byrne, R. and Shacknove, A., 'The Safe Third Country Notion in European Asylum Law', *Harvard Human Rights Journal*, 9 (1996), 185.

Byrne, R., Noll, G. and Vested-Hansen, J. (eds.), *New Asylum Countries? Migration Control and Refugee Protection in an Enlarged European Union* (Dordrecht, The Netherlands: Kluwer Law International, 2002).

Canadian Immigration and Refugee Board, *Guidelines on Women Refugee Claimants Fearing Gender-Related Persecution* (Ottawa: Immigration and Refugee Board, 1993, updated 1996).

Cane, Peter, 'Mapping the Frontiers' in Peter Nirks (ed.), *The Frontiers of Liability, Vol 1* (Oxford University Press, 1994).

314   BIBLIOGRAPHY

Carens, J., 'Aliens and Citizens: The Case for Open Borders', *The Review of Politics*, 49 (1987), 251.

Carlin, James L., 'Significant Refugee Crises Since World War II and the Response of the International Community' *Michigan Yearbook of International Legal Studies*, 3 (1982).

Carrington, K., 'Ministerial Discretion in Migration Matters: Contemporary Policy Issues in Historical Context', Parliament of Australia, *Current Issues Brief*, 3 (2003–4).

Castles, S., 'Towards a Sociology of Forced Migration and Social Transformation', *Sociology*, 37 (No 1 – *Global Refugees*) (2003), 13.

'The Migration–Asylum Nexus and Regional Approaches' in S. Kneebone and F. Rawlings-Sanaei (eds.), *New Regionalism and Asylum Seekers: Challenges Ahead* (Oxford: Berghahn Books, 2007), Chapter 1.

Cholewinski, R., 'Enforced Destitution of Asylum Seekers in the United Kingdom: The Denial of Fundamental Human Rights', *International Journal of Refugee Law*, 10 (1998), 462.

Clayton, G., *Textbook on Immigration and Asylum Law*, 2nd edition (Oxford University Press, 2006).

Cohen, R., 'Response to Hathaway', *Journal of Refugee Studies*, 20 (2007), 370.

Commission of Inquiry into the Actions of Canadian Officials in Relation to Maher Arar, *Report of the Events Relating to Maher Arar* (Ottawa: Public Works and Government Services Canada, 2006).

Committee against Torture, *Conclusions and Recommendations: United Kingdom of Great Britain and Northern Ireland – Dependent Territories*, 10 December 2004, CAT/C/CR/33/3 para. 4(d); House of Lords, House of Commons, Joint Committee on Human Rights, *Nineteenth Report*, Session 2005–06, para. 131, www.publications.parliament.uk/pa/jt200506/jtselect/jtrights/185/18508.htm (accessed 19 April 2008).

Costello, C., 'The Asylum Procedures Directive and the Proliferation of Safe Country Practices: Deterrence, Deflection and the Dismantling of International Protection?', *European Journal of Migration and Law*, 7 (2005), 35.

Covell, C., *The Defence of Natural Law: A Study of the Ideas of Law and Justice in the Writings of Lon L. Fuller, Michael Oakeshot, F.A. Hayek, Ronald Dworkin and John Finnis* (New York: St Martin's Press, 1992).

Cox, A., 'The Independence of the Judiciary: History and Purposes', *University of Dayton Law Review*, 21 (1996), 565.

Craig, P, 'Ultra Vires and the Foundation of Judicial Review' *Cambridge Law Journal*, 63 (1998).

'Formal and Substantive Conceptions of the Rule of Law: An Analytical Framework', *Public Law* (1997), 467.

'Competing Models of Judicial Review' *Public Law*, 428 (1999).

BIBLIOGRAPHY 315

'Public Law, Political Theory and Legal Theory' *Public Law*, 211 (2000).

Cranwell, G., 'Treaties and Interpretation of Statutes: Two Recent Examples in the Migration Context', *Australian Institute of Administrative Law Forum*, 39 (2003), 49.

Crawford, J. and Edeson, W. R., 'International Law and Australian Law' in K. W. Ryan (ed.), *International Law in Australia*, 2nd edition (Sydney: Lawbook, 1984), Chapter 4.

Crawley, H., *Refugees and Gender: Law and Process* (Bristol, UK: Jordans Publishing Ltd, 2001).

Crépeau, F. and Jimenez, E., 'Foreigners and the Right to Justice After 9/11', *International Journal of Law and Psychiatry*, 27 (2004), 609.

Crépeau, F. and Legomsky, S. H., 'North American Responses: A Comparative Study of U.S. and Canadian Refugee Policy' in S. Kneebone and F. Rawlings-Sanaei (eds.), *New Regionalism and Asylum Seekers: Challenges Ahead* (Oxford: Berghahn Books, 2007), Chapter 6.

Crisp, J., 'Forced Displacement in Africa: Dimensions, Difficulties and Policy Directions', UNHCR Research Paper No. 126 (July 2006).

Crock, M, 'Climbing Jacob's Ladder: The High Court and the Administrative Detention of Asylum Seekers in Australia' 15 *Sydney Law Review* (1993).

'A Sanctuary Under Review: Where To From Here for Australia's Refugee and Humanitarian Program?', *UNSW Law Journal*, 23 (2000), 246.

'The Refugees Convention at 50: Mid-life Crisis or Terminal Inadequacy? An Australian Perspective' in S. Kneebone (ed.), *The Refugees Convention 50 Years On: Globalisation and International Law* (Aldershot, UK: Ashgate, 2003), Chapter 3.

Cronin, K., 'A Culture of Control: An Overview of Immigration Policy Making', in J. Jupp and M. Kabala (eds.), *The Politics of Australian Immigration* (Canberra: AGPS, 1993), Chapter 5.

Dauvergne, C., 'Beyond Justice: the Consequences of Liberalism for Immigration Law', *Canadian Journal of Law and Jurisprudence*, 10 (1997), 323.

'Amorality and Humanitarianism in Immigration Law', *Osgoode Hall Law Journal*, 37 (1999), 597.

'Refugee Law and the Measure of Globalisation' in S. Taylor (ed.), *Nationality, Refugee Status and State Protection: Explorations of the Gap between Man and Citizen* (Special edition of *Law in Context*, Federation Press, 2005), pp. 62–82.

Davies, M., *Asking the Law Question* (Sydney: Thomson Lawbook, 1994).

Davies, S. E., 'Redundant or Essential? How Politics Shaped the Outcome of the 1967 Protocol', *International Journal of Refugee Law*, 19 (2007), 703.

de Costa, A., 'Assessing the Cause and Effect of Persecution in Australian Refugee Law: Sarrazola, Khawar and the Migration Legislation Amendment Act (No. 6) 2001 (Cth)', *Federal Law Review*, 30 (2002), 534.

DeWind, J., 'Response to Hathaway', *Journal of Refugee Studies*, 20 (2007), 381.

316   BIBLIOGRAPHY

Department of Immigration and Multicultural and Indigenous Affairs, *Immigration, Population and Citizenship Digest* (Canberra: Department of Immigration and Multicultural and Indigenous Affairs, 2003).

Dicey, Albert Venn, *Introduction to the Study of the Law of the Constitution*, 10th edn (London: Macmillan, 1959).

Divine, R. A., *American Immigration Policy, 1924–1952* (New Haven, CT: Yale University Press, 1957).

Douglas-Scott, S., *Constitutional Law of the European Union* (Harlow, UK: Pearson Education, 2002).

Dworkin, R., *Taking Rights Seriously*, 2nd edition with a Reply to Critics (Cambridge, MA: Harvard University Press, 1978).

A Matter of Principle (Cambridge, MA: Harvard University Press, 1985).

Law's Empire (Cambridge, MA: Belknap Press, 1986).

Justice in Robes (Cambridge, MA; London: Belknap Press/Harvard University Press, 2006).

Dyzenhaus, D., 'The Politics of Deference: Judicial Review and Democracy' in M. Taggart (ed.), *The Province of Administrative Law* (Oxford: Hart Publishing, 1997), Chapter 13.

'Reuniting the Brain: The Democratic Basis of Judicial Review', *Public Law Review*, 9 (1998), 98.

'Recrafting the Rule of Law' in D. Dyzenhaus (ed.), *Recrafting the Rule of Law: The Limits of Legal Order* (Oxford: Hart Publishing, 1999), Chapter 1.

(ed.), *The Unity of Public Law* (Oxford: Hart Publishing, 2004).

Elliot, Mark, 'The Ultra Vires Doctrine in a Constitutional Setting: Still the Central Principle of Administrative Law' 58 *Cambridge Law Journal*, 129 (1999).

European Council of Refugees and Exiles (ECRE), *Country Report 2005*, United Kingdom, August 2006, www.ecre.org/files/ECRE%20Country%20Report%202005rev.pdf (accessed 22 April 2008).

European Union, 'Entry into Force of European Rules on the Qualification and Status of Persons in Need of International Protection', *EU at the UN*, EC06-307EN, 10 October 2006, www.europa-eu-un.org/home (accessed 20 April 2008).

'Green Paper on the Future Common European Asylum System', Press Release, MEMO/07/229, Brussels, 6 June 2007, http://europa.eu/rapid/pressReleasesAction.do?reference=MEMO/07/229 (accessed 31 March 2008).

Feller, E., 'Asylum, Migration and Refugee Protection: Realities, Myths and the Promise of Things to Come', *International Journal of Refugee Law*, 18 (2006), 509.

UNCHR Assistant High Commissioner for Refugees, speaking at meeting of Institute of European Affairs: Jill Donoghue and Johnny Ryan, *Rapporteurs Report* (Ireland: Institute of European Affairs, 23 July 2006), www.iiea.com/images/managed/news_attachments/erika%20feller%20rep%20eport.pdf (accessed 2 April 2008).

Fitzpatrick, J. et al., 'Current Issues in Cessation of Refugee Protection is a Subject of Confusion Mixed with Heightened Interest among States, Refugees and the

United Nations High Commissioner for Refugees (UNHCR)', background paper as part of the Global Consultations on International Protection, www. unhcr.org/protect/PROTECTION/3b3889c28.pdf (accessed 20 April 2008).

Martin, S. F., *Refugee Women*, 2nd edition (Lanham, MD: Lexington Books, 2004).

Forsyth, Christopher, 'Of Fig Leaves and Fairy Tales: The Ultra Vires Doctrine, the Sovereignty of Parliament and Judicial Review' 55 *Cambridge Law Journal*, 122 (1996).

Foster, M., *International Refugee Law and Socio-Economic Rights: Refuge from Deprivation* (Cambridge University Press, 2007).

Frecker, John, *Immigration and Refugee Legal Aid Cost Drivers* (Canada: Department of Justice, 2002).

Frelick, B., 'Abundantly Clear: Refoulement', *Georgetown Immigration Law Journal*, 19 (2005), 245.

'US Detention of Asylum Seekers: What's the Problem? What's the Solution?', *Bender's Immigration Bulletin*, 10 (2005), 159.

Fullerton, M., 'Failing the Test: Germany Leads Europe in Dismantling Refugee Protection', *Texas International Law Journal*, 36 (2001), 231.

Galligan, D. J., *Discretionary Powers: A Legal Study of Official Discretion* (Oxford: Clarendon Press, 1986).

Law in Modern Society (Oxford University Press, 2007).

Galloway, D., 'Liberalism, Globalism and Immigration', *Queens Law Journal*, 18 (1993), 266.

'Criminality and State Protection: Structural Tensions in Canadian Refugee Law' in S. Kneebone (ed.), *The Refugees Convention 50 Years On: Globalisation and International Law* (Aldershot, UK: Ashgate, 2003), Chapter 5.

'Proof and Narrative: Reproducing the Facts in Refugee Cases', (unpublished manuscript on file with Professor Audrey Macklin).

Geiringer, C., 'Tavita and All That: Confronting the Confusion Surrounding Unincorporated Treaties and Administrative Law', *New Zealand Universities Law Review*, 21 (2004), 66.

Gibney, M. J., *The Ethics and Politics of Asylum: Liberal Democracy and the Response to Refugees* (Cambridge University Press, 2004).

'Forced Migration, Engineered Regionalism and Justice Between States' in S. Kneebone and F. Rawlings-Sanaei (eds.), *New Regionalism and Asylum Seekers: Challenges Ahead* (Oxford: Berghahn Books, 2007), Chapter 3.

Gil-Bazo, M.-T., 'Refugee Status and Subsidiary Protection under EC Law: The Qualification Directive and the Right to Be Granted Asylum' in A. Baldaccini, E. Guild and H. Toner (eds.), *Whose Freedom, Security and Justice? EU Immigration and Asylum Law and Policy* (Oxford: Hart Publishing, 2007).

'The Protection of Refugees under the Common European Asylum System: The Establishment of a European Jurisdiction for Asylum Purposes and Compliance with International Refugee and Human Rights Law', Cuadernos

318 BIBLIOGRAPHY

Euopeos de Deusto, No. 36/2007, pp. 153–82, http://ssrn.com/abstract=983722 (accessed 16 April 2008).

Goldberg, P., 'Women and Refugee Status: A Review Essay', *International Journal of Refugee Law*, 7 (1995), 756.

Golding, Martin and Edmundson, William (eds.), *The Blackwell Guide to the Philosophy of Law and Legal Theory* (London: Blackwell, 2005).

Goldsmith, Lord, 'Symposium: Global Constitutionalism: Keynote Address', *Stanford Law Review*, 59 (2007), 1155.

Goodwin-Gill, G., 'Judicial Reasoning and "Social Group" after Islam and Shah', *International Journal of Refugee Law*, 11 (1999), 537.

'Article 31 of the 1951 Convention Relating to the Status of Refugees: Non-penalization, Detention, and Protection' in E. Feller, V. Turk and F. Nicholson (eds.), *Refugee Protection in International Law: UNHCR's Global Consultations on International Protection* (Cambridge University Press, 2003), Part 3.1.

Goodwin-Gill, G. S., 'International Protection and Assistance for Refugees and the Displaced: Institutional Challenges and UN Reform', Paper presented to Refugee Studies Centre Workshop, Oxford, April 2006, p. 4, http://refugee-law.qeh.ox.ac.uk/pdfs/guy-goodwin-gill-institutional-challenges.pdf (accessed 14 April 2008).

'Forced Migration: Refugees, Rights and Security' in J. McAdam (ed.), *Forced Migration, Human Rights and Security* (Oxford: Hart Publishing, 2008), Chapter 1.

Goodwin-Gill, G. S. and McAdam, J., *The Refugee in International Law*, 3rd edition (Oxford University Press, 2007).

Gordon, C., Mailman, S. and Yale-Loehr, S., *Immigration Law and Procedure* (New York: Matthew Bender, 2006).

Gordon, J., *Suburban Sweatshops: The Fight for Immigrant Rights* (Cambridge, MA: Harvard University Press, 2005).

Gorlick, B., 'The Convention and the Committee against Torture: A Complementary Protection Regime for Refugees', *International Journal Of Refugee Law*, 11 (1999), 479.

'Common Burdens and Standards: Legal Elements in Assessing Claims to Refugee Status', *International Journal of Refugee Law*, 15 (2003), 357.

Green, M. S., 'Dworkin v. The Philosophers: A Review Essay on Justice in Robes', *University of Illinois Law Review*, 5 (2007), 1477.

Guest, S., *Ronald Dworkin* (Edinburgh University Press, 1992).

Guild, E., 'The Europeanisation of Europe's Asylum Policy', *International Journal of Refugee Law*, 18 (2006), 630.

Hailbronner, K., 'The Concept of "Safe Country" and Expeditious Asylum Procedures: A Western European Perspective', *International Journal of Refugee Law*, 5 (1993), 31.

BIBLIOGRAPHY 319

'New Techniques for Rendering Asylum Manageable' in K. Hailbronner, D. A. Martin and H. Motomura (eds.), *Immigration Controls* (New York: Berghahn Books, 1998), vol. IV.

Haines, Roger, 'National Security and *Non-Refoulement* in New Zealand: Commentary on *Zaoui v Attorney-General* (No 2)' in Jane McAdam (ed.), *Moving On: Forced Migration and Human Rights* (Oxford: Hart Publishing, 2008).

Harlow, Carol and Rawlings, Richard, *Law and Administration* (London: Weidenfield and Nicholson, 1984).

Hart, H. L. A., *The Concept of Law* (Oxford: Clarendon Press, 1961).

Harvey, C., 'Asylum Seekers, Ultra Vires and the Social Security Regulations', *Public Law*, (1997) 394.

'Refugees, Asylum Seekers, The Rule of Law and Human Rights' in D. Dyzenhaus (ed.), *The Unity of the Public Law* (Oxford: Hart Publishing, 2004), Chapter 8.

'Regionalism, Human Rights and Forced Migration', in S. Kneebone and F. Rawlings-Sanaei (eds.), *New Regionalism and Asylum Seekers: Challenges Ahead* (Oxford: Berghahn Books, 2007).

Harvey, C. and Barnidge, R. P., 'Human Rights, Free Movement, and the Right to Leave in International Law', *International Journal of Refugee Law*, 19 (2007), 1.

Hathaway, J. C., 'The Evolution of Refugee Status in International Law: 1920–1950', *International and Comparative Law Quarterly*, 33 (1984), 348.

The Rights of Refugees Under International Law (Cambridge University Press, 2005).

'Forced Migration Studies: Could We Agree Just to 'Date'?', *Journal of Refugee Studies*, 20 (2007), 349.

Hathaway, J. C. and Neve, R. A., 'Making International Refugee Law Relevant Again: A Proposal for Collectivised and Solution-Oriented Protection', *Harvard Human Rights Journal*, 10 (1997), 115.

Hay, E. and Kneebone, S., 'Refugee Status in Australia and the Cessation Provisions: *QAAH of 2004* v. *MIMIA*', *Alternative Law Journal*, 31 (2006), 147.

Henkin, Louis, et al., *Human Rights* (New York: Foundation Press, 1999).

Home Office, *Asylum Statistics 2002 United Kingdom* (London: Home Office RDSR, 23 August 2003).

Asylum Statistics United Kingdom 2006, 3rd edn. (London: Home Office RDSD, 21 August 2007).

'Public Performance Target: Removing More Failed Asylum Seekers Than New Anticipated Unfounded Applications', *Statistics for First Quarter 2006* (London: Home Office RDSD).

Asylum Statistics: 4th Quarter 2007 United Kingdom (London: Home Office RDSR).

Hopper, R. and Osuna, J. P., 'Remedies of Last Resort: Private Bills and Deferred Action', *Immigration Briefings*, June (1997), 1.

Hull, E., *Without Justice For All: The Constitutional Rights of Aliens* (Westport, CT: Greenwood Press, 1985).

Hutchinson, Allan C. and Monahan, Patrick (eds.), *The Rule of Law: Ideal or Ideology* (Toronto: Carswell, 1987).

Huysmans, J., *Nexus Terrorism/Immigration/Asylum/Refuge in Parliamentary Debates in the UK: Commons Debates since 11 September 2001*, Report for ESRC Project MIDAS (Migration, Democracy and Security) in the New Security Challenges programme, 2 November 2005, www.midas.bham.ac. uk/researchandpolicy.htm (accessed 19 April 2008).

ICAR, 'The History of Kosovars in the UK' in *Navigation Guide*, www.icar.org.uk/?lid=307 (accessed 16 April 2008).

Reporting Asylum: The UK Press and the Effectiveness of PCC Guidelines, January 2007, www.icar.org.uk/?lid=4775 (accessed 17 April 2008).

Immigration and Refugee Board, *Concerning Preparation and Conduct of a Hearing in the Refugee Protection Division: Guidelines Issued by the Chairperson Pursuant to Section 159(1)(h) of the Immigration and Refugee Protection Act* (Ottawa: Immigration and Refugee Board, 2003).

Inter-American Commission on Human Rights, *Report on the Situation of Human Rights of Asylum Seekers within the Canadian Refugee Determination System*, 2000, www.cidh.org/countryrep/canada2000en/table-of-contents.htm (accessed 3 March 2008).

Jackson, V. C., 'Proconstitutional Behavior, Political Actors, and Independent Courts: A Comment on Geoffrey Stone's Paper', *International Journal of Constitutional Law*, 2 (2004), 368.

Jacobson, J. L., 'At-Sea Interception of Alien Migrants: International Law Issues', *Willamette Law Review*, 28 (1992), 811.

Jastram, K. and Cavalieri, S., 'Human Rights in Refugee Tribunals', *Refugee Survey Quarterly*, 24 (2005), 6.

Joint Committee on Human Rights, *The Treatment of Asylum Seekers*, Tenth Report of 2006–07, HL Paper 81, HC 60 (London: House of Commons, 30 March 2007), www.publications.parliament.uk/pa/jt200607/jtselect/jtrights/81/81i.pdf (accessed 18 April 2008).

Government Response to the Committee's Tenth Report of this Session: The Treatment of Asylum Seekers, Seventeenth Report of 2006–7, HL Paper 134, HC 790 (London: House of Commons, 5 July 2007), www.publications.parliament.uk/pa/jt200607/jtselect/jtrights/134/134.pdf (accessed 18 April 2008).

Joint Council for the Welfare of Immigrants, 'Parliamentary Briefing – Clauses 115–122 Special Immigration Status', House of Commons, Second Reading, 8 October 2007, www.jcwi.org.uk/news/jcwi%5B1%5D.cjb.brief.pdf (accessed 20 April 2008).

Jowell, Jeffrey, 'Of Vires and Vacuums: The Constitutional Context of Judicial Review' *Public Law*, 448 (1999).

Kelley, N., 'International Refugee Protection: Challenges and Opportunities', *International Journal of Refugee Law*, 19 (2007), 401.

Kneebone, S., 'The Refugee Review Tribunal and the Assessment of Credibility: An Inquisitorial Role?', *Australian Journal of Administrative Law*, 5 (1998), 78.

'What is the Basis of Judicial Review?', *Public Law Review*, 12 (2001), 95.

'Natural Justice and Non-Citizens: A Matter of Integrity?', *Melbourne University Law Review*, 26 (2002), 355–80.

(ed.), *The Refugees Convention 50 Years On: Globalisation and International Law* (Aldershot, UK: Ashgate, 2003).

'Believable Tales: Proving a Well-Founded Fear of Persecution', *Migration Action*, 25 (2004), 4.

'Bouncing the Ball between the Courts and the Legislature: What is the Score on Refugee Issues?' in T. Davis (ed.), *Human Rights 2003: The Year in Review* (Melbourne: Castan Centre for Human Rights Law, Monash University, 2004), pp. 135–78.

'Strangers at the Gate: Refugees, Citizenship and Nationality', *Australian Journal of Human Rights*, 10 (2004), 33.

'What We *Have* Done With the Refugees Convention: The Australian Way' in S. Taylor (ed.), *Nationality, Refugee Status and State Protection: Explorations of the Gap between Man and Citizen* (Special edition of *Law in Context*, Federation Press, 2005), pp. 83–119.

'Is the Australian Refugee Review Tribunal "Institutionally" Biased?' in F. Crépeau et al. (eds.), *Forced Migration and Global Processes: A View from Forced Migration Studies* (Lanham, MD: Lexington Books, 2006), Chapter 10.

'The Pacific Plan: The Provision of "Effective Protection"?', *International Journal of Refugee Law*, 18 (2006), 696.

'The Legal and Ethical Implications of Extraterritorial Processing of Asylum Seekers: The "Safe Third Country" Concept' in J. McAdam (ed.), *Forced Migration, Human Rights and Security* (Oxford: Hart Publishing, 2008), Chapter 5.

Kneebone, S. and Rawlings-Sanaei, F. (eds.), *New Regionalism and Asylum Seekers: Challenges Ahead* (Oxford: Berghahn Books, 2007).

Kneebone, Susan and Pickering, Sharon, 'Australia, Indonesia and the Pacific Plan' in Susan Kneebone and Felicity Rawlings-Sanaei (eds.), *New Regionalism and Asylum Seekers: Challenges Ahead* (Oxford: Berghahn Books, 2007).

Koser, K., 'Strategies, Stories and Smuggling: Inter-regional Asylum Flows and Their Implications for Regional Responses' in S. Kneebone and F. Rawlings-Sanaei (eds.), *New Regionalism and Asylum Seekers: Challenges Ahead* (Oxford: Berghahn Books, 2007), Chapter 2.

Krause, D. and Knott, I., 'Refugee Determination Processes: A View Across the Tasman', *Alternative Law Journal* 27 (2002), 220.

Kurzban, I. J., 'Restructuring the Asylum Process', *San Diego Law Review*, 19 (1981), 91.

Kushner, T. and Knox, K., *Refugees in an Age of Genocide* (London: Frank Cass, 1999).

BIBLIOGRAPHY

Lambert, H., 'The EU Asylum Qualification Directive: Its Impact on the Jurisprudence of the United Kingdom and International Law', *International and Comparative Law Quarterly*, 55 (2006), 161.

Langfield, Malcolm, *More People Imperative: Immigration to Australia 1901–1939* (Canberra: National Archives of Australia, 1999).

Lauterpacht, E. and Bethlehem, D., 'The Scope and the Content of the Principle of *Non-Refoulement*' in E. Feller, V. Turk and F. Nicholson (eds.), *UNHCR's Global Consultations on International Protection* (Cambridge University Press, 2003).

LaViolette, N., 'Gender-Related Refugee Claims: Expanding the Scope of the Canadian Guidelines', *International Journal of Refugee Law*, 19 (2007), 169.

Legomsky, S. H., 'Forum Choices for the Review of Agency Adjudication: A Study of the Immigration Process', *Iowa Law Review*, 71 (1986), 1297.

Immigration and the Judiciary: Law and Politics in Britain and America (Oxford University Press, 1987).

'Refugees, Administrative Tribunals, and Real Independence: Dangers Ahead for Australia', *Washington University Law Quarterly*, 76 (1998), 243.

'The Detention of Aliens: Theories, Rules, and Discretion', *University of Miami Inter-American Law Review*, 30 (1999), 531.

'Secondary Refugee Movements and the Return of Asylum Seekers to Third Countries: The Meaning of Effective Protection', *International Journal of Refugee Law*, 15 (2003), 567.

Immigration and Refugee Law and Policy, 4th edition (New York: Foundation Press, 2005).

'Deportation and the War on Independence', *Cornell Law Review*, 91 (2006), 369.

'The USA and the Caribbean Interdiction Program', *International Journal of Refugee Law*, 18 (2006), 677.

'Learning to Live with Unequal Justice: Asylum and the Limits to Consistency' 60 *Stanford Review*, 413 (2007).

'The New Path of Immigration Law: Asymmetric Incorporation of Criminal Justice Norms', *Washington and Lee Law Review*, 64 (2007), 469.

Levinson, P. J., 'The Façade of Quasi-Judicial Independence in Immigration Appellate Adjudications', *Bender's Immigration Bulletin*, 9 (2004), 1154.

Lippert, R., *Sanctuary, Sovereignty and Sacrifice: Canadian Sanctuary, Power and Law* (Vancouver: UBC Press, 2005).

Loescher, G. and Scanlan, J. A., *Calculated Kindness: Refugees and America's Half-Open Door 1945–Present* (New York: Free Press, 1986).

Macklin, A., '*Attorney-General v. Ward*: A Review Essay', *International Journal of Refugee Law*, 6 (1994), 362.

'The State of Law's Borders and the Law of States' Borders' in D. Dyzenhaus (ed.), *The Unity of the Public Law* (Oxford: Hart Publishing, 2004), Chapter 7.

Magner, T., 'A Less Than "Pacific" Solution for Asylum Seekers in Australia', *International Journal of Refugee Law*, 16 (2004), 53.

BIBLIOGRAPHY   323

Maher, Gerry, 'Natural Justice as Fairness' in Neil MacCormick and Peter Birks (eds.), *The Legal Mind: Essays for Tony Honore* (Oxford: Clarendon Press, 1986).

Manne, R. and Corlett, D., 'Sending Them Home: Refugees and the New Politics of Indifference', *Quarterly Essay*, 13 (2004), 1.

Martin, S. F., 'Reforming Asylum Adjudication: On Navigating the Coast of Bohemia', (1990) 138 *University of Pennsylvania Law Review*, 1247.

McAdam, J., 'Complementary Protection: A Comparative Perspective', in UNHCR Discussion Paper, No. 2 2005, *Complementary Protection*.

'The Refugee Convention as a Rights Blueprint for Persons in Need of International Protection' in J. McAdam (ed.), *Forced Migration, Human Rights and Security* (Oxford: Hart Publishing, 2008), Chapter 10.

McMillan, J., '*Federal Court v Minister for Immigration*', *Australian Institute of Adminstrative Law Forum*, 22 (1999), 1.

Mertus, J., 'The State and the Post-Cold War Refugee Regime: New Models, New Questions', *International Journal of Refugee Law*, 10 (1998), 321.

Millbank, A., 'The Detention of Boat People' *Current Issues Brief*, 8 (2000–1), www.aph.gov.au/Library/pubs/CIB/2000-01/01cib08.htm (accessed 10 March 2008).

The Problem with the 1951 Convention (Canberra: Department of the Parliamentary Library, 2000–2001), Research Paper 5, www.aph.gov.au/library/pubs/rp/2000-01/01RP05.htm (accessed 1 May 2008).

Miller, T. A., 'Blurring the Boundaries between Immigration and Crime Control after September 11', *Boston College Third World Law Review*, 25 (2005), 81.

Moore, C., *Review of US Refugee Resettlement Programs and Policies* (Washington, DC: US Government Printing Office, 1980).

Mullan, D., *Administrative Law: Essentials of Canadian Law* (Toronto: Irwin Law, 2001).

Murphy, L., 'Concepts of Law', *Australian Journal of Legal Philosophy*, 30 (2005), 1.

Musalo, K., Moore, J. and Boswell, R. A., *Refugee Law and Policy: A Comparative and International Approach*, 2nd edition (Durham, NC: Carolina Academic Press, 2001).

Musgave, Thomas, 'Refugees', in Sam Blay et al. (eds.), *Public International Law: An Australian Perspective* (South Melbourne: Oxford University Press, 1997).

National Association of Immigration Judges, *An Independent Immigration Court: An Idea Whose Time Has Come* (Washington, DC: Government Printing Office, 2002).

Neuman, G. L., 'Extraterritorial Violations of Human Rights by the United States', *American University Journal of International Law and Policy* and *Loyola of Los Angeles International and Comparative Law Journal*, 9 (1994), 213.

Nicholson, F. and Twomey, P. (eds.), *Refugee Rights and Realities: Evolving International Concepts and Regimes* (Cambridge University Press, 1999).

Noll, G., 'Seeking Asylum at Embassies: A Right of Entry under International Law?', *International Journal of Refugee Law*, 17 (2005), 542.

North, A. and Decle, P., 'Courts and Immigration Detention: Once a Jolly Swagman etc', *Australian Journal of Administrative Law*, 10 (2002), 5.

Nyers, P., 'Abject Cosmopolitanism', *Third World Quarterly*, 24 (December 2003), 1069.

'Taking Rights, Mediating Wrongs: Disagreements over the Political Agency of Non-Status Refugees', in Jef Huysmans, Andrew Dobson and Raia Prokhovnik (eds.), *The Politics of Protection: Sites of Insecurity and Political Agency* (London: Routledge, 2006).

Oliver, D., 'Is the Ultra Vires Rule the Basis of Judicial Review?', *Public Law* (1987), 543.

'The Underlying Values of Public and Private Law' in M. Taggart (ed.), *The Province of Administrative Law* (Oxford: Hart Publishing, 1997), pp. 217–42.

Ong Hing, B., 'No Place for Angels: In Reaction to Kevin Johnson', *University of Illinois Law Review*, (2000), 559.

Palmer, J. R. B., 'The Nature and Causes of the Immigration Surge in the Federal Courts of Appeals: A Preliminary Analysis', *New York Law School Law Review*, 51 (2006–7), 13.

Palmer, J. R. B., Yale-Loehr, S. W. and Cronin, E., 'Why Are So Many People Challenging Board of Immigration Appeals Decisions in Federal Court? An Empirical Analysis of the Recent Surge in Petitions for Review', *Georgetown Immigration Law Journal*, 20 (2005), 1.

Passel, J. S., *Estimates of the Size and Characteristics of the Undocumented Population* (Washington, DC: Pew Hispanic Trust, 2005).

Pham, H., 'The Inherent Flaws in the Inherent Authority Position: Why Inviting Local Enforcement of the Immigration Laws Violates the Constitution', *Florida State University Law Review*, 31 (2004), 965.

Phillips, Lord Chief Justice, 'Reflections on the Rule of Law, America's 400th Anniversary at Jamestown Addresses: Rule of Law Conference: Global Issues and the Rule of Law', *University of Richmond Law Review*, 42 (2007), 37.

Pirjola, J., 'Shadows in Paradise: Exploring Non-Refoulement as an Open Concept', *International Journal of Refugee Law*, 19 (2007), 639.

Poynder, N., 'Recent Implementation of the Refugee Convention in Australia and the Law of Accommodations to International Human Rights Treaties: Have We Gone Too Far?', *Australian Journal of Human Rights*, 2 (1995), 75.

'"Mind the Gap": Seeking Alternative Protection Under the Convention Against Torture and the International Covenant on Civil and Political Rights' in S. Kneebone (ed.), *The Refugees Convention 50 Years On: Globalisation and International Law* (Aldershot, UK: Ashgate, 2003), Chapter 7.

Quinn, R. and Yale-Loehr, S., 'Private Immigration Bills: An Overview', *Bender's Immigration Bulletin*, 9 (2004), 1147.

Ramji-Nogales, J., Schoenholtz, A. and Schrag, P. G., 'Refugee Roulette: Disparities in Asylum Adjudication', *Stanford Law Review*, 60 (2007), 295.

Rankin, M. B., *Extending the Limits or Narrowing the Scope? Deconstructing the OAU Refugee Definition Thirty Years On*, UNHCR, New Issues in Refugee Research, Working Paper No 113 (April 2005).

Rawitz, S. B., 'From Wong Yang Sung to Black Robes', *Interpreter Releases*, 65 (1980), 453.

BIBLIOGRAPHY 325

Rawls, John, *A Theory of Justice*, revised ed. (Oxford University Press, 1999).

Rawlings, R., 'Review, Revenge and Retreat', *Modern Law Review*, 68 (2005), 378.

Raz, Joseph, 'The Authority of Constitutions and the Authority of its Authors' in Larry Alexander (ed.), *Constitutionalism: Philosophical Foundations* (Cambridge University Press, 1988).

Robinson, V. and Coleman, C., 'Lessons Learned? A Critical Review of the Government Program to Resettle Bosnian Quota Refugees in the United Kingdom', *International Migration Review*, 34 (2000), 1217.

Scanlan, J. A. and Kent, O. T., 'The Force of Moral Arguments for a Just Immigration Policy in a Hobbesian Universe: The Contemporary American Example' in M. Gibney (ed.), *Open Borders? Closed Societies? The Ethical and Political Issues* (New York: Greenwood Press, 1988), pp. 61–107.

Schoenholtz, A. I., 'Aiding and Abetting Persecutors: The Seizure and Return of Haitian Refugees in Violation of the UN Refugee Convention and Protocol', *Georgetown Immigration Law Journal*, 7 (1993), 67.

'Refugee Protection in the United States Post September 11', *Columbia Human Rights Law Review*, 36 (2005), 323.

Schuck, P. H., 'INS Detention and Removal: A White Paper', *Georgetown Immigration Law Journal*, 11 (1997), 667.

Senate Legal and Constitutional Legislation Committee, *Provisions of the Migration Amendment (Designated Unauthorised Arrivals) Bill 2006* (Canberra: LCLC, June 2006).

Senate Legal and Constitutional References Committee, *A Sanctuary Under Review: An Examination of Australia's Refugee and Humanitarian Processes* (June 2000).

Administration and Operation of the Migration Act 1958 (Canberra: LCRC, March 2006).

Shacknove, A., 'Who is a Refugee?', *Ethics*, 95 (1985), 274.

'From Asylum to Containment', *International Journal of Refugee Law*, 5 (1993), 516.

Shapiro, Scott J., 'What is the Internal Point of View?', 14 October 2006, http://ssrn.com/abstract=937337 (accessed 1 May 2008).

Sheikh Shaghaf, *The Empire Strikes Back: A Critique of Ronald Dworkin's Law's Empire*, April 2007, p. 15, http://ssrn.com/abstract=976312 (accessed 13 May 2008).

Showler, Peter, *Refugee Sandwich* (Montreal: McGill-Queen's Press, 2006).

Singer, P. and Singer, R., 'The Ethics of Refugee Policy' in M. Gibney (ed.), *Open Borders? Closed Societies? The Ethical and Political Issues* (New York: Greenwood Press, 1988), Chapter 4.

Sridharan, Swetha, 'Material Support to Terrorism: Consequenses for Refugees amd Asylum Seekers in the United States', *Migration Fundamentals*, January 2008, www.migrationinformation.org/Feature/display.cfm?id=671 (accessed 16 March 2008).

326 BIBLIOGRAPHY

Steinbock, D. J., 'Interpreting the Refugee Definition', *UCLA Law Review*, 45 (1998), 733.

Stevens, D., *UK Asylum Law and Policy: Historical and Contemporary Perspectives* (London: Sweet and Maxwell, 2004).

Sullivan, K., 'The Year in Detention Law and Policy: Immigration Detention Developments May 2003–April 2004', *Bender's Immigration Bulletin*, 9 (2004), 851.

Tamanaha, Brian Z., *A General Jurisprudence of Law and Society* (Oxford University Press, 2001).

A Concise Guide to the Rule of Law, Legal Studies Research Paper Series, Paper 07-0082, September 2007.

'The Contemporary Relevance of Legal Positivism', *Australian Journal of Legal Philosophy*, 32 (2007), 1.

Taylor, M. H., 'Symbolic Detention', *In Defense of the Alien*, 20 (1998), 153.

Taylor, S., 'The Right to Review in the Australian On-Shore Refugee Status Determination Process: Is It Adequate Procedural Safeguard Against Refoulement?', *Federal Law Review*, 22 (1994), 300.

'The Pacific Solution or a Pacific Nightmare? The Difference Between Burden Shifting and Responsibility Sharing', *Asian-Pacific Law and Policy Journal*, 6 (2005), 1.

Teitgen-Colly, C., 'The European Union and Asylum: An Illusion of Protection', *Common Market Law Review*, 43 (2006), 1503.

Thomas, R., 'The Impact of Judicial Review on Asylum', *Public Law*, (2003), 479.

'After the Ouster: Review and Reconsideration in a Single Tier Tribunal', *Public Law*, (2006), 674.

Towle, R., 'Processes and Critiques of the Indo-Chinese Comprehensive Plan of Action: An Instrument of International Burden-Sharing?', *International Journal of Refugee Law*, 18 (2006), 537.

UK Refugee Council, *Asylum Seekers' Experiences of the New Asylum Model: Findings From a Survey With Clients at Refugee Council One Stop Services* (London: UK Refugee Council, January 2008).

UN High Commissioner for Refugees, *UNHCR Revised Guidelines on Applicable Criteria and Standards Relating to the Detention of Asylum-Seekers* (Geneva: UNHCR 1999), confirming UNHCR Executive Committee, 'ExCom Conclusion 44 (XXXVII)' (1986) *Detention of Refugees and Asylum-Seekers*.

Note on International Protection: Report by the High Commissioner, Geneva, 29 June 2007, A/AC.96/1038.

UNHCR, *Extraterritorial Effect of the Determination of Refugee Status*, 17 October 1978, No. 12 (XXIX) – 1978, para. (a), www.unhcr.org/cgi-bin/texis/vtx/refworld/rwmain?docid=3ae68c4447 (accessed 10 April 2008).

Handbook on Procedures and Criteria for Determining Refugee Status (Geneva: UNHCR, 1979, re-edited 1992).

BIBLIOGRAPHY 327

UNHCR ExCom, 'Conclusion no. 22 (XXXII)' (1981) in *Protection of Asylum Seekers in Situations of Large-scale Influx*, UN doc. A/AC.96/601.

'Conclusion no. 58 (XL)' (1989) in *The Problem of Refugees and Asylum Seekers Who Move in an Irregular Manner from a Country in Which They Have Already Found Protection*, UN doc. A/AC.96/737, part N.

UNHCR, 'UN High Commissioner for Refugees Responds to US Supreme Court Decision in Sale v. Haitian Centers Council', *International Legal Materials*, 32 (1993), 1215.

'Flight from Indochina' in *The State of the World's Refugees 2000: Fifty Years of Humanitarian Action* (Oxford University Press, 2000), Chapter 4.

Statistical Yearbook 2002: Trends in Displacement, Protection and Solutions, July 2004, www.unhcr.org/home/STATISTICS/41206f790.pdf (accessed 16 April 2008).

UNHCR Annotated Comments on the EC Council Directive 2004/83/EC of 29 April 2004, 28 January 2005, pp. 30–1, www.unhcr.org/cgi-bin/texis/vtx/refworld/rwmain?docid=4200d8354 (accessed 1 April 2008).

The State of the World's Refugees: Human Displacement in the New Millennium (Oxford University Press, 2006), Chapter 5.

Quality Initiative Project: Fourth Report to the Minister (London: UNHCR, January 2007).

Statistical Yearbook 2006: Trends in Displacement, Protection and Solutions (Geneva: UNHCR, 2007).

'The Nansen Refugee Award Flash Presentation', www.unhcr.org/cgi-bin/texis/vtx/events?id=3fb359bd4 (accessed 8 November 2007).

Asylum Levels and Trends in Industrialized Countries 2007 (Geneva: UNHCR, 18 March 2008).

Basic Facts, www.unhcr.org/basics.html (accessed 14 April 2008).

'Global Consultations' in *Summary Conclusions: Cessation of Refugee Status*, www.unhcr.bg/global_consult/cessation_refugee_status_en.pdf (accessed 19 April 2008).

US Immigration and Naturalization Service, *1994 Statistical Yearbook* (Washington, DC: Government Printing Office, 1994).

'Country Report: Australia 2007' in *World Refugee Survey*, www.refugees.org/countryreports.aspx?id=1981 (accessed 13 March 2008).

US Committee for Refugees and Immigrants, 'Country Updates: Australia', *World Refugee Survey*, 2001, www.refugees.org (accessed May 2008).

US Congressional Research Service, *Review of US Refugee Resettlement Programs and Policies* (Washington, DC: Government Printing Office, 1980).

US Department of State, US Department of Homeland Security and US Department of Health and Human Services, *Proposed Refugee Admissions for Fiscal Year 2008: Report to the Congress* (Washington, DC: Government Printing Office, 2007).

van Selm-Thorburn, Joanne, "Exceptional Leave to Remain in the United Kingdom" in *Refugee Protection in Europe: Lessons of the Yugoslav Crisis* (The Hague: Martinus Nijhoff Publishers, 1998).

Vasquez, C. M., "The 'Self-Executing' Character of the Refugee Protocol's *Non-Refoulement Obligation*", *Georgetown Immigration Law Journal*, 7 (1993), 39.

Wadham, John, Mountfield, Helen, Edmundson, Anna and Gallagher, Caoilfhionn, *Blackstone's Guide to the Human Rights Act 1998*, 4th edn. (Oxford University Press, 2007).

Wallace, J. C., 'An Essay on Independence of the Judiciary: Independence From What and Why', *New York University Annual Survey of American Law*, 58 (2001), 241.

Walters, M. D., 'The Common Law Constitution and Legal Cosmopolitanism' in D. Dyzenhaus (ed.), *The Unity of the Public Law* (Oxford: Hart Publishing, 2004), Chapter 16.

Hercules as Legal Humanist: Historicising Dworkin's Jurisprudence, Queen's Faculty of Law, Legal Studies Research Paper Series WP No. 07-01 (September 2006), www.ssrn.com/abstract=989609 (accessed 9 May 2008).

Walzer, M., *Spheres of Justice: A Defence of Pluralism and Equality* (Oxford: Basil Blackwell, 1983), pp. 31–63.

Weiss, T. G. and Korn, D. A., *Internal Displacement: Conceptualization and Consequences* (London: Routledge, 2006).

Whelan, F., 'Citizenship and Freedom of Movement: An Open Admission Policy?' in M. Gibney (ed.), *Open Borders? Closed Societies? The Ethical and Political Issues* (New York: Greenwood Press, 1988), pp. 3–39.

Wildes, L., 'The Nonpriority Program of the Immigration and Naturalization Service Goes Public: The Litigative Use of the Freedom of Information Act', *San Diego Law Review*, 14 (1976), 42.

Wishnie, M. J., 'Immigrants and the Right to Petition', *New York University Law Review*, 78 (2003), 667.

Zagor, M., 'Uncertainty and Exclusion: Detention and Aliens and the High Court', *Federal Law Review*, 34 (2006), 127.

INDEX

Adjudication
  formal and substantive theories
    of, 57
  neutrality, and, 293
  standards of, 303
Agenda for Protection, 23
Amnesty International, 250
Asylum seekers
  access to justice, 282
  application of rule of law, and, 1
  denial of access to legal system,
    281
  irregular migration, and, 26
  legal limbo, in, ix,
  measures deterring, 3
  numbers of, 4
  responsibility to process, 8
  restrictive legal measures for, 26
    safe third country notion, 26
  right to seek asylum, 9–11
    refoulement, and, 10
    Refugee Convention, and, 9
    state responsibility, and, 10
    states' duty not to obstruct, 10
    territorial sovereignty claims,
      and, 10
  rise of populism, and, ix,
  routes taken by, choice of, 72
Audi alteram partem, 78
Australia, 171–227
  appeals, 179
  asylum system, 173
  border control policy, 187
  border management, 174
  citizens and non-citizens distinction,
    176
  definition of refugee, 179

  deportation, 186
  designated unauthorised arrivals,
    195
  extra-territorial processing, 171
  Federal Magistrates Court
    role, 184
  Humanitarian Program, 175
    Middle East crises, and, 177
    offshore program, 176
    Vietnamese boat people, 176
  judicial review, 179
    jurisdiction of High Court,
      183
    ouster clause, 297
  mandatory detention policy, 185
    alien status, and, 187
    community responses to, 192
    criticisms of, 188
    detention of children, 189
    entry into Australian community,
      and, 191
    gap between domestic and
      international law, 190
    human rights, and, 189
    implied limitation on, 191
    impracticable removals, 190
    integrity of migration program,
      and, 187
    Migration Reform Act 1992,
      and, 186
    misuse of power, and, 193
    public opinion, and, 192
    reasonably necessary powers, and,
      188
    reform of, 194
    stateless peoples, 189
  mandatory detention regime, 176

330 INDEX

Australia (cont.)
Migration Legislation Amendment
(Judicial Review) Bill, 2001, 183
Migration Legislation Amendment
(Procedural Fairness) Act,
2002, 184
Migration Program, 176
Minister for Immigration, powers,
173, 178
accountability, and, 209
humanitarian discretion, 208
inquiries into, 210
scope, 184
MV Tampa incident, 171
national human rights code, 173
non-refoulement obligation, 202
case law, 203
Minister's humanitarian
discretion, and, 207
protection obligations, and, 204
Refugee Convention
incorporation, and, 202
relevance of effective protection,
206
right to enter and reside, and, 205
safe third country principle,
and, 203
standards for implementation,
203
standards of implementation, 205
offshore and onshore refugees,
175
offshore processing centres, 195
offshore selection of refugees, 174
Pacific Plan, 171
abolition, 197
access to legal system, denial
of, 172
legal limbo, and, 171
legislation for, 171
mandatory detention policy,
and, 193
secondary movers, 178
Permanent Protection Visas, 211
persecution test, 180
post World War II refugees, 174
removal, 175
queue jumpers, 177

Refugee Convention
drafting and establishment, 173
incorporation, 173, 198
indirect incorporation, 198
Minister's discretion, and, 199
protection obligations,
incorporation, 197
refugee definition, 217, 300
application of causation standard,
225
being persecuted, meaning, 218
causation standard, 222
human rights, and, 219
members of social groups, 222
mixed motives for persecution,
223
motivation test, 224
nexus requirement, 222
persecution, meaning, 220
privately motivated persecution,
224
significance of harm, 225
sustained discriminatory conduct,
220
systematic and discriminatory
conduct, 220
threat to life or liberty,
interpretation of, 221
Refugee Review Tribunal, 179
legislative functions, 181
review of adverse decisions, 181
role, 180
refugee status determination, 178
decision-making structures, 179
refugees as constitutional aliens,
174
Constitution, and, 174
parliamentary sovereignty, and,
175
significance of, 174
Temporary Protection Visa regime,
177, 210
border control measure, as, 215
ceased circumstances clause,
and, 212, 306
new measures in, 212
periodic review of status, and, 215
rights under, 177, 211

INDEX

standard of proof, 216
unmeritourious migration litigation,
185
Authority
law, and, 35

Border control
national interest, in, 64
Border controls
burden of asylum, and, 72
Brennan, Sir Gerard
interpretation of legislation, on, 47
neutrality, on, 51

Canada, 78–121
asylum seekers in, 78
asylum system, 80
acceptance rates, 82
accepted claims, 82
conditional removal orders, 83
expedited process, 81
families, 81
full hearings, 81
grounds for ineligibility, 80
humanitarian and compassionate
consideration, 83
Personal Information Form, 81
Pre-Removal Risk Assessments,
83, 290
reasons for decisions, 82
Refugee Protection Officers, 82
rejected claims, 82
safe third country, 81
visa requirements, 80
border controls, 105
asylum seekers stranded on high
seas, 106
smuggling law, 106
Canada-US Safe Third Country
Agreement, 107
9/11, and, 108
appeal regarding, 119
arbitrariness, 118
Charter analysis, 117
criminality exclusions, 115
discretion, and, 118
discrimination, 118
doctrine of ultra vires, and, 119

exceptions, 107
exclusion from asylum for
terrorism, 115
extraordinary rendition to
torture, 117
history of, 107
individualized consideration of
exceptional factors, 118
interpretation of refugee
definition, 116
Land Border Claims, table, 109
NGO challenge to validity of, 109
number of asylum seekers,
and, 108
prohibition against refoulement,
and, 112
rationales supporting, 107
reasonableness, and, 114
refoulement to torture, 116
requirements, 107
security concerns, and, 108
Smart Border Action Plan, 108
success of, 109
US asylum regime, and, 114
US border security concerns,
and, 283
US compliance with international
obligations, and, 113
Canadian Council for Refugees, 308
empirical immigration, 78
Immigration and Refugee Protection
Act, 2001, 79
Immigration and Refugee Protection
Regulations, 79
international law, treatment of, 92
human rights norms, 92
IRB Refugee Protection Division
appointment process, 96
decision-making independence, 97
incompetence, and, 97
level of competence, 96
main tasks of members, 95
political interference with, 96
reputation of, 294
size of, 95
judicial review
access to, 103
application for leave, 103, 297

332 INDEX

Canada (cont.)
docket control, and, 104
exercise of power outside
Canadian territory, 106
grounds for, 103
rejected asylum seekers, and, 103
ordinary courts, access to, 104
post-war refugee admissions, 79
procedural fairness in, 55
Refugee Convention, 79
refugee determination process
single decision maker, 102
refugee determination system, 85
Chiarelli case, 90
credibility of asylum seeker, 95
IRPA process, 101
oral hearings, 89
post 9/11 securitzation of
immigration, and, 90
preventing access to, 95
principles of fundamental justice,
and, 88
prohibition on torture, and, 91
requirements of, 90
right/privilege distinction, 90
security of the person, and, 90
Singh case, 85
Suresh case, 91
refugee hearings
counsel-led questioning, 100
departures from routine, 98
example of, 97
exceptionally vulnerable
claimants, 100
nature of, 100
reverse-order questioning, 98
refugee, definition of, 93, 299
IRB Gender Guidelines, 93
right to be heard, 84
Supreme Court
rights of asylum seekers, and, 105
Cartagena Declaration on Refugees,
1984, 16
refugee, definition, 16
Causation
fear of being persecuted, and, 222
Central America
refugee situation, 16

Children
detention of, 189
Cold War
effects of end of, 19
international migration after, 23
refugee protection, during, 15
Communism
US refugee policy, and, 125
Community
closed borders, and, 67
concept of, 66
conferring membership on
newcomers, 67
exclusion of non-citizens, and,
74
liberal theory, and, 67
political community standard, 70
political culture, and, 74
principle of mutual aid, 68
reciprocity and mutual concern,
and, 70
Comprehensive Plan of Action
for Indo-Chinese refugees
('CPA'), 17
Consistency, presumption of, 63
Constitutional review
originalism debate, and, 44
Convention Against Torture and
Other Cruel Inhuman or
Degrading Treatment or
Punishment (CAT), 9
Convention on the Rights of the Child
(CROC), 289
Convention Plus, 28
Courts of law
refugees' rights of access to, 7
role of, 43
Craig, Paul
ultra vires doctrine, on, 49
Customary international law
non-refoulement as part of, 14

Dauvergne, Catherine
communitarian liberalism, on, 67
Decision-making processes, 293
administrative level, at, 293
neutral adjudication, 293
procedural fairness, and, 294

INDEX

Democracy
judicial review, and. *See* Judicial
review
Detention, freedom from
refugees' rights, and, 8
United States, in, 166
Dicey, Albert Venn
rule of law, on, 35
Diplomatic assurances
use of torture, on, 263
Discrimination
refugees' rights, and, 8
Displacement
root causes of, 20
Dualist legal systems
incorporation of international law,
and, 288
integrity of, 282
Dublin Convention, 107
Due process, 39
neutrality, and, 50
Durable solutions, 17
first use of term, 17
repatriation, and, 17
Dworkin, Ronald
adjudicative principle, and, 46
checkerboard statutes, 59
constitutional review, on, 45
interpretive theory of integrity, xi,
39, 285
adjudication, and, 299
criticisms of, 41
due process, application of, 39
functioning of legal systems, 39
interpretation of legislation,
and, 286
judges, role of, 40
limits to, 304
moral justifications, 40
operation of rule of law, and, 40
sets of laws, 41, 286
state power, and, 41
support for, 41
legal interpretation, on, 48
legislative principle, 57
political morality, 39
procedural fairness, on, 56
rule of law, on, 34

the community, and, 69
theory of adjudication, 46

Education
refugees' rights, and, 7
Ethical
definition, 73
European Charter of Human Rights
national security, and, 229
European Charter of Human Rights
(ECHR)
deportation for national security
reasons, and, 259
torture, prohibition on, 289
European Convention of Human
Rights, 229
UK implementation, 60
European Council of Refugees and
Exiles (ECRE), 257
European Court of Human Rights
Chahal decision, 261
European Union
assistance in regions of origin, 28
burden-sharing arrangements, 242
Common European Asylum
System, 242
harmonization of asylum, 229
harmonized standards, influence
of, 276
influence on UK domestic law, 244
Qualification Directive, 268
aim, 268
asylum shopping, and, 269
cessation of refugee status, 271
incorporation of, 269
international law norms,
and, 270
Refugee Convention, and, 270
revocation of refugee status, 271
rule of law, and, 274
standards for subsidiary
protection, 270
safe third country concept,
and, 27
Exclusionary inclusion, 65
Extraordinary rendition, 117
Extra-territoriality
refoulement and, 12

334 INDEX

Feminism
  refugee, definition of, and, 94
Forced abortion, 133
Forced migrants
  choice, and, 72
Forced migration
  economic development, and, 25
  worldwide phenomenon, as, 122
Freedom of movement
  qualified right, as, 64
  refugees' rights, and, 9

Gibney, Matthew J.
  exclusion of non-citizens, on, 72
Global Commission on International
    Migration
  2005 report, 24

Hailbronner, Professor Kay
  safe third country concept, and, 26
Harm principle
  role of industrialized states,
      and, 73
Hart, Herbert L.A.
  legal positivism, on, 36
Hathaway, James
  Refugee Convention, on, 6
  refugee status, on, 10
  rights under Refugee Convention,
      on, 7
Human rights
  being persecuted, defining,
      and, 219
  detention of asylum seekers,
      and, 189
  Refugee Convention, and, 6

Illegal immigrants, 65
Indo-China
  refugees during 1970s and 1980s, 17
Integrity
  asylum system, of, 33
  ideas of, 33
  law as, 33
  limits to principle of, 304
Interceptions, 8
Interdiction, 8
  defences of, 146

  provisions for interdicted
      passengers, 146
  vessels on high seas, of, 145
Internally displaced persons (IDPs), 4
  first recognition of, 20
  growth in numbers of, 4
  humanitarian assistance for, 21
  policies of containment, and, 21
  ratio of refugees to, 22
  support for refugees, and, 21
International Covenant on Civil and
    Political Rights (ICCPR), 289
International law standards
  inconsistent application of, ix
International migration, 23
  conditions causing, 23
  end of Cold War, and, 23
  irregular, 25
  restrictive measures, justification
      for, 26
International system of refugee
    protection, 3
  development of, 5–9
  Cold War period, during, 15
  refugee crises, 3
  rights of refugees, and, 3
Iraq
  internally displaced persons in, 20

Judicial review, 297–8
  delegated legislative authority,
      and, 50
  democracy, and, 48
  doctrine of separation of powers,
      and, 47
  parliamentary sovereignty,
      and, 49
  red light theory of, 49
  refoulement, and, 48
  restrictions on right to, 297
  role of judges, and, 48
Judiciary
  dependence of refugees on, 55
  moral neutrality, 52
  neutrality, and. See Neutrality
  role of, 40, 44
    activist role, 44
    'law as integrity', and, 46

INDEX 335

conformity of legislation, and, 47
constitutional review, and, 44
conventional approach, 45
legislation, 46
legislative supremacy, and, 46
positivist theory of statutory intention, and, 44
procedural fairness, and, 56
protection of substantive values, and, 45

Jus cogens
refoulement, and, 13

Legal positivism, 36
exclusive and inclusive versions, 37
Legal reasoning
application of standards in, 45
Legislation
compliance with process for introduction of, 59
conformity of, 47
executive arm of government, and, 58
incorporation of treaty obligations, 59
dualist systems of law, under, 60
interpretation of obligations, 60
partial implementation, 61
rights of refugees, and, 60
transnational judicial conversation, and, 61
Vienna Convention, and, 61
interpretation of treaty obligations, 62
conflicting interpretations, 63
justice and fairness, and, 58
legislative principle, 57
legislative supremacy, 46
legislators' powers, exercise of, 58
overturning judicial decisions with, 58
positivist theory on, 58
role of judges, and, 46
ruling government's use of, 58
treaty obligations, and, 58

Mertus, Julie
geopolitical role of states, on, 19

Migration–asylum nexus, 3, 23
developed states' response to, 24
effect of, 3
Mutual aid, principle of, 68

National security
asylum processes, and, 248
Natural justice principle. *See* Procedural fairness
Neutrality
decision makers, of, 51
importance to asylum seekers, 51
judicial independence, and, 50
justifications for, 51
principle of equality, as, 52
procedural fairness, and, 53
refugee status determinations, and, 52
substantive reasons for applying, 52
New Zealand
alliance with Australia, 283
being persecuted, meaning, 218
judicial review, 298
Refugee Convention, incorporation, 291
Refugee Status Appeals Authority, 218
appointment of members, 295
human rights approach in, 293
independence of, 295
powers, 295
procedure, 295
Nexus test, 222
Non-arrival measures
legality of, 10
Non-citizens
exclusion of, 66
government by consent, and, 66
principle of equality, and, 65
refugees, as, 65
Non-entrée measures, 8
Non-governmental organisations (NGOs)
influence in UK, 249
Non-state actors
recognition of claims by, 133

336 INDEX

Offshore processing, 8
Oliver, Dawn
  judicial review, on, 49
Organisation of African Unity
  Convention Governing the
  Specific Aspects of Refugee
  Problems in Africa (OAU
  Convention), 15
  right of asylum, 16

Pacific Plan. *See* Australia
Parliamentary sovereignty
  judicial review, and, 49
  right of *non-refoulement*, and, 66
  rights of refugees, and, 66
  rule of law, and, 36
Participation principle, 54
Persecution
  being persecuted, meaning, 219
  generalised violence, 15
  individualized, 15
  meaning, 6
  right to be free from, 9
  right to flee, 6
Politics
  distinction between law and, 35
Populism
  refugee protection, and, ix
Principle of legality, 63
Procedural fairness
  community membership, and, 70
  decisional independence, and, 157
  exclusion of non-citizens, 56
  ideal of justice, as, 54
  instrumental value, 54
  justice value, 54
  limitations on right to, 55
  neutrality, and, 53
  participation in democratic
    processes, and, 55
  participation principle, and, 54
  principle of practical application,
    as, 54
  principle of universal justice,
    as, 55
  refoulement, and, 53
  substantive and procedural
    standards, 54

Property rights
  refugees' rights, and, 7
Protocol Against the Smuggling of
  Migrants by Land, Sea and Air
  (the Migrant Protocol), 25
Protocol relating to the Status of
  Refugees, 1967, 5
Protocol to Prevent, Suppress and
  Punish Trafficking in Persons,
  Especially Women and Children
  (the Trafficking Protocol), 25
Protracted refugee situations
  definition, 22
  durable solutions for, 28
  locations of, 22
  number living in, 4
  policies of containment, and, 23
  post-Cold War increase in, 19

Rationing
  refugees' rights, and, 7
Refoulement
  judicial review, and, 43, 48
  neutrality, and, 51
  non-refoulement obligation, 11–14
  admission at borders, 11
  application, 301
  application to asylum seekers, 12
  CAT, 12
  'chain' *refoulement*, 12
  customary law, whether, 13
  extra-territorial application, 13, 301
  extra-territoriality, and, 12
  fundamental nature of, 11
  good faith implementation of, 11
  ICCPR, 12
  implementation of, 14
  pre-clearance schemes, and, 12
  principle of *jus cogens*, as, 13
  Refugee Convention, 11
  rejection at frontier, and, 302
  restrictive interpretations of, 14
  scope, 11
  standard of, 12
  state-level interpretations of, 14
  torture, and, 12
  parliamentary sovereignty, and, 66
  procedural fairness, and, 43, 53

INDEX

procedures to protect against, 8
right against, 6
right to seek asylum, and, 10
safe third country principle,
   and, 203
Refugee Convention, 1951, 5
aims, 5
ceased circumstances, and, 213
human rights, and, 5
international cooperation, and, 8
international incorporation of, 288
interpretation, 62
legislative modification of, 61
primary instrument, whether, 300
procedural fairness, and, 53
refugee, definition, 5
refugee status determination
   procedures, 10
'right' to seek asylum under, 9
rights and responsibilities in, 6
status of refugees, 305
Refugee Protocol, 1967, 15
UNHCR mandate, and, 15
Refugees
communitarian liberalism, and, 67
containment, problem of, 28
definition, 5
discriminatory policies towards, 3
international system of protection.
   See International system of
   refugee protection
protracted refugee situations, 4
rates of recognition, 29
rights of
   access to courts of law, 7
   advanced education, 7
   applicable to all, 8
   discrimination, 7
   elementary education, 7
   exclusion of, 69
   freedom from detention, 8
   freedom of movement, 9
   implementation, 1
   incorporation of treaty
      obligations, and, 60
   'lawful' refugees, 7
   lawful 'stayers', 7
   liberty of political participation, 74

non-discrimination, 8
non-penalisation provision, 7
parliamentary sovereignty,
   and, 66
property rights, 7
rationing, 7
refoulement, against, 7
Refugee Convention, under, 6
resettled refugees, 8
states' obligations, 8
taxes, 7
Universal Declaration of Human
   Rights, 9
states' duty to admit, lack of, 10
warehousing, 27
Repatriation
preferred solution, as, 17
voluntary, 18
Restrictive entry measures, 64
Right to be heard
asylum, and, 85
Rule of law
access to legal system, and, 282
application to refugees, 308
democracy, and, 1
development of refugee policy,
   and, 284
evolutionary nature of, 37
formal vision of law, 39
harmonization of asylum law,
   and, 274
implementation at national level, 2
incorporation of international
   treaties, and, 198
law, meaning, 34
legitimacy of justice, and, ix
meaning, 34
morality, relationship with, 37
national and international,
   relationship between, 2
national enterprise, as, 2
operation of, 32
ordinary courts, access to, 104
politics and law distinguished, 35
principle of, ix
reconstructing, ix
right to be heard, and, 84
rights of refugees, and, ix

338 INDEX

Rule of law (*cont.*)
rule-by-law, and, 34
separation of law and politics, 38
thin vision of, 36
UK role in developing, 228
versions of, 75

Safe country of origin, 228, 253
Safe third country, 8, 254
'asylum fatigue', and, 26
non-refoulement obligations,
and, 203
notion of, 26
official recogition of, 27
Security
migrants as risks of, 3
Smuggling, 25
Social groups
family as, 224
Sovereignty
meaning, 36
Soviet Union
break up of, 19
States
geopolitical role of, 19
Sterilization, 133
Stevens, Dallal
UK asylum policy, on, 231
Subsidiary protection, 270

Taxes
refugees' rights, and, 7
Territorial-sovereignty argument, 73
Torture
deporting terror suspects,
and, 264
refoulement, and, 12
Trafficking, 25
Transfer of assets
resettled refugees, and, 8
Trauma
effects of, 85
Treaty obligations
incorporation of. *See* Legislation
interpretation, 61
codified presumptions, 63
common law presumptions, 63
conflict with international law, 63

presumption of consistency, 63
Vienna Convention, 61

Ultra vires doctrine
parliamentary sovereignty, and, 49
United Kingdom, 228–80
accelerated procedures, 254
non-refoulement, and, 257
appeal rights, 234
Asylum and Immigration Appeals
Act, 1993, 236
asylum law and policy in, 231
carriers transporting
undocumented passengers,
232
Former Yugoslavian refugees, 232
number of applications, 233
public debate regarding, 234
refugees with UK connections,
232
terrorism, and, 235
constitutional structure, 244
detention centres, 254
ECHR, incorporation, 240
amending or repealing, 241
declarations of incompatibility,
241
Human Rights Act 1998, and,
240
legislation complying with, 241
prohibition on torture, and, 303
protection for asylum seekers,
and, 240
EU Directives, transposition of, 242
Common European Asylum
System, and, 243
EU Qualification Directive,
and, 268
compelling reasons exception,
278
enforcement, 276
impact of, 277
refugee exclusion criteria, 277
European law, and, 229
Executive action, scrutiny of, 248
human rights commissions, 249
Independent Immigration
Inspectorate, 249

INDEX 339

Joint Parliamentary Committee
  on Human Rights, 248
NGOs, 249
UK Refugee Council, 250
Home Office, 255
  Case Owners structure, 257
  criticism of, 255
  delays in decision making, 255
  measures to address problems
    with, 256
  quality of decision making, 256
Immigration Rules, 239
  nature of, 239
income support
  withdrawal from asylum seekers,
    245
judicial review, 253
  restrictions on, 298
judiciary, 244
  application of asylum law, 244
  checking executive action, 245
  landmark decisions, 244
  national security issues, and, 248
models of adjudication, 296
national security, 259
  applicant's conduct, and, 262
  conduct by non-contracting
    states, 264
  deporting terror suspects, 259
  diplomatic assurances, and, 263
  ECHR, and, 259
  home-grown terrorists, 259
  human rights obligations,
    and, 259
  risk of ill-treatment, and, 262
  scale of threat, 265
  special immigration status,
    260, 306
New Asylum Model, 256
  targets and timetables, 256
Parliamentary supremacy, doctrine
  of, 244
Refugee Convention, incorporation,
  235–9
  asylum regulations, 239
  interpretation of exclusion
    provisions, 237
  policy 'platforms', and, 238

proliferation of legislation, 236
refugee status decision making,
  233, 250
  accelerated procedures, 234
  appeals, 252
  asylum claims, 251
  Asylum Policy Guidance, 251
  Asylum Policy Instructions, 251
  delays in, 234
  Discretionary Leave, 306
  humanitarian protection, 251, 306
  human rights claims, 251
  indefinite leave to remain, 252
  limited leave to remain, 252, 306
  restrictive legal terms, 228
  rule of law, and, 257
  safe country of origin, 253
    criteria for, 254
    meaning, 253
  safe third country, 254
    lists of, 254
    restricted rights, and, 254
  sovereign right to exclude aliens, 292
United Nations Convention against
  Transnational Organised Crime
  (CTOC framework), 25
United Nations High Commissioner
  for Refugees (UNHCR), ix
  1967 Refugee Protocol, and, 15
  asylum systems, and, x
  Convention Plus, 28
  establishment of, 5
  non-refoulement obligations,
    and, 203
  non-refoulement, on, 14
  number of people 'of concern', 4
  role in 1990s, 20
  role of, 8
  rule of law, and, ix
  states' obligation to cooperate
    with, 8
United States of America, 122–70
  administrative and adjudicative
    structures, 128
  appeals, 129
  arrivals at the border, 128
  asylum application process, 128
  immigration judges, 128

340   INDEX

United States of America (*cont.*)
  appeals, 129
    precedents, 130
  asylum in, 127
  availability of, 127
  asylum law and practice in, 122
  communism, 125
  constitutional basis for refugee
    protection, 123
  detail of legal regime, 122
  non-refoulement, 125
  parole, 124
  permanent resettlement program,
    125
  Refugee Act, 1980, 125
  Refugee Convention, 1951, 124
  Refugee Protocol 1967,
    ratification, 124
  refugee, definition, 125
  separation of powers, and, 123
  World War II, during, 124
  cancellation of removal, 139
  displaced persons, 290
  domestic remedies, 136
  discretionary relief, 138
  temporary protected status, 136
  impediments to access, 144
  interdiction of vessels on high
    seas, 145
  strategies for, 145
  independence of adjudicators, 150
  Attorney General, and, 154
  BIA, 152
  courts, 155
  defensive judging, 158
  effect of BIA reassignments, 154
  federal judges, 156
  Immigration Judges, 150
  interpretation of legislation,
    and, 159
  political accountability, 157
  procedural fairness, and, 157
  protection from political process,
    and, 158
  questions of fact, 160
  reassignment, 152
  reassignment of BIA members,
    153

  rule of law, and, 156
  separation of powers, and, 159
  termination of appointments,
    151
  theories of, 157
  unpopular minorities, and, 158
  international human rights
    instruments, 134
  judicial review, 130
  exceptions, 130
  increase in petitions for, 130
  suspensory effect, 130
  legislative powers, use of, 287
  one-off legalization programs, 139
  perceived abuse of asylum system,
    140
  economic impact of
    undocumented immigrants,
    141
  free trade, and, 143
  impact of illegal immigration,
    142
  law enforcement problem, as, 144
  rule of law, and, 141
  violations of border law, 142
  permanent resettlement program,
    126
  family members, 126
  maximum nuber of refugees, 126
  number of admissions under,
    126
  priorities governing, 126
  private bills, 140
  refugee protection system, 123
  registry, 139
  rule of international law, 161
  criminal prosecutions, 169
  detention, 165
  exclusion clauses, 164
  implementation of obligations,
    161
  interdiction on the high seas, 162
  standard of proof, 164
  rule of law, 140
  substandard adjudication of
    claims, 147
  BIA streamlining reforms,
    and, 147

judges, errors by, 150
judicial criticisms, 149
review of system, 150
substantive criteria for refugee
  status, 131
forced abortion or sterilization,
  133
non-state actors, claims by, 133
persecution of social groups, 132
precedent decisions, 132
refugee, definition, 131
temporary protected status, 136
withholding of deportation
  procedure, 290
withholding of removal, 127

Universal Declaration of Human
  Rights (UDHR), 9

Vienna Convention on the Law of
  Treaties, 1969, 61
interpretation of treaty obligations,
  61
Vietnamese boat people
  Australian Humanitarian program,
  and, 176

Walzer, Michael
  community membership, on, 68
World War II
  refugees after, 5

For EU product safety concerns, contact us at Calle de José Abascal, 56–1°, 28003 Madrid, Spain or eugpsr@cambridge.org.

www.ingramcontent.com/pod-product-compliance
Ingram Content Group UK Ltd.
Pitfield, Milton Keynes, MK11 3LW, UK
UKHW020452090825
461507UK00007B/199